Of Poetry and
Music's Power
Humanism and the Creation of Opera

Studies in Musicology, No. 13

George Buelow, Series Editor
Professor of Musicology
Indiana University

Other Titles in This Series

Of Poetry and Music's Power

Humanism and the Creation of Opera

by
Barbara Russano Hanning

RESEARCH PRESS

Produced and distributed by
UMI Research Press
an imprint of
University Microfilms International
Ann Arbor, Michigan 48106

Library of Congress Cataloging in Publication Data

Hanning, Barbara Russano, 1940-
   Of poetry and music's power.

   (Studies in musicology : series 2 ; no. 13)
   Bibliography: p.
   Includes index.
   1. Opera—History and criticism. 2. Libretto.
3. Humanism.   I. Title. II. Series.
ML1702.H36   782.1'09   80-12637
ISBN 0-8357-1071-8

Orpheus personifying *La musica* by
Luca della Robbia. From the Museo
dell'Opera del Duomo, Florence, Italy.
Courtesy of the Alinara/Editorial
Photocolor Archives.

Contents

Contents

Musical Examples

Abbreviations

Encicl. spett.	*Enciclopedia dello spettacolo.*
HLC	Bernard Weinberg, *History of Literary Criticism in the Italian Renaissance.*
JAMS	*Journal of the American Musicological Society.*
MQ	*The Musical Quarterly.*
Madrigal	Alfred Einstein, *The Italian Madrigal.*
PaM	*Publikationen älterer praktischer und theoretischer Musikwerke.*
RMI	*Rivista musicale italiana.*

Preface

Ai lettori:

This study, undertaken as my Yale University doctoral dissertation, was written between 1964 and 1968. Because of the amount of time that has elapsed since its completion, I judged that, were I to re-think the issues raised in it and re-examine all the sources, the result would probably be a new book, and not one which would necessarily belong in this series. Thus, the form in which the work now appears is substantially that of my dissertation, with some minor, largely cosmetic, revisions. Much of the information in Chapter One was reworked and presented in my article, "Apologia pro Ottavio Rinuccini," *JAMS* 26 (1973): 240-62. In addition, I have attempted to give some idea of more recently published research and criticism in this area by expanding the notes and bibliography. Finally, I have added a series of appendices containing the principal texts and libretti discussed in the study, in the hope that these will enhance the usefulness of the volume and prove to be a convenience to its readers.

For the intellectual, moral, and financial support which sustained me during my years of graduate study and those spent in the preparation of this work, my thanks are owed now, as then, to the many persons and institutions whom I cited in 1969 in the preface to my dissertation; my repeating their names here would not reduce my debt to them any more than the intervening years have effaced it. I do wish to acknowledge, with special gratitude, the example and encouragement of Claude V. Palisca and Robert W. Hanning, who, as both mentors and friends, have continued to influence my work mightily. Lastly, I am thankful to Dr. Susan Sommer, of the Music Division of the New York Public Library, for graciously permitting me to publish here, for the first time, the text of the earliest known printed opera libretto — Rinuccini's *Dafne*.

E vivete lieti.

I

Rinuccini and the Power of Music

When the poet-librettist Ottavio Rinuccini (1562-1621) summoned *La Tragedia*, the tragic muse herself, to declaim the prologue to his favola *Euridice*,[1] he epitomized, probably quite consciously, the history of the birth of opera. His decision was surely influenced in part by the prevailing attitude toward antiquity in sixteenth-century Italian literary circles, an attitude of admiration for and imitation of the ancients. Rinuccini himself was a humanist of wide repute, although his classical training was apparently less than rigorous,[2] and a member of two humanistic academies, both of which provided settings for lengthy commentaries, generally Aristotelian in bias, on the relative merits of classical and modern literature.[3] Yet it is precisely because of his classical background that the appearance of Tragedy to introduce his idyllic and truncated version of the tale of Orfeo and Euridice has puzzled many historians of opera, for the ensuing drama has little to do with Aristotle's formulation of the genre of tragedy. Leo Schrade's suggestion that it was simply the "[original] fate of Euridice [which] belonged to tragedy," and which prompted Rinuccini to call the tragic muse upon the scene, must be placed against his own observation that Euridice's fate is here "mellowed" by Rinuccini's *fin lieto*, the happy ending.[4] Nino Pirrotta discusses the meaning of the prologue in similar terms. The poet's invocation of Tragedy, he suggests, is typical of the kind of rhetorical amplification of which the age was so fond, and in this particular case was simply an acknowledgment of the dignity of the royal couple whose nuptials were being celebrated, and of the greatness of the occasion.[5] In all his writings on the subject, Pirrotta contests the importance of the concept of classical tragedy in the formation of opera, and insists (quite correctly) that both of Rinuccini's early libretti, *Dafne* and *Euridice*, belong entirely to the realm of the pastoral clearly defined by Guarini. It was only "the success of *Dafne* [which] emboldened Rinuccini to call *Euridice* a tragedy;"[6] and again, "L'habitude de se parer de classicisme et de s'appuyer sur un *ipse dixit* amena Peri a déclarer... qu'il s'était inspiré des anciens..."[7] In other words, both Schrade and Pirrotta imply that Rinuccini's presentation of *La Tragedia* in the role of

Prologue was a mere token gesture, a gallant bow in the fashionable direction of antiquity.[8]

Persuaded that Rinuccini's Prologue harbors greater significance for the beginnings of opera, I begin this study with an examination of the purposes of the prologue in Renaissance dramatic literature, and of its relevance to the action of the plot or the intention of the author. Sixteenth-century literary theory is not very explicit on this subject, and literary practice, as one would suspect, varied to a great extent.

As a detached preface in which someone addressed the audience on behalf of the author, the prologue was used only in comedy in classical times and was generally foreign to the Renaissance imitations of classical tragedy.[9] Nevertheless, its theoretical function was similar to that of the classical tragic prologue (which, in Aristotelian terms, included everything before the first chorus and which consequently formed an integral part of the drama) — that is, to gain the sympathy and the attention of the reader, and to give him a foretaste of the plot. In the words of Giovanni Talentoni, whose essay in practical criticism was read in 1587 before the Accademia fiorentina (of which Rinuccini was a member), the ancient poets in their prologues "strove to make the listener favorable, to make him attentive to them and aware, and finally to make him well disposed to understand what they say, in the way taught by the rhetoricians."[10] Leone Hebreo de Sommi, in his unpublished dialogue treatise on the art of the theatre,[11] recalls an interesting example of the use of the prologue and insists upon one that is appropriate to the *favola*.

> Veridico: . . . Don't you remember how beautiful was the prologue of that tragicomedy of the last carnival where the poet introduced Comedy and Tragedy in conversation together? . . .
> Santino: Very well; but perhaps not in all comedies would it be possible to find such appropriate prologues.
> Veridico: I grant you that; but when all else fails, one would never be at a loss to introduce things which are suitable to the cities or places where the play takes place, such as introducing the rivers which irrigate them, the first founders who build them, or the famous men and heroes who were born there. . . .[12]

It is noteworthy that the example de Sommi praises — tragedy and comedy talking together in the prologue of a tragicomedy — seems to bear no relation to the actual subject of the drama, but rather to its genre. As early as 1486, Nicolò da Correggio used the prologue of *Cefalo* as a forum for the discussion of genre. Recognizing the difficulty of applying the conventional terms comedy and tragedy to his play, based on an Ovidian myth, of which the ending is altered in a manner resembling the solution presented in Monteverdi's score of *Orfeo*,[13] the author, speaking through the Prologue, decides upon the non-committal subtitles *historia* or *fabula*.[14]

That the prologue could serve, among other things, as a vehicle to convey the author's views on the art of drama was given eloquent expression by a more famous older contemporary of de Sommi, Giraldi Cinthio (1504-73). In *Altile*, his first tragedy with a happy ending, Giraldi has the prologue speak on behalf of "il Poeta nostro" his belief that the prescribed laws of tragedy are not immutable. He is quite sure that if the ancient poets were alive in his day, they would seek to please the different taste of his spectators and would not hesitate to change those laws from which the Greeks themselves often departed. (ll. 4-6,8).[15]

> Dunque hà voluto hora il Poeta nostro
> In questa nova favola serversi
> Di quel, che l'uso, e l'età nostra chiede...
> Per sodisfare à chi sodisfar deve.

Tragedy herself similarly defends the poet's innovations in a verse epilogue entitled "La Tragedia à chi legge" which Giraldi appended to the first edition of *Orbecche* in 1543.[16]   Sentiments very like these are expressed in the prologue to the second edition of Agostino Beccari's *Il Sacrificio* (Ferrara, 1587), generally considered the first pastoral drama. Beccari's prologue argues than any man gifted with a fine talent ("bell'ingegno") will always investigate new paths and methods in order not merely to equal, but to surpass the ancient poets; that is why the contemporary pastoral poem differs so greatly from ancient usage.[17]

The prologue that came to prevail in the pastoral drama was recited by a god or goddess, or sometimes by an allegorical or mythological character. Poliziano's *Orfeo* begins with Mercurio, the messenger of the gods, who announces the play and its argument much like the *angiolo annunziatore* of sacred drama. A fragment of an unpublished pastoral by Giraldi bears a prologue assigned to Amore, who appears again as the petulant child-god in the *Aminta* of Torquato Tasso.[18]   In Tasso's prologue, however, the poet barely refers to the argument of the play, but instead constructs a brief *sinfonia* around Amore himself — whose function as prologue is to transport the reader from the real word "in una sonora atmosfera di sogno, entro la quale si collocheranno senza sforzo le pastorali visioni dei cinque atti successivi."[19]   In Giraldi's pastoral *Eglè* (1545), which was performed in Florence in 1588, the connection of the prologue to the rest of the drama is similarly indirect; the prologue describes how "il poeta" left his own country one day and, wandering in Arcadia to refresh his weary mind ("per ricrear la stanca mente"), came upon two woodland gods discussing Nature.[20]

These examples indicate that the prologue often served as the bold yet defensive expression of an author quite conscious of innovating. At the same time, it functioned to establish the mood, if not to divulge something of the plot, of the poem which it preceded. Finally, as in Guarini's prologue to the *Pastor fido*, written for a wedding celebration at the court of Turin,[21] it frequently presented an encomium to the local rulers, who were generally expected in return to sponsor a performance. These were, one might say, the conventions of prologue-writing in sixteenth-century Italy.

To return to the libretto of *Euridice*, how do these conventions apply to the prologue by Rinuccini? Disregarding for the moment the question of the appropriateness of Tragedy's appearance, we must first discern her message. In the opening strophes Tragedy describes how her ancient role has been modified:

> I, . . . who made the faces of the crowds in the large theatres turn pale with pity, I sing not of blood spilled from innocent veins, not of the lifeless brow of an insane tyrant, unhappy spectacle for human eyes, but about mournful and tearful scenes.[22]

In the third strophe she banishes these sad images and discards her mournful buskins and gloomy garments to awaken in the heart "più dolci affetti." She continues:

> The earth will marvel at this change, so that every gentle soul inspired by Apollo to tread my new path will bring you such renown, O Queen, as may surpass that of Athens or Rome. For you I return and adorn myself with a pleasing mien for the royal nuptials; and I tune my song to happier strings to give sweet pleasure to the noble heart.

The seventh and last strophe is an invitation to hear the song of the Thracian Orfeo, while the royal Seine prepares to receive the new queen.

The elements contained in the prologue, then, are not unusual; but the fact that they are couched in conventional language should not obscure their meaning nor prompt less serious consideration than the words of another author. Tragedy identifies herself as a singer and announces her new aim. The ostensible reason, the happy occasion, is then disclosed and the monarch praised. Finally, the way is briefly prepared for the onset of the *favola*. In other words, Rinuccini uses the prologue to call attention to the innovative character of his work, to flatter the new queen, Maria de' Medici, whose wedding is being celebrated, and to strike the chord for the unfolding of his drama.

The content of the prologue offers, I think, some important evidence for considering the casting of *La Tragedia* in the role of prologue to be relevant to the whole situation; for it raises the questions, What novelty does Rinuccini claim for his poem? and, indirectly, Why should the singer who utters the prologue be conferred with the title Tragedy? The answer to the first question is only partially supplied by the prologue itself. There the poet makes it clear that *La Tragedia* is no longer the ancient spectre of pity and terror, but the sweet songstress of melancholy (tragicomedy), who, precisely by singing, will move the hearts of the audience to new, pleasing emotions.[23] Rinuccini elaborates on this second point in his dedication to the edition of the libretto, printed as a souvenir of the performance.[24] There he states his belief, which "has been the opinion of many," that tragedy in ancient times had been entirely sung. Until his collaboration with Peri, the poet confesses, he thought that the imperfections of modern music rendered impossible such a noble style of performance ("si nobil maniera di recitare").[25] But the music which Peri composed for his *Dafne* completely disabused him of his doubts.[26] Thus it appears that Rinuccini felt justified in invoking Tragedy as the muse which inspired the style, if not the form, of his drama designed to be set "tutta in musica." It was an appropriate testimony to his renewed faith in "the music of our age." Moreover, it symbolized his desire to create a genre which, while its aim was not the same as that of tragedy, simulated the manner of performance of the ancient model, and consequently could approximate its effectiveness.

A gap of almost three years separates the first performance of the first opera, *Dafne*,[27] and Rinuccini's (and Peri's) statements prefacing the libretto (and score) of *Euridice*.[28] This fact has often prompted the remark that poet and composer were merely rationalizing *ex post facto* a "discovery" which they somehow had made in spite of themselves.[29] In one sense, this opinion is upheld by their own statements, for Rinuccini stresses the experimental nature of the creation of *Dafne*: ". . . the favola [was] written by me only to make a simple test of the power of the music of our age" and "Signor Jacopo gave this same fable a better form." In the same place, he expresses the wish that "others, more skillful than myself, may employ their talents to increase and improve the poems thus composed in order that they might not envy those ancients so much celebrated by noble writers."[30] Peri too, by his silence until 1601, implies that his composition of *Dafne* (which was apparently in progress for three years) was merely a proving ground,[31] and concludes his preface to the printed score of *Euridice* with the confession that ". . . I may not have brought this style to the goal I had thought it possible to attain [since the success of *Dafne*], the consideration of novelty having deterred me. . . ."[32]

On the other hand, although the prologue to *La favola di Dafne* lacks any bold statement of novelty (as befitted its experimental nature), it did in every other respect establish the formula for the later prologues.[33] "I, Ovid, who sang so sweetly on the learned lyre about the flames of heavenly lovers . . . I appear to you tonight, o mortals." Then follows the encomium to "l'alta Regina," and finally, setting the stage for the ensuing verses, Rinuccini alludes to the power of love, the sun-god, and the beloved nymph. In addition to the reference in the second quatrain to Ovid as a singer, the penultimate strophe is also noteworthy: "Seeking to use the ancient style, I undertake to show you in a clear example, how dangerous, ladies and gentlemen, it is to underestimate the power of love."[34]   In fact, I consider that the first line of the quatrain — "Seguendo di giovar l'antico stile" — may be understood as a statement of Rinuccini's program, a program which called for the new union of word and music in emulation of ancient drama.

Thus, although *Dafne* was clearly an experiment, the prologue to the first edition contains the germ of what was to flower into the more explicit claims of the later opera libretti. First, as we have seen, in *Euridice* there is the claim of novelty as well as Tragedy's assertion that she, with her new song, will awaken "più dolci affetti." Apollo too, in the prologue of *Arianna*, has a new mission on earth.[35] He comes armed with the kithara, and not with bows and arrows, eager to delight the heart and imprison weighty cares; even haughty ears will yield to the sweet sound of tender lovesongs. The last quatrain in fact contains another echo from the prologue to *Dafne*: Apollo, addressing himself to the royal spouse, expresses the hope that she may admire "l'antico onor ne' novi canti."[36]   The prologue of Rinuccini's *Narciso*,[37] sung in the person of Giulio Romano (i.e., Caccini), exalts the singer's art and refers specifically to the way in which the musician uses the word to attain his effect: "And I tempered sweetly, through the musician's art, the exalted conceits of poetic souls which I, singing in the theatres, used at will in order to make hearts sorrowful and gay" (sixth strophe).[38]   In the next quatrain, he alludes to the voice of Orfeo ("gran cantor") which opened the gates of Hell (*Euridice*), and Apollo's lament over the transformed nymph *(Dafne)*. These two strophes are found again in a later prologue to *Dafne*, newly composed for a performance "in casa del signor Don Giovanni Medici."[39]   This time it is not Ovid, but *La Musica* herself who recites the by now familiar string of formulas.   ". . . I am the goddess, come into the world to teach you, mortals, how to temper artfully high and low sound softly and sweetly."[40]   The usual list of virtues is expanded to include the power to make even the stars dance under the sway of music's kithara, and the required series of compliments is presented to the royal house. Of the two strophes shared in common with the prologue to *Narciso*, the one in which Rinuccini refers specifically to his earlier works includes, in one manuscript, a reference to his newest libretto, *Arianna*.

This brief survey of Rinuccini's prologues is instructive for several reasons. First, the insistence upon certain elements of the formula—namely the marvelous claims of the singer for his art, which we are led to believe is an ancient one, not only by specific reference to antiquity but also by the return of the singer from a distant place and age in every case except that of *Narciso*—reveals Rinuccini's consistent preoccupation with the power of music, a preoccupation which, by his own testimony, had given rise to *Dafne*. Second, the fact that he was fully aware of this preoccupation is given credence not only by his consistent development of it, but also by the poet's several allusions to his own libretti, calling attention, as it were, to their continuity. Now the existence of this continuity does not in itself constitute evidence to disprove the notion that *Dafne* was not a consciously new creation. When, however, it is studied together with the events of the previous decade and with contemporary and post-contemporary witness, it does reveal *Dafne* as the focal point of a series of developments evidently based on certain humanistic ideas about music.

To summarize, *Dafne* was an avowedly experimental work, the composition of which was formally explained by its authors not until almost three years after its first performance. Rinuccini's part of the explanation states that the work was conceived as a vehicle for modern music, in order to afford this music the opportunity to prove itself the equal of ancient music. The favola was to be entirely sung, in imitation of the Greek and Roman manner of performing tragedy. This *de facto* preoccupation with the role and power of music was consistently verbalized and developed in Rinuccini's subsequent opera prologues which, by their adherence to the formal pattern and content of the *Dafne* prologue, as well as by their overt reference to the work, testify at least to Rinuccini's *ex post facto* consciousness of the artistic success of his experiment. Moreover, I think it can be shown that the experiment itself was the conscious result of a program conceived and nourished in the humanist academies of the 1580's and 1590's.

The existence of Rinuccini's preoccupation with the power of music at the actual time of *Dafne's* composition is easy enough to determine. Indeed, the subject was not a matter of concern peculiar to Rinuccini, but exercised the minds of many humanist scholars throughout the sixteenth century.[41] The increasing number of editions and translations of classical poets and rhetoricians heaped upon the ears of Renaissance theorists tale after marvelous tale of the powers of ancient music. For their part, the theorists repeated this lore and arrived at a general conception of ancient music despite the lack of sources. This conception, although differing in certain important details and in the emphasis given to single elements, centered about the use of chromaticism based on the Greek genera, the revival of the ancient modes, the nature of text treatment (wherein the music was generally thought to have been subject to the verse), the use of monody, and the idea that expressivity through the use of either or all these means was the *sine qua non* of effective musical rhetoric. The theorists also differed in the extent to which they wanted to implement the revival of these means, and to incorporate them into modern practice.

For Zarlino, for example, it was obvious that modern music did not produce the same results as ancient; but he attributed this discrepancy to the different aims of contemporary music which sought to dispose its listeners to virtue and, in delighting, to instruct them. This view, based principally on Platonic and Horatian theories of art, remained in contrast to the newly fashionable Aristotelian concept of moving the hearers to various emotions in order to purge them of these emotions.[42] Zarlino's outlook represented a generation convinced that it stood at the apex of the development of the art of music which had flourished anew in counterpoint after the Middle Ages.[43]   But the next generation, represented by Zarlino's pupil Vincenzo Galilei, was persuaded that the apparent lack of effective expression in the highly complex contrapuntal music of its forebears indicated a serious decline in the art, a conviction which stimulated a fervent desire for reform.

It has been fashionable lately to deny the possibility of a fruitful relationship between theory and style in the course of music history, or, as Edward Lowinsky attests, "to disregard the fact that the most significant changes in artistic style may have their origin in a new concept of the art and its function."[44]   I believe that the theorists, poets, and composers who, in the spirit of reform, forged the *stile rappresentativo* were deeply influenced by the Greek, and especially Aristotelian, concept of music.[45]   Both the theories and activities of the group of poets and musicians centered about the "gentlemen composers" Bardi and Corsi, who were to propagate and propagandize this reform, have been well described and documented.[46]   In addition to gaining a new understanding of the ancient modes through the efforts of their most learned and able researcher, Girolamo Mei, they acquired a new sense of the nature and performance of Greek music. Mei, and consequently Galilei, was confident that despite the lengthy passages in the Greek theorists about harmonic ratios, the musical style of the Greeks was in practice almost always monodic. This led him to devalue the great contrapuntal art of the Renaissance and to call for the restoration of music to its pristine simplicity by reuniting it with its sister arts of oratory and poetry.[47] For humanists of Aristotelian persuasion like Mei, music shared with the art of oratory the power to move the affections,

> Ch'io rendo a mio desìr dolenti e lieti
> Con vario canto ne' teatri i petti.[48]

This it did by uniting itself with poetry in the most intimate manner possible, for it had in common with poetry the elements of harmony and rhythm.[49] Music could use these elements to imitate the "conceits of the soul" or the emotions of the singer, rendering the text in such a way as to stimulate the same emotions in the listener.[50]

Rinuccini's participation in what Pietro de' Bardi later called "my father's camerata"[51] has often been taken for granted, but the discrepancy in age between the poet and men like Bardi and Galilei makes his early participation unlikely.[52] Although we do not know when the activities associated with Bardi's côterie were formally terminated, the propagation and cultivation of its ideas certainly did not cease with the publication of Galilei's *Dialogo* in 1581, nor with Bardi's removal to Rome in 1592.[53] Rinuccini's contact with these ideas can be established, for example, through his collaboration with Bardi in the 1589 *intermedi* as well as through his membership in the Alterati academy which included, along with Bardi, Jacopo Corsi and Girolamo Mei.[54]

The *intermedi* of the Florentine wedding festivities of 1589, "invented" and directed by Bardi for three comedies performed on successive days,[55] are not usually thought to embody the theoretical or musical ideals of the Camerata as put forth by Galilei in his *Dialogo della musica antica, e della moderna.* They partook, after all, of a tradition of court entertainment which functioned merely as an ornament to a great occasion; the more important and memorable the occasion, the more elaborate and stupendous was the spectacle. Nevertheless almost all the *intermedi* reveal, at least in their subject matter, that preoccupation with the power of music which I have said resulted from humanist interest and research in ancient music, and in turn stimulated the continuation of that interest and research.[56] It was also the preoccupation with which Rinuccini, by his own admission, was concerned in composing his *Dafne.* Although the utterance of this preoccupation was much less erudite and more general in these *intermedi* than it was to become in Rinuccini's later poetry, it must still be considered a turning point, for there was nothing like it in the poet's previous verses destined for music. For this reason we must consider Bardi's influence on him to have been an important one.

Of the six *intermedi*, Rinuccini was solely responsible for the text of three, and composed the greater part of the verses of two others to which Bardi himself contributed some text.[57] The opening madrigal of the first *intermedio*, which contemplates the "Harmony of the Spheres," is Bardi's and significantly prefigures the standard beginning of Rinuccini's prologues. "I am Harmony, a friend who comes to you, o mortals, from the heavenly spheres escorted by celestial sirens." The rest of the madrigal pays a metaphorical compliment to the ruling couple, as do the following verses by Rinuccini, unnoteworthy except for a reference to the sweet song of the Sirens which makes the planets revolve. But the next *intermedio*, for which the younger poet supplied the verse, dwells upon the virtues and the virtuosity of song. The Pierides compare themselves favorably to Arion and Orfeo, both of whom achieved marvelous results with their sweet singing, and declare that every melody would sound hoarse next to their own. The Muses respond to this challenge by humbly acknowledging their musical talents as a gift of the gods, and they call upon a chorus of nymphs to thank heaven for the pleasure derived from their song. The nymphs in turn condemn the Pierides and pronounce their music to have been but a poor shadow of the *dolci accenti* of the Muses. A basic opposition underlies this meager text, perhaps reflecting the opposition between ancient and modern music with which Bardi and Galilei were so concerned.

This opposition is not portrayed in the music by any basic stylistic changes, for Marenzio sets the choruses both of the Pierides and of the Muses as polyphonic madrigals, the first in six parts, the second in a polychoral texture of twelve parts. Within this conservative framework, however, Marenzio may have been attempting to draw certain distinctions between the two groups by means of precisely those musical details which render a madrigal setting more or less expressive. In the "più soave" chorus of the Muses, for example, he uses a 7-6 suspension twice at cadence points,[58] whereas for the Pierides' chorus he employs only the 4-3 suspension. Also, the increased forces of the second chorus enable Marenzio to vary the texture from an expressive setting of the initial lines on three and four parts, to the simple, polychoral exchanges of short homophonic phrases, and finally the impressive and triumphant double chorus which sings in twelve "real" parts at the close of the madrigal.[59]

The third *intermedio*, depicting the combat between Apollo and the dragon, is again entirely by Rinuccini. Although there are no references to music in his verses, the description of the production by Bastiano de'

Rossi contains some interesting comments about Rinuccini's sources. In describing the appearance of Apollo and the subsequent battle, de' Rossi says:

> . . . In this intermedio the poet wished to represent the Pythic battle in the manner taught by Julius Pollux, who says that when this fight was performed to ancient music, it was divided into five parts. The ability to perform these things with these ancient musical modes being denied us by the ravages and passage of time, and considering that such a battle presented on stage would have had to bring, as it did, perfect delight to the spectators, the poet presented it to us with our modern music, urging with all his might, as a very fine connoisseur of this art, both the imitation and the simulation of the ancient one.[60]

These statements convey several noteworthy facts. We learn first of all that Rinuccini's source gave an important place to music in the representation of this scene.[61] We are also told that the poet, recognizing the impact the ancient performance must have had on the spectators, strove to recapture this effect by urging "with all his might" the imitation of the ancient means. Note too that de' Rossi calls Rinuccini a "very fine connoisseur" of music. Consequently we may judge that this *intermedio* shares with its companion pieces at least an external concern with the power of music.

But there is another respect in which Rinuccini reveals his growing preoccupation with music through this third *intermedio*, and that is, I believe, through the subject matter, slight as it is. In the ancient sources Apollo, god of music and of the sun (one might say, of sweetness and light), of human rationality and of art, becomes hero and victor by destroying the venomous monster who has been terrifying the land of the nymphs and shepherds of the chorus. Order triumphs over chaos, beauty over ugliness as Apollo overcomes the irrational forces represented by the python, and joyous singing and dancing prevail.[62] Apollo, in other words, may be seen as Rinuccini's first artistic spokesman, an adolescent Orfeo. If the *intermedio* is understood in this way, the incorporation of a more developed version of the battle between Apollo and the serpent in the first scene of Rinuccini's *Dafne* deserves greater attention than it has received.[63] For, given the new musical style of *Dafne*, if by extension Apollo can be considered Rinuccini's spokesman specifically for the new art of monody, then it requires only a short leap of imagination to equate the dragon with Bardi's and Galilei's "bête noir" – counterpoint.[64]

The fourth *intermedio* of 1589, written by Giovanbattista Strozzi, again opens with the formula "Io, che dal ciel...," this time sung by a magician who appears on a chariot in the clouds and invokes the "demoni celesti" and "demoni infernali." After the former prophesy "felice eterno canto" upon the marriage of the reigning couple, the "demoni infernali" express their woe at the prospect of a new Golden Age and curse their own fate. According to de' Rossi's description, the rest of the *intermedio* is merely a fantastic depiction of horrors from Dante's *Inferno*.[65]

In contrast to this fourth *intermedio*, in which there are no musical references except for the vague, Platonic association of song with the heavens and with felicity, the fifth centers on Arion, musician *par excellence*. According to Plutarch, Arion was a kitharist and lyric poet who was rescued from oceanic depths by a dolphin attracted to his song.[66] As in the first *intermedio*, both Bardi and Rinuccini devised the verse. Rinuccini's "io" at the opening is the sea-goddess Anfitrite, ascended from the depths of her vast realm to pay homage to the bride and groom: the nymphs echo her sentiments in a madrigal text written by Bardi, whereupon Arion sings Rinuccini's verses, which give eloquent expression to the singer's despair and his urgent plea for help. It is apparent from the musical setting as well as from the highly rhetorical style of the poetry that this was meant to be a *tour de force*, a virtuoso piece designed to illustrate the moving powers of music. The setting, an "Ecco con due risposte," in the earliest known piece by Jacopo Peri, who appeared himself in the role of Arion. In conformity with the dramatic situation Peri composed a solo song which, dazzling in its ornamentation, required all the skill of a virtuoso to perform.[67]

The sixth and final *intermedio* describes music as a gift from the gods, made specifically in "Armonia" and "Ritmo," which attributes provide sweet aid and comfort to belabored mortals. Among the gods, Apollo and Bacchus are named, and the mortals are nymphs and shepherds. The *intermedio* concludes with a *ballo* in which the gods instruct the shepherds in the art of dancing.[68]

It is clear from this brief summary of the 1589 *intermedi* that Rinuccini was already fashioning his interest in the power of music, a theme vaunted by the ancients and avidly discussed by the moderns, and which was to be expressed more fully in his *Dafne* and *Euridice* libretti. Whether this interest was originally kindled by his association with Bardi in 1589 or was acquired through his own humanistic training and participation in the academies, it was surely fostered by Bardi, who also undoubtedly apprised Rinuccini of Mei's and Galilei's theories about the means and effects of ancient music. Consequently, Rinuccini's interest was apparently quite well formed and informed when he became one of those illustrious "cavalieri, letterati, poeti e musici" who, in the last decade of the century, frequented the home of Jacopo Corsi in Florence.[69]

Although the influence on Rinuccini of Bardi and the Camerata has been taken for granted, another influence, that of his contact with Gabriello Chiabrera, has been largely ignored, at least by musicologists.[70] Chiabrera is also named among the famous visitors to casa Corsi during this period, and there the friendship between the two poets, presumably established during his frequent trips to the courts of Florence and Mantua from his residence in Rome, was nurtured. Of the two, Chiabrera was apparently the more rigorous classicist and the more widely recognized poet. After the publication of several collections of early poems (two books of *Canzonette* in 1591 and the *Scherzi e canzonette morali* as well as the *Maniere de' versi toscani* in 1599), he was celebrated as a new Pindar; in contrast, Rinuccini's poems, except for the commemorative libretti, were only published posthumously, in the *Rime e poesie* of 1622. Chiabrera himself, however, lauded Rinuccini at the end of one of his dialogues on the art of poetry, *Il Vecchietti*, and in an elegy composed for the latter's death.[71] Given this amicable relationship, we may well ask what the nature of Chiabrera's influence was.

Rinuccini's debt to Chiabrera is generally discussed in terms of new poetic meters and verse forms imitated by the latter in turn from French poets, especially Ronsard.[72] Although never formally acknowledged by Chiabrera, his acquaintance with the ideas of the Pléiade was formed in Rome through his friendship with Marc-Antoine Muret, the exiled French humanist and follower of Ronsard. Muret had published a commentary to the collection of poems by Ronsard known as *Les Amours* (1552) and had also composed airs for some of these poems in a musical supplement to the original edition.[73] Furthermore, in his *Vita*, Chiabrera describes his relationship with Muret as an intimate one. The influence of French sources, first on Chiabrera and through him, on Rinuccini, is also evident in the external forms of their poetry. The final chorus, for example of *Dafne*, "Bella Ninfa fuggitiva," is identical in meter to Chiabrera's *canzonetta* "Belle rose porporine" from the 1599 collection *Maniere*, which in turn is built upon Ronsard's "Quand je voy dans un jardin."[74] In these examples, the specific innovations are the use in Italian verse (of a courtly rather than popular nature) of mixed *ottonari* and *quatternari* (eight- and four-syllable lines) and of a six-line strophe with the rhyme aab ccb, a form very popular among the Pléiade poets.[75]

But there is another, more subtle respect in which Chiabrera could have influenced Rinuccini; that is by imparting to him the Ronsardian ideal with regard to the union of poetry and music, thereby transmitting not merely new rhythmic patterns but an entire concept of *poesia musicale*. In keeping with his humanist bias, the French poet felt that music was more than an ornament to the words of the poem and that, as in the case of the ancient Greek lyric, their union was both the product and expression of the inspired soul. For Ronsard, "poetry without instruments or without the grace of one or many voices is in no way pleasing, no more than [the sound of] instruments lacking animation from the melody of a pleasant voice."[76] Accordingly, he composed his verses "à la lyre"[77] and to this end he endowed them with certain qualities, such as the regular alternation of masculine and feminine endings, or a symmetrical rhyme scheme (for example, the aab ccb cited above)—qualities which were natural aids to musical organization and expression. Chiabrera was similarly attentive to the musical values of his poetic rhythms and language. The author of the dedication to his *Maniere de' versi toscani* states that the poems were collected and printed "a richiesta di Musici"[78] and in a passage in his dialogue *Il Geri* Chiabrera declares: "composers . . . quickly confess that the variety of the verse renders it more commodious to their enticing the hearer with their notes."[79] Other observations made in *Il Geri* reveal Chiabrera's keen interest in poetico-musical correspondences; for example, with reference to short verses with frequent rhymes, he says, ". . . song is almost their natural medium of expression; for, who doesn't to some extent recite verses in such a way that they are differentiated from ordinary speech?"[80]

Whether this ideal of a poetry naturally and meaningfully suited to music was one to which Chiabrera consciously aspired or whether it was simply the concomitant of his imitation of Ronsardian meters is difficult to know.[81] Nevertheless he was unquestionably aware that he was creating a new *poesia musicale*, based on a model which had already met with great musical success. In addition to the frequent appearance of poems by Ronsard in sixteenth-century miscellaneous editions of chansons, entire collections of his works were set to music by Philippe de Monte, Antoine de Bertrand, and others.[82] Similarly, Chiabrera's poems were to be very popular at the beginning of the seventeenth century, receiving settings by Claudio Monteverdi, Jacopo Peri, Marco da Gagliano, Francesco Anerio, Domenico Mazzocchi, Francesco Rasi, and others.[83] But it was Giulio Caccini who first gave Chiabrera's verses in many respects their most noteworthy settings and praised the poet specifically for his *canzonette*, "quite different from all the rest, offering me a fine opportunity for variety."[84]

Given the tangible evidence, then, of Rinuccini's imitation of Chiabrera's new metric style, and his witnessing of Chiabrera's successful collaboration with Caccini (which was to take the form in 1600 of the stupendous *Rapimento di Cefalo*), it is tempting to see Chiabrera's influence on Rinuccini as an intangible challenge presented to the latter—a challenge to contemplate anew the whole concept of *poesia musicale*.[85] Until *Dafne*, Rinuccini's poetry for music was entirely in the traditional vein of the Cinquecento madrigal. His contact with Bardi, however, had awakened him to the untapped potential of a poetry destined for the most intimate kind of union with music, a union styled after ancient models. It was very likely Chiabrera's example, which consisted in part of Ronsard's ideal of perfect collaboration of music and poetry, that provided the impetus for Rinuccini's "discovery."

But there were still other stimulating factors to Rinuccini in the Florence of the 1590's. An extremely important one which he acknowledged in his dedication to *Euridice* was the "opinion of many" that ancient tragedy was entirely sung.[86] This acknowledgment, however, which was duplicated in Peri's preface to the score,[87] has been taken less seriously than it deserves to be. Pirrotta dismissed their appeal to "l'opinione di molti" as a mere "petition de principe" for, he maintains, the general opinion of scholars was to the contrary.[88]

Most poetic theorists or commentators in the third quarter of the sixteenth century, relying heavily on Aristotle's *Poetics*, did in fact agree that the only musical part of ancient tragedy was the chorus. Benedetto Varchi, for example, in a series of *Lezzioni della poetica* delivered to the Accademia fiorentina in 1553-54, paraphrases Aristotle in saying that the means of poetry, rhythm (*numero*), discourse (*sermone*), and harmony (*armonia*) were all used by the Greeks in their dithyrambic, nomic, tragic, and comic poetry with this difference: "that the dithyrambic and nomic poets employed all three of these things together, . . . whereas the tragic and comic poets used them separately."[89] In his fourth lesson on tragedy, Varchi glosses each phrase of Aristotle's definition. When he comes to the words "embellished language" (*sermone soave*), he points out that Aristotle himself clarifies these words to include "rhythm, harmony, and melody signifying verse by 'rhythm' and 'harmony' and the song of the chorus and music by 'melody' . . .." He goes on to register the contradictory opinion of some who think that by "rhythm" Aristotle must have been referring to "that form of dancing with which the ancients, Latins as well as Greeks, using actions, gestures, and signs performed the tragedies; others say that this passage indicates verse as a requirement for tragedy."[90] By the absence of any further remark at this point on *melodia*, we may assume that Varchi represents the general consensus on the subject of the place of music in the tragedy. Indeed, Giraldi Cinthio, who asserted his discourse on tragedy to be the first exposition of Aristotle's theory of poetics,[91] was one who interpreted "parlar soave" in this passage to mean verse ("che fu detto metro da

Aristotile"), and rhythm to mean dance, or "il movimento del corpo a misura del canto." At the same time, his opinion on the use of melody by the chorus coincides in part with Varchi's, for in his clarification of the means of tragedy he explains:

> although tragedy may imitate with speech, with melody, and with the measured movement of the body which is called rhythm, it does not however use them all together in all its parts, but separately. For example, in the prologue nothing except speech is used. In the first chorus, melody and rhythm together. . . . In the other choruses, only verse and melody are appropriate.[92]

Even Lodovico Castelvetro, who attempted in his commentary of 1570 to refute Aristotle's theory of poetics, accepted the idea of constant alternation of the means of tragedy. "However," declares Castelvetro, "in singing and dancing the chorus does not represent any action as Aristotle supposes."[93] Rather he maintains that these parts are introduced solely for the delight of the spectators.[94] More of a realist perhaps than some of his contemporaries, Castelvetro seems to object to Aristotle's theory of imitation and katharsis principally on empirical grounds. The idea, in other words, that the singing and dancing of the chorus should provide relief from the dramatic tension of the spoken tragedy had, largely through the popularization of Aristotelian poetics, become rooted in the entertainment practice of the day.

Who then are the "many" to whom Rinuccini and Peri refer in their desire to justify the new style of performing their pastorals *Dafne* and *Euridice*? Again, Girolamo Mei seems to have been the first humanist to express the belief that ancient tragedy was entirely sung. In 1573 Mei communicated to his former teacher Pietro Vettori, who was preparing a commentary on Aristotle's *Politics*, some answers to questions Vettori had posed. The answers were contained in the form of the fourth book of Mei's erudite work on the modes of ancient music which had been in progress since 1568.[95] This final section of *De modis* records Mei's opinion and findings on the uses of music in tragedy, comedy, satire, and dithyramb, and incidentally presents Mei's belief that the performance of ancient tragedy included music in all its parts.[96] Although this treatise remained unprinted along with the rest of Mei's writings, it was not unpublished in the strict sense. In the letter accompanying his manuscript, Mei encouraged Vettori to circulate at least this final book of *De modis* among his friends in Florence.[97] Furthermore, among Mei's letters to Bardi and Galilei are several undated folios containing fragmentary notes on the history of Greek music. Among other statements incorporated by Galilei in his *Dialogo* are the following: "La tragedia et la comedia et la satira non sempre havevano il ritmo del saltare, ma la armonia sempre," and "Le tragedie eran cantate à la tibia ma non col coro."[98]

Vincenzo Galilei's important didactic work, the *Dialogo della musica antica, et della moderna*, written for the enlightenment of Count Bardi's côterie,[99] contains numerous references to the manner of performance of ancient tragedy. Although these are almost always buried in discussion concerning the modes or the tuning of instruments, they attest to both Galilei's acceptance and his transmission of Mei's opinion. For example, in a discussion about the uses of the various modes, Galilei says, "in these two tonoi [Dorian and Phrygian] the comic and tragic characters spoke continuously, as did the satyric actors, reciting their verses on stage to the sound of the tibia."[100] Again, in the section on instruments Galilei cites Aristotle's *Problems on Music* and the rubrics of the comedies of Terence as sources for his statement that "the ancient Greek and Latin actors recited their comedies and tragedies to the sound of the tibia and of the kithara, whence it was necessary to adjust them to suit the high, low, and middle ranges, according to the quality of the characters who took part."[101] Finally, near the end of the work, one of the interlocutors (Strozzi), asks the other (Bardi), "You have told me many times that the ancients sang their tragedies and comedies to the sound of the tibia and the kithara, but you have still to show me what might be the authority which has led you to say and believe this." In his reply Bardi opposes the two sources which are responsible for the dilemma:

> You are very right; now listen. That the tragedies and comedies were truly sung (in the way in which you have understood) by the Greeks is said by Aristotle (besides others worthy of credence) in the section on Music, at Problem 49. It is true that in the Poetics, when he comes to the definition of tragedy, it seems that he forgets in part his first opinion.[102]

This Problem was translated by Mei and probably included with one of his letters intended for Galilei, whose references to the modes reflect Mei's terminology.[103]   The pertinent section of Aristotle's text is as follows:

> Why do the choruses in tragedy not sing either in the Hypodorian or in the Hypophrygian mode? . . . Now the Hypophrygian mode has a character of action . . . ; and the Hypodorian is magnificent and steadfast, and so is the most suitable of all the modes to accompaniment by the lyre. Now both these are unsuited to the chorus and more proper for the characters on the stage.[104]

In his monumental work *Della poetica*, Francesco Patrici also discussed several of Aristotle's Problems relating to this subject and concluded from the evidence that "the entire tragedy, which was composed of actors and chorus, was sung."[105]   Subsequently Patrici mentions Galilei and Bardi with reference to the Tables of Alypios which Galilei had published for the first time in his *Dialogo*.   In fact, Patrici had conferred with Bardi on the subject in 1584, and later that same year portions of his forthcoming treatise on poetics appeared on the agenda of discussions for meetings of the Accademia degli Alterati.[106]   It is apparent, then, that Patrici's opinions on ancient music would have been known to Bardi and therefore probably to Rinuccini and Corsi as well.

Patrici in turn is cited by Agostino Michele, whose discourse, published only three years before *Dafne* was conceived, serves here as an example of the extent to which the theory of an entirely sung tragedy was held.   Michele's *Discorso... come si possono scrivere con molta lode le comedie, e le tragedie in prosa* is dedicated to Orsato Giustiniano, whose verse translation of *Oedipus* was presented at Vicenza in 1585 (without the success which was due to such a great poem, according to the author).[107]   His argument against verse tragedies is based on the assumption that ancient tragedy was sung.   It follows that "since verse is necessary for song, [tragedies] were composed in verse, but since the Tuscans perform them without song (except for the chorus) so they should be written in prose."[108]   Michele also provides an indication that opinion was still divided on this matter when he says, "Some assign the music, in tragedy, to the chorus, in which actors used to sing; but I refer to all the parts of the tragedy; because where there is the rhythm of verse, there is necessarily song."[109]

Another member of the Alterati, Lorenzo Giacomini (1552-1598), humanist philosopher and amateur musician, is also credited with having translated Aristotle's *Problems* dealing with music.[110]   Furthermore, Giacomini knew Mei's theories on the subject of the role of music in ancient tragedy, for he referred to them in a discourse on katharsis presented to the Alterati in 1586.[111]   Written in the pseudo-scientific style of the Aristotelian's language, Giacomini's discourse added fuel to the fire originally kindled with Platonic ideas about the power of music by linking the arts of poetry and music, and offering an affections theory to explain the rationalistic achievement of their common expressive goals.

The foregoing summary of the manifestations of musical humanistic activity, of theories and documents emanating from circles in which Corsi and Rinuccini were involved, either as direct participants or as heirs, makes it difficult for me to believe that *Dafne* was inadvertently a beginning.   On the contrary, it provides evidence which upholds the sincerity of Rinuccini's and Peri's motivation and aims as expressed in their prefatory remarks to *Euridice*. They intended their new productions to be tragic in two respects: first, these were representations in the *style* of classical tragedy—signifying, among other things, that they were to be entirely sung;[112] and second, the musical performance was to render this new genre affective in the same way that it did the ancient tragedy. In this light must Rinuccini's avowed intention be understood, "to make a simple test of what the music of our age could do." In other words, as an author of *poesia musicale* newly aware of the moving potential of poetry in union with its sister art, Rinuccini responded to the challenge of the humanists by issuing his own challenge—the first *libretto per musica.*

II

Pathos, Homeopathy, and Theories of the Affections

"... Dafne composta da me solo per far una semplice prova di quello, che *potesse* il canto dell'età nostra..."[1] What did the humanist poet Rinuccini expect to issue from this challenge to the humanist composers who were to set his first libretto? In what was the *potere* of its song thought to consist?

As I have indicated in Chapter One, the ancients, as they were interpreted by the Renaissance Aristotelians, must be seen as the source of Rinuccini's implicit belief in the power of music, and their dramatic theories as his inspiration to provide a new medium through which music could act on men's souls. Aristotle's conception of the basic relationship between music and the affections, or passions of the soul, is given its most provocative expression in the eighth book of his *Politics*.[2]

> Rhythm and melody supply imitations of anger and gentleness, and also of courage and temperance, and of all the qualities contrary to these, and of the other qualities of character, which hardly fall short of the actual affections, as we know from our own experience, for in listening to such strains our souls undergo a change.

Although the precise nature of this change in the soul, and its causes, remained unexplained in Aristotle's treatises,[3] he observed that certain types of melodies always produced certain effects on their listeners. Classifying these melodies into three categories—moral, active, and enthusiastic—Aristotle claimed for each the ability, respectively, to produce moderation of temper (Dorian), to elicit sadness or feeblemindedness (Mixolydian), or to inspire enthusiasm (Phrygian).[4] The melodies of passion or enthusiasm also serve to bring about katharsis or purgation, which Aristotle merely mentions in this section as one of the benefits or functions of music, describing it with these few words:[5]

> For feelings such as pity and fear, or, again, enthusiasm, exist very strongly in some souls, and have more or less influence over all. Some persons fall into a religious frenzy, whom we see as a result of the sacred melodies— when they have used the melodies that excite the soul to mystic frenzy— restored as though they had found healing and purgation. Those who are influenced by pity or fear, and every emotional nature, must have a like experience, and others in so far as

each is susceptible to such emotions, and all are in a manner purged and their souls lightened and delighted.

Either Aristotle's promise[6] to elucidate his term katharsis in speaking about poetry was never kept, or the pertinent passage was recorded in a section of the *Poetics* that has not survived; so that, in fact, it is most often the passage from the *Politics* quoted above which is called upon to interpret Aristotle's theory of purgation in tragedy implied in the *Poetics* (1449b.27).   In any case, these passages concerning purgation not only constitute the point of departure for sixteenth-century theories about the power of both poetry and music to alter the affections, but they also represent a most important point of contact between the two imitative arts.

The vigorous interest with which theories concerning the affections were evolved by the academicians during the last half of the sixteenth century has been documented and largely described in recent studies of Renaissance literary criticism by Bernard Weinberg[7] and Baxter Hathaway.[8]   Most of these theories were the natural by-products of efforts to interpret Aristotle's principle of katharsis, and many, such as the speculations of Piero Vettori, Lorenzo Giacomini, and Torquato Tasso, took account of the parallel between musical and poetic purgations.   Some writers, Tasso and Guarini among them, also extended the function of purgation to types of poetry other than tragedy.

One of the most thorough investigations of the nature of Aristotle's katharsis principle (*Sopra la purgatione della tragedia*, to which I shall return shortly) was presented to the Accademia degli Alterati in Florence in 1586 by Lorenzo Giacomini.[9]   Two years earlier, Giacomini had shown himself to be an Aristotelian in a lecture to the same academy on "whether divine furor is the efficient cause of poetry, and whether art or nature is of greater consequence in the poet."[10]   (The Alterati members had recently discussed the chapter titles of Francesco Patrici's *Della poetica*, then in the process of being published, and presumably Giacomini felt the need to buttress the academy against Patrici's Platonic leanings.)[11]   His conclusions, that "nature"—i.e., talent—is of greater import than art in any type of creativity, and that this quality resides in the creator and not, as it were, beyond him, are symptomatic of Giacomini's belief in the fairly widespread "doctrine of natural sympathy."[12]   Talent, in Giacomini's interpretation of poesis, is a combination of *ingegno* (genius), *giudicio* (judgment), *docilità* (docility), and *memoria* (memory).   A poet well-endowed with these natural gifts has the ability to place himself in a certain affection by "fixing his imagination" (*la fissa imaginazione*), and consequently be moved to find the conceits appropriate to that affection with which to move others.[13] The bond of "natural sympathy" between the poet (or orator) and his audience – the ancients called it "pathos" – was also given implicit expression by authors concerned with the effects of music. This was undoubtedly the principle behind Galilei's statement, for example, that the aim of ancient music was "to induce in another the same passion that one feels oneself;"[14] hence his admonition to composers to observe actors at the theatre and to learn from them the manner of communicating their emotions and conceits.[15] Similarly, Caccini held that the aim of music is to delight and to move the affections of the soul in others, to which end he claimed to have discovered a certain style of ornamentation *più affettuosa*.[16] Its proper use, however, depended upon the singer's first possessing what he wishes to communicate in song.[17]

From the striking but elementary view of poetics presented in his 1584 discourse on divine furor, Giacomini evolved a full-blown theory of the affections which he delivered to the academy in the treatise, *Sopra la purgatione della tragedia* (1586).[18] The contents of this work are paraphrased extensively by Hathaway in his exhaustive summary of Renaissance interpretations of katharsis,[19] as well as by Palisca in his article concerning the Alterati.[20] I wish only to call attention to those places in Giacomini's text which are of particular relevance to the present subject, the emergence of a musical aesthetics from the humanistic assumptions of the late Renaissance – an aesthetics aimed at stirring the passions of the soul.

First among the passages worthy of note is Giacomini's definition of a poem, for he assigns to poetry the same goals given by Aristotle to music:

> An imitation in figurative language reduced to verse, of human actions (by which word we understand even the affections and the interior movements) made according to the art of poetry, proper for purgation, for instruction, for giving recreation or noble diversion.[21]

In breaking down this definition into its various components, Giacomini enumerates the ends of poetry in even greater detail and speaks of their applicability to painting, sculpture, and music as well.

> . . . we say that [poetry] should be used not for one single end but for many, according to the diversity of poems and of listeners, all of which ends we include in the term profit; [1] for the rest and relaxation of the mind from its affairs and labors, and [2] the noble diversion of the mind through the knowledge of the exquisiteness of the work we classify with Aristotle as profitable, along with [3] purgation and [4] instruction. Those first two ends are common to all poetry, but one of them belongs to intelligent men, the other indeterminately to everybody; the other two are proper to special kinds of poetry since purgation does not take

place except where strong passions are expressed, and some poems certainly do not have the power to benefit virtue and improve character.[22]

To the explanation of the function of purgation and how it is brought about specifically in tragedy Giacomini devotes most of the rest of his treatise. As Hathaway indicates, Giacomini's interpretation differs from that of some of the major commentators of the century — such as Robortelli, Speroni, Minturno, Castelvetro, Piccolomini, and Denores — in that he directed his attention principally to developing the analogy between the physiological purgation achieved by the Greek medical practice of homeopathy — in which purgatives were administered to move those bodily humors not capable of moving themselves — and the purgation accomplished by tragedy.[23] In so doing, he gave a prominent position to Aristotle's theory of musical katharsis presented in the *Politics*, which he considered to be equally valid for ordinary poetry. Giacomini saw as a natural concomitant of Aristotle's justification of tragedy his admission of the active and enthusiastic modes for their ability to purge "strong passions," in contradistinction to the ethical modes, which, capable merely of tempering and soothing the passions, were advocated by Plato for the moral training of youth.

> Those who are easily moved to sorrow, pity, and fear, as well as people in general, are purged by harmonies thought to awaken affections, like the Phrygian and the Mixolydian, which had the property of making the soul contracted and a little saddened, and they receive from songs conforming to these modes a purgation, relief, and alleviation not harmful, but actually delightfully salutary.[24]

Stressing as it did the homeopathic implications of katharsis, Giacomini's view of purgation became, in Hathaway's words, "practically a matter of the physical expenditure of emotion." The spectator is moved by tragedy to the emotions of pity and fear, which in turn find physical expression in the movement of bodily humors or "spirits," and this movement constitutes an outlet or relief for his affections. Thus he is rendered temporarily less compassionate and less fearful, even as a person who has cried for a long while may be said to have given vent to his grief and is not likely to cry again soon.[25] In addition, Giacomini repeatedly called attention, as, for example, in the passage quoted above, to a certain pleasure inherent in purgation — i.e., the unburdening of the dolorous conceits and passions of the soul; and in this same "delightfully salutary" relief from sorrow Giacomini also found the justification for purgation — its utility.[26]

Although the homeopathic view of purgation was shared by other sixteenth-century writers, Giacomini went further than most contemporary critics in attempting to explain the relationship between

external stimuli and the affections in physiological terms, and in
exploring the subtleties of humoral psychology. He defined the
affections as "spiritual movements . . . or operations of the soul in which
it is either desirous of and attracted to an object it has come to know, or
abhors it and is repelled."[27] This attraction or revulsion is governed by
the transportation of a certain *potenza* which resides, according to
Aristotle, in the heart, the source of heat and life, and of all the spirits,
but which, Giacomini believed, is carried by the nerves, as by canals, to
the brain, where these extremely hot spirits from the heart are cooled to
perfection, and where they impart the strength of emotion and of every
voluntary movement. It is this *potenza* which, when it receives objects
either agreeable or disagreeable to itself, experiences either pleasure or
pain, and simultaneously causes these same emotions, or more complex
mixtures of them, in the soul.[28] Giacomini went on to explain that every
individual has inclinations of temperament which vary according to the
balance and diversity of spirits in his body.

> Heat, rarity, and agility of the spirits dispose us to gay affections; which is why
> young men are more easily moved than old men to be gay; and by warming and
> rousing the spirits and envigorating the body, food and drink bring forth
> merriment. On the other hand, the overburdening of the sensitive parts [of the
> soul] with agitated and impure vapors, and the lessening of the internal heat leads
> to melancholy and fear, and makes us seem indolent, slow, and useless . . .[29]

To illustrate how the corporeal spirits or vapors operate in his theory of
affections, Giacomini described the process by which tears are condensed
from the many vapors rising to the head when, as the result of some
external stimulus inducing sorrow, the *parti interne* are caused to
contract. The vapors issue in the form of tears, thereby effecting a
purgation of the affection of sorrow by freeing the mind of its excess
vapors.[30] Even more interesting is his description of the causes of *voci
lamentevoli*, which are brought forth, as it were, instinctively

> in order to remove the evil disposition that afflicts the sensitive part [of the soul]
> by shrinking and aggravating especially the heart, which suffers more as it is full
> of spirits and of heat; whence in order to escape pain, and to enlarge and free
> itself from the anguish, the lungs and the other organs of the voice move and
> utter shrieks and moans, unless they be impeded by the intellect.[31]

Certain of Giacomini's ideas seem to me to reveal some important
aspects of the humanistic thought from which the theory, if not the
practice, of monody and opera was born. First is the clarity with which
Giacomini, following Aristotle's lead, links the arts of poetry and music,
insisting on their common functions and aims—recreation or relaxation

of the mind, its noble diversion through the appreciation of beauty (what we might call "aesthetic pleasure"), purgation, and moral instruction. Second is his rationalistic expression of the humanistic desire to understand, and thereby to control, the affections.[32] This is not to claim, however, that Giacomini stands in any direct relationship to the poets and composers who produced the first operas, nor that his lecture on purgation to the Alterati members contains any hint of dissatisfaction with contemporary musical practice, as do the works of Mei and Galilei. But it is easy to see how such a materialistic theory as Giacomini promulgated, explaining how the affections of the soul are aroused by the movement of its spirits, could give rise to the belief that a rapidly moving bass, for example, is more suitable to the expression of happy affections, presumably through its ability precisely to rouse the spirits. Peri testified to his acceptance of this assumption in wishing to regulate the motion of the lines of his composition so that the recitative "might not seem in a way to dance to the movement of the bass, particularly in sad or solemn subjects, although others more joyful naturally require more frequent movements [changes of harmony in the bass]."[33]   In the same place Peri speaks of having devoted himself wholly to discovering that "imitation of speech in song" used by the ancients in reciting their poems. To this end,

> keeping in mind those modes and accents which serve us in our sorrow, in our joy, and the like, I made the bass move in time to these, now more, now less [frequently], according to the affections . . .[34]

Similarly, Caccini cautions against using ornaments which imitate languid affections in *musiche ariose*, or in *canzonette a ballo*; for these require a certain liveliness, usually imparted by the *aria* itself, the motion of which would then be contradicted by the introduction of an affective *maniera*.[35]   Thus the goal of music, like that of oratory — moving the affections — became largely a matter of anticipating and imitating the effects on the listener's *parti interne* of the emotion one wished to evoke.

To be sure, Peri and Caccini do not concern themselves in these prefaces with explanations of the physiological or psychological causes of the effects of their new style, or of music in general; nor do they make reference to other writers' thoughts on the subject. They were not philosophers nor aestheticians, but practical musicians engaged in publicizing their achievements and, to some extent, rationalizing their stylistic position. On the other hand, we may assume that they, as well as their readers were, if not learned, at least literate, and would certainly have been cognizant of some of the aesthetic theories blossoming in the path of classical scholarship and sixteenth-century debates, not to mention the traditional and widespread ideas about humoral psychology. Although Giacomini's theory of the corporeal movement of the spirits, anticipating as it does Descartes' *esprits animaux* and mechanistic view of the passions by more than half a century,[36] was quite new, the concept of a *spiritus* closely associated with music was explicitly postulated as early as 1489 in the works of Marsilio Ficino.[37] According to Ficino (and later, Girolamo Mei),[38] the peculiar power of music (and poetry) resides in the fact that, unlike other sensual stimuli, it is carried by air, which is also the medium of the *spiritus*. It follows that hearing is superior to the other senses because the ear, containing air and thus capable of receiving the movements of music, transmits these movements to the *spiritus*, which, being itself movement, can impart them in turn to the soul.

> Remember that song is the most powerful imitator of all things. For it imitates the intentions and affections of the soul, and speech, and also reproduces bodily gestures, human movements and moral characters, and imitates and acts everything so powerfully that it immediately provokes both the singer and hearer to imitate and perform the same things.[39]

Concerning Ficino's influence on subsequent writers, D. P. Walker offers the suggestion that, since Ficino was to some extent the originator of the "music-spirit" theory, he is also the probable source from which later appearances were derived. After citing its occurrence in Agrippa, Gregor Reisch, Scaliger, and Zarlino,[40] but missing it in Mei, Walker goes on to express his sense of unfulfilled expectations that the theory was not more widely adopted, coinciding as it does so closely with fundamental trends of sixteenth-century musical humanism. My objection to these statements is that together they imply, although perhaps unwittingly, that without Ficino's "music-spirit" theory humanists after Zarlino were at a loss to explain the effects of music on the passions. In other words, Walker appears to leave little room for the influence on musical humanism of the other musico-poetic theories abounding in the late Renaissance, some of which were closely related to Ficino's and were undoubtedly evolved from the same sources. Walker acknowledges, for example, Ficino's debt to both Aristotle and Galen[41] in formulating his definition of *spiritus*, a definition which partakes of both ethical and medical concepts:

> [the] instrument by which [scholars] can, in a way, measure and grasp the whole world . . . by the physicians defined as a certain vapour of the blood, pure, subtle, hot and lucid. And, formed from the subtler blood by the heat of the heart, it flies to the brain, and there the soul assiduously employs it for the exercise of both the interior and exterior senses.[42]

In addition to the Peripatetic writings, such as the physical *Problems, On the Soul,* and *On the Motion and Generation of Animals,* all "rediscovered" during the sixteenth century, the works of Galen appear to have been revived in Latin translation, beginning quite early in the century.[43] It is therefore not surprising to discover that Giacomini not only relies heavily on Aristotle and Galen, citing them several times in this treatise on purgation, but also shares two of the three component elements of Ficino's music-spirit theory enumerated by Walker:[44] the medical concept of *spiritus,* and credence in the ethical power of ancient music and in its therapeutic use. To these Girolamo Mei added the third element, the Aristotelian-Augustinian accounts of hearing and the nature of sound, which he expressed in some unpublished vernacular writings unknown to Walker.[45] Thus, while it is true that Ficino's "music-spirit" theory as such may not be said to have been widely adopted, its component elements certainly retained their seminal qualities and survived in one form or another until the late sixteenth century. Concerning the apparent neglect of Ficino's theory by history, I find relevant Hathaway's opinion on the significance of Giacomini's treatise for his time: "That it did not provoke an answer is evidence that his contemporaries did not find his conclusions upsetting or unthinkable."[46] It may be said, then, that the musical humanists after Zarlino had at their disposal some of the same ideas used by Ficino in the contexts given them by later scholars, such as Giacomini and Mei, among others, who made their own humanistic syntheses of Aristotelian, Platonic, and Galenic concepts.

Another such synthesis, by Francesco Buonamici, will be singled out briefly here because it suggests, as did Giacomini's, a philosophical and psychological theory or rationalization of certain ideas, which, although they remain unexplained by Peri and Caccini, seem clearly to underlie their statements. Buonamici's *Discorsi poetici nella Accademia fiorentina,* published in Florence in 1597, are in fact very closely contemporary to the first operas. Although his view of purgation is an eclectic one and gives place to both homeopathic and allopathic interpretations,[47] Buonamici's explanation of how the purgation is effected was more original — according to Hathaway, even unique.[48] It centered about the concept of the "natural sympathy" uniting the actors with their audience, and led the author to postulate the existence of a ratio between the extrinsic motions of the mind (passions or "commotions" and habits, which may be imitated by the poet on stage or in music) and its intrinsic motions (which are our natural aptitudes). From this, Buonamici created a "psychology of motions" in which purgation was seen as the overcoming or cancellation of intrinsic by extrinsic motions. Thus, for example, an actor or singer, by being moved himself, moves his listener because of the sympathetic response of the human nervous system, and the resulting commotion in the listener, if it is great enough, simultaneously purges and controls his natural aptitudes, which generally tend toward weakness and excess. That Buonamici's formula would not stand up under scientific or logical scrutiny should not deter us from recognizing it among late Renaissance affections theories as one which bears striking similarities, at least in language, to the assumptions made by musical humanists concerning the power of music to move the passions of the soul.

There is one more point raised by both Giacomini and Buonamici — indeed by many other writers toward the end of the century, such as Tasso, Guarini, and Gabriele Zinano — which is here worthy of note, especially in connection with the question of the genre of Rinuccini's early libretti; that is, the belief that all types of poetry (some specified dramatic poetry) were conducive to purgation. By maintaining that the function of tragedy comprehended Aristotle's four goals of poetry and music, Giacomini, for example, was able to defend those tragedies which do not represent an altogether sad action but which progress from *miseria* to *felicità*. These, too, are capable of purging, he argued, for a foreboding evil which seems inevitable is contemplated by the soul as a present reality, and thereby moves it to pity.[49] Presumably, Giacomini felt that if enough tears were provoked by the events leading up to the *fin lieto*, the mind of the spectator could be temporarily relieved of the mournful passions which might otherwise consume it, and a katharsis could thus be accomplished.[50] At the end of this treatise, in enumerating the "artistic" delights of tragedy (and, we may assume, of tragicomedy), Giacomini formally acknowledged that "the compassion of tragedy can also . . . bring delight" because feeling pity is virtuous, and virtue is synonymous with joy.[51]

This revelling in tears, and the emphasis on man's need to weep, evident in Giacomini, was shared by several of his contemporaries and is an interesting portent of the pathetic trend of *seicentismo*. Given the tenor of late sixteenth-century bucolic poetry, it is easy to see how Giacomini's tragic compassion could be transformed into some sort of nameless melancholy, the alleviation of which, for Tasso and Guarini, was one of the most important effects of purgation. The poet whose influence on Rinuccini was greatest, Tasso, was not clear as to how this purgation was brought about and in fact believed in both an allopathic and homeopathic interpretation of Aristotle;[52] but he was convinced that all types of poetry purge the passions, since words are symbols which move the mind "more than spectacles," and hearing is the "sense organ

of discipline and the instrument of the philosophic purgation." Although
Tasso decried the excesses of contemporary poetry and music, and
especially "all that can be attacked as languid and effeminate in the
amorous passions,"[53] he conceded that even "amorous laments" and
"laments for the death of lovers" are useful in purging the
passions[54] — especially the passion of melancholy, since laments
presumably evoke tears and tears relieve the soul of the oppression of
dolorous conceits.   Guarini, wishing to prove in his defense of
tragicomedy that some sort of purgation could be achieved by plays with
happy endings, was even more explicit.   He declared that modern
audiences have no need to be purged of the tragic emotions of pity and
fear, for they, unlike the pagans of antiquity, have the holy precepts of
religion to guide them.   Rather, the driving out of sadness, or
melancholy, was the legitimate concern of the modern playwright, and
this could be accomplished admirably by tragicomedy, the effects of
which he believed (being an allopathist) were closer to comic than tragic
purgation.[55]

It is hardly necessary to point out the sheer delight with which the
poets and composers of the earliest operas imitated the sighs and tearful
plaints of nymphs and shepherds. Indeed, this was not new to opera, as
Einstein's observations on the *Pastor fido* (a "premature opera"), the
Aminta, and the ensuing madrigal literature testify.

For Caccini, too, the key to moving the affections was obviously the
imitation of such effects of the voice as were indicative of a melancholy
state of mind. This is surely the reason behind his describing at such
great length the proper method of employing the ornament *esclamazione*,
that sudden decreasing in volume of the voice on a given pitch, originally
sounded *rinforzando*, which Caccini considered to be the "principal
means of moving the affections." In fact, one of the most characteristic
beginnings of Caccini's monodies is a melodic leap downwards, which,
especially if uttered with the decreasing intensity of *esclamazione*, sounds
indeed like a sigh exploding from an anguished soul.   This is the
"maniera più affettuosa" Caccini claimed to have discovered in his desire
better to attain the goal of music, "to delight and move the affections of
the soul."[56]   Bearing in mind Giacomini's concept of the utility of
tragedy — which depended upon its use of various kinds of *diletto*, among
them being the pleasure of feeling compassion[57] — I don't think it would
distort Caccini's meaning to say that for him, music produced delight
precisely because it was capable of moving the affections (especially that
of melancholy), and thereby, presumably, of purging them.[58]   One has
only to think of the many descriptions of stage presentations around the
turn of the century — descriptions in which audiences are said to have

given lacrimose expression to their enjoyment of these performances — to realize how highly prized and sought after was the evocation and consequent removal of tearful sentiments.[59] This is not to say, however, that the other affections were ignored. At least in theory, the composers of the *seconda prattica* claimed that theirs was a style which could imitate more effectively the entire gamut of emotions. Alessandro Guidotti, Cavalieri's spokesman and editor of his *Rappresentazione di Anima et di Corpo* (1600), remarked that the "type of music regenerated by [signor Emilio del Cavaliere] moves various affections in us, such as pity and jubilation, tears and laughter, and so on . . ."[60] In the preface to Marco da Gagliano's version of Rinuccini's *Dafne*, the composer praised Peri's style both as composer and singer, asserting that no one who has heard him sing has failed to be moved by the grace of his airs and the affection of the words, and is consequently "compelled to weep and rejoice, at the composer's will."[61] Earlier, Galilei had expressed his belief in the ability of ancient music to communicate the "concetti dell'anima" of any person, no matter what his character, age, or station.[62] It was simply that the prevailing literary taste of the late sixteenth century was disposed to favor above all those *meste e lagrimose scene* of which *La Tragedia* speaks in Rinuccini's prologue to *Euridice*. Far from being a misguided and habitual classicizing impulse, then, Rinuccini's evocation of Tragedy in the role of Prologue provides an opportunity for an eloquent defense of tragicomedy, an invitation, as it were, to hear Tragedy's new song and rid one's heart of melancholy. Within the first three quatrains of the prologue, she announces her changed mission — to awaken in her audience not the pity and terror of old, but rather "più dolci affetti," the sweeter affections to which tragicomedy also aspires.[63]

Another Florentine humanist, one who devoted all of his mature scholarly effort to discovering, through careful scrutiny of ancient sources, the nature of the music of the ancients and its effects on the soul, was Girolamo Mei (1519-1594). Mei's reputation in humanist literary circles was such that Giacomini was glad to cite him among the *uomini scienzati* sharing his own view of purgation.[64] Intellectually descended from the so-called Platonic Academy through his teacher, Piero Vettori (1499-1585), Mei also shared elements of Ficino's music-spirit theory which he undoubtedly gleaned from his own study of Aristotle and other classical sources.[65]

Mei's first efforts to come to grips with some of the problems of ancient music were expressed incidentally in two early vernacular treatises, the contents of which to my knowledge have not been discussed by any historians of musical humanism. *Trattato sopra la prosa toscana, e della composizione delle parole in due libri* and *Del verso toscano*[66] were probably written around the time of Mei's admission into the newly formed Accademia de' Umidi in 1540.   Palisca points out how well the subject of the two works coincides with the aims of the academy, which was dedicated to the propagation of the Tuscan language (it soon became known as the Accademia fiorentina) and the translation of Greek and Latin authors.[67]   At the same time, they already revealed Mei's knowledge of Augustine's *De musica* and Aristoxenus' *Harmonics*, sources which he later included in a list of ancient writings on music recommended to Galilei.[68]

Mei's analysis of the elements of vernacular poetry led him to conclude that Tuscan verse is not totally unrelated in essence and form to Greek and Latin poetry, since each is governed by the quantitative proportions of time – the time taken in uttering the words of the verse. The proportions are the same for all three types of poetry, but the way of determining them differs; whereas in Greek and Latin verse the length of the syllables are compared, in the Italian language, which makes no distinction between long and short syllables, the proportions are determined by counting the number of syllables in a line of poetry and establishing the natural position of acute and grave syllables within the line ("positura d'acutezza e gravità quasi naturale").[69]   For Mei it was the alternation of high and low syllables via the intensification and relaxation of the voice that constituted rhythm in language, and meter in poetry.[70] The quality of each syllable – acute, grave, or circumflex – was its accent or inflection,[71] but the word *accento* was also used in a more specific sense to refer to the stress placed upon a particular syllable by elevating its pitch above the others in the same word or verse.[72]

In Mei's system of scanning Tuscan poetry, then, the position of acute or accented syllables determined the ratio or proportion of the verse.   For example if in a seven-syllable line of poetry the accents fall on the third and sixth syllables (e.g., *Misuràt'allegrèzza*) the verse divides itself into the ratio 3:3 and may be said to be governed by the proportion of equality.[73]   Similarly, if the second and sixth syllables are acute (e.g., *Leggiàdra ricovérse*), the ratio is 2:4 and the *maniera* of this verse form is generated by the multiple proportion.   After having thus enumerated all the possible *maniere* of Tuscan poetry, proceeding from the equal, multiple, and superparticular proportions,[74] Mei went on to show how, in his opinion, each verse form must not only be proportionate in itself, but, in order to work on the emotions and be comprehended by the senses, must also be proportionate to the faculties receiving it (i.e., neither too short nor too long),[75] as well as appropriate for the expression of the conceit it intends.[76]   As illustrations, Mei cited the seven-syllable verse forms with the ratios 3:3 and 2:4, both of which appear to the ear to be somehow mutilated; their short duration barely satisfies the senses, and the speed with which they go by is conducive to levity.[77] For this reason, the *maniere* born of these proportions are commonly reserved for treating subjects which correspond to them in nature, either by their excess of affection, or by their frivolity. As examples of this type of poetry, Mei mentioned *canzoni* and *frottole* in which subjects are, if not chosen for their lightness, at least treated lightly, or in which graceful and delicate matters are preferred to grave and serious ones.[78] But when great poets wish to treat serious subjects of some importance, or else graceful and delicate ones with seriousness, they use the eleven-syllable line, generated by the superparticular ratio (4:6), far more frequently than that of seven syllables.[79] Similarly, Mei judged the eight-syllable line (3:4) to be perfect in its own way for simple or light-hearted subjects, such as *laudi* or rhymes pertaining to "peasant things" (*cose villesche*), or *canzoni a ballo*.[80]

For many of the thoughts expressed here as well as in the treatise on prose, Mei was, like his contemporaries, greatly indebted to Aristotelian sources. *On the Soul*, which has as its central preoccupation the nature of sense perception as it relates to the psychology and physiology of the soul, seems to be particularly relevant to *Del verso toscano*. The Italian philologist began his treatise with a discussion of the nature of acuteness and gravity (a question which was to become the central factor in his theory, developed later, of ancient modes), in a passage which has a direct parallel in the Peripatetic work:

> The acuteness and gravity of accent are two effects of the voice, the first of which arises from the speed and the second from the slowness of the movement which produces it, and are opposed to each other as contraries. . . . *Acuteness* and *gravity* are manifestly two terms transferred to the two main differences of tone, the one taken from the form of the angle most able to pierce, and the other from the property of nature least suited to be overcome and forced by unnatural motion. . . . Similarly the effect of the voice generated by speed, by its (for want of a better word) compactness suited to violence, moving as if to make a place by force, pierces more vigorously; whereas that which arises from slowness . . . being easily impeded by an obstacle which comes in its path, tries to oppose it . . . and in this way breaks through rather than pierces.[81]

Mei went on to develop and explore these distinctions in a thoroughly Aristotelian way. For example, his notion that the fastness and slowness which cause the differences in pitch result in turn from the relative strength with which the *spirito* strikes the air[82] is obviously based upon Aristotle's theory that "everything that makes a sound does so by the impact of something (a) against something else, (b) across a space, (c) filled with air."[83] Also rooted in Aristotelian thought was Mei's belief, held in common with Ficino, that hearing is superior to the other senses because the ear, which contains air, receives the impulses of sound transmitted through air, and these, "by playing the right keys, so to speak" can communicate clear and real images to the intellect.[84]   In his treatise on prose, Mei added that the speaker who is attentive to the rhythm of his language (manifested in the alternation of acuteness and gravity) does not allow the ear to become disquieted with tedium, but knows how to renew its interest by pleasing it with the natural imitation of that which is to be understood.   According to his definition, rhythm, called *numerus* by the Latins, is a quality of composition which, "if proportionate to the conceit it wishes to express, upon being heard gives a certain satisfaction to the ear, and in a near-perfect manner, gratifies the intellect."[85]

In the foregoing remarks, which probably date from before 1550, one can witness the emergence of certain concepts very much akin to the cardinal doctrines of musical humanism.   First is the belief in the peculiar power of organized, intelligible sound, which has, as it were, direct contact with the soul via the sense of hearing.[86]   Even in Mei's own "Come potesse tanto la musica appresso gli antichi," an unfinished treatise composed at the end of his life which took him further into the field of aesthetics than any previous effort, the basic Aristotelian assumptions concerning the production of tones and their effect seem to have been taken practically *verbatim* from these early essays.[87]   Second is his precept that sound, in order to work on the emotions and to be comprehended by the senses, must be proportionate to the faculty which receives it, and also proportionate to (i.e., imitative of) the conceit which it intends.   One thinks of Mei's later admonitions to contemporary musicians recorded in his correspondence with Galilei; he objected, for example, to a melody which required a singer to leap to intervals above or below his range, for this violates nature, and does not serve the expression of the conceit.[88]   For the same reasons, Mei criticized the "continual sweetness" of the contrapuntists who, with "a hundred other excessive means of artifice," seeking to delight the ear, at the same time prevent the soul from being moved to any affection at all.[89]   The same precept surely lay behind his condemnation of the modern composer's carelessness with rhythm, "which frequently, not to say always, . . . is contrary to the nature of the object intended by that conceit signified by the words. . . ."[90]   Mei illustrated this tendency by describing a part song in which, at the same time, and on the same text, "the soprano barely moves while the tenor flies . . . (etc.)," an example repeated by both Bardi and Galilei, who condemned the rhythmic inequality of the parts in very similar language.[91]

The third and final assumption emerging in these treatises, one which again prefigures Mei's relationship to a nascent musical humanism destined to form a new style, concerns the notion of imitation. At the end of the discussion of rhyme with which he closed *Del verso toscano*, Mei concluded that imitation and not artifice is the true soul of poetry.[92] For him, as for Galilei, Peri, and Caccini, to express the conceits of the soul meant to imitate the manner or quality of those conceits as they are uttered in human speech;[93] for the manner of man's speech (and action) reveals his character or disposition because it in turn is indicative of certain motions of the soul. Galilei of course ridiculed the type of literal imitation practiced by the madrigalists and contrapuntists of Zarlino's generation, and went on to say that ancient musicians were infintely more capable of moving the passions because, like the orators of old, they understood how to imitate the qualities of tone, rhythm, gesture, etc. — in other words, the motions expressive of those passions.[94] Similarly, Peri sought to imitate in song those accents of speech "which serve us in our sorrow, in our joy, and the like."[95] And Caccini too claimed to have introduced a type of music based on the accents of speech, through which one could almost "speak in song."[96] In another passage, he emphasized the necessity of understanding the conceit of the words before attempting to imitate it, expressing its "flavor" in *corde affettuose* and *con affetto*.[97]

It is possible to trace the development and elaboration of this theory of imitation throughout Mei's writings. To do so is to witness the evolution of a fullfledged theory of affections, one which bore an important relationship, if not to the motivation for the monodic reform and creation of opera, then certainly to their subsequent rationalization. For, if the composers of the second practice had any theory at all, it was the conviction that their new style was eminently more capable of moving the affections; and, as Palisca justly remarks, Mei's greatest influence lay in his view, transmitted through Galilei, that music was an expressive and imitative art, more closely related to rhetoric and poetry than to mathematics or cosmology, as Zarlino believed along with other theorists who had been brought up in the Platonic-Boethian tradition. This was precisely the "new orientation that Galilei passed on to the rising generation of musicians who knew him and read his dialogue."[98]

Mei's first essays in working out an affections theory were conceived in terms of the sounds — consonants and vowels — of language, although the general assumptions concerning sound which emerged in these early treatises served him well in later writings on music. Mei held that each of the sounds, or elements, of language possesses its characteristic *passione* — the quality and distinctiveness of its pronunciation[99] — which is recognized "by some almost incomprehensible sense in us."[100] The chief distinction to be noted in Mei's system is always the acuteness or gravity of the vowel or syllable, for, as he explained more clearly in "Come potesse tanto la musica..."

> gravity and acuteness are actually passions contrary to one another, the one generated by the speed, and the other by the slowness of the motion from which each derives.[101]

Mei felt justified in calling these sounds "passions," for the motions from which they result are in turn created by the muscles of the chest and elsewhere striking the air; and by likening these muscles to "natural keys which obey the soul, involuntarily or necessarily expressing what is dictated by it at that moment,"[102] Mei postulated an exact correspondence between the motions of the soul and the rhythm of language, manifest in the alternaton of acute and grave syllables. Thus he was able to say, in *Trattato sopra la prosa*, that

> . . . just as, naturally, in the range and interval of the voice called by musicians diastematic, in other words, intervallic, the more acute places are a sign of an agitated soul, and the medium ones [designate] a tranquil soul, so in the same way, in the voice also called by them . . . continuous, the natural highness simply compared to the lowness in words retains proportionately the same qualities. Whence those words which have only acute syllables, the more they are strung together, the more able they are than the other kind to create this affection and are thus, for some reason unknown to me, more suitable to a youthful manner than to a serious and old one . . .[103]

With respect to multi-syllable words, Mei reasoned that when the last syllable is grave the effect is temperate, since the grave syllable serves to quiet the ear after it has been struck by the vivacity and strength of the acute syllable. When on the other hand the last syllable is acute, the effect is rousing, and most forceful indeed if the accented syllable were at the end of a long word. In general, the further from the end an acute accent falls, the more its strength will be dissipated by the unaccented syllables which follow; the total effect will be the representation of a noble affection, entirely unsuited for light conceits and for this reason appropriate for discourse which aims at splendor or greatness.[104] In this way, the manner of men's speech (and actions) reveal their character, so that although cowards, for example, may try to hide their true qualities by their appearance,

> [they] are made to show themselves individually and as a group, by their own qualified and modest manner, wherein their skimpy dress, rapid speech, quick step, and shrill voice have nothing at all majestic about them; and the great men

and diligent examiners of noble manners, and of their proprieties have their greatness confirmed in their stately movement, deep voice, and quiet speech.[105]

The core of Mei's theory of affections may be seen in his attempt to explain precisely the relationship between the instruments of imitation and their objects.

Different dispositions are naturally associated with different movements. That is the reason why that which is very hot induces quickness and celerity, and very cold slowness and lethargy, just as the temperate is always associated with evenness and calm. Whence it follows, for the same reason, that from the quality of the vowels it is learned that their tones are heightened, so to speak, by the rapidity of the movements of agitated souls after they have been heated, and when by fear or another affection, [the movements] have been slowed down, [the tones] are lowered; if there is no motion, none of these changes appear.[106]

For these reasons, Mei continued, the angry man and the commander speak quickly and concisely, whereas the person who is fearful and lowly is naturally slow in his speech, and diffuse. Without having any other recourse except to these natural aids, these persons are capable of expressing their characteristic affections.[107] It follows that, in imitating or representing these affections, one must bear in mind the following: since acute and grave syllables are generated by the strength and velocity of the soul's movements, and are capable of expressing only those affections which correspond to these movements, the more one kind exceeds the other in being heard, the more readily its characteristic affections are represented above the other. When acute and grave syllabes are equally represented, a neutral and temperate disposition results,

because each similitude, as though naturally arousing passions like to itself, always moves, in proportion to its ability, similar affections in the object destined to receive it.[108]

That Mei's ideas concerning the effects of high and low pitch did not evolve much beyond this point may be seen in his correspondence with Galilei beginning in 1572, as well as in his last effort, "Come potesse..." However, by placing his discoveries in a somewhat different context, and relating them to his newly acquired knowledge about the ancient modes, Mei provided the stimulus for a renewal of interest in the legendary powers of ancient music. In his first letter to Galilei, dated 8 May 1572, Mei repeated his thoughts on the properties of acuteness and gravity, and added that *tuoni mezzani* are suitable for demonstrating a quiet and moderate temperament, whereas those which are extremely high are signs of an agitated and aroused soul, and those which are very low, of abject and submissive thoughts. In the same way, the extremes of rhythm reveal states of the soul which are *concitato* or *pigro*, and moderate rhythm indicates a poised soul.[109]

Mei carried these assumptions to their logical conclusion when he stated that the marvellous effects of ancient music stemmed precisely from its ability to move the affections; in this, of course, it differed from modern music which has as its goal only the delectation of the ear.[110] In order to achieve its aim, ancient music always presented a single affection embodied in *un aria sola*, wherein all the voices and instruments sang and played the same notes with the same words at the same time.[111] In addition the Greek poet-musician strove

> to express completely and efficaciously whatever he wished to have understood
> through his sung speech by means and through the aid of the highs and lows of
> the voice . . . accompanied with a regulated temperament of the fast and slow,
> articulating the parts of his composition according to these qualities so that each
> one by itself through its proper nature was accommodated to some determinate
> affection.[112]

Mei, who hardly considered himself gifted in the practice of music, believed the modern musician incapable of moving the affections because of the excesses of polyphony wherein each voice sings a different *aria* with different rhythms, causing the words to be broken up and violating the expression of the intended conceit, as well as confusing the intellect by representing a diversity of affections simultaneously.[113] In order to realize its aim, then, music must present a careful imitation to the ear of that which it wishes to represent, and by means of the ear, the intellect will receive an accurate impression of the objects imitated.[114]

A large portion of this first letter, in which Mei also revealed his discoveries concerning the correct disposition of the Greek *tonoi* higher and lower on the greater perfect system,[115] was circulated and later printed under the title *Discorso sopra la musica antica e moderna*.[116] In view of this fact, and also of the close relationship between Galilei and his patron, Giovanni de' Bardi, it is not surprising to find in the latter's discourse *Sopra la musica antica e 'l cantar bene*, addressed to Caccini, the following precepts:

> Those great philosphers and connoisseurs of nature understood well that in the
> low voice is slowness and somnolence, in the medium, quiet, majesty, and
> magnificence, and in the high, shrillness and lament. Now who does not know
> that the drunken and the somnolent usually speak in a low tone and slowly, and
> that men of great affairs converse in a medium voice, quiet and magnificent; . . .
> Concerning all this Aristotle says, at the end of the *Politics*, that in the rhythms
> are the portraits of anger, mildness, strength, temperance, and of every other

moral virtue, as well as of all those qualities which are their contraries, citing the reasons a little further on when he said, in melodies are the changes of character [*costumi*], because one does not remain unchanged upon hearing each of them...[117]

In speaking about the ancient modes, Galilei asserted that the Platonists rejected those that were very high or very low, the former for being *lamentevoli,* the latter, *lugubri.*[118] Elsewhere in the *Dialogo,* he remarked:

It is no wonder that the diversity of sound with respect to highness and lowness, together with the difference of motion, and interval, imparts variety of harmony and affection; for nature does not ordinarily produce similar things with contraries, nor contraries by means of the same quality, but rather with the opposite. When to the consideration of these things were added the suitability of rhythm and the conformity of conceit . . . melody . . . would be capable, as it used to be, of swaying the souls of the hearers in whatever way pleased the skilled musician.[119]

Similarly, when after having derided the practices of modern contrapuntists, Galilei advised them to learn the art of affective expression from actors at the theatre, he directed their attention particularly to the high or low pitch of the voices, the volume and speed with which they are uttered, and the differences among *accenti* and gestures from one character to another.[120]

Mei's last treatise, "Come potesse tanto la musica appresso gli antichi...,"[121] is actually nothing more than a humanist's primer on music, the first section of which serves as an introduction dealing with questions concerning physics, physiology, and aesthetics. Noteworthy is Mei's description of three types of "compositura dell'aria" used by the ancients, each for a different type of expression. The two most common were called "continuous," an almost running style suited to speech, and "intervallic," appropriate to singing because of the extent and certainty of its intervals.[122] Mei added that a third type, described by Aristeides Quintilianus,[123] was "midway between the other two" and "was used by them especially in uttering their verses in reading."[124] Whether or not Mei's manuscript treatises were known to the humanist composers Corsi and Peri, the latter claimed some knowledge of ancient musical practice in his preface to *Euridice*; and the description therein of his concept of ancient dramatic music as "surpassing that of ordinary speech, but falling so far below the melody of song as to take an intermediate form" is, if not a paraphrase of Mei's definition, certainly consistent with it.[125]

In the section of the *trattato* devoted to melopoeia, Mei distinguished among three styles of composition (*modi della compositura*), which formed an important part of the expressive resources of the ancient musicians since each was associated with the representation of a particular manner (*costume*). For example, compositions which represented greatness and magnificence of character, loftiness of spirit, heroic actions, and affections corresponding to these things, were used particularly in tragedy and therefore were said to be in the tragic style. At the other extreme, the so-called nomic style was associated with the representation of submissive and lowly affections, signifying a somewhat oppressed soul and an abject disposition unworthy of man. This style was suited to amorous passions, or to lamentation, pity and the like. The third manner of composition, the dithyrambic, was used for hymns of praise, and for quiet and tranquil states of the soul.[126] These styles not only had characteristic ranges – the tragic, nomic, and dithyrambic "modes" centered respectively about the low, high, and middle strings of the gamut – but they also had characteristic rhythmic qualities. Mei describes these "rhythmic modes" in the section on rhythmopoeia and eventually relates them to the three styles of melopoeia just enumerated.[127] Thus, the more rapid tempo was suitable for the imitation of the humble and submissive affections, the slower one for grandiose and magnificent subjects, and a moderate tempo for tranquil and pacific ones.

Before coming to the last part of his work, which describes the instruments of antiquity and deals with their uses and virtues,[128] Mei made several remarks about the performance of ancient tragedy which bear directly on the beliefs underlying the experiments of the earliest operas. In speaking about the use of rhythm in the ancient poetic genres, he declared that in tragedy, as well as in those comedies and satyr-plays which had a chorus, the principal parts of music (song and rhythm) were always used together and continuously as in the dithyrambs and nomoi, except in those parts in which the chorus was stationary.[129] The chorus itself sang "un aria sola di canto," without the admixture of counterpoint or consonant voices except for the octave, and its aria was "seconded" by one or more instruments chosen according to the ends they were to serve.[130] For example, in tragedy the actors were accompanied by auloi alone which were "accomodati à sopraffar'... ogni tumulto de gli spettatori" and consequently were useful for keeping the performers on key. Most importantly, all accompaniments were adapted to the ends they were to serve, whether these were "necessary" ends – e.g., to maintain law in times of war, or to incite or inflame others to battle – or "voluntary" ones. In this latter category Mei cited public celebrations or rites, such as sacrifices, and private performances, which aimed at "restoring souls" or maintaining certain affections in them as well as producing a purgation or alleviating the passions harbored by the individuals in the audience.[131]

Mei concluded that the role of instruments was an imitative one with respect to the voice, in that the regulation of their highness and lowness varied with the vocal range according to the occasion.[132]

The figure of Girolamo Mei, musical humanist and historian, closes the gap, so to speak, between Aristotle and the Florentine *letterati*, Lorenzo Giacomini and Ottavio Rinuccini, with whom this chapter began. The wheel has come full circle; it remains now to see how the new and unquestionably widespread theories of affections, some of which may be said to have given rise to a poetics of opera, served the new generation of composers which inherited them.

The Orfeo Libretti and the Formulation
of the New Recitative Style

The creation of the *libretto per musica*[1] out of the *poesia musicale* and dramatic genres of the sixteenth century is a subject about which music historians have said very little and literary historians have not said enough. The enormous task of documenting and, to some extent, editing the relevant sources was initiated at the beginning of this century by Angelo Solerti, who compiled and evaluated his materials, naturally enough, from a literary point of view — that is, almost entirely without reference to the musical styles with which the poetry was originally associated.[2] During the several generations since Solerti's work was accomplished, a few voices have attempted to fill the void; studies such as those by Einstein[3] and Ghisi[4] have provided valuable insights into the relationship between the poetry and music (when the latter is extant) of the various forms which were current during the sixteenth century.

Music historians, however, have only recently begun to approach and evaluate the interrelationship between poetry and music in early opera. Anna Amalie Abert, for instance, has gone far beyond Solerti's groundwork in exploring the relationship between the poetry of the new literary genre — the *favola per recitar cantando*[5] — and the "new music" it was in one sense intended to serve.[6] Recent articles by Donald Grout, William Porter, and Nino Pirrotta[7] mark a turning point, I believe, toward the realization of the creative influence of the libretto on the formation of opera. Surely, if one accepts the view set forth in the preceding chapters that Rinuccini's contribution to the creation of opera was an active and formative one, and not merely accidental, then the historian who would comprehend the circumstances surrounding the rise of this new art form, and appreciate the complexity of its first representatives, must inquire into the artisitic goals of the libretto, considered as an independent and unique poetic category. Unenlightening are discussions by those historians who judge, generally with a jaundiced eye, the dramatic qualities of Rinuccini's early works in comparison to the pastorals of Tasso and Guarini, while ignoring the whole question of *poesia musicale* and the suitability of his idiosyncratic verse style for musical setting. Among such discussions I would place, for example, those by Andrea della Corte[8] and Marion Schild,[9] who are concerned with Rinuccini's libretti exclusively as dramatic constructions of more or less forcefulness and psychological depth. On the other hand, the eminent literary historian Attilio Momigliano, who recognizes the failings of such a narrow approach, can do no more than speak about the "atmosfera musicale" of these early libretti, acknowledging his own inability to deal with the subject.[10] His short essay on Rinuccini's libretti, along with those mentioned here above, gives testimony to Einstein's remark that the "history of the libretto is a subject which can be studied adequately only as musical history and not as literary history."[11]

An awareness, then, of the interrelationship of Rinuccini's verse and the musical elements it was intended to serve, and a sensitivity to the ways in which each influences and operates on the other, would seem to be prerequisites for a fruitful examination of early opera. What kind of musical structures are implied by Rinuccini's poetry? Do any larger formal patterns emerge, or devices repeat themselves? Which aspects of Rinuccini's style and technique may be seen as traditional or derivative, and which may be considered as departures from or modifications of sixteenth-century stage practice? In other words, of what importance was the new vehicle of the libretto, created to test the powers of modern music, in shaping the musical style and form of the earliest operas? The relevance of these questions is affirmed by the fact that the *libretto per musica* was the first poetic genre intended specifically for performance by solo voice. Moreover the new *stile recitativo* was avowedly fashioned in imitation of the accents of speech, and the concept of *aria*, as we are now beginning to realize, was inextricably bound to the reality of the inflections or *accenti* of the dramatic text, which became in some way germinal of its own setting.[12] The questions posed above take on further significance when one considers the import of statements concerning Rinuccini's involvement with music and musical humanism,[13] and the implication of several reports which suggest his active participation in collaborating with Peri and Monteverdi,[14] composers whose styles are linked more closely than is generally recognized.[15]

That Girolamo Mei should provide us with an early insight into the development of Renaissance dramatic poetry in the Italian vernacular, and incidentally offer a premature glimpse of the still unborn libretto, is not surprising in view of his interest in the sister arts of poetry and music. Mei recorded his version of the progress of Tuscan poetry from rough beginnings to its highly developed, mid-sixteenth-century state in a discussion of rhyme in his treatise on poetry.[16] There he summed up the literary history of the age as a progression from imperfection to perfection, which coincided with a movement away from the narrative manner of poetry—i.e., the epic—and toward a style known as recitational or *recitativo*.[17] In the first flowering of Tuscan verse, Mei related, poets were occupied with youthful subjects, such as hymns of praise and flattery of women, or love, and similar concerns—in short, subjects which had an idyllic and delicate quality and which were consequently suitable for the narrative manner. But the limitations of this style were realized before long, and a new style was discovered by the poets of the generation preceding Mei. This new manner of imitation, which corrected many of the errors of the former one, was developed with the *rappresentazioni*, or what were soon to be called by the ancient names of tragedy and comedy. Because these works required continuous action the *parti recitative* became longer and more important than the *luoghi oziosi*, or places of inaction or reflection. At first, however, the means of expression of the old style were retained, so that, for example, Poliziano's *Orfeo* and the tragedies of other, minor poets were written in rhyme. Only gradually did it become recognized that this ornament of speech was entirely useless in the representation of action;[18] and for this reason it was finally abandoned by Trissino, Rucellai, and Martelli, especially in those places where it appeared to hinder the purpose of imitation.[19]

In addition to its commentary upon the growth of a literary *stile recitativo*, Mei's account is valuable for its early awareness of the problems inherent in dramatic poetry, problems which inevitably were to confront the composers as well. For the new interest in dramatic poetry was accompanied by the development of a strong tradition of dramatic music, which assumed, however, only the modest role of ornamentation in the *luoghi oziosi*, and in the *intermedi*. Eventually, the sharp contrast between the music, or *intermedio*, and the spoken dialogue was felt increasingly to impede continuity, and the lack of verisimilitude in the incoherent whole became the butt of criticism by the end of the century.[20] Furthermore, the music itself was anything but the subservient bearer of the poetic text, and usually took the form of one of many types of polyphonic compositions which could stand independent of the dramatic context, a fact frequently borne out by madrigal and frottola publications of the time.[21]

Whether it was in the spirit of humanistic reform, or simple experimentation, Emilio de' Cavalieri (1550-1602) was the first composer to set the complete text of a pastoral to music. Although the results of Cavalieri's early labors and the text by Laura Guidiccioni are lost, we know that three of his musical pastorals were presented in Florence even before Ingegneri published his objections to contemporary stage practices.[22] In the opinion of Doni, the Roman-born musician thereby set the precedent for the rebirth of true *musica teatrale*, however primitively.[23]   The historian was careful to explain, though, that Cavalieri's style was not *recitativo*, but rather a style represented principally by "ariette, with a great deal of artifice, many repetitions, echoes, and similar traits."[24]   In other words, these completely musical pastorals performed in the last decade of the century probably consisted of short, strophic verses strung together in a tuneful manner which perhaps fostered stylistic coherence at the expense of dramatic interest or effectiveness.[25]   Yet, insofar as they are recorded in Doni's description, they are among the few presently known documents pointing to the development of a musical idiom specifically intended to suit the needs of representational expression and musical imitation of dramatic action.   In the absence, then, of any extant and independent (as opposed to madrigalistic) tradition of dramatic music previous to the earliest operas,[26] I propose to look first at the poetic tradition to discover what solutions it presented to the problems of dramatic expression.

The Poetic Tradition

There can be no doubt about the literary genre of the early libretti, which were consistently referred to by contemporaries as *favole pastorali* or *pastorali tutti in musica*.[27]   Present-day historians generally dismiss Rinuccini's evocation of the tragic muse as mere pretense,[28] and agree that his operas belong instead to the elegant and artificial sphere of the pastoral, a world set apart from tragedy or comedy by the general absence of strong sentiments, bold passions, and dramatic activity, and marked rather by sensuous language, moralizing conceits, and idyllic settings.   Some of these characteristics have frequently been cited as qualities which rendered the pastoral particularly suitable for musical setting. In the words of Giovanni Battista Doni,

> . . . I would say that since this [pastoral] genre usually has more of the poetic and abstract than comedy and [sacred] representations, and [since] it is almost always composed of amorous subjects, and in an ornate and sweet style, . . . so it might even be granted to have melody in all its parts, especially because there are represented gods, nymphs, and shepherds from that very ancient time in which music was natural and discourse was almost poetic.[29]

In choosing the subjects of the first libretti, Rinuccini could not have acknowledged his debt to the pastoral tradition more clearly, for both the Daphne and Orpheus legends had long been associated with pastoral drama.[30]

Leaving for another time the question of the traditions and origins of Rinuccini's text for *Dafne*,[31] it is instructive to compare the two Orfeo libretti from the first decade of opera, Rinuccini's *Euridice* (1600) and Alessandro Striggio's *Orfeo* (1607), with the earliest secular play in Italian, Poliziano's *Orfeo* (1480). This work was not only a likely source, along with Ovid, for the later treatments, but also the first representative of the pastoral genre.[32] Mei associated Poliziano's dramatic style with the "new manner of imitation" which was quickly adopted by lesser poets;[33] and continued evidence of the widespread popularity of the work may be seen in the numerous editions it received during the sixteenth and seventeenth centuries. Furthermore, its recognition early in the sixteenth century as a milestone in Italian dramatic poetry was witnessed, perhaps paradoxically, by its rapid transformation into the form of a five-act tragedy.[34] In addition to recognizing the pertinence of the Orpheus legend, and its appropriateness to the ideals of musical humanism,[35] one must remember that Poliziano himself had been a favorite and intimate friend of Lorenzo the Magnificent;[36] and perhaps it was partially because of their lifelong association that Rinuccini chose, more than a century later, to resuscitate the *Orfeo* of an earlier fellow-humanist for the marriage of a Medici princess.

The following outline is intended as a summary guide to my discussion of some of the differences and similarities of these three treatments of the Orpheus legend. My readings are based on the edition of Poliziano's *Orfeo* by Carducci,[37] on the original, souvenir publication of the libretto of Rinuccini's *Euridice*,[38] and on the original version of Striggio's *Orfeo* libretto, reprinted by Solerti.[39] Neither Rinuccini's nor Poliziano's poems are divided into acts in the manner of the Striggio libretto, but for convenience I have adopted Solerti's division of the Rinuccini into six scenes. The parenthesized numbers in my outline refer to the lines of poetry as given in the editions cited in the footnotes and in the Appendices to this volume.

Poliziano	Rinuccini	Striggio (1607 libr.)
Mercurio announces the play and gives the argument (1-16).	Prologue: La Tragedia (1-28).	Prologue: La Musica (1-20).
Aristeo, a young shepherd, tells his old companion Mopso of his love for Euridice, and sings a *canzona* in her praise (17-92).	[Scene 1] Chorus summons nymphs and shepherds to celebrate the union of Orfeo and Euridice (29-53).	Act 1. A shepherd summons his woodland companions to invoke Hymen and celebrate the union of Orfeo and Euridice. They respond in the choruses

Tirsi enters with news of Euridice's whereabouts. Aristeo, cautioned by Mopso, exits to seek her (93-124).

Protesting his love, Aristeo tries to arrest Euridice, who flees at his pursuit (125-37).

Answered by a chorus of shepherds, Euridice sings of her joy and invites all to sing and dance (54-84).

Chorus: "Al canto, al ballo, a l'ombre, al prato adorno" (85-100).

"Vieni, Imeneo, deh, vieni" and "Lasciate i monti" (21-68).

At the request of the shepherd, Orfeo and Euridice sing to one another of their joy (69-99).

Reprise of choruses, "Lasciate i monti" and "Vieni Imeneo," in that order (100-117).

Shepherd calls for final chorus of petition, "Alcun non sia che disperato in preda" (118-51).

Orfeo sings a Latin ode in praise of Cardinal Francesco Gonzaga of Mantova, at whose request, it is thought, *Orfeo* was composed (138-89).

A shepherd brings Orfeo news of Euridice's death (190-97).

Orfeo laments and decides to try to regain Euridice by the power of his song (198-213).

[Scene 2] Orfeo sings of his previous sorrows and invokes Venus (101-22). To his rejoicings are added those of Arcetro and Tirsi (123-61).

A messenger (Dafne) enters and is questioned by Orfeo and Arcetro (162-89), before divulging the news of Euridice's death (190-222).

Shepherds lament. Orfeo resolves to pursue his bride to Hades (223-64).

Act 2. Orfeo and shepherds recall his previous unlucky amours, and rejoice in his change of fortune (152-99).

A messenger (Silvia) enters and is questioned by Orfeo and a shepherd (200-213) before divulging the news of Euridice's death (214-38).

Shepherds lament; Orfeo resolves to pursue his bride to Hades (239-56).

Chorus and Silvia bemoan the ill tidings (257-70).

Chorus: "Cruda morte, ahi pur poteste" (265-92).

Final chorus: "Chi ne consola, ahi lassi?" (271-314).

	[Scene 3] Arcetro, in dialogue with the chorus, relates a scene in which Orfeo, having sought out the place of Euridice's demise, wished to kill himself, but was consoled by the miraculous appearance of Venus (293-371). Chorus: "Se de' boschi verdi onori" (372-97). Scene changes.	Scene changes.
Orfeo approaches the inferno singing his laments to the furies (214-29). Plutone overhears him and marvels, but is counseled by Minos to be firm (230-45).	[Scene 4] Venus encourages Orfeo to seek Euridice in Hades (398-417).	Act 3. Orfeo approaches Hades esorted by Hope (Speranza), whom he must leave reluctantly at the gates (315-50). Orfeo encounters the ferry-man Caronte and attempts to sway him with his song. Caronte is impressed but refuses entry. As Orfeo continues singing, the guard falls asleep, and Orfeo, gaining access to the boat, crosses the Styx (351-411). Infernal chorus: "Nulla impresa per uom si tenta in vano" (412-41).
Orfeo entreats Plutone to release Euridice (246-85). Encouraged to mercy by Proserpina, Plutone returns Orfeo's wife to him (286-301).	Hades. Orfeo makes his appeal to Plutone (418-501). The latter, influenced by Proserpina's persuasions and by the advice of Radamanto and	Act 4. Hades. Proserpina pleads with Plutone in Orfeo's behalf while infernal spirits comment in chorus. Plutone yields (442-99).

	Caronte, infernal spirits, yields to Orfeo's song (502-53).	
Orfeo, singing triumphant Latin verses from Ovid, begins to lead Euridice away, but violates Plutone's command not to behold her. Euridice is taken away by one of the furies, who warns Orfeo not to follow (302-21).		Orfeo, praising his lyre, begins to lead Euridice away, but hearing a noise behind him, turns to behold her, whereupon Euridice is led away by a spirit (500-548).
	Infernal chorus: "Poi che gli eterni imperi" (554-83).	Infernal chorus: "E' la virtute un raggio" (549-62).
	Scene reverts to original.	Scene changes.
Orfeo grieves over his fate, scorning love and women (322-53).	[Scene 5] Arcetro and chorus bemoan Orfeo's absence, but Aminta reports having seen the lovers and predicts their imminent return (584-683).	Act 5. Thrace. Orfeo scorning love and women, laments with his echo (563-616).
	[Scene 6] Orfeo and Euridice enter and describe their adventures in response to the questions of the chorus and their companions (684-742).	
One of the Baccanti summons her companions to avenge their god against Orfeo. She exits and returns with Orfeo's head (354-69).		He withdraws as Chorus of Baccanti appear singing praises to Bacchus and revenge to Orfeo.

Chorus in honor of	Final chorus: "Bion-	Refrain chorus: "Evo-
Bacchus: "Ognun se-	do arcier che d'alto	hè, padre Lieo"
gua, Bacco, te"	monte" (743-90).	(617-78).
(370-400).		

Even from such a skeletal comparison as this, it is apparent that the more striking similarities of treatment relate to content rather than to form; and for this reason, although it will often be difficult to separate the two, I shall discuss the poetry first from the point of view of content, and later, from that of form.

In addition to sharing certain characteristics of Poliziano's retelling of the Orpheus legend – its combination of the mythological and the idyllic, and its emphasis on the winning power of Orpheus' song – the later poets also adopted certain devices, which are present in Polizano's work and which, out of deference to classical models, had become conventional during the Renaissance. One such convention was the use of the messenger, who, by unburdening his ill tidings upon a static scene, and provoking the players to react to his news, serves as a catalyst to carry the drama forward. It is interesting to see how the later poets, while adhering to his principle, elaborate upon it. In Poliziano's work, the messenger-shepherd reveals the news of Euridice's death to Orfeo swiftly and without any preface, in the space of two lines (*Orfeo*, ll. 190-91):

> Crudel novella ti rapporto Orfeo,
> Che tua ninfa bellissima è defunta.

The simple description of how Euridice was bitten by a venomous serpent fills the rest of the octave. Compare the same place in *Euridice*: from the point in the drama where the nymph Dafne enters until she completes her recitation, Rinuccini composed no less than sixty lines of verse. He took the occasion to describe in great detail various aspects of the woodland scene in which Euridice met her death, and accordingly Dafne postpones the core of her announcement until the close of her recitation (*Euridice*, ll. 220-22):

> . . . E, volti gli occhi al cielo,
> Scolorito il bel viso e i bei sembianti,
> Restò tanta bellezza immobil gelo.

In addition to filling in the details of the offstage events, Rinuccini's intention here was surely virtuosic, for the sixteenth century delighted in such idyllic scenes, as the madrigal literature testifies. True, it has the effect of delaying rather than accelerating the action, but it also gives the composer a chance to treat a developed, narrative text. Although the basic structure of Striggio's messenger scene is close to that of Rinuccini, Silvia in *Orfeo* is a model of conciseness, with the result that her appearance is perhaps more effective from a dramatic point of view.[40]

Another device used in all three works under discussion, the quotation of isolated lines of poetry from famous sources, may be considered a direct and conventional acknowledgment of their authors' debt to the past. For just as Poliziano owed his clarity of style and his inspiration to the Latin poets, especially to Virgil and Ovid, so did Rinuccini and Striggio, along with many of their contemporaries, draw on Dante and Petrarch. Poliziano's Orfeo sings a few verses from Ovid as he leads his spouse out of the darkness of Hades (ll. 302-305).[41] Similarly Striggio assigns the famous line from Dante's *Commedia*—"Lasciate ogni speranza o voi ch'entrate"—literally enough to Speranza (Hope), who, having escorted Orfeo to the gates of Hell, abandons him there (Act 3, l. 338). In the opening scene of *Euridice*, during the celebration by nymphs and shepherds of the heroine's nuptials, Rinuccini cites a line from Petrarch's wedding sonnet, "Due rose fresche e colte in paradiso,"

Non vede un simil par d'amanti 'l sole!

and, directly following its initial statement (l. 53), Peri underscores it with a threefold repetition by assigning it first to a shepherd, then to Arcetro, and finally to a five-part chorus.[42]

Once one acknowledges the possible influence of the weight of Medici tradition upon Rinuccini,[43] his choice of the Orpheus legend as a triumphant successor to the experimental *Dafne* may be considered self-evident. The logical expression of the musical humanism which Rinuccini inherited from Bardi and Corsi in the last decade of the sixteenth century, it also echoes the traditional lore concerning the marvels of ancient music and musicians transmitted through the Middle Ages and repeated even more frequently during the Renaissance.[44] Able to charm even the beasts of the wilderness and the infernal deities with his music, Orpheus became a symbol no less appropriate to Rinuccini and Striggio than he must have been to Poliziano, whose master, Marsilio Ficino, counted among the most prized classical disciplines to have been revived in the Florence of his day the art of singing to the Orphic lyre.[45] Indeed, Orpheus appeared with a lute and surrounded by animals, as the personification of Rhetoric on the north side of Giotto's campanile, which towers beside the Duomo in the center of Florence, in a marble bas-relief executed by Luca della Robbia in 1437.[46] The figure of

Orpheus also symbolized the neo-Platonic attempt to reconcile pagan mythology with Christianity.[47]   Reflecting a strong clerical, Latin tradition, which had its origins in early Christianity, medieval and early Renaissance scholars, poets, and artists had compared Orpheus to David, "the magical musician who played in the wilderness, and to the Christ, the Good Shepherd, whose words drew all mankind and who prophesied the day when the lion would lie down with the lamb."[48]   In fact, the opening scene of Poliziano's play contains an obvious reference to the parallel between Orpheus and Christ in the dialogue concerning the lost white calf (prefigurative of Euridice), which Tirsi retrieves before the main action begins.[49]

Given these traditions, it is reasonable to argue that the climactic moment of the tale of Orpheus and Eurydice for the Renaissance humanist was not the moment in which Orpheus transgresses by turning to behold Eurydice, but rather that moment in which, by his art, he gains Eurydice's release from the shadowy realm.[50]   This idea is, in fact, supported by the manner in which each of the poets handles the scene in question, setting it apart in some way from the rest of the action. Poliziano gives the distraught lover no less than five stanzas of ottava rima at this point (ll. 246-85) – the longest monologue in the work except for the Latin encomium to Cardinal Gonzaga, which occurs near the beginning of the play (ll. 138-89) and which bears no relation to the plot. Moreover, Poliziano stresses the formal nature of Orfeo's "performance" by directing that the singer recite these strophes, beginning "O regnator di tutte quelle genti," while kneeling before Plutone.[51]   The entreaty itself contains some of the most virtuosic and, for want of a better word, "musical" verses of the entire poem.   To illustrate I quote part of the third octave (ll. 262-67), which is full of word repetition and alliteration.

> Ogni cosa nel fine a voi ritorna,
> Ogni vita mortale a voi ricade:
> Quanto cerchia la luna con suo' corna
> Convien ch'arrivi alle vostre contrade:
> Chi più chi men tra' superi soggiorna;
> Ognun convien che cerchi queste strade:...

Compared to the prolongation of this central point in the drama, the events following it – Orfeo's second loss of Euridice, his lament, and his execution at the hands of the Baccanti – occur swiftly and without the same emphasis on lyricism that renders climactic the scene in Hades.

Rinuccini in fact omits these later events altogether by making the Underworld god's surrender of Euridice an unconditional one, with the result that his truncated version of the legend has surprised and mystified latter-day critics and scholars. I am persuaded that, by eliminating the conditional nature of Euridice's rescue, whether Rinuccini's intentions were merely to lighten the action of the play to suit the festive occasion, or whether they also reflected his artistic judgment not to distract attention from Orfeo's triumphant moment, the librettist succeeded in emphasizing the poet-musician's confrontation with the powers of Hell as the highpoint of the action. Following Poliziano's example, Rinuccini also imparted a greater formality to Orfeo's plea to Plutone ("Funeste piaggie," ll. 418-47), not by binding them into a regularly repeating metrical and rhyme scheme—for Rinuccini shunned this type of organization of monologues, and evolved instead, as we shall see, a verse which was more free to develop according to the exigencies of the sentiments it expressed—but rather by unifying the irregular stanzas with a refrain device unique among Orfeo's lines. Later in Rinuccini's poem, Orfeo himself calls attention to these stanzas when, in a dialogue with the chorus (ll. 725-30), he relates having awakened pity in Plutone's implacable heart with

> Modi or soavi, or mesti,
> Fervidi preghi e flebili sospiri...

Furthermore, by making Orfeo's victory unconditional and final, Rinuccini did more than simply transform the ending of the fable from tragic to happy. He also altered the meaning of the Orpheus myth, the original artistic significance of which is interpreted in the following way by Joseph Kerman:

> It is the problem of emotion and its control, the summoning of feeling to an intensity and communicability and form which the action of life heeds as death provisionally respects. All this Orpheus as artist achieves. But as man he cannot shape his emotions to Pluto's shrewd decree; face to face with the situation, he looks back, and fails. Life and art are not necessarily one.[52]

Seen in these terms, then, Rinuccini's eradication of Orfeo's weakness from the plot may be said to reveal his own, more simplistic attitude toward the problem of art. For, if Orfeo's artistic success is unfettered by his human failing in *Euridice*, and if the problem of artistic control is here equated rather than juxtaposed with that of emotional control, then the libretto is in effect an allegory of the doctrine that art and life *are* one, or at least inseparable because art imitates life. Indeed, Rinuccini's poetry and Peri's recitative, which it in a sense informed, have been both praised and condemned for their close imitation of life—according to whether the results are seen as natural lyricism or as stereotyped expression which fails to rise above the level of ordinary speech.

Although Striggio's treatment of the myth adheres closely, as does Poliziano's, to the legendary events, he distributes them among five acts, making each act a self-enclosed unit with its own climax.[53]   Noteworthy is the fact that, like the poets before him, Striggio again emphasizes the central importance to the drama of Orfeo's artistic triumph by making it the matter of Act 3 at the very midpoint of the story.   This time, however, Orfeo's performance is directed not at Plutone, but rather at the ferryman Caronte, who is charmed to sleep by the song, with the result that Orfeo, still very much a mortal, gains access to Hades.[54]

Striggio's insertion of this scene, with its curious dialogue between Orfeo and the half-comic keeper of the Styx has piqued the imaginations of many students of *Orfeo*, for it is difficult in some respects to reconcile the tone of Act 3 with the rest of the opera.[55]   However, if Striggio's plan is compared with the other treatments of the legend discussed here, the addition of the Caronte scene serves, I believe, to de-emphasize Orfeo's failure of Act 4 as the main event of the action — i.e., his failure to retrieve Euridice permanently — by seeking to establish and emphasize his artistic prowess in the third act.   In fact, the protagonist does not appear at all in the opening of Act 4, in Hades, where the dialogue consists entirely of exchanges between the Underworld gods; instead Orfeo, having demonstrated his skill before the act began, remains mute as Proserpina pleads in his behalf for Euridice's release.   In this way, Striggio removes from the setting of Hades Orfeo's formal and virtuosic petition, "Possente spirto e formidabil nume" (Act 3 ll. 363-81), and makes it the substance of a self-contained act at the center of the drama. Thus did Striggio create a pyramidal scheme for his entire libretto with "Possente spirto" at its apex, and with the events following Act 3 forming the counterparts of those preceding it.

3. Orfeo's triumph

2. First loss   4. Second loss
    of Euridice   of Euridice

1. General rejoicing   5. General lamenting

Monteverdi's setting, particularly in its tonal scheme, strongly reinforces Striggio's placement of "Possente spirto" at the psychological climax of the fable;[56] for the tonal progression of the entire opera forms a large *Bogen*, in which the furthest point from the beginning tonal area is reached in the third act, in the recitative between Orfeo and Speranza preceding Orfeo's magnificent solo.[57]

Prologue	1	2	3	4	5
d-G	d-G	g-G	c-G	g-D	g-D

In addition to placing Orfeo's *preghiera* in a position central to the events of the drama, Striggio accentuates the formal nature and virtuosity of "Possente spirto" by writing six strophes of terza rima, or tercets with the progressive rhyme pattern ABA, BCB, CDC . . . . Nowhere else in his libretto does Striggio resort to this archaic and greatly revered meter, associated with Dante, as well as with the improvisatory recitations on traditional musical formulas of the Renaissance lyric or dramatic eclogue.[58] By setting these verses apart from the rest of the poem, therefore, Striggio not only calls attention to Orfeo's skill, as did his predecessors, but he also provides a medium eminently suited to display Orfeo's talent.[59]

The Poetic Structures and Their Musical Implications

In embarking upon a discussion of the form and metrical structure of the three Orfeo poems, we might profitably return to Mei's remarks concerning dramatic poetry and consider them as a point of departure for further observations. Mei's "history" of the rise of Italian dramatic poetry indirectly raises two important questions. How, if at all, is the formal distinction between the *parti recitative* and the *luoghi oziosi* reflected in the style and structure of the poetry? What are the musical implications of these distinctions?

Mei himself partially supplies the answer to the first question, for the entire digression occurs in his argument against rhyme, which is in his view "entirely useless in the representation of action."[60] The Florentine humanist, himself the author of several tragedies, inveighs against this ornament of speech principally because it hinders the purpose of imitation in poetry, and particularly in representational poetry, where the dialogue should give the impression of being spontaneous.

> Because, if you wish to move in others anger or fear or love or any other emotion, you usually see to it that the means you employ to this end strongly appears through your words to be something true, and not studied or premeditated; . . . for otherwise everything seems false and it is obvious to others that you do not speak from the heart. And he who is aware that something is not said from the heart, but with artifice and deceitfully, fearing betrayal, is cautious and does not believe such things; and not believing them, does not allow himself to be carried away by their words, and is not moved. Now being preoccupied with such . . . excessive refinements [of rhetoric], which are all products of the intellect that is reflective and detached from every affection, one quickly and certainly eliminates in others all belief.[61]

We may infer from these statements that Mei certainly would have excluded the use of rhyme from the *parti recitative*.

Another inference may be drawn from Mei's distinction between "narrative" poetry and that which is recitational or dramatic.[62] The first type – what we call, for example, epic poetry – was always formalistic in nature and adhered to a particular scheme, such as the ottava or terza rima. While Mei considered these suitable to convey the type of expression found in the infant style of vernacular poetry, which was mainly narrative, descriptive, and idyllic, he found fault with Poliziano's *Orfeo* precisely because of its use of repetitive verse patterns and conventional rhyme schemes. Presumably Mei might have accepted rhyme in the *luoghi oziosi* as a vehicle for more lyric sentiments, or for a prepared song or dance, but he certainly believed its use in the *parti recitative* to be contrary to verisimilitude and an obstacle to moving the affections.

Because Mei was arguing against rhyme as an unnecessary evil in dramatic poetry,[63] his tacit condemnation of Poliziano's versification left him no room to consider *Orfeo's* subtler qualities. A closer examination of this early work demonstrates that there are actually clearly wrought distinctions between places of action or dialogue, and places of inaction or lyrically heightened sentiment. Although Poliziano's verse throughout is characterized by rhyme, it is not restricted solely to ottava rima, nor therefore is its style as inflexible as Mei implies. In fact, in breaking the rhythm of the *ottave*, Poliziano departed from the only tradition of vernacular drama then in existence – that of the *rappresentazioni sacre*. Among the sacred plays in d'Ancona's voluminous anthology, those which are most closely contemporary to Poliziano are composed entirely in ottava rima.[64] Only later do variations in this metrical norm, such as are brought about by the interpolation of passages in terza rima or of strophic *canzoni* or *laudi*, appear regularly in this genre.[65]

Whether or not Poliziano initiated the practice of varying the verse style to accord with the tone and purpose of the speaker, in his *Orfeo* the principle appears to have been carried out with unusual consistency and, as I have indicated above, according to certain recognizable criteria. The Prologue, presenting within two strophes of ottava rima a straightforward and concise narration of the events which are about to take place, introduces the octave as the basic unit of the poem. One is surprised, then, by the *terzine* of the ensuing dialogue (ll. 17-84), comprising the entire opening scene, wherein Mopso and Aristeo converse about two utterly discrete but not unrelated subjects – a calf which strayed from their flock and Aristeo's passionate desire for the nymph Euridice.

Poliziano brings this static scene to its climax in a lyrical "Canzona," a series of four sestets, each punctuated by the refrain couplet,

> Udite, selve, mie dolci parole,
> Poi che la ninfa mia udir non vôle.

in which Aristeo complains that his attentions to Euridice fall on deaf ears (ll. 54-84).

Immediately Aristeo completes his song, the meter returns to the octave scheme of the Prologue. As though to accentuate this structural change, Poliziano writes dodecasyllabic instead of hendecasyllabic lines throughout the first octave, using dactylic rhymes (*versi sdruccioli*) at the end of each verse (ll. 85-92).[66] At this point a third shepherd, Tirsi, returns with the recovered calf and reveals his discovery of a beautiful nymph (Euridice) gathering flowers nearby. Tirsi, almost in the capacity of a messenger, provides the impetus for the action, which commences as Aristeo leaves his companions in pursuit of the "gentil donzella." The octaves, which set this new pace for the play, move swiftly and easily and are often broken into quatrains and paired, or even single, verses to accommodate the more excited dialogue of the shepherds (ll. 85-124).[67] Again Poliziano concludes the scene with a lyrical climax as Aristeo sings a short interlude to the fleeing Euridice ("Non mi fuggir donzella"), and the octaves are set aside for more rapid tercets of seven- and eleven-syllable verses (ll. 125-37).

Orfeo's first appearance in the drama provides the occasion for a long ode in Latin (ll. 138-89), which, as I noted above, has little to do with the argument of the play.[68] Only after this solo, which serves to establish Orfeo's dramatic presence, does the fluent meter of the octaves resume. The action continues as Orfeo is presented with the news of Euridice's death and confronts the infernal deities with his song (ll. 190-301).

The next departure from ottava rima occurs at the end of the Hell-scene, when Euridice is newly taken from her too-anxious consort and led back to Hades (ll. 306-21). The meter here reverts again to short strophes of mixed seven- and eleven-syllable lines as Orfeo and Euridice give voice to their new anguish ("Ohimè, che 'l troppo amor"). Following the pattern established in the foregoing verses, the ultimate scene, in which Orfeo scorns love and women and then meets his punishment at the vengeful hands of the Baccanti (ll. 322-400), also moves from octaves to a final refrain text similar to the earlier *canzone* sung by Aristeo. But here the Baccanti's sestets are more dance-like and composed mainly of seven-syllable lines, of which the last syllables are accented (*rime tronche*).

The plan which emerges, then, in Poliziano's attempt to "represent" his partly pastoral, partly mythological version of the Orpheus legend involves an alternation of poetic meters to accommodate his verses to the pace of the action. It is significant that the poet chose the relatively new form of the octave to carry the action forward and to sustain the *parti recitative*. Brought to perfection by Poliziano, the octave was the mode of the romance, of narration and description, as well as of the less pretentious *rappresentazione sacra*, and in the hands of Ariosto it was to assume an almost classical dignity. With the rise to popularity of the octave, the older terza rima, the medium of Dante's *Commedia* and of a host of Trecento and Quattrocento imitators, became conventional, didactic, and prosaic in the sense that it was felt to be closest to prose.[69] This is undoubtedly the reason why Poliziano set in *terzine* the opening dialogue between Aristeo and Mopso, who are not yet the noble characters of the idealized pastoral world of the sixteenth century. Similarly, it explains why he turned to octaves only after Orfeo's appearance, and used them throughout the central part of the action and for the protagonist's climactic "performance" before the Underworld gods. De Sanctis sums up the distinction, already observed by Poliziano, in speaking of Ariosto's *Satire*:

> The *ottava rima* sang; the *terzina* discoursed, joked, satirized, expressed the prosaic and realistic side of life.[70]

The only chorus in Poliziano's *Orfeo* is provided by the Baccanti, whose appearance at the end of the play serves as a postlude to the action. Although there are no choral interludes in the body of the drama, Poliziano does mark off each scene with static, lyric moments, or *luoghi oziosi*, the function of which in the later works is elaborated by the chorus.[71] It is significantly in these places – Aristeo's *canzone*, Orfeo's and Euridice's matching laments after the abortive rescue from Hades – that the poetry deviates, in ways described above, from the flowing rhythm of the octaves.

In the case of the fifteenth-century *Orfeo*, an examination of the musical implications of its apparently carefully executed poetic structure is hampered by the fact that the musical portions have not been preserved.[72] According to Einstein, the work must have been a mixture of spoken declamation and song, both improvised and composed.[73] The latter type is represented by Aristeo's *canzone* with its sestets of hendecasyllabic lines, the last one of which always rhymes with the refrain verse, as well as by the refrain chorus of the Baccanti which, because of its short lines and strong rhythm, Einstein called a *frottola*. He guessed that the stanzas of Orfeo's invocation to Plutone (ll. 246-85)

must have been sung also, although Baccio Ugolini, a friend of Lorenzo
the Magnificent who represented Orfeo, probably improvised the music
following one of the simple, conventional schemes used for singing ottava
rima.[74]   In addition to these, I should think that other, analogous
passages were sung, such as Orfeo's Latin ode at the moment of his
initial appearance on the scene (ll. 138-89),[75] the triumphant Latin verses
from Ovid (ll. 302-05), and Aristeo's tercets, recited as the young
shepherd pursues the fleeing Euridice ("Non mi fuggir, donzella").
Finally, and closely related to the foregoing, are the brief exclamatory
stanzas of the spouses, who are forced to exchange a last farewell after
Orfeo violates Plutone's restriction (ll. 306-21).   Along with Aristeo's
"Non mi fuggir," these stanzas are in the freer, lyrical style of the
previously discussed interludes. For Orfeo and Euridice, Poliziano writes
two sestets of mixed seven- and eleven-syllable lines, with irregular
rhymes.

The structural freedom characteristic of such interpolations in an
otherwise unvaried procession of uniform strophes anticipates the style of
madrigal poetry; and their regular association with *luoghi oziosi*—that is,
with lyrical or climactic interludes—became a common feature in the
literature of the infant pastoral drama, the so-called dramatic eclogues, of
which *Orfeo* was the prototype.   It is easy to imagine that these
interludes would have been heightened by music.[76] Following Einstein's
lead and extending his assumptions, it seems quite plausible that, for
example, the Latin verses cited above in my expanded, hypothetical list
of musically performed sections would have been sung to conventional
tunes;[77] for schematic music specifically intended for improvisation on
Latin and vernacular verses may be found scattered through the *frottola*
collections at the beginning of the sixteenth century.[78] Although the
verses of Aristeo's *terzine*, "Non mi fuggir," are not of uniform length
and do not adhere to the progressive rhyme scheme of true terza rima,
they too could have been adapted to one of the conventional airs,
specifically to the flexible scheme of the *capitolo*, which, at the turn of
the century, provided the basis for the improvisation of those climactic
strophes of a dramatic eclogue in terza rima designated for vocal
performance.[79] As for Euridice's "Ohimè, che 'l troppo amore" and the
verses following, recited by Orfeo and one of the Furies, who warns him
not to return to Hades (ll. 306-21), either these would have been set in
the style of a *madrigale*, or, what is more likely, they too would have
been sung to the air of the *capitolo*.   Perhaps they were even richly
ornamented, in the manner of the alternately declamatory and highly
florid setting of a similar text by an unknown composer, the second
tercet of which begins similarly—Aimè ch'a torto vo biastemando

amore—and which was preserved in Petrucci's Sixth Book of *Frottole*.[80] Although the print dates from 1505, the music of this particular text is considerably older. (See musical example 1, below).[81] It is not impossible that a similar style might have been appropriate to a hypothetical setting of Euridice's verses for the infant *teatro italiano* which, until Poliziano's *Orfeo*, had known only the archaic sacred plays.

Ignoring for the moment the whole development of the pastoral drama which occurred during the intervening century and a quarter, I think it will be instructive to juxtapose the Poliziano *Orfeo* and its successors in order to compare, not from a historical, but from a structural point of view, the interaction of the poetic and musical forms before attempting to bring the results into a historical perspective. To begin with a most important question for their new genre of *poesia musicale*, what structural distinctions did Rinuccini and Striggio make in their treatment of the *parti recitative* as opposed to the *luoghi oziosi* of their libretti? What means did they adopt to convey the different functions of the dialogue, now narrative or descriptive, now expressive or pathetic, and of the chorus, which serves sometimes as a stationary commentator providing lyrical interludes to the action, and sometimes as an active participant in the drama?

Even a cursory examination of the later libretti reveals that the scheme of Poliziano's poem, with its neat, functional divisions into strophic, narrative verse on the one hand and more flexible, lyrical verse on the other, is here entirely reversed. Unlike the meter of the greater part of Poliziano's tale, and equally unlike the *sacre rappresentazioni* preceding it or the pastoral dramatic eclogues following it, the basic meter of these libretti consists in the freely developing and changing rhythm of eleven- and seven-syllable lines, forming a continually varying rhyme scheme that defies standardization. The equivalent of the conventional and uniform octaves or tercets of Poliziano, these irregular verses are precisely what carries the action of the plays forward by means of narrative and dialogue sections. Collectively, they generally constitute the *parti recitative* of the drama, which were literally translated into the free, declamatory, and expressive accents of recitative.[82] Conversely, whereas Poliziano deviated from his strophic scheme to introduce protomadrigals of mixed seven- and eleven-syllable lines at lyrical climaxes, Rinuccini and Striggio generally wrote more organized, formalistic poetry for such places—that is, stanzas in which the verses are of uniform length and the rhyme schemes are closed and conventional. This was the manner reserved for the static parts of their dramas, where soloists or chorus give voice to simple lyrical or reflective sentiments. In short, it was this style that clearly distinguished the *luoghi oziosi* from the rest of

Example 1
Petrucci, *Frottole Libro Sexto* (1505), no. 4

the action, and the formal structures therein presented to the composer exerted in most cases a formidable and binding influence on the shape of the musical setting. This relationship became so commonplace during the seventeenth century that few composers felt the need to challenge or modify the structural implications of their texts.[83] Closer examination of Rinuccini's libretto accordingly provides important insights into the initial and highly influential assumptions of operatic poetry.

There are several specific, noteworthy characteristics of the verse structure of *Euridice*. The opening scene presents the protagonist in the idyllic, pastoral setting against which the "tragedy" is to take place. Although Rinuccini concentrates upon Euridice, perhaps in deference to the occasion, and postpones Orfeo's appearance until the second scene, the parallel with Poliziano is clear; in both plays the static opening dialogue among the shepherds reveals a situation which contains, at least potentially, the suggestion of a plot. In *Orfeo*, Mopso learns that Aristeo is enamored of Euridice, and the latter's pursuit of the nymph ultimately results in her downfall as well as that of Orfeo. Similarly, in *Euridice*, the pastoral celebration of Euridice's nuptials, with her companions singing and dancing in the woods, provides the background whence Dafne later brings the news of Euridice's unhappy fate. But instead of the periodic cadencing of tercets, as in Poliziano, we hear the casual alternation of rhyming lines (*rime incrociate*) interspersed frequently with the prominent sound of couplets (*rime baciate*). A good example is the little speech in which Euridice extends her invitation to make merry (ll. 73-81):[84]

> In mille guise e mille
> Crescon le gioie mie dentro al mio petto,
> Mentre ogn'una di voi par che scintille
> Dal bel guardo seren riso e diletto.
> Ma deh, compagne amate,
> Là tra quell'ombre grate
> Moviam di quel fiorito almo boschetto,
> E quivi al suon de' limpidi cristalli
> Trarrem liete carole e lieti balli.

The stanza contains two separate thoughts, the first of which is concluded at the end of the fourth line. Were it not for the unexpected reappearance of the rhyme from the second and fourth lines in the middle of the second thought, we should have a simple octave unfolding in the space of two quatrains. By breaking up the metrical structure with heptasyllables, and by inserting the seventh line, Rinuccini here succeeds in transforming a conventional octave formula into something assymmetrical and irregular.[85]

a B A B   c c B D D

This technique is characteristic of his "recitative" style, and the result is a poetic manner which, while never foregoing its most musical quality (rhyme), attempts to understate, if not obscure, its allegiance to any formal structure or recurring series of rhymes. Such a flexible style obviously harbors important implications for a musical setting designed to imitate the accents of speech.[86]

Another trait of Rinuccini's poetry that renders the use of rhyme less obvious is the frequent pairing of hendecasyllables and heptasyllables, the latter being a verse form which, according to Mei, is too fleeting to satisfy the ear. Hence, the endings of the short verses are presumably less readily perceived by the listener, and the effect is to increase the possibility of enjambment and render the poetry closer to the style of prose. In addition, Rinuccini occasionally inserts unrhymed lines into the texture of his fabric. These are always isolated, as though they had been added intentionally to disfigure the design, and they are usually, though not without exception, verses of seven syllables. For example, of the lines recited by the shepherds who address Euridice in the opening scene ("Qual in sì rozzo core," ll. 61-72), the first and fifth (italicized in the following scheme) are unrhymed.[87]

a B B C *d* c E e f F G g

Furthermore, not one of the three couplets at the end has lines of equal length.

While Rinuccini usually avoids formal and conventional constructions, especially in the *parti recitative* of his libretto, there are sections in *Euridice* in which he seems to employ a modification of the old framework of terza rima to accommodate his dialogue. Of course, there is no question of a schematic meter such as Poliziano used in his *Orfeo*, for Rinuccini's verses are often too short, his tercets too flexible, and the deviations from the traditional scheme too many. Yet the antecedents of his verse are obvious, and I believe Rinuccini's approximation of the original norms indicates his quest for some kind of structural organization to serve as a guide for the creation of a new poetic language, suitable to dramatic dialogue and speech-like song. At the same time, his use of tercets provides a basis for the musical structuring of the recitative into symmetrical exchanges, which in turn fosters rhythmic and tonal coherence.

It is interesting to compare Padre Agostino Manni's libretto for Cavalieri's *Rappresentazione di Anima et di Corpo*, performed in Rome in

February, 1600, and printed about a month before the first performance of *Euridice*, with Rinuccini's new dialogue technique.[88]   In Manni's libretto the entire dialogue between Anima and Corpo following the initial soliloquy of Il Tempo[89] occurs in rapid tercets, each harboring one unrhymed line.   This is in marked contrast to the monologue verse, in which rhymed couplets succeed one another without deviation.   A schematic representation of the dialogue between Anima and Corpo follows:

Corpo:	Anima mia che pensi?	a
	Perchè dogliosa stai	b
	Sempre trahendo guai?	b
Anima:	Vorrei riposo e pace	c d d
	[etc.]	

Corpo:	e f f	Anima:	g h h
	i j j		k l l
	m n n		o p p
	q r r		s t t
			t U U

There is one important difference to be noted in the comparison between Manni's and Rinuccini's verse style; that is the stylization of the pattern in Cavalieri's work in contrast to the flexibility and variety with which Rinuccini manipulates the same idea.   The unfailing regularity of Manni's verse extends even to the length of the lines, which are, as indicated in the diagram here above, uniformly heptasyllabic.[90]   By his own admission, Cavalieri wished to strengthen the "poetic" elements of his score in order to reinforce the "beauty of the music;"[91] in contrast, Rinuccini apparently sought to minimize these elements in order to better approximate natural speech and perhaps also to provide a more flexible structure in which the merits of "our music" could come to the fore.

The irregular tercets of *Euridice* seem to be associated particularly with those sections wherein the pace of the action quickens and the dialogue becomes more pertinent to the development of the plot—e.g., in scene 2, after Dafne's message is announced, and scene 4, which takes place in Hell.   But even at the beginning of the second scene of *Euridice*, which is somewhat in the lyric vein of the first, Orfeo's cadences begin to fall into tercets (ll. 110-122):

Ma deh, perchè sì lente
Del bel carro immortal le rote accese

Per l'eterno cammin tardano il corso?
Sferza, Padre cortese,
A' volanti destrier le groppe e 'l dorso,
Spegni ne l'onde omai,
Spegni o nascondi i fiammeggianti rai.
Bella Madre d'Amor, da l'onde fòra
Sorgi, e la nott'ombrosa
Di vaga luce scintillando indora.
Venga, deh venga omai la bella sposa
Tra 'l notturno silenzio e i lieti orrori
A temprar tante fiamme e tanti ardori.

(*a*B C b C d D E f E F G G)

Immediately following Tirsi's decorative arietta (ll. 144-53) the dialogue becomes heightened, if not more excited, by Dafne's appearance and reluctance to divulge her message. Rinuccini's use of free tercets, cast roughly in the mold of terza rima, to signal the rise in intensity at this point in the drama is striking; for their rapidly changing end-rhymes, their swift cadences and frequent unrhymed lines propel the scene forward, at the same time permitting parallelisms and interplay among the interlocutors (ll. 170 ff.):

Arcetro:	Ohimè! che fia già mai?
	Pur or tutta gioiosa
	Al fonte de gli Allor costei lasciai.
Orfeo:	Qual così ria novella
	Turba il tuo bel sembiante
	In questo allegro dì, gentil donzella?
Dafne:	O del gran Febo e de le sacre Dive
	Pregio sovran, di queste selve onore,
	Non chieder la cagion del mio dolore.
Orfeo:	Ninfa, deh sii contenta
	Ridir perchè t'affani,
	Chè taciuto martir troppo tormenta.

(a *b* A c *d* C E F F g *h* G)

The last scene (sixth in Solerti's scheme) serves to illustrate the notion that Rinuccini probably conceived of this style as a latter-day substitute for, or extension of, terza rima. The only section of true terza rima in the libretto occurs at the lyrical opening of this scene, as Orfeo sings "Gioite al canto mio, selve frondose" (ll. 684-90). At the close of this brief air, Euridice and the chorus embark upon a dialogue (ll. 691 ff.) in which, although the framework of tercets remains, the conventional meter and rhyme scheme of terza rima is dissolved by the poet's interposition of heptasyllables, and by his avoiding rhyme in at least one line in each tercet, as in the aforesaid passage from scene two. As I have suggested above, by mixing the dignified hendecasyllables with shorter lines, Rinuccini is here able to exaggerate the already prosaic quality of the terza rima. Moreover, by ignoring the traditional interlacing rhyme scheme of the *terzine*—whereby the unrhymed verse of one strophe becomes the rhyme for the outer verses of the next (ABA BCB C . . .)— and instead, by beginning each new strophe independently, he sets up a pattern in which the tercets move forward with even greater rapidity than in true terza rima.

Returning to scene two, one sees that the motion of the tercets, begun immediately following Tirsi's song, is interrupted by Orfeo's couplet; by repeating the rhymes of the previous tercet, Orfeo fittingly and conventionally signals the conclusion of the celebration which occupied the entire opening scene and this much of the second (ll. 154-61):

Arcetro:	Deh come ogni bifolco, ogni pastore
	A' tuoi lieti imenei
	Scopre il piacer ch'entro racchiude il core.
Tirsi:	Del tuo beato amor gli alti contenti
	Crescano ognor, come per pioggia suole
	L'onda gonfiar de' rapidi torrenti.
Orfeo:	E per te, Tirsi mio, liete e ridenti
	Sempre le notti e i dì rimeni il sole.

Rinuccini rarely uses this sort of close rhyme in dialogue (AbA CDC CD); instead he treats it basically as a cadential device which retards and punctuates the flow of discourse. Elsewhere in *Euridice*, it is twice more employed to signal the approach of a turning point or mark the end of a section.[92] So here, Orfeo's aphorism is followed immediately by the entrance of the messenger, whose tidings jar what had been up to this point an idyllic and lyrical mood. This helps to explain the sudden change in style of the poetry, for Dafne's verses are organized into quatrains rather than tercets, although they retain the forward-moving characteristics of the tercets (ll. 162-69):[93]

Dafne, nunzia:		
	Lassa! che di spavento e di pietate	A
	Gelami il cor nel seno!	b

Miserabil beltate,	a
Come in un punto, ohimè! venisti meno.	B
Ahi! che lampo o baleno	b
In notturno seren ben ratto fugge,	C
Ma più rapida l'ale	d
Affretta umana vita al dì fatale.	D

From this point on, until the action slows down again in the final scene, the tendency we have already noted in Rinuccini's recitative style to avoid or disguise conventional rhyme patterns becomes much more pronounced. The number of unrhymed lines increases suddenly, and the 1:3 ratio noted in the tercets immediately following Dafne's entrance above (ll. 169 ff.) continues to be the norm as Orfeo and his companions react to Dafne's long narrative. The frequency of these unrhymed lines decreases somewhat in the third scene, which is entirely narrative in character, but increases again in the fourth and fifth scenes, where Rinuccini also employs his modified *terzine* as, for example, in Orfeo's dialogue with Plutone at the height of the drama (ll. 448 ff.). The return to a continuous series of rhymed lines toward the end of this scene appears to mark the decline of dramatic tension, as first Proserpina and then Plutone yield to Orfeo's request. In fact, it is interesting that only after the decision to free Euridice is made do Orfeo and Plutone share a quatrain, signifying, as it were, their mental accord (ll. 531-34):

Plutone:	Romper le proprie leggi è vil possanza	A
	Anzi reca sovente e biasmo e danno.	B
Orfeo:	Ma de gli afflitti consolar l'affanno	B
	E' pur di regio cor gentil'usanza.	A

It is evident that the stylistic distinctions drawn by Rinuccini are more subtle than the simple division between *luoghi oziosi* and *parti recitative* established in Poliziano's poem. The *luoghi oziosi* are of course primarily the choral sections, which serve as interludes at the end of each scene, and the strophic dance-songs, which enliven the static moments during the course of the play. These all share a uniform style, to be discussed separately. The poetry of the recitative sections, however, varies according to the function and place of the monologue or dialogue in relation to the drama. The recitative style of the static opening scene of jubilation, or of the narrative third scene belonging to Arcetro, is not that of the rapid exchanges following Dafne's announcement in scene two, nor the emotionally pregnant dialogue of the Hades scene. In the first examples (from scenes 1 and 3), the poetry is characterized by more obvious and more frequent rhymes, usually the *rime incrociate* and *rime baciate* found in Euridice's "In mille guise e mille";[94] in the second (from scenes 2 and 4), it becomes more speech-like, contains a greater number of unrhymed lines, and proceeds often in the more rapid rhythm of the tercets described above.[95]

There are then three styles or manners of poetry in Rinuccini's *Euridice* libretto (the third being that of the choral interludes), a fact which in itself has not been remarked either by the literary or by the musical historians of these early operas. What is still more remarkable, however, is that each of the three styles may be seen to correspond to one of the three types of melopoeia into which Giovanni Battista Doni divides all those stage representations which he feels may appropriately use music throughout – that is, pastoral tragicomedies, sacred representations, eclogues, and other dramas not bound by the more rigid conventions of tragedy and comedy.[96] Doni's divisions are comprised of (1) the narrative or recitational, (2) the affective or expressive, and (3) the madrigalistic styles. The first type of melopoeia, or style of composition, to which Doni refers has the same characteristics as Rinuccini's first poetic manner, as I have described it in the first, third, and final scenes of *Euridice*, and in Dafne's narration from scene two. In the poetic genres cited by Doni, the composer

> should be able to exercise greater freedom, even making use of that simple style, which we can call narrative; because it is used in the narrations of certain messages, descriptions, and similar calm dialogue; or properly recitational, because it suits those recitations in song of certain epic poems or romances, which indeed are heard to the commonly sung tunes of these ottave rime.[97]

The second style of composition in Doni's hierarchy (corresponding to Rinuccini's second poetic manner) is reserved for more affective discourse, which may be imitated successfully only by careful observation of the precise accents and inflections of the natural tones heard in speech.

> He who would like, therefore, precisely to express these very accents and inflections of pitch which are naturally uttered in speaking . . . will need to pay great attention, to practice at length, and to use suitable means; but above all [he will need] an extremely sensitive ear.[98] For this reason he should diligently observe which syllables are intoned with a uniform and steady accent, and on which ones the voice is raised or lowered, and to what note or interval, considering those rapid transitions which occur between the accented syllables, and all the varieties which are made principally by the most artful and expert speakers, according to the manner, affection, and sentiment of that which is spoken, for example, interrogations, threats, and all kinds of interjections and representational speech.[99]

Doni's brief discourse on the ways and means of imitating affective discourse, interpolated into his summary of the styles of representational music, stresses verisimilitude above all else – the precise imitation of the external manifestations of those affections to be represented.   This accords well with Rinuccini's second manner, in which he attempts to impart a prose-like quality to the more affective and dramatic parts of his libretto by means of the rapid and irregularly rhyming tercets of the second and fourth scenes of *Euridice*, as well as the increase in the appearance of short, unrhymed lines in those scenes of heightened dramatic tension.   Finally Doni speaks of the type of melody which is derived from the most graceful madrigals, and which lends variety, charm, and effectiveness to the whole.   No doubt, this is precisely the style in which Rinuccini intended his *luoghi oziosi* to be set.[100]

The parallels drawn here are enlightening not only because they suggest important relationships between poetry and music in this new and humanistic marriage of the two arts, but also for their implications concerning the far-reaching influence of Rinuccini's creative role in shaping the new art form.   It must not be thought that the parallels between Doni's hierarchy of melodic styles and Rinuccini's levels of poetic expression are coincidental, for the earliest historian of opera frequently illustrated his remarks with particular reference to the score of Peri's *Euridice*; and, although these bear only incidentally on the libretto, it is through such references that Doni indirectly establishes his (and Peri's) indebtedness to the formal structure of Rinuccini's libretto.

Let us examine more closely the characteristics of Doni's stylistic categories.   To illustrate the first and simplest style of recitative, Doni cites three works – *Due lettere amorose*, two solo madrigals "in genere rappresentativo" by Monteverdi, published in his seventh book (1619), and "Per quel vago boschetto," Dafne's account of Euridice's death in Peri's score.   Doni finds this the least appealing style of the new music, for the modern composers of recitative, in attempting to simulate ordinary speech as closely as possible, neglected to make their melodies varied and tuneful enough.   Far from being able to delight or move the listener, this simple recitative style can become tedious.   That is why, he says, it is used by good composers only in narrative discourse devoid of strong affections.[101]

Doni seems satisfied, however, with the qualities of "Per quel vago boschetto," for "it uses rapid notes judiciously, remaining on one note a lot of the time; because the same thing is done even when something is recounted in simple speech."[102]   Simple as it is, this remark constitutes an accurate description of the essentials of recitative and, along with others in the treatise, can be understood only in the light of Peri's own formulation of dramatic recitative[103]—his "imitation of speech in song"—upon which the historian evidently based his observation.[104] In the preface to *Euridice*, Peri stated:

> I knew likewise that in our speech some vowels are so intoned that harmony may be based upon them, and that in the course of speaking one passes through many others that are not so intoned until one returns to another [vowel] capable of [supporting a] progression to a fresh consonance. And keeping in mind those modes and accents which serve us in our sorrow, in our joy, and the like, I made the bass move in time to these, now more, now less [frequently], according to the affections, and I held it stable through the dissonances and consonances until, running through various notes, the voice of the speaker came to a word that, being intoned in ordinary speech, opened the way to a new harmony. And I did this not only in order that the flow of discourse might not distress the ear (as though stumbling among the repeated chords it encountered with the more frequent consonances) and [not only] in order that it might not seem in a way to dance to the movement of the bass, particularly in sad or solemn subjects, although others more joyful naturally require more frequent movements [changes of harmony];[105] but also in order that the use of the dissonances might either diminish or cover up whatever advantage might derive from our having to intone every note, which perhaps the ancient musicians had less need of doing.[106]

The two basic principles of *stile recitativo*, formulated here by Peri in painstaking detail—the simulation of the inflections of ordinary speech by the use of free dissonance and unsupported consonance in the "rapid notes" of the vocal part, and the regulation of the movement of the harmony in accordance with the affections of the text—are the underlying assumptions of Doni's brief comment about Dafne's narrative, "Per quel vago boschetto," with its "judicious" use of "rapid notes" and its sustained chords. Peri derived these principles from his conviction that "the ancient Greeks and Romans . . . used a harmony, which, surpassing that of ordinary speech, fell so far below the melody of song as to take an intermediate form."[107] He goes on to say, with reference to the classical poets,

> This is why we find their poems admitting iambic verse, a form less elevated than the hexameter but said to be advanced beyond the confines of familiar conversation.[108]

Here Peri is referring to the fact that, while classical heroic verse was typically in dactylic hexameter, the usual verse of dramatic dialogue was iambic trimeter because it approached the more prosaic accents of ordinary speech.[109]

Insofar as Peri's formulation of the recitative style incorporated the idea of imitating the inflections of speech in melody, it did not differ radically from other modes of singing, such as psalmody, or improvised solo recitations of certain types of poetry on a given tune, nor even from some of the declamation found in the madrigals and solo songs dating from the late sixteenth century. It was not in the melodic element of recitative that Peri's unique contribution to monody appeared, but rather in the rhythmic and harmonic elements. For, as Claude Palisca has stated, the real novelty of Florentine recitative was not its dependence upon "an interaction between speech inflection and melody" but rather "between speech rhythm and measured rhythm, and between free dissonance and triadic harmony." Indeed, the recitative melody was "at once free from and controlled by harmony and measured rhythm."[110]

The ingredients of Caccini's formulation of the new style, which was apparently evolved simultaneously with Peri's, are rooted essentially in the same tenets—imitation of speech inflection, rhythmic flexibility, and harmonic freedom.

> It occurred to me to introduce a kind of music by which others might be able, as it were, to talk in harmony, using in that style (as I have said at other times) a certain noble nonchalance (*sprezzatura*) in singing, passing now and then through certain dissonances, but holding the bass note firm, except when I wanted to avail myself of the common practice, and with the inner voices played on an instrument in order to express some affection, these being of no use for anything else.[111]

Notwithstanding the objections to recitative raised by Doni and to some extent by the rest of history, it must be seen as "a truly progressive solution" to the "new demands" of text-setting because it incorporated "the most recent advances in triadic harmony and controlled dissonance."[112] The nonchalance of the new style from a harmonic point of view consisted precisely in the disregard of the old contrapuntal practice (the *prima prattica,* referred to by Caccini above as the "common practice"), wherein the movement of the parts supporting the melody was controlled by specific intervallic relationships, which usually resulted in the harmonization of virtually every note of the text-bearing voice. Obviously the repudiation of the contrapuntal rules of the Renaissance theorists was possible only after the single "aria" came to be accepted as the most effective means of conveying the conceits of a text, and once the tonal language necessary to support and enhance the aria had evolved in the non-linear continuo realizations of the lutanists and theorboists who, like Peri, accompanied their own solo songs. Caccini defines the subordinate role of the harmonic accompaniment when he links the color and disposition of the inner voices to the expression of some affection, for "these are of no use for anything else."[113]

Although Caccini clarifies the relationship between harmony and text-expression in the new style, it is Peri who affirms the correspondence between rhythmic motion and the affections. In so doing, Peri realizes the musical implications, for example, of Giacomini's mechanistic affections theory,[114] although his knowledge of this theory was probably limited to the more general statements found in Bardi and Galilei, who, of course, relied upon and helped to spread the opinion of Girolamo Mei. Once again it is tempting to draw a direct parallel between Peri's formulation of the role of rhythm in the new style and Mei's description of the Greek poet-musician, who accompanied his song "with the regulated temperament of the fast and slow, articulating the parts of his composition . . . so that each one by itself through its proper nature was accommodated to some determinate affection."[115] The importance of Peri's insistence on the relationship between rhythmic motion and the affections in representational music should not be overlooked, for the rhythmic solutions of the new style are just as "progressive" as the harmonic ones. The Baroque style in music came to be characterized not only by the exploitation of triadic harmony for expressive purposes, but also by two extremes of rhythmic motion: the flexibility of recitative style, with its free rhythms based upon speech inflections, and the repetition of certain stereotyped rhythmic patterns, derived from dance tunes or from poetic meters.[116] Many of these became associated with specific affections and gradually evolved into a common vocabulary of "motions" which, while arousing similar motions in the listener, determined the expressive character of a particular piece. Although not codified until the eighteenth century, this idea was inherent in certain humanist principles of the early monodists. For example, Bardi, paraphrasing Aristotle's *Politics*, affirmed that "in rhythms are the portraits of anger, mildness, strength, temperance, and of every other moral virtue, as well as of all those qualities which are their contraries."[117] In addition, Mei and Galilei linked the air style, because of its "characteristic movement," with moving the affections.[118]

Just as the musical solutions to the problems of affective solo singing on stage may be called progressive, so must the poetic solutions; for Rinuccini developed a new style of *poesia musicale* which, while it incorporated some of the expressive idiom and techniques of the late sixteenth-century pastoral and madrigal literature, was uniquely suited to "talking in harmony." Just as Peri considered his recitative style to be midway between "ordinary speech" and the "melody of song," so must Rinuccini have judged the flexible intermingling of seven- and eleven-syllable lines in his *parti recitative* to partake of the qualities of both familiar conversation and elevated verse. Specifically, the librettist must have believed that the introduction into the shepherds' discourse of *settenari*, a verse form said by Mei to be too fleeting to satisfy the senses (which we may interpret as meaning that it was too short to be heard as verse),[119] functioned in a way similar to the iambic meter of ancient dramatic dialogue. Peri shunned a continually moving bass lest it be allowed to dominate the upper part and communicate an affection without regard to the text; instead he avowedly "made the bass move in time to the [modes and accents of speech], now more, now less [frequently], according to the affections." Similarly, by shunning conventional verse patterns throughout the *parti recitative*, Rinuccini must have intended that metrical regularity not be allowed to subvert his more immediate concern – the variety of expression and potency (*potere*) of the dramatic melody, which takes its existence from the rhythms and inflections of the dramatic text. Thus the irregular mixture of seven- and eleven-syllable verse renders the conversations of his shepherds more natural and less stylized than, for example, the dialogue in Cavalieri's *Rappresentazione*, between interlocutors who generally speak in isometric couplets or tercets. In the same way that Peri desired to free the voice from the tyranny of its rhythmic and harmonic accompaniment, Rinuccini apparently wished to release it from the requirements of conventional verse forms.

Not only in its use of meter, but also in the disavowal or distortion of conventional rhyme schemes does the librettist's recitative style conform to this picture. Rinuccini orders the rhymed endings of his verse in such a way as to negate the impression that they are part of a preordained arrangement or scheme. The occurrence of a series of rhymes thus cannot usually be anticipated by the reader, especially during the more affective and rapidly moving sections, wherein the freely-rhyming texture is significantly interwoven with unrhymed verses. Such flexibility yields the impression that each part of the dialogue is freshly wrought and subject only to its own laws of form and expression. At the same time, it is important to recognize that, far from abandoning rhyme, Rinuccini depends upon it to lend coherence and structure to his verse. His method here, too, is analogous to that of Peri, who, while relegating the harmonic accompaniment of his vocal line to a subsidiary position, nevertheless derives musical coherence from its support. With the above considerations in mind, I suggest that even Rinuccini's new *poesia musicale*, with its studied disregard for metrical and rhyme patterns, possesses that "noble" quality so highly regarded by the composers – *sprezzatura*.[120]

Prized most of all by Caccini as the factor enabling his new manner of singing to approach ordinary speech,[121] *sprezzatura* was also undoubtedly that quality of performance for which Peri lauded Vittoria Archilei:

> This lady has always made my compositions worthy of her singing, adorning them not only with those trills and those long colorature, simple and double, which with her lively talent she invents continually (more to comply with the usage of our times than because she considers the beauty and force of our singing to reside in them) *but also with those graceful ornaments that cannot be written or, if written, cannot be learned from writing.*[122]

In making a distinction between the quantity of written colorature and those ornaments which depend upon the quality and modulation of the performer's voice, Peri was no doubt denying the expressiveness of the current usage of ornamentation and criticizing Caccini, who, a few months earlier, had claimed to have invented it.[123] Yet both Caccini and Peri recognized the importance of the unwritten inflections and accents of the voice, these subtle and often spontaneous modifications of tone—faster or slower, louder or softer—which reflect the conceits of the soul and which Caccini indeed tried to notate in his *Nuove musiche*. However, I maintain that this emphasis upon spontaneity and naturalness, and the desire to communicate faithfully a particular moment of affection are not unique to the composers and performers of the new theatrical style; for they may be likened precisely to that mode of poetic representation for which Rinuccini was obviously striving in his *libretti per musica*.

Rinuccini's recitative verse style has much in common with some sections of the pastoral plays of Tasso and Guarini. Yet it is easily differentiated from these by the fact that its style is consistent within the general outlines established by the poet, whereas the larger works are marked by a diversity of versification for which there seems to have been no reason other than a justifiable interest in variety and virtuosity of expression. The libretto was created principally as a vehicle for musical expression, whereas the late-Renaissance pastoral was a *tour de force*, the form of which, however controversial, nevertheless presented a fine vehicle for displaying the range of the poet's own skill and the technical mastery of his peculiar artistic means. This is apparent in Guarini's definition of the "instrumental end" of tragicomedy—i.e., its form—which results from the combination and moderation of traits belonging to both tragedy and comedy.[124]

> . . . it takes from the one the great persons, but not the action, the plot which is verisimilar but not true, the passions which are aroused but blunted, pleasure but

not sadness, danger but not death. From the other, laughter which is not dissolute, moderate pleasures, a fictional plot, a happy reversal, and above all the comic order.[125]

Not only was the form of the new genre a mixture of two extremes, but its verse and diction were to assume a stylistic position midway between the weighty and the humble. Consequently the poet of the *Pastor fido* claimed that

. . . the verse is not turgid, not noisy, not dithyrambic. Its periods are not prolonged, not short, not intricate, not hard, not difficult to understand; . . .Its diction is clear but not low, proper but not vulgar, figurative but not enigmatical, beautiful but not affected, sustained but not inflated, pliant but not languishing; and, to conclude in a word, such as is not remote from common speech and yet not close to that of the common herd; it is not so elaborate that the stage abhors it nor so vulgar that the theater condemns it, but rather it can be played without trouble and read without labor.[126]

One can easily see that Rinuccini must have been influenced by this stylistic formulation of tragicomedy. At the same time he did not follow Guarini's example to the extent that he allowed the preoccupation with stylistic virtuosity to distract him from his main task—the creation of a drama to be sung entirely in music. It is surely not unimportant for the musical setting of such a drama that Rinuccini's libretto coheres so well as an artistic unit. More than anything else, this coherence is a function of stylistic consistency. In contrast, Guarini's play, and to some extent Tasso's *Aminta* as well, give the impression of being complex, but somewhat amorphous structures. In the *Pastor fido*, this impression is fostered by the melange of verse forms which flow into one another within a continuum ranging from close rhyme to blank verse, and including a great deal of rhythmic variation in the combination or separation of long and short lines. It is difficult to know whether Guarini's norm is the irregular mixture of heptasyllables and hendecasyllables, usually punctuated at the cadences or periods by rhymed couplets, that characterizes a great part of the dialogue (e.g., I. 1, 4), or the long passages of blank hendecasyllables found in some scenes involving narration (I. 3) or soliloquy (I. 5 and II. 4). Sometimes the dialogue moves without warning into more lyrical moods wherein short lines and close rhymes predominate (I. 4, ll. 831 ff.).

With Tasso, the basic unit of dialogue seems to be hendecasyllabic verse, although he, too, frequently intermingles shorter lines to a greater or lesser extent.[127] Rhyme generally gives place to assonance in Tasso's verse, as well as to a device with even greater structural potential—repetition or refrain. The same kind of stylistic variation is extended in these pastoral tragicomedies to the choruses, which will be discussed more fully below.[128]   Suffice it to say here that the verse style most nearly resembling that of Rinuccini's *parti recitative* may be found in several of the closing choruses in both works,[129] choruses with a through-composed (as opposed to strophic) design, and possessing the same rhythmic flexibility and free use of rhyme that carry forward the *parti recitative* of Rinuccini's libretti.   Whether or not these choruses were intended to be sung,[130] there can be no doubt that both Guarini and Tasso associated this style with a greater degree of lyricism than is found in their dialogue sections.   With this tradition to draw from—and Rinuccini was obviously influenced by the pastoral poets most of all—it is significant that the librettist chose the somewhat lyrical, though loosely organized style used primarily in the pastoral choruses, rather than blank verse, for his music dramas.

Although the number of musical settings inspired by Guarini's play is more than five hundred from printed sources alone (with at least that many probably not yet uncovered in manuscript sources), there are only two scenes which have received dramatic settings in their entirety.[131]   Act 2, scene 6 (Corisca, Satiro) was composed as a *dialogo musicale a 2 voci* (Venice, 1623) by T. Merula, and Act 3, scene 2, "Giuoco della cieca," survives as a full-fledged cantata in *stile rappresentativo* by Giovanni Ghizzolo[132] in his first book of *Madrigali et arie* (1609).[133]   Since the latter was composed within the first decade of operatic activity, and since the style, as indeed the title of his work, obviously reflects the influence of Caccini, a comparison between the recitative styles prompted by Guarini's text and Rinuccini's *Euridice* is both justified and instructive.

It is important to note that Guarini intended only the four choral responses, which organize and buttress the scene, and formalize the playing of the "game," to be set to music.   Consequently, there is a significant difference between the verse of the chorus of nymphs—successively rhymed couplets which adhere to a carefully organized metrical scheme[134]—and the unrhymed, seven- and eleven-syllable lines in which the dialogue of the "players" is cast.   The following passage, an exchange between Amarilli (blindfolded) and her lover Mirtillo, is framed by the dancing and singing of the nymphs' chorus, and thus constitutes a short, closed section of recitative:[135]

> Am.:   In buona fè, Licori,
> ch'i' mi pensai d'averti presa, e trovo
> d'aver presa una pianta.
> Sénto ben che tu ridi.

Mirt.: Deh, foss'io quella pianta.
Or non vegg'io Corisca
tra quelle fratte ascosa? E' dessa certo;
e non so che m'accenna,
che non m'intendo, e pur m'accenna ancora.

Not only is there no rhyme, but the few long lines are broken up by enjambment and frequent commas, which heighten the similarity of the verse to ordinary speech by obscuring its structure. The musical setting, however, is in direct contradiction to this principle. Presented with a text whose only structural prop, so to speak, was its regular fragmentation into short phrases, Ghizzolo seems to have seized upon this means to organize the passage into a coherent musical whole. Thus, the parallel rhythmic construction of the phrases, the relatively fast harmonic rhythm, and the use of motivic repetition (as in Mirtillo's line beginning "Tra quelle fratte. . .") are traits more indicative of madrigal and air style than of recitative. (See example 2.)[136] In fact, this passage is more similar to Peri's setting of Tirsi's arietta (ll. 144-48), with its regularly inserted caesuras at the half-line, than to Peri's or Caccini's recitative style. (See example 3.)[137]

Nel puro ardor de la più bella stella
Aurea facella — di bel foco accendi,
E qui discendi — su l'aurate piume,
Giocondo nume, — e di celeste fiamma
L'anime infiamma.

This is not to say that a composer with closer ties to the Florentine school than had Ghizzolo, whose activity seems to have centered in the Veneto, would not have set the Guarini text differently. However, such a composer would have encountered the same problematic traits, which in Ghizzolo's setting are reinforced, but which are not present in Rinuccini's recitative sections.

Here follow a few lines of quiet dialogue from *Euridice*, from the passage immediately preceding Dafne's entrance in the second scene, the verse characteristics of which have been recounted above (ll. 154-61):[138]

Arcetro:	Deh come ogni bifolco, ogni pastore	A
	A' tuoi lieti Imenei	b
	Scopre il piacer ch'entro racchiude il core.	A
Tirsi:	Del tuo beato amor gli alti contenti	C
	Crescano ognor, come per pioggia suole	D
	l'onda gonfiar de' rapidi torrenti.	C
Orfeo:	E per te, Tirsi mio, liete e ridenti	C
	Sempre le notti e i dì rimeni il sole.	D

Example 2
from G. Ghizzolo, *La Cieca* (1609)

Example 3
Peri, *Euridice*, p. 11

Rinuccini's dialogue, with more hendecasyllabic lines and fewer internal pauses, has a sustained quality not present in the preceding example by Guarini. In general, since Rinuccini's verse is of mixed length and since the phrases extend through three or four lines, there is no striking rhythmic unit to lend musical coherence. Rather, this is supplied by rhyme, which, by emphasizing the line endings, provides melodic and cadential goals.

These factors are reflected to a greater or lesser degree in the musical settings by Peri and Caccini. (See examples 4 and 5.) For example, in Peri's setting, Arcetro pauses only at the end of the first verse, breaking his remark into unequal halves. The caesura within the verse (after "ogni bifolco") is expressed by a brief retardation of rhythmic movement, which, however, detracts little from the progression of the vocal line toward its main goal ("core"), especially since the supporting harmony remains stable. Similarly, the ending of the second, short verse ("Imenei"), is subordinated to the following one, this time by

Example 4
Peri, *Euridice*, p. 12

Example 5
Caccini, *Euridice*, p. 11

means of harmonic acceleration to the final cadence. Taken as a whole, then, the passage may be said to consist of two asymmetrical phrases, one static, the other dynamic. The closing word of the first phrase, "pastore," is thrown into relief by a rest, creating the expectation of a concluding rhyme, which subsequently becomes the goal of the dynamic half. The same principle is even more clearly visible in the next pair of phrases, which, I think, must be seen as extending through Orfeo's lines to the end of the passage. The point of division here occurs at the G-major cadence on "torrenti," which maintains the harmony of the opening cadential motion of Tirsi's phrase, thus rendering it static, while Orfeo's response, which proceeds to a cadence on A-major, constitutes the dynamic member of this pair.

In connection with this second pair of phrases (in example 4) it is interesting to note that Peri has altered Rinuccini's libretto at Orfeo's couplet (ll. 160-61). Instead of the original

> E per te, Tirsi mio, liete e ridenti
> Sempre le notti e i dì rimeni il sole

the score has

> E per te Tirsi mio rimeni il sole
> Sempre le notti, e i dì lieti e ridenti.

The only possible motive for this reversal must have been Peri's desire to change the disposition of the rhymes from ABA AB to ABA BA. In this way, the expectations aroused by the first phrase (ABA), with its slow-moving harmonies which remain in the area of G major, are fulfilled in the second phrase (BA) by the corresponding end-rhyme. At the same time, the achievement of this melodic goal is aided by the faster harmonic rhythm in the second phrase, which advances to a cadence in a new tonal area, A-major—the same, incidentally, as the close on "core" above. Thus I suggest that the main cohesive principle and driving force in Peri's recitative style is the element of tension and relaxation created by the erratic rhyming pairs of Rinuccini's verse and mirrored in Peri's skillful manipulation of harmonic rhythm, to which the composer himself attached great importance in speaking about the new style.[139]

One can see to what structural advantage Peri employs his librettist's irregularly rhymed verse by comparing his setting with Caccini's of the same passage (example 5).[140] Caccini uses the text exactly as it appears in the libretto, and does not distinguish the verse endings musically from one another. (Almost all except the last line of each speech receive the same rhythmic close of two minims.) Combined with Caccini's more active harmonic rhythm, this equalization results in shorter, less sustained phrases and repeated interruptions of the larger goals by melodic and rhythmic cadences that have been prompted by the interior verse endings.

On the other hand, such finely wrought lines in Caccini's score as Orfeo's couplet preceding Dafne's entrance ("E per te, Tirsi mio. . .") give evidence that the composer frequently affirms, as he does in the preface to *Le nuove musiche*, the value of purely musical expressive means. This may be seen again in Euridice's solo in the first scene, "In mille guise, e mille" (ll. 73-81), which closes in a flourish of coloratura prompted by the words, "Trarrem liete carole, e lieti balli." But there are other, more subtle indications of musical domination of the text in Caccini's setting. (See example 6.) For example, the trochaic rhythmic pattern set up in the first verse serves as a model for the beginnnings of subsequent, longer verses, creating an almost isometric effect, which is only partially dispelled by the syncopated climax of the fourth verse. Compare this with Peri's setting (example 7), which exhibits somewhat more sensitivity to declamation in its variety of rhythmic detail.[141]

In manner similar to the rhythmic patterning, Caccini's harmonic progressions here seem to follow a logic which is independent of the text structure. Each verse has its own, rather arbitrary, harmonic direction, accompanied by a fairly regular harmonic rhythm. The entire passage is loosely organized into two roughly complementary phrases.

Example 6
Caccini, *Euridice*, p. 5

Example 7
Peri, *Euridice*, p. 6

Peri's setting, on the other hand, depends upon Rinuccini's rhyme scheme for its harmonic and melodic goals; for Peri derives structural coherence from the poetry by controlling the harmony and rhythm of his accompaniment in such a way that the members of a rhyming pair complement each other either in the direction of the harmony (toward or away from a cadential goal) or in the degree of the harmonic rhythm (slower or faster), or both. Thus, in Euridice's solo (example 7), the first four verses form a unit wherein the principal rhyming pair ("petto-diletto") represents two phrases, the first of which suggests a particular tonal area, while the second departs from that area (. . . B . . . B). At the same time, the harmonic rhythm in the second phrase is approximately twice as fast as it is in the first, accelerating the motion to the expected rhyming close. The same static-dynamic relationship occurs in the next pair of phrases, the first comprised of two short verses (rhyming "amate-grate") and balanced by a long one whose ending ("boschetto") recalls a previous rhyme (c c B). Finally, the passage concludes with a hendecasyllabic couplet, the second phrase of which returns to the tonality of the initial cadence (D D).

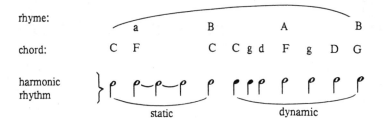

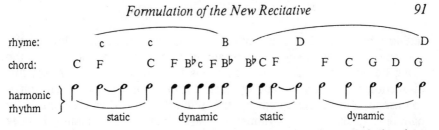

rhyme:		c	c		B	D		D
chord:	C F		C	F B♭c F B♭	B♭C F	F	C G D	G

The point is that Peri creates a musical logic, evident here and elsewhere in his score, which is firmly rooted in and inspired by Rinuccini's poetic structures.

Another example is supplied by Dafne's long account of Euridice's demise, which Doni considered an illustration of simple, narrative recitative (ll. 190-222):

Part I	a	Per quel vago boschetto,
	b	Ove rigando i fiori
	B	Lento trascorre il fonte de gli allori,
	a	Prendea dolce diletto
	C	Con le compagne sue la bella sposa.
	c	Chi violetta o rosa
	d	Per far ghirlande al crine
	D	Togliea dal prato e dall'acute spine,
	e	E qual posando il fianco
	f	Su la fiorita sponda
	F	Dolce cantava al mormorar de l'onda.
Part II	g	Ma la bella Euridice
	H	Movea danzando il piè su 'l verde prato,
	i	Quando, ria sorte acerba!
	h	Angue crudo e spietato,
	I	Che celato giacea tra' fiori e l'erba,
	J	Punsele il piè con sì maligno dente,
	j	Ch'impallidì repente
	K	Come raggio di sol che nube adombri,
	l	E dal profondo core
	m	Con un sospir mortale
	L	Sì spaventoso ohimè! sospinse fuore,
	m	Che, quasi avesse l'ale,
	N	Giunse ogni Ninfa al doloroso suono,
	n	Et ella in abbandono
	O	Tutta lasciossi allor ne l'altrui braccia.

etc.

Peri divided his setting into two parts, one dominated by a single tonal area (B-flat), and the other characterized by movement through various chords quite removed from the tonality of the opening section. This broadly conceived structural duality corresponds to the content of Dafne's message. Starting with a calm description of the woodland setting where Euridice and her companions were gathering flowers, the messenger continues with a more animated and detailed portrait of the dying heroine, pierced by the venomous tooth of a serpent. Again this distinction between static and dynamic members of a large formal unit is confirmed and underscored by the interaction of rhyme-endings and harmonic goals. In the symmetrical disposition of the opening phrases (ll. 190-200) and in the musical parallels between them (see example 8 part I), Peri's setting is not very different from that of Caccini.[142] The musical symmetry results from the nearly equal groups of verses, all but one terminating in a rhymed couplet:

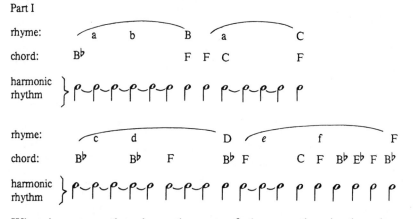

Part I

What is noteworthy about the rest of the narration is that the more dynamic harmonic movement may be seen to coincide with a more disjointed rhyme scheme, wherein couplets are separated and poetic phrases terminate in unexpected and unrhymed verses:

Part II

rhyme: m   N n   O   P   O p

chord: G   F B♭ DG G   A D D   G C   D

harmonic rhythm

Such structural asymmetry, which provides less opportunity for periodic, and thus anticipated, cadences, contributes to the dynamic feeling of this section by propelling the melody forward. Furthermore, it simulates the realism of an evolving narrative speech in contrast to the stylized expression of, for example, the inflexible patterns of the *Rappresentazione di Anima et di Corpo*.

Cavalieri's music is so bound by the formalized and continuous couplets and tercets of his libretto that it never rises above a stereotyped level of expression. This composer's avowed intention—to have the poetry serve the music—is surely reflected in his score, for the rhyming pairs of the text encourage motivic repetition, equalize the length of phrases, and determine the regular occurrence of harmonic goals. The results may be seen in the opening monologue of *La rappresentazione* sung by Il Tempo (example 9).[143]

It is interesting to compare this setting with Monteverdi's treatment of a text consisting entirely of rhymed heptasyllabic couplets. The following is the *Partenza amorosa a voce sola in genere rappresentativo*, one of the so-called *Due lettere amorose* cited by Doni as a model of narrative recitative.[144]

Se pur destina e vole	a
Il Cielo almo mio sole	a
Ch'in tenebre mi viva	b
Ascolta alma mia diva	b
Ciò che potrà ridire	c
Fra cotanto martire	c
Di sconsolato Amante	d
Lingua fredda e tremante	d
O del cor luce e speme	e
Odi le voci estreme	e
Odile e del bel seno	f
Una lagrima almeno	f
Bagni la viva neve	g
Rimira ah come lieve	g
etc.[145]	

Instead of adhering, as Cavalieri does, to the rhymed cadences of the poetry for musical form, Monteverdi obscures some of the verse endings

Example 8
Peri, *Euridice*, pp. 14-16

Example 9
Cavalieri, *Rappresentazione di Anima et di Corpo*, p. II

by fusing them rhythmically and melodically with the beginning of the next line. (See, for example, "vole" or "martire" in example 10.) Elsewhere, he destroys the integrity of a couplet with rests in the vocal line, and half cadences in the bass (e.g., "viva-diva" or "neve-lieve") in order to foster musical continuity. It is significant, however, that at the points of articulation punctuated by harmonic cadences, Monteverdi usually proceeds in a manner which correlates with the poetic structure. In his avoidance and manipulation of the stylized patterns characteristic of this particular text, Monteverdi seems to be striving toward a musical flexibility which utilizes the formal potential of rhyme without being restricted by its every structural detail. Such flexibility is inherent in Rinuccini's dramatic poetry; and to the extent that Monteverdi may have been consciously imitating the Florentine style in these works "in genere rappresentativo," he seems to have solved the problem of stylized poetic expression in a manner akin to, if not modeled upon, Peri's recitative style.[146]

A fragment of recitative from *Dafne*, discovered by William Porter in a Ms. from the Brussels Conservatory,[147] sheds light on the matter of the Florentine treatment of poetic texts in the initial stages of development of the new dramatic style. The text, beginning "Qual nova meraviglia," is recited by a messenger narrating the central event of the story—the nymph's transformation into a laurel tree. In the Brussels version the narrative is considerably abbreviated compared to the libretto, and the choral comments are eliminated. In fact, Porter suggests that the Brussels version is the earlier one, dating from about 1598. The text bears the same features as the expanded narrative sections of the printed

Example 10
Monteverdi, "Partenza amorosa a voce sola in genere rappresentativo,"
in *Opere*, VII, 167-8

Dafne and *Euridice* libretti—mixed long and short, rhymed and unrhymed verses arranged in such a way as to promote rhythmic and melodic continuity. The implication is that, from the inception of the new genre to its fruition at the turn of the century, the flexible qualities in Rinuccini's dramatic *poesia musicale* played an essential role in molding the new recitative style.

In a new setting of *Dafne* in 1608 the Florentine composer Marco da Gagliano added one refinement to the structural details of Peri's formulation of narrative recitative.[148] Although he held fast to the basic directives of the poetry, Gagliano increased the recitational flow by reducing the rhythmic prominence of the verse endings. In his original score, as in Peri's and Caccini's, the basic units of recitative are ♩ and ♪, but the rhyming words are usually expressed by semi-minims (♩ ♩) as opposed to the more sustained values (𝅗𝅥 𝅗𝅥) of Peri's setting. Correspondingly Gagliano notates the broad cadences in minims (𝅗𝅥 𝅗𝅥); however, since Peri rarely uses semibreves, but usually sets the closing words of his speeches in minims as well, he does not translate the distinction between internal line-endings and closing cadences into a rhythmic hierarchy such as Gagliano creates in the later score.

In all other matters of declamation, and in harmonic movement, Gagliano seems certainly to have accepted and utilized Peri's solutions. The same dual principle of harmonic and rhythmic control of the phrase in conjunction with the avoidance or attainment of rhyme-endings that characterized Peri's style may be seen in Gagliano's work. For example, the revised version of the narrative of Dafne's transformation, "Quando la bella Ninfa" (ll. 322-49), is parallel both in poetic and musical structure to Peri's "Per quel vago boschetto."

a   Quando la bella ninfa,
B   Sprezzando i prieghi del celeste amante,
B   Vidi che per fuggir movea le piante,
c   Da voi mi tolsi anch'io
C   L'orme seguendo l'acceso Dio.
d   Ella, quasi cervetta
D   Che innanzi a crudo veltro il passo affretta,
e   Fuggia veloce, e spesso
E   Si volgeva a mirar se lungi o presso
b   Avea l'odiato amante;
. . . .
I   Sciolse la lingua: et ecco in un momento
J   Che l'uno e l'altro leggiadretto piede,
I   Che pur dianzi al fuggir parve aura o vento,
j   Fatto immobil si vede,
K   Di salvatica scorza insieme avvinto,
L   E le braccia e le palme al ciel distese
m   Veste selvaggia fronde:
m   Le crespe chiome bionde
N   Più non riveggo e 'l volto e 'l bianco petto;
n   Ma dal gentile aspetto
O   Ogni sembianza si dilegua e perde;
O   Sol miro un arboscel fiorito e verde.

The recitative has a short first section consisting of symmetrical phrases which balance each other in the degree of motion of the harmonic rhythm and in the direction of the harmonic progression. (See example 11.) The phrases may be described again as alternately static and dynamic. Each is built upon a poetic unit with a self-contained rhyme.

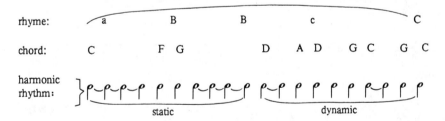

As in the example from Peri, the initial section contrasts markedly with the rest of the piece, which contains more distant harmonic cadences in conjunction with unrhymed lines. Characterized by "open" groups of verses and changing harmonic goals, the latter part of the narrative is governed by more dynamic movement in relation to the previous, closed section:

Example 11
Gagliano, *Dafne*, pp. 38-40

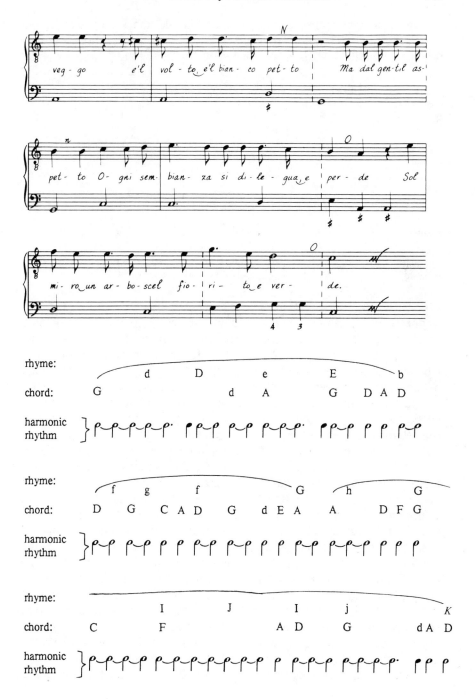

As the messenger approaches the end of his tale, the verses are aligned once again in a series of rhymed couplets, and the harmony returns briefly to the tonal area of the opening verses of the speech.

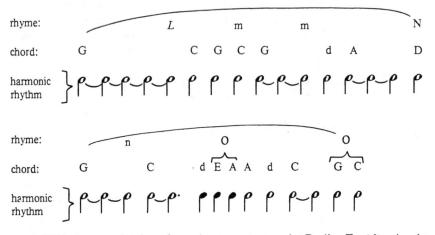

Differing at the last from its counterpart in Peri's *Euridice* in the reappearance of closed couplets and in the return to the original tonal area, this narration from *Dafne* is still more striking for its tonal logic. Although the progression of the bass by fifths away from and back to the area of C utilizes the stopping points provided by the poet, the rounded harmonic plan, in which each pause occurs on the chord most nearly related to that of the previous cadence, is essentially independent of the poetic structure.   Such tightly constructed harmonic movement is characteristic of the entire score by Gagliano, but is notably absent in Peri.   On the other hand, Peri's accompaniment bears little resemblance to that basso continuo style which, during the Baroque era of keyboard accompaniment, became regulated by and associated with certain rules of linear conduct.   It is interesting to note that Gagliano's teacher in composition was Luca Bati, a traditionalist with respect to the contrapuntal legacy of the sixteenth century; furthermore Gagliano's position as *maestro di cappella* for San Lorenzo in the early years of the seventeenth century no doubt required him to spend many hours at the organ.[149]   In contrast, Peri was trained principally as a performer, and his skill as a composer must necessarily have been influenced, as Pirrotta suggests, by his experience in playing the theorbo or *chitarrone*.[150]   On such instruments, which have little sustaining power compared to the organ, a bass line could not possibly acquire the directive force that it did on the keyboard instrument.   Instead, it remained a supporting accompaniment whose existence was justified only by its relation to the vocal part. According to Peri and Caccini this relationship was determined by the expressive needs of the text and its delivery, which meant in practice that the vocal line was discontinuously colored by changing harmonies. Particularly in Peri's score, the more affective the passage is, the more rapid and "colorful" are the harmonic changes. In Gagliano's *Dafne*, on the other hand, even the most affective passages seem to be controlled by a harmonic plan encompassing more than the resolution of an isolated, free dissonance. In fact, unprepared dissonances appear less frequently in Gagliano's score than in Peri's, with the resulting impression that tonal coherence takes precedence over tonal color in Gagliano's narrative recitative, as well as in passages of rapid dialogue, where the continuity of the recitative owes more to the force and logic of the harmonic progressions than to the rhyme scheme.[151]

To return to an examination of the *Euridice* libretto and a comparison of Peri's and Caccini's settings, it is notable that the stylistic gap between the two composers[152] narrows somewhat with the appearance on the scene of the messenger Dafne. (See examples 12 and 13.) The harmonic pace of Caccini's recitative here slows down considerably, approaching the more sustained style of Peri. Even more striking is Orfeo's tercet a few lines later (example 14) wherein Peri's technique of using "false proportions" or dissonant intervals above a sustained bass is perfectly imitated. On the other hand, Peri's vocal line is broken by more frequent rests and syncopations than Caccini uses in these affective passages. Still, the similarity of such passages as Dafne's "O del gran Febo" (examples 15 and 16) is due, I believe, not to any borrowing on the part of one composer from the other, but rather to both composers' faithful imitation of the text, here representative of Rinuccini's affective style. Short, exclamatory verses and assymetrically disposed rhymes within the framework of rapidly moving tercets are an excellent medium for the expression of heightened emotions, for they allow the vocal line greater freedom, particularly from expected rhythmic or melodic goals. In this respect Cavalieri's tercets possess qualities which are diametrically opposed to Rinuccini's verses; the former are bound by a stylized expression through which the poetry is made to serve the "beauty of the music" rather than the music being called upon to enhance the affections of the poetry. In order to realize the degree of Rinuccini's musical sensitivity in creating a poetry suitable to convey a truly expressive style, one need only compare the settings by Peri and Caccini to the dialogue between Anima and Corpo by Cavalieri (example 17), wherein little variation is admitted in matters such as phrase structure, cadential goals, and rhythmic motion.[153]

Example 12
Caccini, *Euridice*, pp. 11-12

Example 13
Peri, *Euridice*, pp. 12-13

Example 14
Caccini, *Euridice*, pp. 12-13

Ninfa deh sii contenta Ridir perchè t'affanni, Che taciuto martir troppo tormenta.

Example 15
Peri, *Euridice*, pp. 13-14

O del gran Febo, e delle sacre Dive Pregio sovram di queste selve onore Non chieder la cagion del mio dolore

Example 16
Caccini, *Euridice*, p. 12

O del gran Febo, e delle sacre dive Pregio sovran di queste selve onore

re Non chie-der la ca - gion del mio   do - lo - re.

Example 17
Cavalieri, *Rappresentazione*, p. V

Corpo:
Al-ma d'o-gni al-tra co - sa Tu sei più bel-la, e va - ga In te dun-que ci ap-pa - ga.

Anima:
Gia non mi fe - ci io stes - sa, E co - me in me po - tre - i Que-tar gli affetti mie-i?

Corpo:
Las - so! che di noi si - a? Se ri-tro-sa sei tan - to, Sta-rem ci sem-pre in pian-to.

Anima:
Ques-to nò, se m'as-col - ti; E se me-co ri-mi - ri A più al-ti de - si - ri.

However, granted the more fluid structure of Rinuccini's tercets, how does one account for the sameness of Peri's and Caccini's musical responses to this section of the libretto? The explanation surely lies in their concept of imitation. The imitation of an anguished outcry, for example, by means of a descending leap, or of an excited mental state by the more frequent interruption of a phrase with rests, are devices common to both settings which correspond to Doni's (and Galilei's) suggestions for composing affective melody.[154] The principle at work here is of course not the madrigalistic one of pictorial or auditory representation of the images in the text, but rather the imitation of the manner and inflections of the person reciting, in an attempt to express the emotions accompanying the text.[155] Another example of this type of imitation is the semitone or whole-tone rise of the vocal part at a cadence where the mode of the text is interrogative.[156]

In more affective or dramatically heightened portions of the libretto, therefore, the structuring of recitative passages (especially by Peri) into large units governed by the tension and relaxation accompanying the initiation and achievement of rhyming goals, gives way to another means of organization – the repetition of small units, be they exclamatory motives, cadence patterns, or even a word or phrase of text. (See examples 15, 16, 17, and 18.) In fact, in both scores, the entire section from Dafne's entrance to her narration of Euridice's death ("Per quel vago boschetto") hangs together largely by the repetition of the exclamatory descent at the beginning of virtually every phrase. Elsewhere in the second scene of *Euridice*, Orfeo's reaction to Dafne's news provides an example of word repetition as a means both of imitating an emotion-laden recitation and of giving some degree of organization to its affective expression (ll. 226-36):

> Non piango e non sospiro,
> O mia cara Euridice,
> Chè sospirar, chè lagrimar non posso.
> Cadavero infelice,
> O mio core, o mia speme, o pace, o vita!
> Ohimè! chi mi t'ha tolto,
> Chi mi t'ha tolto, ohimè! dove se' gita?
> Tosto vedrai ch'invano
> Non chiamasti morendo il tuo consorte.
> Non son, non son lontano:
> Io vengo, o cara vita, o cara morte.

Rinuccini used this same expressive style in the opening of the sixth scene of *Arianna* for the famous *Lamento* (ll. 783 ff.):[157]

> Lasciatemi morire,
> Lasciatemi morire,
> E chi volete voi che mi conforte
> In così dura sorte,
> In così gran martire?
> Lasciatemi morire.
>
> ....
>
> O Teseo, o Teseo mio ,
> Sì che mio ti vo' dir, che mio pur sei,
> Benchè t'involi, ahi crudo! a gli occhi miei.
> Volgiti, Teseo mio
> Volgiti, Teseo, oh Dio!
> Volgiti indietro a rimirar colei
> Che lasciato ha per te la patria e il regno,
> E in queste arene ancora,
> Cibo di fere dispietate e crude
> Lascerà l'ossa ignude.
> O Teseo, o Teseo mio,
> 　　　　　　　　　　etc.

In the following examples (18, 19 and 20)[158] from both Peri's and Caccini's *Euridice* scores, and from Monteverdi's setting of Arianna's impassioned verses, the repetition of text, sometimes in combination with musical repetition or sequence, serves the same function as it does in rhetoric—at once to intensify and to imitate the force of the emotions being expressed.[159]

Different from the motivic play and textual fragmentation of the madrigalists,[160] who were motivated as often by the purely musical consideration of phrase extension as they were by the desire for heightened expression, musical repetition in the context in which it occurs in these excerpts is clearly subordinated in quality and degree to the rhetorical intentions of the poet and to the limitations of dramatic verisimilitude. Nevertheless, Caccini's response to the lines "O mio core, o mia speme, o pace, o vita! / Ohimè! chi mi t'ha tolto / Chi mi t'ha tolto, ohimè! dove se' gita?" is basically the rather literal one of a madrigalist, for he seizes upon the text repetitions as an opportunity to write musical sequences. The effect is inevitably more lyric than dramatic. Peri, on the other hand, translates the expressive content of the text into a pervasive stylistic device with which he conveys, subtly and with consummate skill, the emotional manner of a shaken but undaunted Orfeo. The device consists in the rhythmic syncopation of the vocal line, which creates harmonic as well as rhythmic tension by anticipating the new harmony of the bass. The resulting dissonances, intolerable by the standards of the "prima prattica," are rendered even more effective by the sustained movement of the bass, for

Example 18
Peri, *Euridice*, p. 17

ch'in va - no Non chia-mas-ti mo- ren-do il tuo con-sor-te Non

son non son lon-ta - no io ven-go, o ca - ra vi - ta, o ca - ra mor- te.

Example 19
Caccini, *Euridice*, pp. 15-16

Orfeo:

Non pian - go, e non so - spi - ro O mia ca - ra Eu - ri -

di - ce Che so-spi - rar, che la-gri- mar non pos- so Ca-da-ve-ro in-fe-

Example 20
Monteverdi, "Lamento d'Arianna," in *Opere*, vol. 11, pp. 162-63

Peri's harmonic rhythm is almost twice as slow in this passage as in the corresponding section of Caccini's score. However, it should be noted that, in keeping with Peri's insistence upon the expressive function of the rhythm of the bass, he accompanies the determined sentiments of the last lines of Orfeo's speech:

> Non son, non son lontano,
> Io vengo, o cara vita, o cara morte

with the appropriate change—a marked increase in harmonic movement—and the corresponding absence of syncopation or emphasized dissonance. In contrast, there is no reflection of Orfeo's changed mood in Caccini's setting. This comparison reinforces the distinction between the two composers. Although Caccini propagates the new *stile rappresentativo*, he remains basically a songster; but Peri creates a recitative style for the stage which, by paralleling the emotion-laden text in the intensity of its expression, and by imitating the manner of its delivery, may justly be said to be dramatic.

Monteverdi shows himself to be a master of the techniques of both his predecessors in his setting of Arianna's expressive recitative. (See example 20.) The initial motive on "O Teseo, o Teseo mio" (l. 792), the interval of a descending third immediately repeated in sequence a third higher, reappears literally after several lines, and is soon reiterated in an expanded form to accommodate the phrase, "Volgiti, Teseo mio, / Volgiti, Teseo, oh Dio!" (ll. 795-96). Although the motivic recurrence was obviously suggested by the repetition of these phrases in Rinuccini's libretto, Monteverdi transforms it into a point of tonal and emotional stability, against which the rhythmic syncopations and driving dissonances of Arianna's anguished monologue resound even more pathetically. Furthermore, by returning to Arianna's initial exclamation at intervals throughout the lament, Rinuccini provides the composer with a broader set of formal goals in addition to those supplied by the rhyme endings, thereby enabling Monteverdi to control on a larger scale the formal organization of an otherwise unwieldy recitation.[161]

All three of these examples of affective recitative, with their use of textual and musical repetition as well as of syncopated dissonances against a sustained bass, techniques which we often associate with the lyrical effusions of "aria," are nonetheless composed according to the same basic principles which govern narrative recitative. This corroborates Pirrotta's view that the composers themselves had a "catholic conception of the style . . . embracing . . . the full range of nuances from the most prosaic and matter-of-fact utterances, to the most lyrical and even florid outbursts."[162]   Despite Pirrotta's estimation of the "ineffectual theorizing"[163] which preceded and accompanied the first operas, such a view actually betrays a willingness to accept the validity of Peri's own remarks concerning his "imitation of speech in song," and of Doni's reduction of the new style, based largely on an examination of Peri's score, to various levels of recitative.

Approaching Monteverdi's *Orfeo*[164] in the light of the foregoing observations and examples, one recognizes that, although Alessandro Striggio adhered more closely than did Rinuccini to the version of the Orpheus myth recounted by Poliziano, he was nevertheless guided by Rinuccini's example in more detailed matters. I refer specifically to the fact that, in his own libretto, Striggio carried the stylistic distinctions suggested by his predecessor's varied versification to their logical conclusion.   That is to say Striggio used *versi sciolti*, or blank verse, as the basis for his *parti recitative*; rhyming verses were admitted only occasionally, for example, to punctuate the ends of speeches. In the more affective portions of the dialogue, he generally refrained from rhyme altogether and resorted entirely to blank verse. However, because Striggio's libretto is a more complicated work than Rinuccini's, seemingly designed to explore the variety of ways in which a dramatic situation builds to an effective climax, the poetry of *Orfeo* does not lend itself easily to the neat stylistic divisions which can be seen, with Doni's aid, in the *Euridice* libretto.

The texture of Striggio's fabric is subject to more subtle as well as more rapid variation than that of its predecessors. Each act has its own laws of versification, laws which vary according to the direction and structure of the drama. For example, the motion of the second act, from a series of entirely static, rhymed quatrains accompanying the dance-songs of Orfeo and his companions, to the blank verse of Orfeo's simple lament, "Tu se' morta" — i.e., a motion from inaction to action, from *luogo ozioso* to *parte recitativa*, from strophic song to heightened speech — is completely reversed in the third act. There the blank verse of Orfeo's quiet conversation with Hope, as the two approach Hades, gives place to the static, strophic stanzas of his confrontation with Caronte. Thus the act progresses from recitative to lyricism, from simple speech to virtuosic song. However, Orfeo's blank verse at the beginning of Act 3 cannot have the same effect as his "Tu se' morta" near the end of Act 2 because its position with respect to the dramatic climax of the third act is insignificant. The difference, then, between the narrative and affective moments in Striggio's libretto and between climaxes and decorative strophes, cannot be determined, as with Rinuccini, by the style of the poetry alone, but must be judged in relation to the dramatic structure of the act. It is precisely the variety attained by Striggio's juxtaposition of styles that makes each of the acts of his libretto formally interesting as well as dramatically effective.

The first act of *Orfeo* offers a good illustration of this juxtaposition, as well as a splendid example — perhaps one without parallel in the first two decades of opera — of the way in which Striggio invested an otherwise amorphous pastoral scene with formal interest. Donald J. Grout has observed that the greater part of this act assumes the form of an arch, or *Bogen*, beginning and ending with the chorus "Vieni, Imeneo, deh vieni" (ll. 37-42 and 112-17).[165] Striggio's short text for this choral invocation,[166] with the scheme

abbAcC

is given a five-part homophonic setting by Monteverdi. Almost a strophic extension of the text of the chorus, the following solo ("Muse, onor di Parnaso, amor del Cielo") is assigned to one of the nymphs of the chorus (ll. 43-50):

ABbACcdD

This is one of the few *rhymed* solo pieces of mixed heptasyllables and hendecasyllables in the entire work — another is Euridice's "Io non dirò" on the opposite side of the arch (ll. 94-99) — and, as such, its style conforms well to the lyrical mood of the choruses connected by it. Monteverdi's music is agreeably simple and recitational, in what Doni would have called the narrative style.[167]

After the strophic, choral balletto "Lasciate i monti," containing only short, dance-like verses of five and seven syllables, one expects the same rhymed recitative as Striggio provided in the nymph's octave preceding the balletto. Instead the high point of the *Bogen* is formed by Orfeo's encomium to his bride, "Rosa del ciel," in which the rhyme scheme initiated in the first four verses appears to break down, as it were, in a surfeit of emotion. The rest of the solo, then, is in blank verse of mixed length, with some word repetition and assonance (ll. 75-93):

> Rosa del ciel, gemma del giorno, e degna
> Prole di lui che l'universo affrena,
> Sol, ch'il tutto circondi e 'l tutto miri,
> Da gli stellanti giri,
> Dimmi, vedesti mai
> Alcun di me più fortunato amante?
> Fu ben felice il giorno,
> Mio ben, che pria ti vidi,
> E più felice l'ora
> Che per te sospirai,
> Per ch'al mio sospirar tu sospirasti:
> Felicissimo il punto
> Che la candida mano
> Pegno di pura fede a me porgesti!
> Se tanti cori avessi. . .
>   etc.

Unlike the second act, where the messenger's entrance breaks the idyllic mood of the pastoral setting and prompts the abrupt introduction of blank verse, nothing happens in Act 1 to require such a change of style. Rather, Striggio here provided a psychological climax, suddenly intensifying and personalizing the comunication among the shepherds at the words "Ma tu, gentil cantor..." (l. 69) in preparation for Orfeo's first solo. Monteverdi's response was perfect: he set Orfeo's encomium to his bride as an emotionally charged, expressive recitative, the effect of which is all the more striking by contrast to the other, rhymed solos in the act.

Successful as this scheme is, Striggio did not repeat it, for it suited only the structure of his first act. In fact, the poet's sensitivity to dramatic detail permitted a complete reversal of this plan for the central psychological climax of the drama—Orfeo's confrontation with Caronte. The third act begins in blank verse and progresses through Orfeo's rhymed octave of mixed seven- and eleven-syllable verse, sung in heightened recitative (ll. 343-50):

Dove, ah, dove te 'n vai,	a
Unico del mio cor dolce conforto?	B
Poichè non lunge omai	a
Del mio lungo cammin si scopre il porto,	B

Perchè ti parti e m'abbandoni, ahi lasso,	C
Su 'l periglioso passo?	c
Qual bene or più m'avanza	d
Se fuggi tu, dolcissima Speranza?	D

The formalization and stylization of expression continues with Caronte's pompous quatrains, entirely of hendecasyllables (ll. 351-62):

O tu ch'innanzi morte a queste rive	E
Temerario te 'n vieni, arresta i passi;	F
Solcar quest'onde ad uom mortal non dassi,	F
Nè può coi morti albergo aver chi vive.	E
Che? vuoi forse nemico al mio signore,	G
Cerbero trar da le Tartaree porte?	H
O rapir brami sua cara consorte,	H
D'impudico desire acceso il core?	G
etc.	

and culminates in Orfeo's tour de force in *terzine* (ll. 363 ff.):

Possente spirto e formidabil nume,	J
Senza cui far passaggio a l'altra riva	K
Alma da corpo sciolta in van presume,	J
Non viv'io no, che poi di vita è priva	K
Mia cara sposa, il cor non è più meco,	L
E senza cor com'esser può ch'io viva?	K
etc.	

It cannot be overemphasized that Striggio here provided Monteverdi with a carefully constructed poetic climax, wherein a progressive formalization of elements paved the way for Orfeo's *preghiera.* Monteverdi followed his librettist's cues by setting the intransigent Caronte's verses as a strophic recitative, and Orfeo's climactic *terzine*—climactic in a completely different style from the affective recitative, "Rosa del ciel"—as a set of increasingly virtuosic strophic variations, the form of which was undoubtedly inspired by the extraordinary (not to say anachronistic) use at this highpoint of the action, of conventional terza rima, with its progressive and interlocking series of rhymes.[168]

These observations concerning the structure of Striggio's libretto now prompt an important question: How is the poet's attention to dramatic detail and versification reflected in Monteverdi's setting? Orfeo's solo from the first act, "Rosa del ciel," offers a good illustration. Not simply a connective or narrative recitative, "Rosa del ciel" is set apart in its passionate rhetoric by the disintegration of the close rhymes characteristic of Striggio's versification until this point. Consequently, after the initial four lines, the unrhymed and freely alternating heptasyllables and hendecasyllables provide no formal melodic goals upon which the composer might depend for a degree of musical coherence. Verse endings are not related except by occasional assonance (e.g., "porgesti-avessi"), and cadence points occur only at the ends of complete phrases, and without the reinforcement provided by the sound of rhyming couplets.

It seems to me that Monteverdi's musical setting of "Rosa del ciel" gives evidence of a clear distinction in his treatment of rhymed and unrhymed verses in this context. The opening four lines of the solo, rhyming AABb, correspond to the initial musical section, which is harmonically static for the duration of twelve semibreves. (See example 21.) All the motion in this section is carried by the melodic line, and simultaneously the entire burden of formal organization falls upon the rhymed verse-endings of the vocal part. The parallel with Peri's affective style is very close. On the other hand, in the next section, beginning "Dimmi, vedesti mai," when the rhymes disappear and the verse endings, no longer clearly marked, are subordinated to the whole phrase in a continuous drive toward the next cadence point, the contrast with Peri's style is greater. Because of the absence of rhyme in all but the opening quatrain of Monteverdi's recitative, the piece depends more completely upon the harmonic motion of the bass line for its formal coherence and logic. In "Rosa del ciel," then, the different musical results occasioned by two distinct versification procedures are neatly juxtaposed – one controlled by the melodic cadencing of paired rhymes, the other driven by a harmonic plan independent of the text, although deriving its goals from the irregularly spaced cadences of the blank verse. The harmonic plan that emerges in this example, following the static opening phrase on the chord of g minor, is the progression of the bass line through the entire B-flat major traid. An outline of the corresponding cadence points in the libretto and score indicates the degree of harmonic organization of this solo:

Rosa del ciel...	giri	g (pedal)
	... amante	B♭
	... sospirasti	d
	... porgesti	F
	... maggio	B♭
	... contento	d

Further indication of Monteverdi's developed sense of harmony as a

Example 21
Monteverdi, *Orfeo* (1609 ed.), Act I, pp. 13-14

gi͜ mi fa con-ten - to͜.

structural prop is given, it seems to me, by the frequently large leaps and generally wider range of his vocal line, as compared to Peri's.

A comparison of "Rosa del ciel" with another recitative from the first act, this one in rhyme—"Muse, onor di Parnaso" (ll. 43-50)[169]—reveals that the harmonic rhythm is considerably slower in the rhymed recitative. Consequently, although the bass of "Muse, onor di Parnaso" often proceeds by fifths, it does not function in a linear fashion to hold the piece together; rather, the rhythmically accentuated and rhymed endings of the vocal part provide the melodic goals, the successive attainment of which is the principal cohesive force of this type of recitative. As I have indicated above, in these passages characterized by harmonic *sprezzatura* and a strong reliance upon the disposition of rhyming verses to lend melodic coherence, Monteverdi's recitative style is closest to Peri's model.

Another interesting comparison may be made between Peri's and Montevedi's settings of rapid dialogue following the messenger's entrance with the news of Euridice's death.[170] At this point in his libretto, Striggio employed an even more drastic change in verse style than Rinuccini had achieved with rapid and partially unrhymed tercets. From the messenger's first words—"Ahi, caso acerbo!" (l. 200)—until the end of the act, Striggio emphasized the contrast with the strophic dance-songs of the idyllic first half of the act by resorting entirely to *versi sciolti*. Monteverdi emphasized and prolonged this stylistic contrast, using Peri's principle of the expressive potential of faster or slower harmonic rhythm. Thus, the shepherd who had been the last one to speak in rhymed verse before the entrance of Silvia (*Messagiera*), and who was then accompanied by a quickly-moving harmonic rhythm, continues at first to question Silvia in the style characteristic of the early part of the act. Meanwhile, the messenger divulges her grief to the more sustained accompaniment of "un organo di legno e un chitarone," while the harmonic rhythm of the score is abruptly retarded to one half of what it had been. Also similar to Peri's treatment is the sudden change in tonal color, with the introduction of chromatic tones into Silvia's affective cries.

Monteverdi underscores this contrast in color by indicating a change in instrumentation for Silvia's accompaniment, while the shepherd continues to be heard against the background of "clavicembalo, chitarone e viola da braccio," — i.e., the same group of instruments which played the ritornello of Orfeo's dance-song immediately preceding the interruption of the festivities.   Moreover, the messenger's declamation is full of characteristically short, exclamatory phrases, which for the Florentine composers probably represented the inflections of the spontaneous human cry.   Monteverdi uses large downward leaps, free dissonance, rhythmic syncopations, and frequent rests for Silvia, whereas in the quiet manner of the shepherd's melody, the stepwise motion and longer, rhythmically uncomplicated phrases of narrative recitative prevail. However, despite the absence of rhyme in this section of Striggio's libretto and Monteverdi's use of disparate styles, the passages of rapid dialogue following the messenger's entrance cohere because their stylistic alternation is regularly reinforced, not only by contrasting degrees of harmonic rhythm and instrumental groups, but also by the consistent juxtaposition of discrete tonal areas.   The shepherd's accompanying chords centered around C-major suddenly and repeatedly give place to the ambiguous A-major/minor area of Silvia's shrill tones.   Orfeo's entrances in the darker, flat keys are equally unprepared though no less effective.[171]   Thus Monteverdi's score at this climactic moment is not more poignant nor more dramatic than its counterpart in Peri's *Euridice*; rather it is endowed with a higher degree of artistic unity, which is at once indicative of and related to Monteverdi's greatness.

One last observation about the recitative style in the second act of *Orfeo* concerns the remarkable similarity of Monteverdi's affective style to that of Peri in setting Orfeo's reaction to Euridice's death.[172] Striggio's text, "Tu se' morta, mia vita, ed io respiro?/Tu se', tu se' pur ita/Per mai più non tornare, ed io rimango?" (ll. 247 ff.) has much in common with Rinuccini's "Non piango e non sospiro" (*Euridice*, ll. 226-36) in that some of its verses are composed entirely of cumulative or repetitive exclamations, or short phrases which parallel one another in their construction.   Monteverdi extends this technique to Orfeo's vocal line, where its effect is to simulate the incoherency of speech that results from intense emotion. (See example 22.)[173] As in Peri's setting, the initial phrases are broken by many rests, so that the verse endings are hardly distinguishable.   With the occasional rhymed endings of Rinuccini's affective verse thus de-emphasized, the stylistic resemblance of the two settings is even more striking.   In addition to the text repetition, Monteverdi employs two musical devices which are obviously related to Peri's score.   One is the pervasive use of rhythmic syncopation, which

Example 22
Monteverdi, *Orfeo* (1609 ed.), Act 2, p. 39

alternately retards and accelerates the flow of the vocal line in a manner appropriate to Orfeo's state of emotion.   The other is the sudden acceleration of the harmonic rhythm at the point in Orfeo's solo coinciding with the changed sentiments of the text: "No, che se i versi alcuna cosa ponno...." Both of these devices have been discussed above at length in connection with Peri's preface to and score of *Euridice.*

Before discussing the verse and musical characteristics of the choruses and airs of *Euridice* and *Orfeo*, and of Rinuccini's later libretti, I should like to voice an unorthodox opinion concerning the discrepancy between the endings of Striggio's play and Monteverdi's opera.   I have already noted that the original version of the libretto adheres closely to the ending of Poliziano's representation of the legend, whereas Monteverdi's score of 1609 resorts to a *deus ex machina.*[174]   In addition, the *luoghi oziosi* at the ends of the acts are somewhat shortened by Monteverdi, who eliminates one, sometimes two, of Striggio's strophes from the final choruses.   Perhaps his intention was to prevent the choruses from becoming independent *intermedi* by preserving the immediate relevance of their comments to the drama.   More difficult to explain is the change of events in the last act, unless one accepts the hypothesis that the old ending was as unacceptable to the tastes of the courtly Mantuan audience as it would have been to the Florentine wedding guests who viewed the first performance of *Euridice.*

Whatever the reason, this kind of alteration of a pagan myth has a precedent as old as Nicolò da Correggio's *Cefalo*, which, published in 1486, anticipated the pastoral dramas of the sixteenth century.   Like Poliziano's *Orfeo, Cefalo* was based on an Ovidian myth, the ending of which Correggio himself altered, taking as his model the *sacre rappresentazioni.* But instead of relying on the miraculous intervention of the Virgin to reunite the wronged heroine with husband or lover (in the religious plays, she would have been a saint or martyr who underwent persecution at the hands of a stepmother, mother-in-law, or some similar representative of evil), in the last act Correggio introduced the goddess Diana, who revives and restores the dead Proci to the penitent Cefalo.[175]

When W. W. Greg discounted the possible influence of *Orfeo* and *Cefalo* on later writers of the pastoral, he could not have been thinking of the early opera librettists.[176]   The very probable connection between Poliziano's work and the later *Orfeo* libretti has already been discussed. It is not implausible to speculate that a pastoral play by a close contemporary of Poliziano could have attracted the attention of Rinuccini or Striggio who, indebted as they were to the *Aminta* and the *Pastor fido*, did not stop at these sources for fresh and appropriate materials.

Certainly, the parallel between Monteverdi's happy ending and that of the final act of *Cefalo* is very great.

Whether or not *Cefalo* served as a model for Monteverdi's reforms, the structure of the altered fifth act is inconsistent with the rest of Striggio's work, as many have remarked. Although I say "Monteverdi's reforms," I do not mean to imply that the composer himself was responsible for the poetry of the happy ending—he was far too pressed for time and weighed down with musical and financial responsibilities to have undertaken this task. On the other hand, Striggio was a purist and too much of a dramatist to be interested in such a mechanical solution as the descent of Apollo on a cloud to rescue Orfeo, if not from the Bacchantes, then from his own self-pity.[177] I believe that, after the successes in 1608 of the *Ballo delle Ingrate* and *Arianna*, the latter of which also concludes with the miraculous appearance of two gods, Monteverdi turned to his new librettist, Rinuccini, to provide a happy ending for the printed score of *Orfeo*. Apollo's entrance is suggestive in itself, for Apollo was Rinuccini's initial spokesman, the protagonist of his first opera (*Dafne*) and Orpheus's ancestor according to legend.[178] Furthermore, a close stylistic analysis of the revised libretto printed by Solerti reveals, it seems to me, certain traits which are much more characteristic of Rinuccini's poetry than they are of Striggio's. Following Orfeo's lament, Apollo's first verses mark the change in style:[179]

Apollo:	Perch'a lo sdegno et al dolor in preda	*A*
	Così ti doni, o figlio?	b
	Non è, non è consiglio	b
	Di generoso petto	c
	Servir al proprio affetto.	c
	Quinci biasmo e periglio	b
	Già sovrastar ti veggio	*d*
	Onde movo dal ciel per darti aita;	E
	Or tu m'ascolta e n'avrai lode e vita.	E
Orfeo:	Padre cortese, al maggior uopo arrivi	F
	Ch'a disperato fine	*g*
	Con estremo dolore	h
	M'avean condotto già sdegno et amore.	H
	Eccomi dunque attento a tue ragioni,	I
	Celeste padre; or ciò che vuoi, m'imponi.	I
Apollo:	Troppo, troppo gioisti	*j*
	Di tua lieta ventura,	k
	Or troppo piagni	*l*
	Tua sorte acerba e dura. Ancor non sai	*M*
	Come nulla qua giù diletta e dura?	K
	Dunque se goder brami immortal vita	N
	Vientene meco al ciel ch'a sè t'invita.	N

The more than occasional use of unrhymed lines interwoven with paired verses suggest Rinuccini's hand, for Striggio tends to save his unrhymed lines for the sections in blank verse. Also, the internal rhyme occurring in Apollo's speech "Troppo, troppo gioisti" at the fourth verse ("ventura-dura"), and the way in which the final, unpaired syllable of the same verse ("sai") is enchoed four lines below in Orfeo's couplet

> Se non vedrò più mai
> De l'amata Euridice i dolci rai?

are techniques extremely reminiscent of *Euridice* but are not to be seen in the original version of Striggio's libretto.

In addition to the development of certain poetic conventions associated with the *parti recitative*—the more or less formal devices which in turn influenced the shaping of the new musical recitative style—the conventionalization of *luoghi oziosi* or passages of reflective or lyrical sentiment in the early libretti also had a bearing upon the musical setting; for the occurrence and, to some extent, the musical characteristics of chorus and solo song depended directly upon the poetic cues. It is, finally, to these *luoghi oziosi*, and the interrelationship between their poetic and musical aspects, that I now direct your attention.

IV

Lyric Conventions: Chorus and Solo Song

The theoretical position of the sixteenth-century dramaturgists and musical humanists concerning the function of the chorus was again rooted in Aristotelian thought, particularly in the stipulation that the chorus be not merely an ornament, unrelated to the drama, but rather an integral part of the action, serving either as an interlocutor or as a dramatically justified and articulate, though anonymous, spectator.[1] In practice, however, the chorus in early opera was frequently needed "both for variety and as a means of achieving definite musical shape and coherence in an otherwise relatively formless flow of monodic recitative."[2] However, there was room for a variety of treatments, based to a greater or lesser degree on theoretical considerations, for the early opera libretti and scores testify that the chorus was used in all these ways — as actor in the drama, as spectator, as form-giver, and as interlude or *intermedio*. In Rinuccini's *Euridice* the chorus frequently participates actively in the dialogue, although it does not further the action except by prompting the narration of offstage events by a messenger or another character to whom it addresses questions. On the other hand, Striggio's chorus in *Orfeo* either gives shape to and reflects the prevailing mood of the drama, or comments upon it in a detached manner. Whereas Rinuccini employs the chorus in his opening scene almost continuously, as one of the interlocutors in the dialogue, Striggio buttresses the structure of his first and second acts with symmetrical repetitions of entire choral phrases or sections. In short, although the concept of the chorus' function was received from the theorists, its treatment in the hands of the early librettists is characterized by the same variety found in the contemporary pastoral play; the two poets are as divergent in their styles as Tasso and Guarini.

For the purpose of analyzing the relationship between poetry and music, or libretto and score, it is important to isolate the design conceived by the librettists from that completed by the composer. Admittedly this is not an easy task when one considers the close rapport that usually existed between the two architects. Nevertheless it is misleading to assume, as Grout does in his discussion of *Euridice*,[3] that Rinuccini's plan was consistently realized by Peri; for even the discrepancies are pertinent to the problem of determining the formative influence of these early libretti on their musical settings.

For example, a close examination of the opening scene of *Euridice* reveals that Peri's score does not always agree with Rinuccini's intentions as they are implied in the printed libretto. In fact Rinuccini's design is in some respects closer to Striggio's first-act scheme than it is to Peri's setting, and might even have served the Mantuan poet as the model for *Orfeo*. The opening recitative of Peri's score, summoning the community of shepherds and nymphs to rejoice in the approaching nuptials, was designated "Coro" by Rinuccini, and the ensuing speeches, with the exception only of Euridice's lines, were assigned to choral groups of nymphs and shepherds ("Ninfe" and "Pastori" are the plural nouns indicated by Rinuccini). In other words, by far the greater number of verses in this scene were seemingly intended for recitation by the chorus, albeit a chorus reduced in number and divided into homogenous vocal ranges, with the only solo part being the sixteen lines (54-60 and 73-81) sung by Euridice. The parallel with Striggio's first act lies in the placement of Euridice's initial verses, like Orfeo's "Rosa del ciel," at the center of a chorus-dominated scene, with the possible intention that her more personal sentiments be thrown into relief as a lyrical highpoint.

By using this *coro spezzato* in a quasi-dialogue in the opening scene of *Euridice*, Rinuccini was adhering to his own plan for the first scene of *Dafne*. According to the earliest printed version of the libretto (1597/8)[4] this opera too began with brief exchanges between parts of the chorus, progressed to a single solo of heightened affection, and culminated in a choral finale.[5] It is interesting to recall that a similar concept of choral writing prevailed in the opening of the third *intermedio* of 1589, the subject of which provided Rinuccini with the basis for his first opera. In Rossi's *Descrizione* of the court festivities of that year, the author relates that nine couples of men and women in quasi-Greek costume appeared from opposite sides of the stage. Each group sang its own short madrigal before joining forces in a prayer of deliverance from the Pythic monster.[6]

Elsewhere in *Dafne* (scene 5) and *Euridice* (scenes 3 and 6), the chorus is employed to elicit narrative, as it does in *Pastor fido* (IV.3) and in *Aminta* (II.1, IV.1 and 2), thereby adopting the role of actor in the drama. Rinuccini's innovation, of course, lies in his conviction that the chorus was to be sung in its participant as well as in its reflective role, as it had been in the early Attic tragedies, in which the chorus was the predominant element. In the initial scene of *Dafne* and *Euridice* the implications of this conviction are reflected in the librettist's treatment of the chorus, for the poetry is in the same fluid style of mixed heptasyllables and hendecasyllables as that which characterizes the *parti recitative* generally. A later libretto sheds some light on the question of how these "choral recitatives" were to be performed. In *Narciso* (1608),[7] Rinuccini employs a *Coro di Ninfe stabile,* — i.e., one which is continually present on stage — at the same time assigning it two different modes of participation in the dialogue. In act 2 (ll. 273 ff.) the librettist calls upon individual members of the chorus to recite the only verses given to the nymphs in the entire scene, designating simply "Una Ninfa" and "Altra Ninfa." This is in distinct contrast to the latter part of Act 1 (ll. 176 ff.), where Rinuccini writes only "Coro" above every few lines of recitative.[8] The implication is that, as in the opening scene of his early libretti, Rinuccini conceived these lines to be divided between *cori spezzati* and chanted as monodic choral recitative.

No music is known to have survived for *Narciso*; in fact, the libretto, having been rejected by Monteverdi in 1608 and two years later by Loreto Vittori, was probably never set at all.[9] Among the surviving fragments of the first *Dafne*, there are no examples of choral recitative. Judging by *Euridice*, however, either Peri felt that Rinuccini's conception was impractical from a musical point of view, or he simply preferred to avail himself of the widely accepted practice of representing the role of the chorus with a single member from the group.[10] Peri consistently assigns the choral speeches in the first scene to individual nymphs and shepherds, all anonymous except for Aminta, who shares with a nymph the recitative, "Qual in si rozzo core" (ll. 61-72), assigned by Rinuccini to a group of "Pastori."[11] The composer must have indeed considered the possibility of setting these choral verses monodically; for elsewhere in the favola, notably in the third and fifth scenes, he occasionally accepted the implications of Rinuccini's libretto by setting in choral monody isolated passages of recitative, usually a single interrogative verse or a fleeting *terzina* preceeded by the rubric "Coro."[12] But in scene 5, for example, the more lengthy passages of the chorus' interrogation of Aminta are consistently given to Arcetro, and in the final scene the words of the chorus are uttered throughout by single characters.[13] On the other hand, Caccini follows the librettist's cues rather consistently throughout the narrative scenes 3, 5, and 6, apparently employing choral monody for all but a few of the passages where it is indicated.[14]

Gagliano's 1608 score for *Dafne* leaves no room for doubt as to who sang the passages assigned to "Ninfe" and "Pastori" in the opening scene of Rinuccini's libretto, for the copy of the printed score in the Magliabecchiana collection has inscribed at its head the handwritten names of the performers comprising the chorus. The same names appear individually at the beginning of each subsequent "choral" passage, indicating that these were, with few exceptions, performed as solo recitatives, while two quatrains of a refrain chorus were composed for two voices.[15]

Concerning the manner of performance of the participant chorus, a further complicating factor must be acknowledged — that is, the ambiguity of the meaning of the term "coro" as it appeared in early opera. For example, the annotations to Gagliano's score corroborate the fact that the "full chorus" composed in a five-part texture was, more correctly speaking, a "madrigal chorus," ostensibly performed by the company of seven singers whose names appear in the score. Grout summarizes his findings based upon evidence collected from the musical prints by stating, "the pieces called choruses in early opera are certainly not intended for large choruses in the modern sense, but are either ensembles of solo voices, or, at most, small bodies of singers with not more than two or three voices to a part."[16] In fact, at one point in the Gagliano score, four lines of monodic recitative are assigned to "Tonino. Cecc.º"[17] Since the rubric in the score indicates "Ninfa del Coro" (the libretto has the plural "Ninfe"), it is unlikely that one of the singers could have sung the bass part. The alternative — that both sang the same line of recitative — is in my opinion quite acceptable.[18] Reasoning from this, it is possible that the monodic choruses in the Peri or Caccini scores could have been performed by two or three singers without destroying their characteristic *sprezzatura* nor hampering the intelligibility of the text.

In Striggio's *Orfeo*, the chorus is generally confined to the more limited role of "articulate spectator," rarely taking an active part in the dialogue. Although Striggio frequently writes mixed seven- and eleven-syllable verse for the chorus, even blank verse as at the end of Act 2, evidently neither the librettist nor the composer equates this with *stile recitativo*. Instead, Monteverdi usually employs a five-part homophonic choral texture, such as in "Vieni Imeneo" (ll. 37-42) and "Ahi caso acerbo" (ll. 257-62),[19] choruses which, as prayer and lament, express collective responses to given situations in the drama. Significantly, when in the fourth act of *Orfeo* the librettist does write choral recitatives — i.e., passages in which the chorus partakes in the dialogue by addressing itself to specific characters and helping to shape the course of events — Monteverdi assigns these verses to various soloists from the chorus, and never to the entire group. The first instance of this is at "O de gli abitator de l'ombre eterne / Possente Re..." (ll. 475-82), where the Infernal Spirits (or one of their number, as in Monteverdi's version) attempt to influence Plutone's decision. Interestingly enough, in the midst of a section of *versi sciolti*, Striggio sets their invocation in the formal hendecasyllables of ottava rima, a meter which he uses nowhere else in the libretto.[20] The second deviation of a similar nature occurs at the words with which Euridice is condemned to Hades forever, "Torna a l'ombre di morte, / Infelice Euridice," (ll. 539-42); once again, the rubric at this point in the score reads "Uno spirito del coro canta."[21]

As Grout observes, the chorus in early opera often became a powerful structural device in that, by means of repetition and refrain, it served to buttress and unify a scene which was, in other respects, without any formal design.   In most but not all cases, the repetition was indicated in the libretto. For example, the climax immediately before the recitation of Euridice's first verses, consisting of a four-fold repetition of the line from Petrarch—"Non vede un simil par d'amanti 'l sole!"[22]—simply does not occur in the printed, souvenir edition of Rinuccini's libretto.   The logical conclusion is that Peri alone was responsible for the repetition of the verse, three times by soloists from the chorus, each in a different vocal range, and a fourth time by the chorus in a five-part setting.[23]   This is the first utterance of the full chorus in the score, although presumably it has been on stage since the beginning; then it remains silent again until the five-part refrain, "Al canto, al ballo," at the end of the scene. In this way Peri, independently of his librettist, employs the chorus as a formal device, to mark the goals toward which the recitative sections move—i.e., Euridice's first lines, "Donne, ch'a' miei diletti" (ll. 54 ff.) as she, not Orfeo, is the protagonist of Rinuccini's version, and the communal jubilation of the *balletto*, which closes the first scene.

Except for the implicit use of the *coro spezzato*, alternating between nymphs and shepherds in the opening scenes of *Dafne* and *Euridice*, Rinuccini seems to have confined the chorus as a form-giving device in his first works entirely to the reflective interludes or *luoghi oziosi*, which generally conclude the *parti recitative*, and thereby define the scenes or acts of the drama.[24]   His apparent aversion to the formal structures he had used earlier in the court masques and *intermedi*, and that Striggio was to use in *Orfeo*, was perhaps based on a fear of marring the continuity and verisimilitude of the recitative, the element he undoubtedly considered to be the most novel, indeed the most vital one of the new genre.[25]   On the other hand, one might say that Striggio profited from Rinuccini's negative example by realizing that the contrast provided by formal repetition was indispensable to the greater effectiveness of the *parti recitative*. Thus the internal choruses of *Orfeo*, which are generally commentative or reflective and detached from the flow of discourse, sometimes serve to punctuate the recitative and provide a supportive frame within which the action unfolds. In the first act, for example, the two choruses ("Vieni Imeneo" and "Lasciate i monti") are symmetrically placed on either side of the lyrical climax of the act, thereby at once creating and executing a formal scheme which lends interest and variety to an otherwise uniformly jubilant and Arcadian series of utterances.[26] In the second act, Striggio uses a refrain device, involving the chorus, which unifies the latter half of the act, at the same time providing a stylized and striking backdrop for the various reactions to Euridice's death. The refrain couplet

> Ahi caso acerbo! ahi fato empio e crudele!
> Ahi stelle ingiuriose, ahi cielo avaro!

is introduced by the messenger bearing the news of Euridice's death (ll. 200-201).   Striggio subsequently assigns it first to one of the shepherds who receives the news (ll. 239-40), and then to the five-part chorus (ll. 257-8), which comments on the verses, finally using them as the refrain of the lament at the end of the act (ll. 271 ff.).   The repetitions, cleverly spaced as they are at ever diminishing intervals, seem to record the gradual realization of, and resignation to, the message's import as well as give momentum to the act as it moves toward conclusion.   At the same time, by supplying the poetic and dramatic goals for this section of intense passion, which is suddenly devoid of rhyme, the refrain becomes an important cohesive force in the progression of the musical setting.

Striggio's use of the chorus in the first and second acts of *Orfeo* is similar to Guarini's treatment of the nymph's chorus in *Pastor fido* III.2, wherein the shepherds play the "giuoco della cieca."[27]   Grout analyzes the tight formal structure of this set of four choruses, rhymed in consecutive couplets and inserted periodically into a free, unrhymed dialogue of mixed hendecasyllables and heptasyllables.   Although he maintains that Guarini probably intended them to be spoken rather than sung, he notes the obvious analogy between "the formal structure of these choruses and that of a musical composition."[28] However, according to Guarini's own testimony, the choruses were sung and danced, and their verses were actually written after the music had been composed.[29] Evidently, at this point in history, the Ferrarese poet did not assume as much responsibility as did the later poet-librettists for creating the shape of their dramatic structures in music.

It is significant that Striggio employs a form-building device — in this case, textual and/or choral refrain — only in conjunction with two scenes, in both of which the solo texts have no formal implications at all. One is the second half of Act 2, just mentioned, which is the longest portion of the opera entirely in blank verse; the other is the final act, which was dominated in the original libretto by the Bacchantes' choral ritornello, "Evohè, padre Lieo" (ll. 617-23), and which opens with a long and amorphous solo by Orfeo, partially in rhyme with echo responses, and partially in blank hendecasyllables. I find relevant here Grout's remark that "as Italian opera toward the middle of the seventeenth century began to develop satisfactory large forms for the solo aria, the chorus, no longer necessary as a form-giving element, began to disappear."[30] However, a period of even greater participation by the chorus came first, along with the expansion and greater formalization of the *luoghi oziosi*, a period which is reflected in Rinuccini's post-*Euridice* libretti.

In order to characterize the poetry of the *luoghi oziosi* of the early opera libretti, we must consider the structure of those internal choruses which function as spectators rather than actors, as well as of the final or interlude choruses at the ends of the scenes or acts. Finally, we will examine the few proto-arias designated for solo performance.

Without exception Rinuccini's interlude choruses in *Dafne* and *Euridice* are organized into rhymed strophes, usually isometric in design. Moreover, two of the choruses in each opera are unified to an even greater degree by the use of one or two refrain verses.[31] In *Euridice* the refrain choruses occur at the ends of the first and second scenes — "Al canto, al ballo," the woodland *balletto* (ll. 85-100), and the lament "Cruda Morte, ahi pur potesti" (ll. 265-92), wherein the final pair of lines from the first strophe is repeated after each succeeding strophe:

> Sospirate, aure celesti,
> Lagrimate, o selve, o campi.

Interestingly enough, Striggio places his only refrain chorus, "Chi ne consola, ahi lassi" (ll. 271-97), in the same position as Rinuccini's choral lament — i.e., at the end of Act 2 of *Orfeo*, where the two-line refrain ("Ahi caso acerbo...") echoes the earlier reaction of Orfeo's companions to Dafne's distressing news.[32] Although Striggio's dance-chorus of the first act does not actually have a refrain, he invests it with a similar function by repeating the whole structure in the second half of the act. Certain parallels in the text design are carried over into the musical realm, although the settings of Peri and Monteverdi are generally more dissimilar than they are alike. Peri alternates the five-part madrigal refrain "Al canto, al ballo" with solo strophic variations in recitative style (as does Caccini).[33] Monteverdi's choral *balletto*, "Lasciate i monti," is cast entirely in madrigal style for five parts, although the second strophe is homophonic in texture and set in the triple meter reminiscent of the internal couplet ("A le bell'onde e liete / Tutti, o pastor, correte") of

Peri's choral refrain in *Euridice*.[34] In the lament, however, the similarities of textual organization are reflected in their musical treatments. There, Monteverdi also employs the device of framing solo passages sung by members of the chorus with polyphonic choral refrain. However, unlike Peri and Caccini, who again rely upon strophic repetition, Monteverdi writes a through-composed madrigal duet accompanied by a basso continuo of *organo di legno* and *chitarrone*.[35]

On the whole, however, the structural similarities between the two poets' treatments of the chorus are less striking than are the differences. Fully half of the choruses in *Orfeo* are single stanzas of freely developing madrigal verse, with mixed seven- and eleven-syllable lines. For example, the chorus of Infernal Spirits which terminates Act 4, "È la vertute un raggio,"—remarking that only the master of one's own passions is worthy of eternal glory—consists of fourteen lines of mixed length, organized into the sonnet-like shape of a sestet followed by two quatrains. However, Striggio is careful not to repeat the structure of the first quatrain exactly in the second to avoid the implication of musical repetition. In fact, Monteverdi went even further by eliminating the first of the two quatrains from his setting, a five-part, pseudo-contrapuntal madrigal.[36] "Alcun non sia," at the end of the first act, has an even more amorphous design, and is almost completely in blank verse, a manner which Striggio elsewhere reserves for affective solo passages.[37] Significantly, the only other chorus in blank verse is the strophic lament "Chi ne consola, ahi lassi?" at the end of Act 2, and here Striggio substitutes assonance for rhyme much of the time. Even among the strophic choruses, mixed heptasyllables and hendecasyllables are the rule, the only exceptions being the dance-choruses of the first and final acts.

In contrast, the interlude choruses in Rinuccini's *Euridice* all seem, as I have suggested, to be the result of a single concept of choral writing. Four of the five employ the shorter, more conventionally song-like verse of seven or eight syllables. (Except for Striggio's chorus of Baccanti, which was probably a *balletto*, the only parallel in *Orfeo* to Rinuccini's use of octosyllabic verse occurs precisely in the final chorus, "Vanne, Orfeo, felice a pieno," of the revised last act, the authorship of which I have questioned.[38]) Striking is the fact that, unlike his contemporary, Rinuccini deliberately avoids expressive madrigal verse in his choruses—that is, single stanzas of metrical irregularity, with no allegiance to a strict order of rhymes. The question is, Why did Rinuccini employ exclusively strophic and frequently isometric forms for his interlude choral texts? I suggest that one answer may lie in the necessity to differentiate the function of the participant chorus from that of the lyrical one, a need which is not present in Striggio's libretto. Thus

Rinuccini may have chosen to reserve the mixed heptasyllables and hendecasyllables for use in the participant, recitative choruses and solos, whereas the imposition of strophic organization and more formal rhyme schemes on the lyrical, interlude choruses emphasized the contrast between *parti recitative* and *luoghi oziosi,* and incidentally provided the musician with occasions for delighting the senses.

Perhaps another factor influencing the strophic form of Rinuccini's choruses, and I believe the source of his desire to differentiate the form of the interlude chorus, was the poet's awareness of the structure of the classical Greek tragedies wherein the choric odes, also lyrical extensions of the mood of the action, were similarly strophic in design. They were usually composed of strophe and antistrophe, stanzas which were exactly alike with respect to rhyme, meter, and melody, and which were then followed by a third stanza, differing in form from the other two, known as the epode. This scheme is to some extent reinforced by Peri's treatment of the text of "Cruda Morte" at the end of scene 2. Although the strophes are somewhat differently disposed (four different stanzas of music being distributed among seven quatrains, each followed by the same musical and textual refrain), the idea of the concluding epode is preserved.[39]

I		II		III		IV	
Chorus		1st nymph		2nd nymph		trio	
(1)	R	(2)	R	(3)	R		
				(4)	R		
		(5)	R	(6)	R	(7)	R

Other examples are provided by the settings of "Poi che gli eterni imperi" and "Biondo arcier, che d'alto monte," at the ends of scenes 4 and 6 respectively. The first chorus terminates the scene in Hades with the Infernal Spirits organized into two groups. Five strophes of *settenari* are given three stanzas of music, with the two choruses joining forces for the final strophe, in the following manner:[40]

I	II	III
1st chorus a 4	2nd chorus a 4	Radamanto
(1)	(2)	(3)
(4)	1st and 2nd	
	choruses, together	
	(5)	

This arrangement accords well with the description of the chorus which sang Andrea Gabrieli's music for the 1585 performance of *Edipo tiranno* at Vicenza. According to one chronicler, the chorus was composed of fifteen persons, seven on each side of the stage, with their leader in the center.[41]   Gabrieli's choruses, however, abiding by the translation of Sophocles' play by Orsato Giustiniani, were not strophic, but rather in a free *canzone* style with unrhymed verses of mixed length divided into stanzas from three to seventeen lines according to themes rather than any fixed poetic pattern.   Although the structure of the Greek chorus was generally known by about 1570, the freedom and irregularity displayed by Giustiniani's choral translations seem to have been preferred by Italian translators and dramatists, who continued to write choral *canzoni*.[42]   Thus it is possible that Rinuccini consciously bypassed one aspect of contemporary stage practice in an effort to restore the ancient manner of performing the choruses.

Perhaps the best illustration of the classical sequence of strophe, antistrophe, and epode in Peri's score is provided by "Biondo arcier" at the end of the opera.[43]   Here, two strophes, sung successively to the same music, are followed by a third, which receives a different setting for three voices.   This pattern is repeated several times, together with a short instrumental *ritornello*.

I			II	
Chorus a 5			Trio	
(1)	(2)	R	(3)	R
(4)	(5)	R	(6)	R
(7)	(8)	R		

Except for Caccini's setting of "Poi che gli eterni imperi,"[44] which follows Peri's scheme in every detail, the rival composer of *Euridice* apparently took no pains to preserve the concept of alternately contrasting or matching pairs of strophes.   Thus, although the first and last strophes of "Cruda Morte" are composed for monodic chorus and trio respectively, quatrains two through six constitute a series of strophic variations over the same bass—a time-honored technique employed frequently by Caccini in *Le nuove musiche;* and the final dance-chorus of the opera, "Biondo arcier," is provided with only one stanza of music.[45]

Further evidence of the deliberateness with which Rinuccini turned to the strophic construction of choruses may be seen by comparing *Dafne* and *Euridice* with his previous efforts at dramatic choral writing—specifically, the *intermedi.*   Four of the six *intermedi* of 1589 have choral finales, although each one concludes a scene already dominated by choral madrigals.   Only two of these, at the ends of the third and sixth *intermedi*, are in strophic form and significantly, both are "canzoni col ballo."   Nevertheless these are not as dance-like as Rinuccini's later octosyllabic and isometric choruses; rather they are marked by the same mixture of seven- and eleven-syllable lines characteristic of the madrigals. In addition to isometric choruses of *settenari* and *ottonari*, *Dafne* does have one strophic chorus of mixed verse — "Non si nasconde in selva" at the end of scene 4 — but there the hendecasyllables are broken into halves by the device of internal rhyme, with the resulting six- and five-syllable half-lines seeming to match the *settenari*. Thus, it appears evident that Rinuccini employed the short, isometric, strophic chorus particularly in association with the first operas. Furthermore, a comparison of their form with the choruses of other types of dramatic poetry in the sixteenth century, such as the pastoral tragicomedy or neo-classical Italian tragedy — in each of which the chorus was elaborated in the irregular manner of the free *canzone* described above[46] — reveals that the use of the strophic chorus on the musical stage was one of Rinuccini's most original and personal contributions.

It is interesting to note that Girolamo Mei in 1581 had already made the connection between the ancient manner of strophic poetry and that of "some of our poets [who] respond to [it] in part in their *canzoni*, wherein all the stanzas must be alike."[47] Equally arresting in connection with the choruses of *Dafne* and *Euridice* are remarks made by Mei in his earlier writings on poetry concerning the characteristics of *ottonari*, the eight-syllable verse found so frequently in Rinuccini's choric interludes. Having observed by means of his hierarchic scheme of metric proportions that this verse form, governed by the sesquialter proportion (3 : 4) and therefore furthest alienated from the proportion of equality, somehow appears awkward, even uncouth to the refined ear, Mei remarked that it has nevertheless always been exquisitely suited to the manner of certain types of poetry. To illustrate he mentioned poems of deliberately simple character, which are intended to express an uncomplicated subject — that is, one which involves a pure and solitary affection (elsewhere Mei spoke of an excessive or extreme affection) — or poems which express simple or somewhat vulgar conceits. As examples, Mei cited respectively the *laudi*, "written by devout persons," and the *canzoni villesche*, which are commonly called *canzoni a ballo*. These are effective, he added, precisely because their lesser degree of artifice allows the affection to manifest itself with greater force.[48] Mei concluded his little defense of the *ottonari* with the reminder that

> . . . such compositions, being sung, were intended to be heard rather than simply read, whence such of their defects as [simplicity and awkwardness], being easily covered by the song with its air and modes, were less apt to be observed, and for that reason more freely disregarded by their makers. This occurred even among the ancient Greek poets in the days when the same persons were accustomed to be poets and musicians, about whom one reads that all those who accompanied

their own verses with song were not as strict in observing every detail as were
others who wrote [verses], in their measure and disposition indeed exquisite, as if
they were intended only to be read.[49]

Notwithstanding the fact that they were intended to be heard rather than
simply read, *canzoni* texts appeared in many anthologies printed in the
sixteenth century.[50]   In general they were strophic texts with refrains,
written in isometric and usually octosyllabic verse.[51] Their characteristics
indeed corroborate Mei's association of *ottonari* with popular strophic
song and with the statement of a single strong affection.   Surely
Rinuccini was in part influenced by these qualities in his choice of
ottonari and *settenari* for passages where he intended the rustic,
polyphonic song appropriate to the simple inhabitants of the pastoral
world as opposed to recitative — in other words, in the lyrical, interlude
chorus as opposed to the reciting or participant chorus.

In addition to the general association of Rinuccini's interlude
choruses with the rejuvenation of the old *canzone a ballo*, there is a
specific connection with a particular strophic form created by Gabriello
Chiabrera, who, approximately forty years after Mei recorded his
observations concerning the simplicity and awkwardness of eight-syllable
verse, exalted these qualities to new heights in his *canzonette*.[52] The final
chorus of *Euridice* ("Biondo arcier, che d'alto monte" [ll. 743 ff.]) reveals
an unusual structure, but one that is consistent with a group of poems
occupying a peculiar position in the early literature of solo song.   The
chorus consists of eight strophes, each of which is a sestet divisible into
completely symmetrical halves:

| Syllables per line: | 8 | 4 | 8 | – | 8 | 4 | 8 |
| Rhyme Scheme: | a | a | b | – | c | c | b |

In his article on *Dafne*, William Porter identifies the pieces in this group
as Chiabrera's "Belle rose purpurine," which appears in Caccini's *Nuove
musiche* (1602), Rinuccini's "Mille dolci parolette," which is found in the
1662 anthology of his poetry, and "Bella ninfa fuggitiva," the final chorus
of *Dafne*, and finally a terza rima from Sannazaro's Arcadia, "La
pastorella mia spietat' e rigida."   All are found in at least one of two
large manuscript collections of solo songs dating from the end of the
sixteenth century.[53] The Chiabrera poem is known to have been set to
music by Caccini, and the excerpt from *Dafne* is attributed to Jacopo
Corsi in the Brussels manuscript, where it appears in a monodic version,
probably reduced from an originally homophonic chorus; however, the
other two settings are anonymous.   Porter singles out these pieces not
only for their similarity of poetic structure, but also because of the

striking resemblance in the first lines of their musical settings, suggesting the possibility that each piece may have had as its starting point the same musical formula. Rinuccini himself seems to have considered the poetic structure as a formula, for he used it at the close of three of his libretti.[54] In the same way that his prologues all adhere to the metrical form established in his first opera, both the final choruses of *Euridice* and *Arianna* employ the *canzonetta* structure found in the closing scene of *Dafne*. That Rinuccini succeeded in making this a convention of operatic composition is evident in Striggio's use of at least the initial part of the formula for the original closing chorus of Baccanti in *Orfeo*:

> Evohè, padre Lieo
> Bassareo
> Te chiamiam con chiari accenti...

Chiabrera himself utilizes this convention in each of three *favolette da recitarsi cantando: Oritia, Il pianto di Orfeo,* and *La Galatea,* all probably written before 1608.[55] As there are no known settings of the final choruses of these works, it is impossible to say whether they reveal any similarities indicative of a common musical origin.[56] It may be significant, however, that in the description of the 1608 performance of *Arianna* by the Mantuan court chronicler Federico Follino, from which Solerti culls the libretto, the chorus is called an *aria da ballo*.[57]

In the opening phrase of Caccini's setting of the *Euridice* chorus, "Biondo arcier, che d'alto monte," which he too labels "aria," there is still a close resemblance in the contour, if not in the exact pitch relationships, to those settings quoted by Porter and best represented by the chorus from *Dafne*. (See examples 23 and 24.) Although the uppermost part of Peri's setting of "Biondo arcier" deviates from these examples, it can be argued that there is some relationship between Peri's bass line and that of Caccini's setting, a relationship consistent in all but the fourth and fifth lines. (See example 25.) Even without the assurance of further evidence, to guess that the composers availed themselves of a pre-existent musical formula in setting these strophes is not untenable. Certainly the least that may be imagined is that the creators of this new musical genre, following the lead of their librettists, and supported by a long tradition of composition or improvisation on established schemes, borrowed from their own recent successes in solo song as well as in *stile rappresentativo,* and thereby built up a musical vocabulary, which, from this distance in time, seems indeed formulaic in its expression.

For the most part, Rinuccini remains faithful in his later libretti to the concept of strophic choruses, although isometric verse is generally superseded by a more sophisticated array of schemes involving mixed

Example 23
Caccini, *Euridice*, p. 51 (outer voices only)

Bion-d'ar-|cier che d'al-to mon-te Au- reo fon- te Sor-ger

fai di sì bell' on - da, Ben può dir-si al-ma fe- li- ce, Cui pur

li- ce ap-pres- sar l'al-te- ra spon-da l'al-te- ra spon-da.

Example 24
Corsi, *Dafne*; from Brussels Ms., fols. 53-54 (Porter, p. 183).

Bel- la nin - fa fug-gi- ti - va, Sciol- t'e

pri - va Del mor-tal tuo no - bil ve - lo,

Example 25
Peri, *Euridice*, pp. 50-51 (outer voices only)

heptasyllables and hendecasyllables. At the same time, he expands the octosyllabic strophic chorus to include a separate refrain or *ritornello* stanza, thereby transforming it into a refrain *canzona* in which the last verse of each strophe returns to the rhyme of the refrain stanza. Examples are "Alma Dea, che l'arco tendi" (*Narciso*, Act 4, ll. 954-81), and "Stampa il ciel con l'auree piante" (*Arianna*, scene 3, ll. 458-97). Both adhere to the typical *canzonetta* rhythm (◡◡ / ◡ / ◡ / ◡) although there is no indication in the libretti that the fishermen in *Arianna* or the nymphs in *Narciso* (here following) danced to their strophes.

> Alma Dea, che l'arco tendi
> Per campagne e per foreste,
> Alma Dea, nume celeste,
> Spegni tu d'amor gl'incendi.
>
> Tu di casti e bei desiri
> Arma, Diva, i nostri petti,
> Onde invan l'arco saetti

Stral d'affanno e di martiri.
Non più lagrime o sospiri
Eschin fuor dai tristi seni:
Tu le notti e i dì sereni
Fanne, o Dea ch'in ciel risplendi.

Alma Dea, che l'arco tendi
etc.

It is likely, however, that dancing was the rule in such an interlude chorus as this; after all, the alternation of new strophes with a short refrain stanza, to which they are linked by a particular rhyming device, is exactly the pattern established by the so-called *canzoni a ballo* in the sixteenth century.   Significantly, this type of refrain structure also provided Chiabrera with a model for the final chorus of *Il rapimento di Cefalo* (ll. 608-37).[58]

There is some evidence in the texts themselves to suggest that Gabriello Chiabrera's dramatic poetry dating from the first decade of opera composition exerted considerable formal influence on Rinuccini's 1608 libretti and even on Striggio's *Orfeo*.[59]   In *Cefalo* both the large allegorical cast, brought together more for purposes of scenic and mechanical display than for dramatic development, and the treatment of the chorus betray the close relationship of Chiabrera's earliest libretto with the traditions of the *intermedi*. There are choruses of hunters (the only group which allies the world of *Cefalo* to the *favola pastorale*), of tritons, of cupids, of heavenly bodies, and of gods.   Except for the concluding choruses of Acts 4 and 5, the non-strophic style of the choral verse implies a musical setting akin to the madrigal.   However, even in *Cefalo*, which has as many strophic soli as there are in *Dafne* and *Euridice* together, the poet's characteristic predilection for strophic forms in both solo and choric passages is evident.[60]

Chiabrera's position was ambiguous concerning the use of rhyme in dramatic verse, and of the chorus in dramatic action.   In the dedication to one of his non-musical works for the stage, *Meganira* (a *favola boschereccia* written at about the same time as *Il rapimento di Cefalo*), Chiabrera remarked:

. . . Indeed some people, thinking that dramatic verse represents mutual conversation, want rhyme to be entirely abandoned so as to better represent verisimilitude.   Others consider that, deprived of rhyme, Tuscan verse remains deprived of its real sweetness and strength, and they have used rhyme on stage, but without specific pattern, and with great license; whence results the achievement of the grace of the poetry, and the fulfillment of the exigencies of the stage.   I do not know which opinion is better; I believe that one can write faultless poetry in one or the other style.   And for now I have decided not to abandon rhyme. . . . Concerning the chorus, I feel that the populace, which it represents, should not have a place in intimate action, whence I refrained from interposing it.[61]

Although Chiabrera does not abandon rhyme in this play, he employs it more sparingly than in *Cefalo*, and with particular care to avoid couplets; indeed a cursory reading of *Meganira* reveals that rhyme is ornamental and incidental to the primarily metrical thrust of the poetry. Moreover, almost in illustration of his point about the validity of "the other opinion," which would ban rhyme from the stage, Chiabrera composed a companion play, *Gelopea*, entirely in blank verse.[62] Thus it seems that for Chiabrera, as well as for Rinuccini, rhyme was upheld as an indispensable quality of *poesia per musica*.

The absence of the chorus in *Meganira, Gelopea,* and a third work from his period, *Alcippo*, raises an interesting question. If Chiabrera considered the role of the chorus to be intrusive and unwarranted in "intimate action," its contemporaneous appearance in *Cefalo* must be excused as an admissable ornament to a subject which could hardly be called intimate. But how does one explain Chiabrera's persistent use of the chorus in his succeeding libretti, *Oritia, Polifemo geloso,* or *Galatea*?[63] These actions, involving the usual love intrigues of Arcadia, are no less intimate that those presented in *Meganira*. Why, then, is Galatea surrounded by a chorus and Gelopea not, when the difference between these two characters lies merely in one being a "pescatrice," the other a "pastorella"? The answer, I believe, may be found in the poet's recognition of the diversion and structural potential offered by the chorus in a dramatic medium intended to be entirely sung.

Chiabrera's stylistic position vis-à-vis his contemporaries is epitomized by a comparison of his *Galatea* (1608)[64] with Rinuccini's *Euridice* and Striggio's *Orfeo*. From such a comparison it becomes obvious that, with respect to content, Chiabrera learned much from Rinuccini, whereas from the point of view of structure, his technique is more closely related to that of Striggio. In fact, Chiabrera's formal imagination, as exhibited in his earlier works, probably spurred Striggio's own concern with structural coherence, in the same way that it seemed to have influenced Rinuccini's composition after *Euridice*.

A *favola marittima, Galatea* has a plot strikingly similar to that of *Euridice* and *Orfeo*, with the same mixture of pastoral and mythological elements. However, Chiabrera's portrayal of Polifemo's sentiments as those of a spurned rival renders it a more complicated and lengthy fable than the Orfeo operas, wherein the heroine's death is simply attributed to the poisonous serpent rather than to any motive of vengeance.[65] In *Galatea* it is Aci, the object of Polifemo's jealousy, who is deprived of life in the first flowering of his love for the heroine. In the end she, lamenting Aci's death to the ocean with "il flebil suon de' mesti accenti," gains the pity of Proteus, who restores her lover to life. Except in the second scene, the chorus is present throughout the action, serving the same functions as in Rinuccini's plays, and indeed dominating the first and fifth scenes as well as some of the third. Indicative of the expanding ornamental and structural role of the chorus, the first scene revolves around (rather than concluding in) a strophic refrain chorus (ll. 42-60), which grows out of the opening dialogue between the joyful Aci and his companions. The refrain,

> Vieni, deh vieni, o Galatea vezzosa,
> Rida al seren de' tuoi soavi lumi
> Sovra l'arena d'òr l'onda amorosa.

— almost a parody of the recurring invocation, "Vieni Imeneo, deh vieni," from the first act of Striggio's libretto—frames a five-line, hendecasyllabic strophe assigned to individual members of the chorus and ending always in the rhyme of the refrain.[66]

1st Fisherwoman:	k L m L n o P O (recitative)
Chorus:	A B A
2nd Fisherwoman:	C D D C A
Chorus:	A B A
Fisherwoman a 2:	E F F E A
Chorus:	A B A

In addition, the structure of the three-line refrain is subtly echoed at the end of the scene in Aci's solo, "Son tuoi begl'occhi, o Galatea gentile," composed of a series of *terzine*, rhyming A B B, C D D, E F F, G H H (ll. 110-21). The other refrain chorus in *Galatea* also recalls Striggio's libretto, for it occurs as the collective response to the messenger's announcement (in the fifth scene) of Aci's slaying by Polifemo. Here, as in Striggio's work, a line of solo recitative—"Piangete, o scogli, e lacrimate, arene" (l. 319)—is repeated by the chorus and taken up as the last verse of a choral lament.[67]

1st Fisherman:	a a B b c C
Chorus:	C
2nd Fisherman:	d E E d F c C
Chorus:	C
Chorus:	g H g H g C C

It is important to remember that these verses are sung by the participant chorus rather than as an interlude; then, following this passage, a single, reflective choral stanza in the style of the expressive madrigal concludes the scene (ll. 335-46).

Rinuccini's later libretti, as may be seen in the poet's revision of his *Dafne* for the 1608 festivities, bear the marks of Chiabrera's influence. Anna Abert remarks that Rinuccini expanded his earliest libretto in the direction of the pastoral play and away from the "Intermedienhafte Kürze," of the early works by increasing the participation of the nymph's simple woodland companions;[68] the only scenes which did not undergo substantial revision or expansion are those in which the gods Venus, Cupid, and Apollo converse among themselves, and where the gist of the dialogue has little to do with the main event of the action (scenes 2 and 4). One direct result was, inevitably, an increase in the number and size of the choruses, and a new interest in varying the manner of choral participation as well as the actual choral structures. Thus, in the first scene of the 1608 version, Rinuccini interpolated a refrain chorus of supplication between the opening dialogue and the echo piece, "Ebra di sangue" (ll. 44 ff.), which is assigned to individual members of the chorus.[69] Before the end of the scene, however, there are two more choral pieces—the added madrigal "Oimè! che veggio," sung by the company as they witness the battle between Apollo and the python,[70] and the closing strophic chorus "Almo Dio, che 'l carro ardente" from the original libretto (ll. 67-90).[71] The addition of the refrain chorus, which grows out of the static situation that prevails before the battle and provides a structured means of expressing the fear and prayer of the inhabitants threatened by the monster, serves the same function as the refrain chorus from the opening scene of Chiabrera's *Galatea*, which it obviously recalls. Gagliano treats the refrain chorus, "Se lassù tra gli aurei chiostri," in the manner of Peri's chorus "Cruda morte" (which the poetry closely resembles in meter and construction), except that, in addition to the five-part refrain, he employs the technique of strophic variation to relate the two stanzas of music assigned to the soloists.[72] As the following diagram shows, the first and last strophes are assigned to a single shepherd, the others to a pair of shepherds, whose duet, largely in parallel thirds, is accompanied by a sustained instrumental bass undoubtedly in imitation of the characteristic sound of pastoral music. (See example 26.)

I	Refrain	I′	Refrain
Shepherd	Chorus a 5	Shepherds a 2	Chorus a 5
(1) a b \[a b\]	\[a b\]	(2) c d c d	\[a b\]
		(3) e f e f	\[a b\]
(4) g h g h	\[a b\]		

Example 26
Gagliano, *Dafne*, pp. 3-4

The parallel between the revised *Dafne* and Chiabrera's *Galatea* is further reinforced when, in the narrative fifth scene, Rinuccini employs a single refrain verse — "Piangete, o Ninfe, e con voi pianga Amore" — to punctuate the cries of lamentation as the nymphs and shepherds of the chorus respond to the news of Dafne's transformation. As in Chiabrera's work, and the second scene of Striggio's *Orfeo*, the refrain is employed to unify a non-strophic passage dominated by the musical styles of expressive recitative and madrigal.[73]

Nymph:	$\boxed{A}$	B	b	C	C		
Chorus (a2 + b.c.):	$\underline{D}$	e	D	E	e	A	$\boxed{A}$
Chorus a 5:	$\boxed{A}$						
Chorus a 6:	F	g	g	F			
Shepherd:	a	$\boxed{A}$					
Chorus a 5:	$\boxed{A}$						

The formal expansion represented by the 1608 *Dafne* is also evident in *Arianna* and *Narciso*, the former having eight scenes and the latter as many as fifteen. Almost necessarily, this expansion coincides with a greater interest in form-building, which continues to be especially marked in scenes involving the chorus, although it is also visible in some monologues. *Arianna* in fact has three different choruses in its cast — two groups of soldiers comprising the companies of Teseo and Bacchus respectively, and the chorus of simple fishermen surrounding Arianna.[74] The first two groups appear only in the second and last scenes of the play, but the fishermen's chorus is present in various capacities in every intervening scene. In scenes 4 and 6 it assumes the role of an interested spectator, commenting upon the events as they occur — a function which it did not have in *Dafne* and *Euridice* and which, according to Abert, brings the play closer to the realm of tragedy.[75] The chorus also maintains the role of eliciting narrative from a messenger (as in scenes 5 and 7), and marking the scene-endings with *luoghi oziosi*. These are sometimes expanded to include a dialogue, usually between the two halves of the chorus and presumably in recitative style, which is then followed by the reflective, strophic verse characteristic of the earlier operas. In the fourth scene, for example, various parts of the chorus remark, in freely rhymed and mixed verse, the effect of Teseo's desertion upon the heroine (ll. 576-618) before summarizing their observations in four sententious strophes. Elsewhere, at the end of the first act of *Narciso*, the entire third scene and a good part of the second are given over completely to the chorus of nymphs who lie in wait for a glimpse of the stony-hearted protagonist (ll. 176 ff.). This tendency to expand the summarizing and concluding role of the chorus in the interludes points to the opera's eventual "absorption" of the *intermedio*—i.e., those choral scenes of little or no relevance to the drama characteristic of Roman opera, which replaced the originally simple choric interlude with elaborate musical and scenic display—a process to which Grout refers in his discussion of Stefano Landi's *Morte d'Orfeo* (Rome, 1619).[76]

The second scene of *Arianna* provides a good example of the expanded role of the ornamental chorus in the later libretti. Preceded only by the prologue (Apollo) and a dialogue between the gods Venus and Cupid, this scene actually initiates the action of the play by presenting for the first time the principal characters, Teseo (with his counselor) and Arianna, each of whom is surrounded by choruses of soldiers and fishermen respectively. The first forty-three lines consist of lively exchanges between Teseo and his soldiers on the eve of their victorious departure for homes and families. Although the section is not as long as the *luoghi oziosi* of *Euridice*, Rinuccini's versification is more formal and more closely knit than in the earlier libretto. The chorus begins with a short strophic song in *canzonetta* rhythm—three quatrains of *ottonari*, rhyming abba (ll. 154-67):

> Coro: Se d'Ismeno in su la riva,
> Per ornar d'Alcide i vanti,
> Fa sentir celesti canti
> Nobil suon di cetra argiva,
>   etc.

After Teseo addresses his companions in a brief recitative (ll. 166-72) the chorus continues, either *spezzato* or in the voices of individual members, now conversing with Teseo and his counselor in quatrains which, having lost their isometric quality, are cast in the freely alternating seven- and eleven-syllable lines characteristic of simple recitative (aBbA, cdcD, EFfE, etc.; ll. 173 ff.):

> Coro: Dolce i teneri figli,
> Dole sposa gentil raccorsi in seno;
> Ma dolce ancor non meno,
> Per bellissimo onor, rischi e perigli.
> Ove più ferve il cielo,
> Ove più il mar s'inscoglia
> Ov'ha più duro gelo
> Scòrgine pur s'alto desio t'invoglia.
>   etc.

Finally, Teseo's words suddenly take on a more intimate tone as he addresses his wife, and Rinuccini begins to admit unrhymed verse into the fabric at this new, heightened level of dialogue between the inter-locutors (*A* B *c* b *D E f* G g; ll. 198 ff.):

> Teseo: Quai segni di timor nel tuo bel volto
> Veggio, o parmi vedere, o core, o vita?
> Deh, rasserena omai
> L'alma beltà smarrita:
> Tosto vedrai de la famosa Atene
> Le gloriose mura e gli aurei tempi,
> Ove, mia cara sposa,
> Regina regnerai tranquilla e lieta,
> Qual già vivesti in Creta.

The scene ends with an unrelated interlude chorus provided by the native fishermen who, unaware that they are about to be hosts to an abandoned queen, remain on the beach after the exit of the royal company. In twelve lines of recitative verse (ll. 286 ff.), interpolated into the series of strophes after the fishermen have begun their song, Rinuccini attempts to justify the interlude and to establish its relationship to the events of the preceding scene. The recitative was probably assigned to a member of the chorus, who describes the coming of nightfall, speaks of the removal of the day's catch, and sets the stage for the concluding strophes (ll. 295-97):

> . . . .
> Noi qui, posando intanto
> Al lume de le stelle
> I dolci sonni alletterem col canto.

Thus, in addition to demonstrating the perseverance of the various levels of organization in Rinuccini's verse style, the second scene of *Arianna* illustrates how the chorus continued to be employed as a frame for the main action and more important sections of dialogue, in this case lending support to Teseo's exuberant mood and providing a foil for Arianna's troubled spirits.

There were many solutions, then, to the problem of representing a chorus on the musical stage. The libretti discussed here by Rinuccini, Chiabrera, and Striggio, dating from the first decade of opera, illustrate that the dramatic poets sought to expand the role of the chorus and to vary its function in order to enhance and support the structure of their infant art-form. I believe that, in the wake of Peri's and Caccini's experiments with a monodic and dramatically justified chorus, the librettists were influenced to provide a greater opportunity for musical variety by composers, like Marco da Gagliano and Claudio Monteverdi, who did not share the severe humanist's scorn for the expressive polyphonic madrigal,[77] nor abide by the theorist's limitations concerning the use of the chorus. As the solo song had not yet evolved large forms independent of the strophic air—for so firmly did it adhere to the ideals of expressive recitative in the early decades of opera—the chorus was the logical medium with which to achieve such form and variety.

What was the role in these early libretti of soloistic expression outside of the *parti recitative*? Or, what part did solo song play in the *luoghi oziosi*? The transition in Rinuccini's *poesia musicale* intended for solo singing, from *intermedio* verse to the first operas, is characterized by a development parallel to that of the choruses—the suppression of the free verse style of the madrigal in favor of more formal structures.[78] All the solo passages of the 1589 *intermedi* are couched in the freely rhyming verse of mixed meter and set in the highly ornamental style of the pseudo-monodic madrigal.[79] On the other hand, two of the three surviving solo fragments from *Dafne* are strophic, and both may be considered "song" as opposed to recitative. They are "Chi da lacci d'amor vive disciolto" (ll. 151-58), a single stanza of ottava rima probably set by Peri, and "Non curi la mia piant'o fiamm'o gelo" (ll. 388-97), three strophes of terza rima plus the concluding rhyme, attributed to Jacopo Corsi in the Brussels Ms.[80] By analogy with the libretto and score of *Euridice*, it would seem that these were the only two solo songs in the entire *Dafne* score, in addition to the strophic prologue.[81] When these fragments are added to the three solo songs of *Euridice*, two of which are in strophic form with conventional rhyme and metric schemes,[82] one must conclude that Rinuccini abandoned madrigal verse as the vehicle for solo song in his operas, and chose instead to rely upon the poetry of the air.

As we have seen, the tendency toward strophic solo composition is even more pronounced in Striggio's *Orfeo*, especially in the first three acts. In the fourth act as well, Orfeo sings three strophes of a triumphant song as he leads Euridice out of Hades, until doubts begin to assail him as to whether his spouse is indeed following (ll. 500 ff.). In choosing the meters of ottava and terza rima, or in setting up any pattern which then became the model for succeeding strophes, the early librettists were surely aware of the musical implications inherent in such regular forms. Isometric strophes necessarily meant musical repetition, phrases of equal length, and frequent full cadences. The single stanzas of madrigal verse required a more complex musical development, capable of carrying the poem to a logical conclusion. The latter style frequently involved word and phrase repetition, and required more sustained phrases as well as greater variety of rhythmic and melodic motion to aid the continuous progression of the poetry to a single final close.

The question then arises, Why is the style of the air favored over that of the madrigal in the non-recitative sections of these early operas? The answer lies partially in the fact that the air had been the traditional vehicle for solo performance during the Renaissance — for the minstrel reciting the octaves of Ariosto, for the courtier composing a sonnet to his lady, for the actors singing the interludes of the *sacre rappresentazioni*, and for the *zanni* impersonating the stock characters of the *commedia dell'arte*.

As the time-honored medium for solo song, then, the strophic air was the natural means of expression for figures like Orfeo, who were renowned for their musical prowess, or like the nymphs and shepherds of the Golden Age, to whom "music was natural" and speech was "almost poetic."[83] Thus Rinuccini assigns strophic airs to Tirsi ("Nel pur ardor") and Narciso ("Se d'amor nel regno crudo"), the latter graciously condescending to entertain his sylvan admirers with the words (ll. 400-05)

> Io vi vo' far contente
> Fin ch'apparisca il sol su l'orizzonte,
> Leggiadre ninfe; e voglio,
> Se fede il canto impetra,
> (Porgimi la tua cetra)
> Tanti affanni quetar, tanto cordoglio.

The quatrains following this passage in *Narciso* are the counterpart in mood and style to Orfeo's dance-song, "Vi ricorda, o boschi ombrosi" in the second act of Striggio's *Orfeo*. In fact, their poetic structures are so similar that Narciso's solo could easily have been sung to Orfeo's music.[84] Similarly, the formal terze rime by which Orfeo can convey his unrestrained joy at the return of his bride in *Euridice* ("Gioite al canto mio, selve frondose" [ll. 684 ff.]) are equally appropriate for his virtuosic plea to Caronte in Striggio's libretto ("Possente spirto e formidabil nume" [ll. 363 ff.]).

Another factor which deserves to be mentioned here is the prominence of the strophic air in the newly formed corpus of monodic literature, a corpus in which Rinuccini's poetry was well represented.[85] Obviously the rise of a new manner of singing and the creation of a literary genre to test its merits are not historical coincidences; rather, they are both manifestations of a single fashionable concern in the last quarter of the sixteenth century — the preoccupation with the affections. It was quite natural, therefore, that the later genre, opera, should have availed itself of the already proven merits of the strophic song or air, at the same time disassociating itself from the discredited sixteenth-century madrigal. Half a century earlier, Girolamo Mei had written that the short strophic songs of *settenari* or *ottonari* were appropriate to the uncomplicated but intense affections of simple folk.[86] Presumably Mei would have admitted the affairs of nymphs and shepherds into his classification of "cose villesche," but he was not yet so explicit as Galilei was to be in developing this idea at the end of the century.

In one of his last essays, intended as a supplement to his own complete but unpublished counterpoint treatise, Galilei turned his attention to certain practical problems from which he had remained aloof in his *Dialogo* — particularly the matter of composing melody and accompaniment.[87] Maintaining the humanistic position inherited from Mei concerning high and low pitch and fast and slow rhythm, Galilei reasoned further that, since the ancient Greek poets were limited to kitharas constructed with only four strings, the secret of their legendary art lay in the limitation and suitability of the means which it employed.[88]

> And, if someone were to ask me, since it is natural for a man to be able to reach with his voice eight or ten notes without straining, whether therefore all notes outside of the three or four used by Olympos were to be scorned — I would reply in this way. The three or four that Olympos used in one song were not apt for expressing all the passions and affections of the soul. The three or four notes that a tranquil soul seeks are not the same as those which suit the excited spirit, or one who is lamenting, or a lazy and somnolent one. For the tranquil soul seeks the middle notes; the querulous, the high; and the lazy and somnolent, the low. Thus, also, the latter will use slow meters; the tranquil, the intermediate; and the excited, the rapid. In this way the musician will tend to use now these and another time others according to the affection he wants to represent and impress on the listeners.[89]

Galilei held up as examples of this theory certain popular tunes or airs very much celebrated in his day, "such as the *Romanesca* and the *Passamezzo*, considered however in their primitive simplicity and not adorned with the artifices of today."[90] Claude Palisca has studied the music of the airs mentioned specifically in Galilei's treatise, and has noted that, by extolling their characteristics, Galilei was actually reaffirming the homophonic idiom of Italian popular music by calling for a return to the simple air-dominated (and, in most cases, strophic) songs heard on the lips of shepherds and workers in the fields. Galilei also asserted that among the most commendable qualities of these songs was a certain characteristic movement peculiar to each and able to awaken a particular affection.[91] It is hardly necessary to point out that such "characteristic movement" is first of all inherent in the rhythm of the poetry; and it was precisely this quality which the strophic airs of

Striggio's *Orfeo* or the octosyllabic choruses of Rinuccini's *Euridice* offered to the composers of the *seconda prattica*, who allowed themselves to be guided as a matter of principle by the rhythms and inflections of their texts.

In the light of Galilei's remarks, it is interesting to consider that Caronte, for example, confronts Orfeo with rhymed hendecasyllabic quatrains rather than free verse, quatrains which Monteverdi sets as strophic variations in the "somnolent" range of the baritone voice.[92] (It will be recalled that Caronte, while not moved to pity by Orfeo's performance, is easily charmed to sleep soon thereafter, allowing Orfeo to pass into the realm of the immortals.) Although Monteverdi rightfully did not compose a tuneful shepherd's air for this imposing Underworld figure, he employed simple strophic repetition in a style which greatly resembles that of the prologues, with their more measured quality than ordinary recitative, resulting in part from the metrical uniformity of the verse.[93] The four lines of music serve for each succeeding quatrain except for the slight rhythmic changes necessitated by variations of inflection in the new verses. Since the passage is an excellent example of Monteverdi's attention to the details of declamation, I have reproduced Caronte's melody in full, placing the corresponding verses of each new strophe under one another (example 27). Dramatically as well as musically, Caronte's strophic recitation is analogous to the prologue, for in its position at the beginning of the Hell scene, with the ferryman guarding the Tartarean gate, it serves the same function as La Musica's introduction to the pastoral world.

Elsewhere in *Orfeo*, Striggio's isometric quatrains supply strophic aria texts in similarly appropriate situations — for example, the shepherd's solo "Mira ch'a se n'alletta" and the duet "In questo prato adorno" at the beginning of Act 2, for both of which Monteverdi writes simple, stepwise tunes, each with a range contained within one octave, and set off by dance-like instrumental ritornelli.[94] The *canzonetta* rhythm of "Vi ricorda o boschi ombrosi," Orfeo's strophic dance-song completing the series of airs before the messenger's arrival in Act 2, is replaced in Act 4 as Orfeo leads his bride out of the shadowy realm[95] by the stately, "walking" bass of "Qual onor di te fia degno," with its continuous procession of quarter notes through the gamut of the G-major scale. Again, Monteverdi adheres to the formal implications of the quatrains by composing a series of strophic variations in which Orfeo is free to elaborate upon the virtues of his "cetra omnipotente." Here the characteristic movement may be found in the steadily moving bass, which was undoubtedly intended to generate the excited and triumphant mood

Example 27
Monteverdi, *Orfeo*, pp. 50-51

of the solo until the interruption of that mood, signaled by the sudden cessation of its rhythmic motion and the abrupt introduction of g-minor.

In Rinuccini's libretti, the appearance of strophic quatrains is usually limited to the prologues and choruses, which, as we have seen, often stimulated the composers to write strophic variations for individual members of the chorus. In the *Ballo delle Ingrate*, however, Rinuccini assigns seven strophes of rhymed hendecasyllabic quatrains (ABBA) to Plutone, who describes the prudes' fate to the women of the audience in the manner, once again, of the recitational prologues of the early operas.[96] While the music of Plutone's recitation, "Da 'l tenebroso orror de 'l mio gran regno," is very similar to the quasi-air style of the initial strains of *Euridice* and *Orfeo*, with the measured recitative occasionally punctuated by flourishes of colorature at the end of a verse or strophe, Monteverdi here uses a more sophisticated variation technique, so that the contour of both bass and melody undergoes a greater degree of transformation from one strophe to another.[97]

Among a wide variety of strophic forms intended for solo performance, Chiabrera also employs the rhymed hendecasyllabic quatrain internally in four different libretti including his first, *Il rapimento di Cefalo*. I list them here, giving their incipits, the number of quatrains, and insofar as is possible, indicating their place in the libretto.

"Nella magion stellante e luminosa" Berecintia in *Cefalo*, Act 4, ll. 357 ff.; see Solerti, *Albori*, vol. 3, p. 47.	(5 quatrains) ABBA
"Se più meco mirar non è speranza" Orfeo in *Pianto d'Orfeo*, ll. 187 ff.; see ibid., 97 ff.	(6 quatrains) ABBA
"Quante mai liete gioie in sè raccoglie" Apollo in *Amori di Aci e Galatea* (1617); see ibid., pp. 135-6.	(3 quatrains) ABBA
"Coppia real, che di sua mano insieme" Imeneo in Prologue to 1608 performance of Guarini's *Idropica*; see ibid., pp. 211-12.	(5 quatrains) ABBA
"O Galatea, che 'l pregio sei" Polifemo in *Galatea*, ll. 133 ff.; see Appendix G below.	(4 quatrains) ABAB

The last solo is actually part of a larger monologue, which presumably began and ended in recitative while the central section constituted Polifemo's formal complaint to Galatea. These quatrains differ in structure from the others in that they consist of alternating ten- and nine-syllable verses with an interlacing rhyme scheme—i.e., ABAB.

Although no music is known for any of the strophic songs by Chiabera enumerated above,[98] one can guess that their musical settings may well have been similar to the strophic variations of Caronte or Plutone. In fact, not only are the poetic structures virtually the same, but also their contents have much in common. In each case (except for Polifemo's complaint) the verses are directed toward forces outside of the dramatic setting—Berecintia addresses "eterni alberghi" in her tirade against Cupid, Orfeo invokes the powerful "stelle d'Amore" to rid him of painful memories, Plutone offers the lesson of the damned souls to the ladies in the audience, and Imeneo delivers an encomium to the royal couple whose nuptials were being celebrated by the 1608 festivities. In each case, the message consists of a straightforward recitation of grievances or praises, which generally neither fosters the movement of the play nor expresses a particular affection;[99] instead it presents a situation basic to the development or outcome of the drama, in a manner closely resembling that of the prologues. Thus the recitation of these quatrains in the somewhat neutral, unadorned style of the strophic prologues—a style which Doni called *proprio recitativo*,[100] but which was capable nevertheless of being elaborated as the text warranted—would certainly have been appropriate.

Another medium for overt song in early opera was terza rima. In the last scene of the original *Dafne* libretto, Apollo sings an encomium to the transfigured nymph in traditional *terzine*—"Non curi la mia pianta o fiamma o gelo" (ll. 388-97). The preceding verses, again presumably set in recitative style, call attention to the formal nature of the song which, we are led to believe, he is about to improvise in homage to the laurel (ll. 385 ff.):

> Ma deh! se in questa fronde odi il mio pianto,
> Senti la nobil cetra,
> Quai doni a te dal ciel cantando impetra:
>
> Non curi la mia pianta o fiamma o gelo,
> Sian del vivo smeraldo eterni pregi,
> Nè l'offenda già mai l'ira del cielo.
> > etc.

This precedent was apparently followed by both Chiabrera and Striggio, who similarly resort to terza rima in situations where formal lyricism is appropriate. Here follows a list of songs in *terzine* which appear in the libretti we have been discussing.

Rinuccini
"Non curi la mia pianta o fiamma o gelo" (3 tercets)
Apollo in *Dafne,* ll. 388 ff.; see Appendix A below.

"Gioite al canto mio, selve frondose" (2 tercets)
Orfeo in *Euridice,* ll. 684 ff.; see Appendix B below.

"Ecco splendere in ciel quel dî giocondo" (6 tercets)
L'Angelo Gabriele in celebrations for the
Feast of the Annunciation on 25 March 1620;
see Solerti, *Albori,* vol. 2, p. 351.

Chiabrera
"Chi mi conforta ahimè! chi più consolami?" (5 tercets)[101]
Titone (solo per aria) in *Cefalo,* Act 2, ll. 130 ff.;
see idem., *Albori,* vol. 3, p. 37.

"Son tuoi begl'occhi, o Galatea gentile" (4 tercets)
Aci in *Galatea,* ll. 110 ff.; see Appendix G below.

"Or che se 'n va rinchiuso in forme nove" (2 tercets)
Glauco in the second *intermedio* to 1608
performance of Guarini's *Idropica*; see Solerti,
Albori, vol. 3, p. 220.

Striggio
"Possente spirto e formidabil nume" (6 tercets)
Orfeo in *Orfeo,* Act 2, ll. 363 ff.; see Appendix E below.

Although there are no terze rime in *Arianna* and *Narciso,* the last text cited above in the Rinuccini group occurs in a late fragment—a short sacred drama composed for the Feast of the Annunciation and performed in music in the Medici chapel of San Lorenzo.[102]

There are two settings of "Non curi la mia pianta"—one attributed to Jacopo Corsi in the Brussels manuscript[103] and the other by Marco da Gagliano in his 1608 score of *Dafne*—as well as two of "Gioite al canto mio," one in each of the *Euridice* settings. It is interesting to note the similarities among the three earliest compositions—those by Corsi, Peri, and Caccini. (See examples 28, 30, and 31.) Notwithstanding the fact that "Gioite al canto mio" is set each time in triple meter, the last phrase of the Peri and Corsi pieces and the third in Caccini have the same harmonic and melodic contour. Furthermore, the first few bars of Caccini and Peri are similar as well. While one is not surprised to find

Example 28
Corsi, *Dafne*; from Brussels, fol. 52 (Porter, pp. 181-82)

Example 29
Petrucci, *Frottole*, XI. 44 (Einstein, *Madrigal*, III, no. 9)
(excluding two inner parts)

Example 30
Peri, *Euridice*, pp. 46-47

Example 31
Caccini, *Euridice*, p. 47

such parallels among composers who worked together for a short time in such close association, it is another matter to discover that a *capitolo*—i.e., a strophic composition especially designed for singing terza rima—dating from the early sixteenth century, bears a striking resemblance to the later songs. The *capitolo*, a setting by Joannes Lulinus Venetus of the first of a long series of tercets by an anonymous poet, is from Petrucci's eleventh book of *frottole*, printed in 1514 (example 29).[104] Its relationship to the later works is seen most clearly by comparing it with Corsi's "Non curi la mia pianta" (see example 28), of which the entire progression of the first line, the discant of the second, and the bass of the third, are extremely similar to their counterparts in the *capitolo* air.

Another factor to be noted is that the terza rima settings by Peri and Caccini both contain a repetition of the third phrase of music, or (as in Caccini's piece) a variation of it, paralleled by a repetition of the third verse of the text. In the case of "Gioite al canto mio," this repetition seems justified by the text itself, which contains a reference to Orfeo's echo reverberating in the vales ("Eco rimbombi da le valli ascose").

However, an examination of other examples of the *capitolo* reveals that the form traditionally called for four lines of music, presumably in order to accommodate the additional line of text at the end of the poem, since the ultimate stanza in a series of terze rime always consists of four lines, rhyming YZYZ. Einstein refers to a farewell letter, written in the form of an *aria di capitolo* and printed as the final piece in a *frottola* collection of 1515, in which an instrumental interlude separates the strophes and also provides the music for the concluding verse.[105] It might be argued that Monteverdi's ritornelli separating Orfeo's strophic variations ("Possente spirto") serve the same function since no final ritornello occurs at the end of the last strophe, but only the additional line of text.[106] In another *frottola* print (1519), an item labeled *capitolo*, obviously a model for the improvisation of terza rima, again consists of four lines of music for only three verses (example 32).[107] Moreover, the declamation, which is reduced to its simplest form, is characterized by a rhythmic break at the sixth syllable of each hendecasyllabic line, a typical feature of many airs intended for terza and ottava rima. The fact that this break also occurs in Peri's and Caccini's settings of *terzine*, and reappears frequently as a caesura after the fifth or sixth syllables of Monteverdi's "Possente spirto," and Gagliano's setting of "Non curi la mia pianta," provides further evidence to link these airs of early opera with the style of the traditional *arie* of sixteenth-century improvisation.

Caccini's setting of the *terzine* from *Il rapimento di Cefalo*[108] may be classified with Monteverdi's *preghiera* and Gagliano's setting of the piece from *Dafne*[109] as a "frozen improvisation" in the highly ornamental style of late sixteenth-century solo song. All are in the form of strophic variations, except for "Chi mi confort'ahimè," where Caccini writes out only two stanzas — one to serve for the first four *terzine*, and a more elaborate one for the ultimate strophe. It should also be noted in connection with the relationship of their form to that of the *capitolo* that Caccini and Gagliano both compose the equivalent of four lines of music, so that no new music need be supplied at the conclusion. However, the "extra" bars are taken up by long colorature (as in the extended second line of Gagliano's "Non curi") or by simple repetition of the last line of the tercet (as in Caccini's aria), rather than by an instrumental interlude. If, as Palisca and Porter have already suggested, the strophic airs of the first operas retain a real as well as an ideal link with the Italian tradition of vocal monody — real to the extent that certain melodic formulas, perhaps less renowned than the *Romanesca* or *Ruggiero*, might actually have been employed as the basis for these solo songs — then the whole matter of the relationship of music and poetry in the new art form becomes double-edged. One must consider not only

Example 32
Fioretti di frottole barzelette capitoli strambotti e sonetti libro secondo (1519) no. 20. (excluding two inner parts)

the extent to which conventional and new poetic forms shaped the musical style of these works, but also how much traditional musical styles influenced the nascent libretti.

The last group of texts to be considered, the ottave rime, is also the largest, especially if the closely related quatrains of the prologues and epilogues of early opera are included, as I believe they should be. To begin with, however, it must be remembered that ottava rima in its traditional form of strophic recitation (ABABABCC) dominated a large segment of the Italian stage during the sixteenth century, in the still-popular *sacre rappresentazioni*, and the pastoral eclogues or romantic epics in the style of Poliziano's *Orfeo* or Tasso's *Gerusalemme liberata*. As late as 1579, Rinuccini found a convenient structure for his early court masques[110] in the stately, hendecasyllabic octaves; for, their prefabricated strophic design, traditionally used to convey a recitational text, must also have been easily accommodated to the stylized dance movements of the masquers. Sometimes narrative or descriptive, the texts were also frequently representational, in the manner of the later opera prologues, in that the singers presented themselves in the guise of Amazzoni, Bergiere, or Gentildonne, and either preceded or accompanied the dancers with their song.[111] Rinuccini's *Maschere di Bergiere* (1590) consists of eleven strophes of ottave rime, beginning "Serenissima donna il cui gran nome."[112] According to a setting preserved in two manuscript collections of solo songs,[113] "La Signora Lucia di Giulio Romano" sang them in an ornate, improvisatory style in which the simple, recitative-like declamation periodically dissolved in a flourish of coloratura. Stripped of its ornamentation, the music provides the aria for only four verses and must therefore be repeated in order to present the rest of the stanza. (See example 33.)

Einstein indicated the existence of a connection between the recitational style of such octaves and the "popular declamation-formulas," such as the *Ruggiero* and the *Romanesca*.[114] These formulas were incorporated into the madrigal literature as *ostinati* in the uppermost part of a vocal texture, particularly in connection with Ariosto's octaves.[115] As an example, Einstein printed a madrigal by Francesco Corteccia on a stanza from *Orlando*, "Io dico e diss' et dirò fin ch'io viva" (1547), in which the melody of the first two verses (AB) is thrice repeated to a varying accompaniment.[116] A similar principle is probably at work in the abbreviated *arie* for singing ottava rima and *strambotto* texts in the Bottegari Lutebook, where it is to be imagined that the lutanist took the two lines of music as a model to be used in improvising a set of lute variations with which to accompany the melodic repetition of the rest of the text.[117] It is almost certain, then, that Signora Lucia, following the same harmonic and melodic contours which are preserved in this, her own improvised setting of the first strophe of the *Maschere di Bergiere*, performed the ten succeeding strophes in the same manner, changing only the *accenti* and *passaggi* of the melody according to the requirements of each new stanza of text. This is undoubtedly the same style in which Caccini's daughters, a generation later, sang a group of Rinuccini's *ottave* in the *Mascherata di Ninfe di Senna*, performed in

Example 33
Maschere di bergiere (1590) (from Ghisi, *Alle fonti della monodia*, p. 47)

Se-re-nis-si-ma don - na il cui gran no - me Di

mil-le fre-gi a-dor-na al - to ri-suc - na

De la cui re-gia man - de le cui chio - me . De - gno'l

mon-do non ha scet-tro o co - ro - na, Stan-ch'et op-pres so - ma

da l'as-pre so - me Del fu-ri-bon-do Mar - te' di Bel-

Florence in 1611 for the wedding of Mario Sforza and Arnea di Lorena.[118] A letter by Jacopo Cicognini describing the festivities records that

> . . . the . . . octaves were set to music by the same ladies who sang them: the first ["Donne, dal cui sembiante Amor sì belle"] was sung by signora Vittoria Archilei of Rome with her usual beautiful and angelic voice; the second ["Scòrgela a reverir gentil pensiero"] with all the greatest perfection by signora Settimia; and the third ["Ma dove di Loren quel nobil sole"] with the customary ease [which inspired] general admiration by signora Francesca, both daughters of the widely celebrated Giulio Romano. And the fourth octave ["Cosmo, che in su 'l mattin degli anni a pena"], composed by the same signora Francesca in a most graceful and beautiful style, was sung by all three of them together with such beautiful fugues and ornaments. . . .[119]

In the case of the first three strophes it seems unlikely that each of the performers would have been responsible for more than the improvised ornamentation of her particular text, once a basic tune had been chosen. Similarly, a note by Caccini preceding each of the solo strophes of the refrain chorus "Ineffabile ardore" from *Il rapimento di Cefalo* indicates that the performers indeed sang these "airs" with their own embellishments.[120]

The ottava rima survived in early opera, then, as another vehicle for traditional solo singing in the *luoghi oziosi*, to provide variety and relief from the simple dialogue of the *parti recitative*, as well as in some cases to give the soloist his coveted opportunity to impress the audience with his skill. The following is a list of octaves appearing in the early libretti, either as strophic compositions, or single stanzas. Beginning with *Dafne*, the list excludes the early court masques of Rinuccini which were composed almost entirely in ottave rime. It will be noted that the form continues to be associated particularly with the *Mascherate* and *Balli*, which I include here for the sake of completeness, although the music for many of these compositions has not yet been discovered.[121]

Rinuccini
"Chi da lacci d'amor vive disciolto"   (1 octave)
Venere in *Dafne*, ll. 151-58; see Appendix A below.

"Udite, donne, udite i saggi detti"   (1 octave)
Venere in *Ballo delle Ingrate*; see Solerti,
Albori, vol. 2, p. 251.

"Serenissimi regi, a cui s'inchina"   (3 octaves)
Senna in *Mascherata di Ninfe di Senna* (1611);
see ibid., p. 271.

"Torna, deh torna pargoletto mio"   (1 octave)
Venere in *Mascherata di Ninfe di Senna*;
see ibid., p. 278.

"Donne, dal cui sembiante Amor sì belle"   (4 octaves)
Tre Ninfe (alternately) in *Mascherata di ...Senna*;
see ibid., pp. 287-88.

"Su 'l dorso alter di inaccessibil monte"   (1 octave)
Pallade in *Comparsa degli Eroi Celesti* (1613);
see ibid., p. 310.

Chiabrera
"Non vedran gli occhi miei piaggie fiorite"   (2 octaves)
Reina in *Oritia*, ll. 304-19; see Solerti,
Albori, vol. 3, pp. 72-3.

"Indarno Febo il suo bello oro eterno"   (1 octave)
Orfeo in *Pianto d'Orfeo*, ll. 57-64; see ibid., p. 93.

"Chi 'l bell'arco possente e la faretra"   (1 octave)
Galatea in *Galatea*, ll. 509-16; see Appendix G below.

"Ha cento lustri con etereo giro"   (4 octaves)
Manto in Prologue to *Idropica*; see Solerti,
Albori, vol. 3, pp. 209-10.

"O ben felici Amanti, ora ch'Amore"   (1 octave)
Mercurio in *Vegghia delle Grazie* (1615), ll. 145-52;
see ibid., p. 198.

Striggio
    "O degli abitator de l'ombre eterne"   (1 octave)
    Uno spirito del Coro di spiriti infernali in *Orfeo*,
    Act 4, ll. 475 ff.; see Appendix E below.

The two settings of "Chi da' lacci d'amor" — one, from the solo song manuscripts, probably by Peri[122] and the other from Gagliano's setting of *Dafne*[123] — are interesting for their lively air style, which, like "Gioite al canto mio," involves a rhythmically active bass. Again, the unit of repetition is four lines, with the second half of the octave performed to a variation of the music of the first half. (Gagliano writes out the music for the second half, but in the manuscript version of Peri's setting the variations were presumably left to the performer.) Other similarities between the two settings, such as the harmonic sequences common to the second and fourth lines of both pieces, suggest the possibility that they are related in a way that goes beyond the use of the same text. (See examples 34 and 35.)

Two other settings of the ottave rime listed above are by Monteverdi — one from Rinuccini's *Ballo delle Ingrate*, the other from Striggio's *Orfeo*.[124] The first is again divided into musically equivalent halves and separated by an instrumental *sinfonia*. In both of the Monteverdi settings, however, the musical style is not so obviously "airy" as it is in "Chi da' lacci d'amor," but rather falls into the category described by Doni as *proprio recitativo* or "properly recitational," which the same author associates with ottave rime.[125]

The question of formulaic construction must also be raised in connection with the uniform poetic style and musical similarities among the prologues of these early works. Although they stand aloof from the rest of the poem and constitute a category of their own, the prologues share to a great degree the characteristics of the recitational octaves and quatrains discussed above, serving a narrative rather than dramatic function. It will be recalled that Poliziano's brief prologue to the fifteenth-century *Orfeo* is a single stanza of ottava rima, which may

Example 34*
Peri (?), *Dafne*; from Florence cod. 66, fols. 154-154v (Porter, p. 179)

Chi da' lac-ci d'a- mor vi - ve di-sciol-to

Del - la sua li- ber-tà go- da pur lie - to ,

Su - per- bo no : d'os-cu - ra nu - be in- vol- to

Stas-si per noi dal ciel l'al- to de-cre - to

* A second quatrain of text follows, to be sung to the same four lines of music.

Example 35*
Gagliano, *Dafne*, pp. 19-20.

Chi da lac-ci d'a-mor vi - ve di-sciol-to

Del-la sua li-ber-tà   go -   da pur lie - to

Su - per-bo nò   d'o- scu-ra nu -   be in-vol-   to

Stas-   si per noi del ciel   l'al - to de- cre - to.

* A second quatrain of text is sung to essentially the same music, differing only in ornamentation and in the repetition of the last verse.

indeed have been recited to a conventional tune associated with the recitation of octaves. Porter identified an anonymous setting of an octave from Tasso's *Gerusalemme*, "Giunto alla tomba ove al suo spirto vivo" (canto XII, stanza 96) as having music very similar to the prologues of both *Dafne* and *Euridice*.[126] The composer wrote down the music for the entire octave, but according to Porter the second quatrain is sung essentially to the same music as the first. Although he gives a line-by-line comparison of the basses of these three pieces, I believe it is equally important to take cognizance of their melodic parallels; for if the generation of such compositions did not actually utilize the principle of melodic or harmonic variation on a pre-existent formula, then it was certainly based upon the imitation of a common recitational *style*, which by its nature produced certain types of melodies. Thus, for the sake of completeness, and in order to complement the comparison made by Porter, I reproduce in line-by-line fashion the vocal lines of "Giunto alla tomba," and the Peri prologues from *Dafne* and *Euridice* (see example 36), adding to these the Caccini setting of "Io, che d'alti sospir." It will be noted that Caccini's version (transposed in the example one whole tone below the original in order to facilitate comparison) resembles the anonymous setting particularly in the descent of its first line, but in all other respects approximates the contours of Peri's composition.

Similarly, the opening melody of "O degli abitator" from Monteverdi's *Orfeo* (which is the only through-composed ottava rima among our examples) resembles the group surrounding "Giunto alla tomba" (example 37); and the opening of La Musica's prologue to *Orfeo* (example 38) is reminiscent of Signora Lucia's octave, "Serenissima donna," discussed above.[127]   Finally I include, side by side, Gagliano's setting of the prologue to *Dafne* and Venus' "Udite, donne, udite" from Monteverdi's *Ballo delle Ingrate* to point out their parallels, especially in their first, second, and last lines (examples 39 and 40).

One can easily see the difficulty that would be involved in any attempt to isolate one or more prototypes in this group of compositions on prologue or ottava rima texts. The deviations are so numerous as to make it almost impossible to decide which melody or bass, or combination thereof, is to be regarded as the basic design. Perhaps it is worth noting in this connection that, despite all its association with traditional sixteenth-century forms, the poetic structure of the prologue Rinuccini invented for *Dafne* has been singled out by some literary historians as one of the poet's most original stylistic accomplishments.[128] One cannot exclude the possibility, therefore, that Peri's own music for that prologue, notwithstanding the similarities discovered by Porter between it and the stanza from *Gerusalemme*, became the paradigm — one which followed Galilei's admonition to return to the simple air-dominated style of the Italian popular idiom, whether it be by imitating the regional tunes of the shepherds and laborers, or, as in this case, the *arie* in which Ariosto's verses were recited by unskilled as well virtuosic singers.[129]

In conclusion, I wish to make two brief observations concerning Rinuccini's later works. The first is that in composing *Arianna* and *Narciso* Rinuccini seems suddenly to have put aside the strophic and conventional aria in favor of more flexible and original solo passages, which depend for their form not only upon metrical regularity and rhyme, but also upon refrain and other types of expressive text repetition as in the "Lamento d'Arianna." With the exception of the prologues, these libretti no longer contain airs resembling terza or ottava rima; instead, they reveal a notable increase in the use of the chorus, a trend

Example 36
Prologue melodies of *Dafne* and *Euridice* compared with an ottava rima

Example 37
Monteverdi, *Orfeo*, p. 76

Example 38
Monteverdi, *Orfeo*, Prologue (p. 1)

Example 39
Gagliano, *Dafne*, Prologue (p. 1)

Go - don-si all'om - bra de fron-do - si Mir - ti,

I gra-di - ti del Ciel fe-li - ci spir - ti

Mo - strom'in que-sta not-te a voi mor-ta-li .

Example 40
Monteverdi, *Ballo delle Ingrate* (*Opere*, Vol. 8, Part 2), p. 317.

Venere :

U - di - te Don - ne, u - di - te i sag - gi det - ti

Di ce-le- ste par - lar nel cor ser - ba - te

which implies a corollary to Grout's hypothesis concerning the decline of the chorus.[130]

    Where the chorus was not prominent—i.e., in the court masques—the use of strophic air forms, especially ottava rima, did survive until much later. However, and this is my second point, Rinuccini's ascendancy as a librettist did not last through the second decade of the century until his death in 1621, but ceased apparently in 1613 or before. This corresponds to a general decline in the arts at this time at the Florentine court, and a shift in the production of opera to other important cities, such as Mantua and Rome. Rinuccini's dramatic *poesia musicale* from this late period reflects a poet not at the height of a glorious and successful career, but continually groping to accommodate his verses to new situations and occasions. Thus the *Mascherata di selvaggi*, a *ballo* performed in the Palazzo Strozzi in February, 1611, is unique in that it lacks a chorus, and is written entirely in free verse with irregular rhyme.[131] At the same time, the dramatic *versi sacri* of 1619-20[132] are almost entirely in strophic form, although they betray the same brevity and reduction of forces that characterize the *Mascherata di selvaggi*. Had Rinuccini lived beyond the age of fifty-nine, he would probably have been persuaded to turn his attention to the rising form of the solo cantata, leaving to others the dramatic celebration of the Orphic legend.

Notes

Chapter 1

1. "*L'Euridice / d'Ottavio / Rinuccini, / rappresentata / nello sponsalitio / della Christianiss. / Regina / di Francia, e di Navarra. / ...* in Fiorenza. 1600. / nella stamperia di Cosimo Giunti. / ...." The first performance took place on 6 October 1600 at the Pitti Palace in Florence on the occasion of the marriage of Marie de Medici and Henry IV of France. A copy of the printed edition of the libretto in the possession of the library of the Yale School of Music was made available to me. The text was reprinted in the posthumous collection of Rinuccini's *Poesie* (Florence: C. Giunti, 1622) and more recently (with slight variations) in *Drammi per musica*, ed. Andrea della Corte (Collezione di classici italiani... 2d series, vol. 50, Turin [1926], 289-326; in Angelo Solerti, *Gli albori del melodramma*, 3 vols. (Milan, 1904-5, repr. 1969), vol. 2., pp. 105-42; and in *Drammi per musica, dal Rinuccini allo Zeno*, ed. A. della Corte (Turin, 1926, repr. 1958), vol. 1, pp. 69-106.

2. See Chiabrera's elegy for Rinuccini partially quoted in Raccamadoro-Ramelli's critical biography, *Ottavio Rinuccini* (Fabriano, 1900), p. 35: "... egli non studiò scienza nessuna, ed anco della lingua latina poco fu esperto." Nino Pirrotta considers the artistic pose which characterized Rinuccini's entire output one of "classicismo moderno" – that is, midway between the absolute reverence for classical models professed by Bardi and the excessive lightness of Cavalieri's pastorals. See his sketch of the poet in *Enciclopedia dello spettacolo* (hereafter *Encicl. spett.*), vol. 8 (Rome, 1961), col. 1003.

3. Rinuccini was elected while still a young man to the Accademia fiorentina and in 1586 became a member of the Accademia degli Alterati in which he bore the name "Sonnacchioso", or "Sleepy". See Raccamadoro-Ramelli, p. 36. Also on Rinuccini, see Jacopo Rilli, *Notizie letterarie, ed istoriche intorno agli uomini illustri dell'Accademia fiorentina*, part 1 (Florence, 1700), pp. 258-62. For the subjects of some of the papers read before these academies, see Bernard Weinberg, "Argomenti di discussione letteraria nell'Accademia degli Alterati (1570-1600)," *Giornale storico della letteratura italiana* 131 (1954): 174-94, and idem, *A History of Literary Criticism in the Italian Renaissance* (hereafter *HLC*), 2 vols. (Chicago, 1961), passim.

4. Leo Schrade, *Tragedy in the Art of Music* (Cambridge, Mass., 1964), p. 56.

5. "... il prologo dato alla Tragedia nell'Euridice fu soltanto un'iperbole cortigiana, nata dalla tradizione che associava il genere tragico all'idea della regalità." *Encicl. spett.*, vol. 8, col. 1004. Pirrotta reiterates this view in a more recent article; see "Monteverdi e i problemi dell' opera," in *Studi sul teatro Veneto fra Rinascimento ed età barocca*, ed. M.T. Muraro (Florence, 1971), p. 333.

6.   Pirrotta, "Temperaments and Tendencies in the Florentine Camerata," *MQ* 40 (1954): 188.

7.   Pirrotta, "Tragédie et comédie dans la camerata fiorentina," *Musique et poésie au XVIe siècle* (Paris, 1954), p. 295.   Jacopo Peri was the composer for whom Rinuccini originally wrote the libretto.   Rinuccini's language in his dedication to *Euridice* is similar to Peri's in its reference to, and praise of, antiquity.   See Chapter One, p. 5.

8.   Pirrotta dismisses *La Dafne* as the starting point, "not because the dates of its various performances are uncertain and a complete score missing, but because both the text and the few surviving fragments of the music make this work seem immature and preliminary compared to the full-fledged vitality of *Euridice*."   See his essay, "Early Opera and Aria," in *New Looks at Italian Opera*, ed. William Austin (Ithaca, 1968), p. 39.   The essay also appears in Italian in Pirrotta, *Li due Orfei, da Poliziano a Monteverdi* (Turin, 1969; repr. 1975), pp. 276-333.   For Pirrotta's evaluation of my views on *La Dafne*, see his note on 86a on p. 329. Cf. also Gary Tomlinson, "Ancora su Ottavio Rinuccini," *JAMS* 28 (1975): 351-56, and my "Communication" in ibid. 29 (1976): 501-3.

9.   B. Giraldi Cinthio was an innovator in the use of a detached prologue in his tragedy *Orbecche*, and in his succeeding tragicomedies.   See Chapter One, p. 3.

10. *Lettione sopra'l principio del Canzoniere del Petrarca*, pp. Av.-A2.   The citation and translation are from Weinberg, *HLC* 1: 224.

11. De Sommi was a Mantuan Jew whose little-known comedies and his *Dialoghi in materia di rappresentazioni sceniche* remained primarily in manuscript form.   He probably died in 1590 according to Alessandro d'Ancona, *Origini del teatro italiano*, 2 vols. (2d ed., Turin, 1891). See vol. 2, pp. 403 ff.

12. The passage appears in Leone de Sommi, *Quattro dialoghi in materia di rappresentazioni sceniche*, ed. F. Marotti (Milan, 1968), p. 69; it is also printed by d'Ancona in *Origini*, vol. 2, p. 420.

Veridico:... Non vi ricorda egli come riuscî vago il Prologo di quella tragicomedia del carnevale passato, dove il poeta introdusse la Comedia e la Tragedia a colloquio insieme?...

Santino: Benissimo, ma non a tutte le comedie si potrà trovar forse così appropriati prologhi.

Veridico: Ve lo concedo, ma quando il tutto manchi, non mancarà mai introdur cose che abbiano convenienza con le città o lochi dove si recita, come introdur i fiumi che le irrigano, i primi fondatori che le edificarono, o gli uomini famosi et gli eroi che vi son nati....

13. See Chapter Three, pp. 128 ff.

14.   See Madeleine Doran, *Endeavors of Art, A Study of Form in Elizabethan Drama* (Madison, Wis., 1954), p. 189.

15.   "Et egli tien per cosa più che certa, / Che s'hora fusser quî i Poeti antichi / Cercherian sodisfare à questi tempi, / A spettatori, à la materia nova, / E che sia ver, che varin queste leggi, / Vedesi che più volte i Greci istessi / Si sono da i primi ordini partiti /...." Prologue to *Altile*, p. 7, 14-20. I cite the complete edition of *Le tragedie de M. Gio. Battista Giraldi Cinthio...* (Venice, 1583) in which the plays are bound together but have separate pagination.

16.   One of the innovations in question is the introduction of a prologue separated from the body of the play. La Tragedia argues that she cannot be blamed "però che i tempi / Ne' quai son nata, e la novità mia, / E qualche altro rispetto occulto fammi / meco portarlo;... /" See *Le tragedie, Orbecche*, p. 130, 12 ff.; for Giraldi's further thoughts on the prologue, see his *Discorso intorno al comporre delle comedie e delle tragedie* in *Scritti estetici*, ed. G. Antimaco (*Biblioteca rara*, vol. 52-53 [Milan, 1864], pp. 72-78.

17.   Printed in *Parnaso italiano, ovvero, Raccolta de' poeti classici italiani*, ed. A. Rubbi, 54 vols. (Venice, 1784-91); see vol. 17, pp. 233-34.

18.   This pastoral fragment has often been called *Amore* because of its opening. The fragment is published by G. Carducci, *Su L'Aminta di T. Tasso* (Florence, 1896), pp. 115-29.

19.   See L. Fassò's commentary to his third edition of the *Aminta* (Florence [1932]), p. 9.

20.   The pastoral is printed in *Parnaso italiano* 24 (Venice, 1786). See p. 195.

21.   It is questioned whether this performance actually took place; see d'Ancona, *Origini* 2: 536, and V. Rossi, *Battista Guarini ed il Pastor fido* (Turin, 1886), pp. 183 ff. The encomiastic nature of the prologue, however, is undisputed.

22.   The Italian text appears in Appendix B of this study, pp. 271-72. Marion Schild (*Die Musikdramen Ottavio Rinuccinis* [Univ. of Munich, Ph. D. diss., 1933], p. 14) sees in these strophes Rinuccini's disavowal of the Cinquecento tradition in which the bloodthirsty plots of Senecan tragedy provided the model, along with Aristotle's *Poetics*, for sixteenth-century tragedians.

23.   See Chapter Two, p. 31, where I suggest that Rinuccini embraces in his prologue the aim of tragicomedy—i.e., the purgation of melancholy. Tragedy throws off the trappings of the ancient theater and instead sings of the melancholic and tearful emotions proper to tragicomedy, emotions which she will then purge by using "happier strings" and awakening "sweeter affections."

24.   See note 1, above. The dedication is reprinted in Solerti, ed. *Le origini del melodramma* (Turin, 1903; repr. 1969), pp. 40-42; a translation appears in O. Strunk,

Source Readings in Music History (New York, 1950), pp. 367-69. For the reader's convenience a complete text is provided in Appendix B of this study, pp. 269-70.

25. Rinuccini was the author of a good deal of *poesia musicale*, having composed the texts for several *maschere* in honor of the Medici weddings of 1579 and 1586. His role in the 1589 *intermedi* will be discussed below.

26. "E' stata openione di molti... che gl'antichi Greci, e Romani cantassero su le Scene le Tragedie intere, ma sì nobil maniera di recitare non che rinnovata, ma ne pur che io sappia fin quì era stata tentata da alcuno, e ciò mi credev'io per difetto della Musica moderna di gran lunga al l'antica inferiore, ma pensiero sì fatto mi tolse interamente dell'animo M. Iacopo Peri,... mise gratia sotto le note la favola di Dafne composta da me solo per far una semplice prova di quello, che potesse il canto dell'età nostra,..." (in Solerti, *Le origini*, p. 40). See also Appendix B below, p. 269.

27. In the preface to the 1608 edition of his score, Marco da Gagliano gives Carnival, 1597 as the date of the first performance of *Dafne*. (See Solerti, *Gli albori*, vol. 2, p. 68.) Because the Florentine calendar year began on 25 March, da Gagliano's date refers presumably to February or March, 1598. From Jacopo Peri's preface to his setting of Rinuccini's *Euridice* of 1600 (cf. ibid., p. 110), we learn that *Dafne* was performed during three consecutive carnival seasons in Florence. Thus the dates of the earlier versions of *Dafne* are generally assumed to be 1597/8, 1598/9, and 1599/1600. Most recently, F.W. Sternfeld has written about the chronology of *Dafne* ("The First Printed Opera Libretto," *Music and Letters* 59 [1978]: 121-38), concluding that the undated libretto extant in the New York Public Library belongs to the first performance of 1597/8. In a letter to the editors of *Music and Letters* (59 [1978]:522-23), Tim Carter argues against this hypothesis, but acknowledges that the New York copy of the libretto antedates the 1600 edition of *Dafne*.

28. Rinuccini's preface is dated 4 October 1600, and Peri's dedication bears the date 6 February 1600 (1601, modern style).

29. See, for example, Pirrotta: "But those who personified the almost unconscious ambitions of which I have spoken sought to rationalize them and to present them on the stage in a plausible manner; later they invented the ideas and theory of 'speaking in song'" ("Temperaments and Tendencies . . . ," p. 187). Although Donald J. Grout admits that "The Florentine opera in the beginning was the outgrowth of a limited musical theory applied to an artificial, stylized poetic form," he then reminds us that its founders, "all actuated by an enthusiastic misconception of antiquity . . . have often been compared to Columbus, who set out to find the East Indies and accidentally discovered a new continent." Grout himself perpetuates the misconception that the Florentines were "seeking to revive Greek drama" and thereby "opened the way to modern opera." (See his *Short History of Opera*, 2d ed., New York, 1965, pp. 49-50). Similarly, Ambros is extremely contemptuous of the humanist element in Galilei's theories. (See his *Geschichte der Musik*, vol. 4, 3d ed. revised by Hugo Leichtentritt [Leipzig, 1909], pp. 285-346.) Fabio Fano does not go so far as to denigrate the humanistic efforts of the Florentines but does maintain "che il classicismo stava in realtà in

quelle discussioni come mero pretesto teorico; tutt'al più si potrà concedere ch'esso abbia qualche volta inceppato sia il naturale sviluppo del pensiero estetico che il libero volo dell'ispirazione artistica dei primi autori di drammi in musica" (*La Camerata fiorentina, Vincenzo Galilei*, Milan, 1934 [Istituzioni e monumenti del l'arte musicale italiana, vol. 4], p. xlix, note 2). Only Leo Schrade (*Tragedy in the Art of Music*, pp. 53-54) and Claude Palisca (*Girolamo Mei: Letters on Ancient and Modern Music*, Musicological Studies and Documents, no. 3 [1960], Introduction pp. 40 ff.) recognize the precise nature of the Florentines' "discovery" and the existence of a continuity between their "program" and its results.

30. "... onde, preso animo, e dato miglior forma alla stessa favola, e di nuovo rappresentandola in casa il Sig. Jacopo, fu ella... udita e commendata." "... cominciando io a conoscere quanto simili rappresentazioni in musica siano gradite, ho voluto recare in luce queste due, perchè altri di me più intendenti si ingegnino di accrescere e migliorare sì fatte poesie, di maniera che non abbiano invidia a quelle antiche tanto celebrate da i nobili scrittori." (See dedication to *Euridice*, in Solerti, *Le origini*, p. 41, and note 26 above. Also see Appendix B below, p. 270.)

31. Another indication of the experimental nature of *Dafne* is the fact that no full score survives, which prompts one to wonder if it had ever been printed. This situation contrasts markedly with the immediate nature of the publicity received by *Euridice*, publicity that is still in evidence. On the other hand, the explanation for this difference may lie in the occasional nature of the first performance of *Euridice*—the royal nuptials, for which at least the libretto had souvenir value—whereas the earliest performances of *Dafne*, according to Rinuccini, were played at Corsi's apartments before a private gathering. For a description of the pomp and ceremony attached to the occasion, see Claude Palisca, "The First Performance of 'Euridice'," in the *Twenty-fifth Anniversary Festschrift of Queens College* (New York, 1964).

32. "... io non sia arrivato, con questo modo, fin dove mi pareva di poter giungere, essendo stato freno al mio corso il rispetto della novità..." The preface is reproduced in Solerti, *Le origine*, pp. 45-49, and in translation in Strunk, pp. 373-76. See Appendix B below, pp. 297-99.

33. Solerti (*Albori*, vol. 2, pp. 74-104) reprints the edition of 1600, giving the variants of 1604 and 1608 in the notes. The libretto is also reproduced in Andrea della Corte, *Drammi per musica*, vol. 1, pp. 45-68, and in *Parnaso italiano*, vol. 17, pp. 347-66. William Porter, in his illuminating article, "Peri and Corsi's *Dafne*: Some New Discoveries and Observations," (*JAMS* 18 [1965]: 170-96), alludes to possible predecessors of Rinuccini's prologue when he cites the "many . . . Prologues to musical productions of the time, particularly those written by Rinuccini, . . . in the form either of an ottava rima or with a structure similar to the *Dafne* and *Euridice* Prologues—that is, with four line stanzas requiring the same type of music as an ottava rima" (p. 189). It is interesting to note, however, that among those verses (in Solerti's collection of late 16th- and early 17th-century *poesia musicale*) which antedate *Dafne*, the only ottave rime (ABABABCC) belong to the *Maschere*, and these may be considered to be prologues only insofar as they preceded the dancing. On the other hand, those verses in the 1589 intermedi which served a function similar to the *Dafne* prologue ("Io, che...," or "Siam

noi...,") are not in ottava rima, nor even in regular four-line stanzas, but are usually of mixed seven- and eleven-syllable lines, arranged in irregular patterns. One must conclude that the *Dafne* prologue was quite deliberately new in its structure.

34.   See Appendix A, ll. 21-24 on p. 246 below.

35.   For the text of *Arianna*, see Solerti, *Albori* vol. 2, pp. 143-87 and della Corte, vol. 1, pp. 111-56. The prologue is given in Appendix C below, p. 301.

36.   *Arianna* is actually subtitled "tragedia" by Rinuccini: however, I do not believe it follows, as some writers have assumed, that the earlier libretti were trying to be tragedies, but did not succeed. (See, for example, Marion Schild's treatment of the libretti, especially p. 14.) It merely reflects the change in taste which was beginning to occur over the turn of the century from a preference for uncomplicated pastoral plots to what A. Abert has called "Intriguen-drama" (*Claudio Monteverdi und das musikalische Drama* [Lippstadt, 1954], pp. 100-122).

37.   The libretto of *Narciso* was probably written for the wedding celebrations in Mantua in 1608, but the occasion never materialized, and the wedding was postponed until October of that year. From the prologue, which is assigned to Giulio Romano, we may speculate that the libretto was intended for a setting by Caccini (detto Romano) who was, with Rinuccini, among the members of the newly instituted Accademia degli Elevati in Florence.

38.   See Appendix D below, pp. 303-4. The complete libretto is printed for the first time in Solerti, *Albori*, vol. 2, pp. 189-239.

39.   See Solerti, ibid., pp. 103-4. The prologue was found by Solerti in two versions in the Vatican manuscripts Trivulziano 1006 and Palatino 249.

40.   See the first quatrain, Appendix A below, p. 260. Since the Palatine version of this prologue refers to the libretto of *Arianna* (1608) as well, it was probably written after Striggio's *Orfeo* libretto, in which the prologue is also sung by *La Musica*. But the version in Trivulziano may well be earlier than *Orfeo* (1607).

41.   D. P. Walker feels that "the problem of the 'effetti,' – i.e., the desire to revive the ethical power of ancient music" was the single primary concern of disparate theories of the sixteenth century." See his article, "Musical Humanism in the 16th and Early 17th Centuries" (*Music Review* 2 [1941]: 1-13, 111-21, 220-27, 288-308; 3 [1942] 55-71), p. 3, note 12, upon which this paragraph is largely based.

42.   See the discussion by Claude Palisca in his introduction to *Mei: Letters*, pp. 43 ff. and Chapter Two, below.

43.   *Le istitutioni harmoniche* (Venice, 1558), Proemio, p. 2. A facsimile of this edition was published by Broude Bros. (New York, 1965); the 1573 edition is also available in facsimile (The Gregg Press, 1966).

44. Lowinsky, Review of *Der musikalische Humanismus im 16. und im fruehen 17. Jahrhundert*, by D. P. Walker, in *MQ* 37 (1951): 285.

45. Lowinsky feels that even Walker underestimated the contribution made by 15th- and early 16th-century theory to the revival of ancient musical thought and literature (loc. cit., p. 287).

46. See the articles by Nino Pirrotta, Claude Palisca, D. P. Walker, H. Martin, and Angelo Solerti cited in this chapter and in the bibliography.

47. See Letter no. 1 (ed. Palisca), pp. 90 ff., and cf. Galilei, *Dialogo della musica antica, e moderna* (Florence: Giorgio Marescotti, 1581), pp. 80-90; facsimile editions by Fabio Fano (Rome, 1934) and Broude Bros. (New York, 1967).

48. From an alternative second quatrain of the *La Musica* prologue to Rinuccini's *Dafne*, found in the Trivulziano manuscript and printed by Solerti, *Albori*, vol. 2, p. 103.

49. See, for example, the definition of "practical music" in Giovanni de' Bardi's *Discorso sopra la musica antica e 'l cantar bene* (printed in G. B. Doni, *Lyra Barberina* (Florence, 1763), vol. 2, p. 234, but dating from about 1580; translation as given in Strunk, p. 292): "a combination of words arranged by a poet into verses made up of various metres with respect to the long and the short, these being in their movement now fast and now slow, now low, now high, and now intermediate, approaching the sound of the words of the human voice . . ."

50. These ideas, which are implicit in the prefaces of Peri and Caccini, were stated explicitly by Lorenzo Giacomini in his discourse delivered to the Accademia degli Alterati, *Sopra la purgatione della tragedia* (1586), and by Girolamo Mei in several of his works. See below, p. 18, and Chapter Two.

51. See the younger Bardi's letter to G. B. Doni (1634), reprinted in Solerti, *Le origini*, pp. 143-47, and translated in Strunk, pp. 363-66. Also see Claude V. Palisca, "The *Camerata Fiorentina*: A Reappraisal," *Studi musicali* 1 (1972): 203-35.

52. See Pirrotta, "Rinuccini," in *Encicl. spett.*, vol. 8, col. 1003; and Palisca: "Ottavio Rinuccini, born in 1562, would not likely have been active in the group before around 1582, though the proximity of the Rinuccini palace at 6 Via de' Neri at the corner of Via de' Rustici to that of Bardi on the Via de' Benci would have made his frequent presence likely" ("The *Camerata Fiorentina* . . . ," p. 208).

53. Pirrotta considers the probable performance of Galilei's *Lamentations of Jeremiah* in 1582 to be the last documented manifestation of the Camerata "vera e propria" ("Camerata fiorentina," in *Encicl. spett.*, vol. 2, col. 1564). On the other hand, Caccini remarks that he sang some songs from his *Nuove musiche* at Bardi's Camerata. (Cf. his Preface translated in H. Wiley Hitchcock's edition of *Le nuove musiche* (Madison, Wis., 1970), especially pp. 44-45 and note 84 below.) This could not have been earlier than about 1585 if we may judge by the style of the music – the seventh madrigal in *Le nuove musiche*, "Vedrò il mio sol," is

stylistically very close to Caccini's contribution to the fourth *intermedio* of 1589, "Io che dal ciel cader"—and by Pirrotta's own remark that Caccini's first monodic experiments date from 1585 (cf. "Bardi," in *Encicl. spett.*, vol. 1, col. 1499). Palisca expresses the opinion that Caccini "scored his first successes with the monodic style around 1590, since Bardi moved from Florence to Rome in 1592, and his Camerata did not survive that date" (*Baroque Music* [Englewood Cliffs, New Jersey, 1968], p. 26). Also see his discussion of chronology in "The *Camerata Fiorentina . . . ,*" pp. 203-8.

54. See Palisca, "The Alterati of Florence: Pioneers in the Theory of Dramatic Music," in *New Looks at Italian Opera*, ed. W. W. Austin (Ithaca, New York, 1968), pp. 9-38.

55. On May 2 with Bargagli's *La Pellegrina*, on May 6 with *La Zingara* played by the Comici Gelosi, and on May 13 with Isabella Andreini's *La Pazzia* (A. Einstein, *The Italian Madrigal* [Princeton, 1949] 3 vols., p. 730).

56. "These masques conclude, and in a sense symbolize, a cycle of abstract theorizing and Platonic longing for the music of antiquity . . ." (Pirrotta, "Temperaments and tendencies . . . ," p. 175). Cf. Aby Warburg ("I constumi teatrali per gli intermezzi del 1589," in *Commemorazione della riforma melodrammatica* [Atti dell'accademia del R. Istituto musicale di Firenze, Anno XXXIII], p. 108): "Tutti questi intermezzi... sono pantomime sul gusto antico... sul *potere della musica*, e, come si ha incontestabilmente dalla descrizione del De' Rossi, sono modellati dietro le indicazioni degli antichi scrittori."

57. The text is reproduced by Solerti (*Albori*, vol. 2, pp. 15-42) from Bastiano de' Rossi's *Descrizione dell'aparato e degl'intermedi...* (Florence, 1589), with the variations that appear in Cristofano Malvezzi's print, *Intermedii et concerti fatti per la commedia rappresentata in Firenze* (Venice, 1591), as well as in the volume edited by D. P. Walker and J. Jacquot, *Musique des intermèdes de 'La Pellegrina'* (Centre National de la Recherche Scientifique), Paris, 1963, pp. xxxiii-lviii. The surviving music for the *intermedi* is discussed by Pirrotta in *Li due Orfei*, pp. 237 ff. and by Howard M. Brown, *Sixteenth-Century Instrumentation: The Music for the Florentine Intermedii* (American Institute of Musicology, 1973), pp. 107 ff., among others.

58. In both cases the text seems to have called forth this pleasing dissonance: "dolcezz'accenti o suono" at pp. 42-43, and "Quanto di bello il Ciel intend'e vede" at p. 44.

59. Walker's negative claims are, in my opinion, somewhat exaggerated, when he states that Marenzio's madrigal settings, and those by Malvezzi in the other *intermedi*, are in no way humanistic or expressive (except in their general tendency toward careful declamation); "ni dans l'ensemble, ni dans le détail, la musique ne semble varier selon le sense du texte." He goes on to offer as an explanation for this lack of expressivity the existence of a probable musical tradition for these court spectacles which was necessarily "simple mais riche de sonorité, à laquelle il ne fallait pas trop faire attention—pas d'audaces harmonique, pas de contrepoint ou

de fugues qui serait trop difficiles à comprendre..." See "La musique des intermèdes florentins de 1589" in *Les fêtes de la renaissance* (Paris, 1956), pp. 138-39; also in the edition cited above (note 57), p. xxvi. On the other hand, F. Ghisi argues, "... l'utilisation des choeurs a plusieurs voix semble justifiée par les principes esthétiques même de l'antique tragédie grecque..."; "... l'art du madrigal... était tout ce que l'on pouvait offrir de mieux." See "Les fêtes florentines et les origines de l'opéra," ibid. p. xvii.

60. "... ci volle il poeta in questo intermedio rappresentar la battaglia Pitica nella guisa che c'insegna Giulio Polluce, il quale dice che in rappresentandosi con l'antica musica questa pugna, si dividea in cinque parti... Essendo a noi dalla malvagità e dalla lunghezza del tempo tolto di poter così fatte cose rappresentar con quei modi musici antichi, e stimando il poeta che tal battaglia, rappresentata in scena, dovesse arrecare, si come fece, sommo diletto agli spettatori, la ci rappresentò con la nostra moderna musica, a tutto suo potere sforzandosi, come intendentissimo di quest'arte, e d'imitare e di rassomigliar quell'antica" (*Descrizione...*, p. 44). Unfortunately, the music (a *sinfonia*) corresponding to the battle scene does not survive. Those documents, however, which describe the scene—i.e., de' Rossi's souvenir booklet, some prints by Caracci, and the drawings by the architect Buontalenti—all testify, according to Ghisi, to "un effort d'interprétation admirable des mouvements du choeur dans l'antique tragédie grecque" ("Les fêtes florentines...," p. xvii).

61. Actually, Julius Pollux (2nd century A.D.) ascribes the invention of the Pythian Nome to Sacadas (*Onomasticon* 4. 78), who was victorious with the flute at the Pythian Games at Delphi. However, it is Strabo, writing in the 1st century, who describes the Pythian Nome:

And to the citharoedes they [i.e. the Amphictyons] added [i.e. to the other Delphic Games] both flute-players and citharists who played without singing, who were to render a certain melody which is called the Pythian Nome. There are five parts of it: *angkrousis, ampeira, katakeleusmos, iambi* and *dactyli,* and *syringes.* Now the melody was [described] by Timosthenes, the admiral of the second Ptolemy...; and through this melody he means to celebrate the contest between Apollo and the dragon, setting forth the prelude as *anakrousis,* the first onset of the contest as *ampeira,* the contest itself as *katakeleusmos,* the triumph following the victory as *iambus* and *dactylus,* the rhythms being in two measures, one of which, the dactyl, is appropriate to hymns of praise, whereas the other, the iamb, is suited to reproaches (compare the word "iambize"), and the expiration of the dragon as *syringes,* since with *syringes* players imitated the dragon as breathing its last in hissings.

See *The Geography of Strabo* 9.3.10, trans. H. L. Jones (Loeb Classical Library, London and New York, 1927). I am indebted to Professor Joseph Solodow for this reference.

62. Warburg ("I costumi teatrali..., p. 129) points out the agreement between Bardi's conception of a "rappresentazione mimica con coro" and Francesco Patrici's idea of the delphic festival, wherein "e cantando e sonando fece un coro intorno al tempio d'Apolline Delfico danzare. E questo appo Greci, fu la prima origine del

choro" (*Della poetica, la deca disputata* [Florence, 1586], p. 180). Undoubtedly it was the choreography associated with this scene which was responsible for the sections of triple meter in the opening madrigal. (See *Musique...,* p. 58 ff.) Walker calls particular attention to these sections in denouncing Marenzio's music as inexpressive and nonhumanistic ("Les intermèdes..., p. xxvi).

63.   Further on this aspect of the libretto, and on the political and iconographical relevance of the Apollo and Daphne legend to the Medici court, see my article, "Glorious Apollo: Poetic and Political Themes in the First Opera," *Renaissance Quarterly* 32 (1979): 485-513.

64.   See Galilei's section of Apollo-lore, wherein the god is called "inventor della musica" (*Dialogo,* pp. 142-43).

65.   Warburg comments that this fourth *intermedio,* the only one of the six which is not concerned with ancient music, "conviene molto meno al concetto generale... Questo forse deriva dal non essere stato messo in versi come gli altri da Ottavio Rinuccini..." (p. 108, note 1). D. P. Walker suggests that the dantesque subject of this *intermedio* was introduced in order to permit Bardi to present an infernal scene, which was "de rigeur dans les intermèdes, probablement pour faire contraste avec la joie monotone qui, pour célébrer un mariage royal, était nécessaire dans la plupart des scènes." See "Les intermèdes...," p. xxix. On the tradition of infernal scenes and their instrumentation in the sixteenth century, see Robert L. Weaver, "Sixteenth-Century Instrumentation," *MQ* 47 (1961): 370-71.

66.   Arion is mentioned by practically all the sixteenth-century humanist theorists. Galilei relates how *La Musica* liberated Arion from death as one illustration of the marvelous effects of ancient music (*Dialogo,* p. 86). Especially noteworthy, however, is Patrici's quotation from Suida: "Si dice che fu trovatore del modo Tragico. E primo haver constituito il choro. E cantato il Ditirambo." See his *Della poetica, la deca istoriale* (1586), p. 370.

67.   See *Musique des intermèdes,* p. 98. Both the situation and Peri's treatment of it are remarkably similar to Monteverdi's later setting of Orfeo's petition to the Underworld god, Plutone.

68.   De' Rossi's reproduction of Rinuccini's text for this final *intermedio* differs considerably from the version given by Malvezzi – cf. "Notes critiques..." in the edition, pp. li ff. There Rinuccini's verses for the final *ballo* were replaced by those of Laura Guidiccioni. For a summary of the complexities of the situation, see ibid., pp. xxxiv-xxxv. The fact that Guidiccioni's verses for the dance were reportedly composed after the music has been remarked with surprise by some historians. However, an indication that this was not an unusual procedure may be found in Guarini's notes to the 1602 edition of *Il pastor fido,* wherein the poet describes the composition of the dance chorus in Act III, scene 2, cast in the form of the game "blindman's bluff." According to Guarini, the choreography was composed first, in imitation of the ordinary motions of "il giuoco della cieca." Then "Luzzasco" wrote the music, and finally the poet invented the words, "il che cagionò la diversità del verso, ora di cinque sillabe, ora di sette, ora di otto, ora

di undeci, secondo che gli conveniva servire alla neccessità delle note." Quoted in the edition of *Il pastor fido* by Luigi Fassò (*Teatro del seicento*, Milan [n.d.], La letteratura italiana; storia e testi, vol. 390, pp. 97-323. See Chapter Four, p. 136. Also see Warren Kirkendale, *L'Aria di Fiorenza, id est il Ballo del Gran Duca* (Florence, 1972), pp. 42 ff.

69. "In essa si concertavano e si provavano le cocchiate, le feste, i balli accompagnati da musica, ed ivi nacque per opera di Ottavio Rinuccini, poeta celebre, e di Iacopo Peri, gran maestro d'armonia, lo stile recitativo per uso delle scene" (Carlo Roberto Dati, cited by Solerti, *Albori*, vol. 1, p. 48).

70. This is probably because the subject is usually thought to belong solely to the literary sphere. But see the very limited discussion by G. Maugain, *Ronsard en Italie* (Paris, 1926), Chapitre 3, "L'influence de Ronsard sur l'ode légère et le mélodrame de Chiabrera," and the more penetrating remarks by Carlo Calcaterra in a collection of essays entitled *Poesia e canto, Studi sulla poesia melica italiana e sulla favola per musica* (Bologna, 1951), especially "Discussioni sul Ronsardismo italiano," pp. 191-212.

71. *Il Vecchietti,* or *Del verso eroico volgare*, was printed with the *Vita* in *Dialoghi dell'arte poetica con altre prose e lettere* (Venice, 1830); the elegy, in *Rime* (Rome, 1718) 2: 295.

72. Calcaterra acknowledges this debt and recapitulates his views on the matter thusly: "In altre parole, non è proprio studiare i primi nostri melodrammi sotto l'aspetto ritmico senza tenere presente l'azione particolare che ebbe sopra alcune forme, sopra tutto sui cori, la metrica chiabreresco-ronsardiana" (*Poesia e canto*, p. 195).

73. See Maugain, p. 114.

74. F. Neri cites the more famous fifth strophe of Chiabrera's poem. See *Il Chiabrera e la Pleiade francese* (Turin, 1920), pp. 53-54.

> Se bel rio, se bell'auretta
> Tra l'erbetta
> Sul mattin mormorando erra,
> Se di fiori un praticello
> Si fa bello,
> Noi diciam, ride la terra.
> (*Rime* 2 [1718] : 99)

> Quand je voy dans un jardin
> Au matin
> S'esclorre une fleur nouvelle,
> J'accompare le bouton
> Au teton
> De son beau sein qui pommelle.
> (*Oeuvres* 1 [Paris, 1914] : 198)

Bella Ninfa fuggitiva,
Sciolta e priva
Del mortal tuo nobil velo,
Godi pur pianta novella,
Casta e bella,
Cara al mondo, e cara al cielo.
(*Dafne*, 1600 libretto, ll. 398-403)

75.　According to G. M. Monti (*Le villanelle alla napolitana e l'antica lirica dialettale* [Naples, 1925], pp. 205-8), the rustic Neapolitan villanella, examples of which survived, for instance, in the courtly repertory of songs from Cosimo Bottegari's lutebook, dating from the last quarter of the sixteenth century, contributed to the formation of a new lyric style in Florence. He sees the essence of this new style as the imitation of old popular forms combined with and given new life by French meter, imitated by Chiabrera and Rinuccini from Ronsard and the Pléiade poets.

76.　"La Poesie sans les instrumens ou sans la grace d'une seule ou plusieurs voix n'est nullement agréable, non plus que les instrumens sans estre animez de la mélodie d'une plaisante voix" (*Oeuvres* 7: 16 ff; cited by Maugain, p. 109). In speaking of the development of a new *poesia musicale* around the turn of the century, F. Ghisi defines further the nature of the new concept: "il ne réside pas en fait dans une union entre la poésie et la musique, mais bien dans les rapports entre les divers éléments musicaux inhérents a la parole même, laquelle en vertu de ses accents et de ses inflexions vocaux donne lieu à une déclamation chantée correspondant aux sentiments et aux mouvements expressifs de l'âme" ("Les fêtes florentines...," p. xx). One can see how clearly Ronsard's thought anticipates the prefaces of, for example, Orazio Vecchi and Adriano Banchieri, and the early opera composers.

77.　See Maugain, p. 110: "Entendons par là qu'il les organisait pour être mis en musique."

78.　See Neri, p. 96.

79.　"... i maestri di canto... confessano prontamente che dalla varietà de' versi si presta loro comodità di più allettar l'uditore con loro note" (*Dialoghi*, p. 78).

80.　"... cantarsi è quasi loro qualità naturale; perchè chi recita versi o tanto o quanto non dà loro un aria onde si discompagnano dal comune parlare?" (*Dialoghi*, p. 92). Cf. Ronsard's opinion of short verses, which "sont merveilleusement propres pour la musique.... Quand tu les appelleras lyriques, tu ne leur feras point de tort, tantost les allongeant, tantost les accourcissant, et apres un grand vers, un petit,... au choix de ton oreille, gardant toujours le plus que pourras une bonne cadence de vers propres... pour la musique..."; and his admonition to poets: "Je te veux aussi bien advertir de hautement prononcer tes vers en ta chambre, quand tu les feras, ou plus tost les chanter,... car cela est bien une des principalles parties que tu dois le plus curieusement observer" (*Oeuvres* 7: 60; cited by Maugain, p. 130, note 1).

81. I tend to agree with E. N. Girardi (*Esperienza e poesia in G. Chiabrera* [Milan, 1950]) , who says with reference to the quotation in the text above from *Il Geri*, "è certo una e non l'unica testimonianza di un accentuato interesse ritmico-musicale, ma non va poi considerata più che come corollario giustificativo di una poesia nuova,... che... deve la sua novità anche ad una versificazione fortemente ritmata e facilmente cantabile" (p. 40).

82. See C. Comte and P. Laumonier, "Ronsard et les musiciens du XVIe siècle," *Revue d'histoire littéraire de la France* 7 (1900) 341-81 and J. Tiersot, "Ronsard et la musique de son temps," *Sammelbände der internationalen Musikgesellschaft*, Jahrgang 4 (1902-1903): 70-142.

83. See the list of publications given by Maugain, pp. 119-20.

84. "... assai diversificata da tutte l' altre... prestandomi egli grande occasione d' andar variando." See Caccini's Preface to *Le nuove musiche* (Florence, 1602 [1601, Florentine style]); translation as given by Hitchcock, p. 46. Caccini also implies that the compositions on Chiabrera's texts were among his more recent works. They are nos. 3, 9, and 10 among the *arie*: "Ard'il mio petto misero," "Belle rose purpurine," and "Chi mi confort'ahimè," and "Deh, dove son fuggite" among the madrigals.

85. Pirrotta implies this possibility in discussing the importance for the development of opera of the last decade of the sixteenth century, "... sia che i tempi fossero più maturi con l'inclinare del linguaggio musicale... a una più accentuata espressività, sia che il gioco della emulazione e delle rivalità... stimolasse gli impegni." See "Camerata fiorentina," in *EncicL spett.*, vol. 2, col. 1565.

86. See above, note 26, and Appendix B below, p. 269.

87. *Le Musiche di Jacopo Peri... sopra L'Euridice...* (Florence, 1601 [1600, Florentine style]): "... veduto che si trattava di poesia drammatica e che però si doveva imitar' col canto chi parla... stimai che gli antichi Greci e Romani (i quali, secondo l'opinione di molti, cantavano su le scene le tragedie intere)...." See Appendix B below, p. 297.

88. See "Tragédie et comédie..." p. 295, and "Early Opera and Aria," pp. 80-81. In the latter, Pirrotta upholds his position that Rinuccini's and Peri's assertions were motivated more by practical than theoretical concerns.

89. "... che i poeti Ditirambici, e i nomici usavano tutte tre queste cose insiememente... dove i Tragici e i comici l'usavano separatamente." See *Lezzioni di M. Benedetto Varchi Accademico Fiorentino, Lette da lui publicamanete nell'Accademia fiorentina, sopra diverse materie, poetiche, e filosofiche...* (Florence, 1590), p. 605. Cf. Aristotle, *Poetics* 1447 b: "There are, again, some arts which employ all the means above mentioned – namely, rhythm, tune, and meter. Such are Dithyrambic and Nomic poetry, and also Tragedy and Comedy; but between them the difference is that in the first two cases these means are all employed in combination, in the latter, now one means employed, now another." Quotations

of Aristotle in this study are from *The Works of Aristotle*, trans. E.S. Forster, et al.; ed. W. D. Ross and J. A. Smith (12 vols., Oxford, 1910-1952).

90. "... intende per *sermone soave* quello, nel quale si ritrova numero, armonia, e melodia, significando per numero, e armonia il verso, e per melodia il canto de i Cori, e la musica, benché alcuni vogliono, che per numero si debba intendere quel modo di saltare col quale gli antichi cori Greci, come Latini, usando atti, gesti, e cenni, rappresentavano le Tragedie; dicono ancora alcuni, che di questo luogo si trae manifestissimamente, che nelle Tragedie si ricerca di necessità il verso" (*Lezzioni*, p. 659).

91. It was dated 1543, although not published until 1554. See Weinberg, *HLC* 1: 433 ff.

92. "... Quantunque la tragedia imiti col parlare, con la melodia e col misurato movimento del corpo che è chiamato numero, non gli usa però ella tutti insieme in tutte le sue parti, ma separatamente. Perocchè nel prologo non ha luogo se non il parlare. Nel primo coro alle volte la melodia e il numero.... Agli altri cori conviene solo il verso e la melodia." See *Discorso intorno al comporre delle comedie e delle tragedie*, pp. 9-10.

93. "Percioche il choro non suona ne balla rappresentando attione alcuna, come presuppone Aristotele." See his *Poetica d'Aristotele vulgarizzata et sposta* (Vienna, 1570), p. 33.

94. See, for example, *Poetica*, p. 146: "Nel quinto e ultimo luogo è da riporre la melodia... con tutto che sia parte molto difficile da essercitare, & dilettevole da vedere & da udire, non pertenendo alla tragedia a modo niuno per far vedere la favola, la sentenzia, ei costumi... Ma questa parte è stata introdotta non per necessità niuna, ma per diletto, & per far pruova, quanto quelle arti possano fare vedere, & udire con le figure, o co movimenti del corpo, o con le voci, o co suoni la favola, & la sentenzia, e i costumi."

95. See Palisca, *Mei: Letters*, Introduction, p. 31, and "The *Camerata Fiorentina* . . . ," p. 221.

96. The manuscript in the Vatican Latin collection (5323) is entitled *Hieronymi Meij Fiorentini De modis musicis antiquorum ad Petrum Victoriarum Libri iiii*. The relevant passage is from the fourth book (separately paginated in the manuscript), p. 18: "Melicorum poetarum permista genera extiterunt, qui omnes tum ab instrumentorum diversitate tum a suo poemate appellari consueverunt. In citharoedes enim et aulaedos primum sunt dispersiri; quod si ad citharum aut lyram, ad Tibiam isti, quam aulos graeci dicunt sua poemata canere instituerunt. Hic vero illud non est omittendum Tragoedos et Comoedos perpetua Tibijs usos fuisse: quod etiam et de satyris, ni fallor, est existimandum."

97. As early as 1577 Mei's theory was discussed by Giorgio Bartoli in a letter to Lorenzo Giacomini, who had probably solicited his opinion. But Bartoli, confused by Aristotle's own lack of consistency on this subject, ultimately concluded that the practice of singing the entire tragedy could not have been very successful.

Bartoli's views are summarized by Claude Palisca, "The Alterati of Florence: Pioneers in the Theory of Dramatic Music," in *New Looks at Italian Opera*, pp. 33-34.

98. See *Mei: Letters*, p. 145.

99. Palisca aptly calls the work, "a humanist's introduction to music."   See *Mei: Letters*, Introduction, p. 79.

100. "... ne quali due Tuoni parlavano continuamente le persone comiche e tragiche, & così parimente quella della Satira, al suono della Tibia nella scena del Teatro recitando i poemi loro" (*Dialogo*, p. 63).

101. "... gli antichi Strioni Greci & Latini, recitavano le Comedie e le Tragedie loro al suono della Tibia, & della Cithara; la onde ne conveniva adoperare in tale affare, della acute, delle gravi & delle mediocri, secondo la qualità delle persone che in esse intervenivano" (*Dialogo*, p. 100).

102. "STR.   Voi mi havete piu volte detto, che gli antichi cantavano al suono della Tibia & della Cithara, le Tragedie & Comedie loro, ne m'havete per ancora mostrato qual sia l'autorità che vi hà mosso à dire & creder questo...

BAR.   Havete mille ragioni; hor avvertite che le Tragedie, & le Comedie fussero veramente (nella maniera che avete inteso) cantate da Greci, ve lo dice (oltre a li altri degni di fede) Aristotile nella particola dell'harmonia, al Problema quarantanove.   Vero è che nella Poetica, quando viene alla diffinitione della Tragedia, pare che egli scordi in alcuna cosa da quel primo parere" (*Dialogo*, p. 145).

103. See *Mei: Letters*, pp. 178 ff., and Palisca's notes 35 and 36.

104. The Problem (922b. 10-27) is numbered 48 in the complete edition, *The Works of Aristotle*, ed. Ross and Smith, 12 vols. (Oxford, 1910-52).

105. "Da che si comprende, che tutta la Tragedia, che di attori era composta, e di choro si cantava." (*La deca istoriale* [Ferrara, 1586], p. 285.)

106. Weinberg mentions these meetings in "Argomenti di discussione letteraria...," entry of 12 June 1584.

107. Venice, 1592. See p. 5.

108. "Perche al canto è necessario il verso perciò in versi le composero, e perche i Toscani senza alcun canto (eccetto che ne' chori) le rappresentano, da lor deono essere spiegate in Prosa" (p. 6).   Michele later makes a remark which is interesting and ironic in light of aesthetic developments by the end of the century.   For the ancients, he admits, "il canto era talmente caro, e gratioso à gli ascoltanti, che con lui recitavano le Tragedie intere, et hor che ciò facesse sommo fastidio, et indicibile noia arrecarebbe" (p. 37).

109.   "Alcuni attribuiscono il canto delle Tragedie al choro, nel quale cantavano gl'Histrioni; ma io à tutte le parti della Tragedia lo riferisco; percioche ove è il numero del verso, è necessario, che vi sia il canto" (p. 6).

110.   A manuscript attributed to Giacomini in the Riccardiana collection in Florence is mentioned by Palisca, "The Alterati of Florence," pp. 22-23.

111.   *Lezione... di Lorenzo Giacomini Tebalducci Malespini... sopra la purgatione della Tragedia.* The discourse was published in 1597 (*Orationi e discorsi di L. Giacomini*) and again in *Prose fiorentine raccolte dallo Smarrito* (Florence, 1729), vol. 4, part 2, pp. 212-50. For a discussion of the discourse, see Chapter Two, below.

112.   In the preface to the 1608 score of *Dafne* by Marco da Gagliano, the composer reaffirms the idea that Rinuccini desired principally to emulate the style used in performing the ancient tragedies, rather than their form or content. "Dopo l'avere più e più volte discorso intorno alla maniera usata dagli antichi in rappresentare le lor tragedie, come introducevano i cori, se usavano il canto e di che sorte, e cose simili, il signor Ottavio Rinuccini si diede a compor la favola di *Dafne*." See Solerti, *Le origini*, p. 80; the preface is also reprinted in Solerti, *Albori*, vol. 2, pp. 67-73.

Chapter 2

1.   From Rinuccini's dedication to *Euridice* (italics mine). See Chapter One above, notes 1 and 24, and Appendix B below, pp. 269-70.

2.   viii.5. 1340a. 19-24. The translations of Aristotle used throughout this chapter are taken from the edition by W.D. Ross and J.A. Smith, *The Works of Aristotle*, 12 vols. (Oxford, 1910-52).

3.   In the tracts of the Peripatetic school following Aristotle however, especially in the *Problems*, may be seen a new awareness of the physics and physiology of aesthetic perception. See Edward A. Lippman, *Musical Thought in Ancient Greece* (New York and London, 1964), pp. 142 ff.

4.   *Politics* viii.5. 1340b. 1-4. Lippman (pp. 129-30) points out how, generally, the melodic types further the various musical functions — "moral" for the benefit of instruction, "enthusiastic" for purgation, and "active" for noble diversion and relaxation. See below, pp. 23-24.

5.   *Politics* viii.7. 1342a. 5-15. Indeed, Aristotle seems to have culled this function from a passage in Plato's *Laws* (vii. 790-91) in which he describes how the frenzied affection of the Bacchantes became quieted by the violent motion of external rhythm. Plato did apparently admit the enthusiastic Phrygian mode because of its ability to stir up bellicose affections; it was the enfeebling Mixolydian and the sensuous tones of the aulos to which he objected. See *Politics* 1342a. 32-1342b. 7 and Lippman, p. 71.

6.   *Politics* viii.7. 1341b. 37-39.

7. *A History of Literary Criticism.* . . . See Chapter One above, note 3.

8. *The Age of Criticism: The Late Renaissance in Italy* (Ithaca, New York, 1962), pp. 205-300.

9. Hathaway considers it "the most exhaustive . . . to be found in sixteenth-century Italian criticism" (p. 251).

10. "Il Mesto [i.e., Giacomini.].. lesse una lezione; le Proposizioni furono se il Furor divino è cagione efficiente della Poesia e se nel Poeta l'arte è di più Momento o la Natura." See Weinberg, "Argomenti...," cited under the date "10 luglio 1584."

11. Patrici's erudite treatise was not actually published until 1586, but according to the Diary of the Alterati, one of its members — viz., Count Giovanni de' Bardi — had just returned from the northern cities of Mantua and Ferrara where he had visited Patrici. (See page 18 above, and note 106 to Chapter One.) The first chapter of *Della Poetica: La deca disputata* is devoted to a defense of the "furore poetico."

12. Hathaway remarks the importance of Giacomini's tenet, recorded in the 1586 treatise on purgation, but implicit in his earlier work, that "the motive force" in the effect achieved by tragedy is "the natural sympathy that exists between people (*la naturale simpatia*), for the doctrine of natural sympathy was the keystone in the arch of the psychologizing done in the Renaissance . . ." (p. 255).

13. Giacomini's 1584 lecture was later published in *Orationi e discorsi* . . . (Florence, 1597); my summary is based on the one given by Claude Palisca, "The Alterati of Florence: Pioneers in the Theory of Dramatic Music," in *New Looks at Italian Opera*, ed. W. W. Austin (Ithaca, N.Y., 1968), pp. 22-23; see also Weinberg, *HLC* 1 (1961): 322-24.

14. *Dialogo*, p. 89 (translation in Strunk, p. 317).

15. Ibid.; Galilei goes on to express his belief that "every brute beast has the natural faculty of communicating its pleasure and its pain of body and mind, at least to those of its own species, nor was voice given to them by nature for any other purpose" (Strunk, p. 318).

16. "Ma perchè... anzi sono andato sempre investigando più novità a me possibile, pur che la novità sia stata atta a poter meglio conseguire il fine del musico, cioè di dilettare e muovere l'affetto dell'animo, ho trovato essere maniera più affettuosa...." Cf. Preface to *Le nuove musiche* (1602), reprinted in Solerti, *Le origini*, p. 63; also see Hitchcock's translation, p. 49. (The translation by Playford which appears in Strunk is archaic and even unreliable in places.) In view of Caccini's articulation of the aim of music, it is interesting to note that he placed at the head of his collection a setting of "Movetevi à pietà" ("Be ye moved to pity").

17. Caccini felt that the excesses and abuses of contemporary singing stemmed from the fact that "il musico non ben possiede prima quello che egli vuol cantare: e se ciò fosse, indubitamente non incorrerebbe in cotali errori..." (in Solerti, *Le origini*, p. 61). Cf. Hitchcock, p. 48.

18. See Chapter One above, note 111. My references are to the edition in *Prose fiorentine...*, vol. 4, part 2, pp. 212-50.

19. See part three, "A Purgation of Passions," pp. 205-300; on Giacomini in particular, pp. 251-59.

20. See "The Alterati of Florence...," pp. 24 ff.

21. "E poema nella più propria significazione definiamo: *imitazione con parlare favoloso ridotto in versi di azione umana* (sotto nome di azione comprendiamo anco gli affetti, e le operazioni interne) *fatta secondo l'arte poetica, atta a purgare, ad ammaestrare, a dar riposo, o nobile diporto" (Sopra la purgatione*, pp. 219-20).

22. "... diciamo essa doversi usare non per un fine solo, ma per molti, secondo la diversità de' poemi, e degli uditori, i quali fini tutti comprendiamo sotto nome di giovamento, poichè ed il riposo, e l'allentamento dell'animo da' negozi, e dalle fatiche, e 'l nobile diporto della mente per la conoscenza dell'esquisitezza dell'opera con Aristotile al giovamento riduciamo, siccome anco la purgazione, e l'ammaestramento. Quei due primi fini sono a tutte le poesie comuni, ma uno pertiene agli uomini intelligenti, l'altro indeterminatamente a ciascuno; gli altri due s'appropriano a speziali poesie, poichè la purgazione non ha luogo, se non dove si esprimono gagliardi affetti, ed alcuni poemi è certo non aver forza di giovare alla virtù, e di migliorare il costume" (ibid., p. 221). Cf. *Politics* viii.7. 1341b. 35-40.

23. See *The Age of Criticism*, p. 253.

24. "... tanto coloro, i quali sono gagliardamente volti alla mestizia, alla compassione, ed al timore, quanto universalmente tutti gli uomini, ricevon dalle armonie, che vagliono a destar affetti, quale è la Frigia, e la Mixolidia, di cui era proprio render l'anima ristretta, e per poco addolorata, e da canzoni purganti conformi alle armonie, ricever, dico, purgazione, sfogamento, ed alleggiamento non dannoso, anzi salutevole con diletto" (*Sopra la purgatione*, p. 233).

25. Ibid., pp. 242-43.

26. "E questa purgazione, ed alleggiamento fa ella con qualche diletto... il quale, come usava dire Posidonio, referendolo Galeno, ne porge questa utilità, che satolla le passioni dell'animo da dogliosi affetti ingombrato" (ibid., p. 230).

27. "... e spiritali movimenti (per usare la parola di Dante) ed operazioni dell'anima, in quanto dopo aver conosciuto l'oggetto, lo vuole, e si spiega, o non lo vuole, e l'aborrisce" (*Sopra la purgatione*, pp. 235-36). Compare this definition and the passage following it, for example, with Galen's statement that "there must exist in almost all parts of the animal a certain inclination toward, or, so to speak, an appetite for their own special quality, and an aversion to, or, as it were, a hatred of the foreign quality. And it is natural that when they feel an inclination they should attract, and that when they feel aversion they should expel." See *On the Natural Faculties* iii.6 (tr., A.J. Brock [London, 1916], p. 249). The tendency to "physicize" biology and to "biologize" psychology is evidently found everywhere

in Galen's works. (Cf. ibid., Introduction, p. xxvii, et passim.) On his importance for the sixteenth century, see p. 28 and note 43.

28. "...[nel cerebro], ove i troppo ardenti spiriti del cuore si riducono a temperamento, ed a perfezione, e dove si fa l'immaginare, e 'l vedere [etc.] ..., e onde per li nervi, quasi canali, si compartiscono le virtù del sentimento, e d'ogni movimento volontario. Questa potenza se riceve gli oggetti convenevoli a se, gli abbraccia, e sente diletto, se sconvenevoli, gli aborrisce, e pruova dolore.... il piacere, e 'l dolore, i quali si ritrovano nella prima apprensione dell'oggetto avantichè l'anima lo desideri, o speri, o tema, della mischianza de' quali atti si compongono gli altri affetti, che non son semplici, nè puri" (*Sopra la purgatione*, pp. 226-27).

29. "Il calore, la sottigliezza, e l'agilità degli spiriti ci preparano ad affetti giocondi; il perchè i giovani più de' vecchi si muovono ad essi, ed il cibo, ed il vino riscaldando, e destando gli spiriti, e rinvigorendo il corpo, partorisce letizia. Dall'altra parte l'aggravamento della parte sensitiva per li vapori torbidi, ed impuri, e la diminuzione del calore interno preparano a mestizia, ed a timore, e ci fanno parere pigri, tardi, ed inutili..." (ibid., p. 229). Cf. Aristotle's *Rhetoric* ii. 12 and 13, in which the characters of young and old men, respectively, are dissected. Concerning the young, Aristotle says, "They are hot-tempered and quick-tempered. . . . They are sanguine; nature warms their blood as though with excess of wine. . . . The hot temper prevents fear. . . ." Of old men he declares, "They are cowardly . . . ; unlike that of the young, who are warm-blooded, their temperament is chilly; fear is, in fact, a form of chill. . . . They do not feel their passions much, and their actions are inspired less by what they do feel than by the love of gain." In the following section, Chapter 14, Aristotle describes men in their prime as having a temperament free from the extremes of the young and old, and a character midway between the two.

30. *Sopra la purgatione*, p. 229.

31. "... per rimuovere cioè la mala disposizione, che affligge ristringendo, ed aggravando la parte sensitiva, e 'l cuore principalmente, che, come pieno di spiriti, e di calore, più patisce; onde per iscuotere il dolore, e per allargarsi, e liberarsi dall'affanno si muove, e muovesi il polmone, e gli altri organi della voce, e fansi strida, e gemiti se dall'intelletto non sono impediti" (ibid., p. 230).

32. D. P. Walker acknowledges the widespread concern among musical humanists for both these aspects of ancient music. Cf. "Musical Humanism. . . ," p. 3, note 12: ". . . The keystone of nearly all these theories is the problem of the 'effetti,' – i.e., the desire to revive the ethical power of ancient music;" and on p. 8: "The subjection of music to verse was a perversion of the union believed to have existed in antiquity." Also see pp. 7-8 and note 41 of Chapter One.

33. "E questo... perchè il corso del ragionare... non paresse in un certo modo ballare al moto del basso, e principalmente nelle cose o meste o gravi, richiedendo per natura l'altre più liete più spessi movimenti...." (See the preface to *Euridice* [1601], in Appendix B below, pp. 297-98.

34. "Et avuto riguardo a que' modi et a quegli accenti che nel dolerci, nel rallegrarci et in somiglianti cose ci servono, feci muovere il basso al tempo di quegli, or più or meno, secondo gli affetti...." By *modi* Peri surely intended those modes of speech, enumerated by the rhetoricians and grammarians, which are determined particularly by the condition of the verb, and which indicate in a general sense the disposition of the speaker. Cf. the meaning given by the *Vocabolario degli Accademici della Crusca* (5th printing, Florence, 1863 ff.), vol. 10 (1907), where the following excerpt from Benedetto Buomattei (*Della lingua toscana*, Florence, 1760) is quoted in illustration: "Sappiamo in oltre che gli affetti umani son varj; perchè uno semplicemente ragiona, altri ragionando comanda, altri nelle parole dimostra voglia; ed ecco onde viene il *modo*" (p. 413, under entry 23). By extension of its grammatical meaning, the word *modo* could also be taken for "Una determinata forma o disposizione di pensieri o di parole," and an example of its rhetorical usage is quoted from Bartolomeo Cavalcanti (*La Retorica*, Venice, 1559 [italics mine]): "il modo... accompagna la cosa... in tali maniere, quali sono: apertamente, ascosamente, con violenza, con fraude, *lentamente, con prestezza*, umilmente, con superbia, allegramente, con dolore, ed altrimenti: da i quali modi si potranno trarre argomenti massimamente per fare la cosa più o meno verisimile, degno di lode o di biasimo, e per innalzarla e per abbassarla" (*Vocabolario*, p. 412, entry 19). Finally, the word could mean, simply, "Locuzione, frase" (see ibid., entry 18. For meanings of *accenti*, see below, notes 71 and 72.

35. "... intendo per conseguenza che nelle musiche ariose, o canzonette a ballo, invece di essi affetti, si debba usar solo la vivezza del canto, il quale suole essere trasportato dall'aria istessa, nella quale... si deve lasciare l'istessa vivezza, e non porvi affetto alcuno che abbia del languido" (*Le nuove musiche*, Preface; in Solerti, *Le origini*, p. 63).

36. *Les passions de l'âme* was written in 1646 but not published until 1649 in Amsterdam.

37. See D. P. Walker, "Ficino's *Spiritus* and Music," *Annales musicologiques* 1 (1953): 131-50.

38. See pp. 33-34.

39. Quoted and translated by Walker from the third book of Ficino's *De triplici vita: De vita coelitus comparanda* 3, xxi ("Ficino's *Spiritus*...," p. 139).

40. Zarlino expounded Ficino's theory quite fully in his *Istitutioni harmoniche* of 1558 (1, iv and vii; 2, viii), introducing at the same time a confusion of medical and Christian *spiritus*. (See Walker, ibid., p. 149.) In practice, however, Ficino's Platonic emphasis on beauty, virtue, and universal harmony led the composers and theorists of Zarlino's generation to dilute the humanistic formulation of the function of music into a much less exacting one – edification of the soul through the senses. Cf. Palisca, *Girolamo Mei: Letters*, Introduction, p. 43: "That modern music lacked the emotional power of ancient music seemed no serious indictment to him. . . . Besides, sensuous qualities were most vital for Zarlino, because to him the function of music was basically constructive recreation – *docere delectando*. . . ."

41. Of Aristotle, *On the Motion of Animals* and *Generation of Animals* are cited particularly, and Galen's commentary on Hippocrates and Plato; Cf. "Ficino's *Spiritus...*," p. 133.

42. Quoted and translated from *De triplici vita* by Walker, ibid.

43. *De naturalibus facultatibus* (1523), *Definitiones medicae* (1529), *De temperamentis* (1538), and *De elementis* (1558) seem to be among the most relevant examples of the revival editions of this extremely prolific disciple of Hippocrates. Also see notes 27 and 41 to the present chapter.

44. See "Ficino's *Spiritus...*," p. 147.

45. See p. 31 ff.

46. *The Age of Criticism*, p. 259.

47. "Just as the body is said to be purged when the bad humors are drawn off or corrected, so also poetry purges the mind by removing excess passions or by correcting them by their contraries, both melancholy passions by means of music and laughter and insolence in prosperous turns of fortune by means of pity and fear with the example of good men." The translation of this passage from *Discorsi poetici* is Hathaway's; see ibid., p. 277.

48. See his seventh discourse, "On Tragedy," which is summarized in Hathaway, pp. 278-84.

49. "... come possa quella tragedia... compire questa purgazione, non rappresentando caso doloroso, onde la compassione si tragga; e la risposta non è malagevole a darsi,... perciocchè diciamo anche in tragedia tale aver luogo il compatimento, e lo spavento, poichè il male vicino, che senza speranza di scampo è per accadere, dall'anima è considerato come presente, e come tale muove compassione" (*Sopra la purgatione...*, p. 249).

50. Guarini had a similarly medicinal and humoral view of purgation, and likened it to the process by which physicians, "who when they wish to purge, say, choler . . . intend . . . to take away merely that part which by overflowing its natural bounds corrupts the symmetry of life, from which infirmity arises." In another passage he commented that tragicomedy purges melancholy "in the same way that music purges that emotion which, as Aristotle teaches us, the Greeks called *enthousiasmos* or in the way Sacred Scripture tells us David drove out, with the harmony of his sound, the evil spirits from Saul. . . ." (Both these passages, from the *Compendio della poesia tragicomica* [1601], are quoted in translation by Hathaway, pp. 268 and 294.) Also on Guarini, see p. 30 and note 55.

51. "... essendo il compatire atto di virtù, e sendo ogni operatione secondo la virtù, o a la virtù somigliante per natura gioconda, può anche per questo riguardo, la compassione de la Tragedia apportare diletto" (*Sopra la purgatione*, p. 240).

52. Tasso's most complete exposition of his view of purgation is recorded in a late work, *Del giudizio sovra la Gerusalemme*, summarized by Hathaway, pp. 260-63.

53. In a more youthful dialogue, *La Cavalletta, ovvero Della poesia toscana*, Tasso disapproved of what he called "degenerate music which has become soft and effeminate," and added, "I do not blame sweetness and grace, but I should like to see them combined with moderation." (See Einstein, *The Italian Madrigal*, vol. 1, p. 220.) As Einstein points out (ibid., p. 216) music was most often called *suave* and *dolce* – i.e. soothing and sweet – in the sixteenth century. The fact that a humanist as late as Giovanni de' Bardi could say "la Musica altro che dolcezza non è; che chi cantar vuole, conviene, che dolcissima Musica, e dolcissimi modi ben regolati dolcissimamente canti" (*Discorso sopra la musica antica*, in G.B. Doni, *Lyra Barberina*, vol. 2, p. 248), is further evidence, I think, of the corruption of Platonic ideas concerning music's function, and the shift in emphasis from ethical qualities to sensual ones. See note 40 of the present chapter.

54. ". . . with both kinds of laments, however, I have wanted to purge the passions, following rather the judgment of Aristotle and the other Peripatetics than that of Plato, of the Academicians, and of the Stoics and Epicureans, who . . . seem to agree concerning what pertains to the evacuation of the emotions and to the tranquility of the mind." (Quoted in translation by Hathaway, p. 260.) It is significant and extremely interesting that Galilei's first experiments in the *stile rappresentativo*, which were to set the tone for the new style, were laments – one from Dante (Count Ugolino's lament from *Inferno*, Canto xxxiii), and the other a portion of the Lamentations of Jeremiah from the liturgy of Holy Week. (See Pietro de' Bardi's letter to Doni, reprinted in Solerti, *Le origini*, pp. 143-47; translation in Strunk, p. 364.)

55. "... dico che se mi sarà domandato che fine è quello della Tragicomedia, dirò, ch'è d'imitare con apparato scenico un azione finta e mista di tutte quelle parti Tragiche, & Comiche che verisimilmente, e con decoro possano star insieme corrette sotto una sola forma dramatica, per fino di purgare col diletto la mestizia de gli ascoltanti" (*Il Verrato* [Ferrara, 1588], fol. 29 v.). Further on Guarini's theories, see Hathaway, pp. 268 ff.; Weinberg, *HLC* 2: 656 ff., and 1074 ff.; Marvin T. Herrick, *Tragicomedy* (Urbana, Illinois, 1962), pp. 130-42; and N.J. Perella, "The Autonomy of Poetry in Battista Guarini's Polemical Tracts," *Forum Italicum* 7 (1973): 338-52.

56. "... ho trovato essere maniera più affettuosa lo intonare... la prima voce scemandola, però che l'esclamazione, che è mezzo più principale per muovere l'affetto (et l'esclamazione propriamente altro non è, che nel lassare della voce rinforzandola alquanto)... spesse volte diviene acuto, et impatibile all'udito, come in più occasioni ho udito io. Indubitamente adunque, come affetto più proprio per muovere, miglior effetto farà l'intonara la voce scemandola, che crescendola" (*Le nuove musiche*, Preface, in Solerti, *Le origini*, pp. 63-64). Cf. Hitchcock, p. 49.

57. See above, pp. 24 and 29.

58. For example, cf. Caccini's statement, "mi venne anco pensiero, *per sollevamento tal volta degli animi oppressi,* comporre qualche canzonetta a uso di aria..." (*Le nuove musiche,* Preface, in Solerti, *Le origini,* p. 58; italics mine).

59. A few examples that come to mind are Guidotti's relation of how Vittoria Archilei "mosse meravigliosamente a lacrime" in her role in Cavalieri's *Disperazione di Fileno,* performed in Florence in 1590 (Preface to *Rappresentazione di Anima et di Corpo* [1600], reprinted in Solerti, *Le origini,* p. 5); Cavalieri's own description of the success of his *Rappresentazione* in Rome, in a letter in which he boasted that his music moved the audience "to tears and laughter and pleased them greatly," (see Palisca, "Musical Asides in the Diplomatic Correspodence of Emilio de' Cavalieri," *MQ* 49 [1963]: 351); and Vittoria Archilei's rendition of Arianna's lament in the Monteverdi-Rinuccini production of 1608, reported first by Marco da Gagliano in the Preface to the readers of his *Dafne* score (reprinted in Solerti, *Le origini,* p. 82) and many times thereafter repeated by writers on music.

60. See Solerti, *Le origini,* p. 5: "... questa sorte di musica da lui rinovata commova a diversi affetti, come a pietà et a giubilo, a pianto et a riso, et ad altri simili..."

61. Ibid., p. 81: "... non può interamente comprendere la gentilezza e la forza delle sue arie chi non l'ha udite cantare da lui medesimo, però che egli dà loro una sì fatta grazia e di maniera imprime in altrui l'affetto di quelle parole, che è forza e piangere e rallegrarsi secondo che egli vuole."

62. "... i quali concetti vestiti prima dal Poeta di scelte parole à bisogno tale opportune, gli esprimeva poscia il Musico in quel Tuono, con quelli accenti, e gesti, con quella quantità e qualità di suono, e con quel rithmo che conveniva in quell'attione à tal personaggio" (*Dialogo,* p. 90; translation in Strunk, p. 319).

63. The prologue in full is reproduced below in Appendix B, pp. 271-72. My translation appears in Chapter One above, p. 4.

64. See *Sopra la purgatione,* p. 237. Mei's judgment on purgation is expressed in the fourth book of *De modis musicis antiquorum* (1573), pp. 35 ff.

65. See pp. 33-34 and note 86.

66. Both treatises exist only in manuscript form (cf. Palisca, *Girolamo Mei: Letters,* p. 196). The sources to which I refer in the following discussion are 1) Florence, Biblioteca Nazionale Centrale, Magliabecchiana, Cl. 6, cod. 34 ("Trattato di Girolamo Mei sopra la prosa toscana, e della composizione delle parole in due libri"), an autograph Ms. in 72 folios, and 2) Biblioteca Riccardiana, Ms. Ricc. 2597 ("Del Verso Toscano Trattato del Signor Hieronimo Mei Gentilhuomo fiorentino distinto in tre libri"), a seventeenth-century copy in 91 folios. My attention was directed to these sources by Prof. Palisca, who generously let me use his microfilms of both works.

67. See Palisca's Introduction to his edition of the letters, *Girolamo Mei ...,* p. 21.

68. Cf. Letter no. 1 (8 May 1572), pp. 118-22: "Nota di scrittori di musica che ancor oggi si trovano et che io ho veduti."

69. *Del verso toscano*, fols. 4r-5r and fols. 22r-23v.

70. Certain humanists dissented from this position maintaining on the contrary that the rhythm of Italian verse forms was determined by the alternation of long and short syllables. Thus, for example, Giorgio Bartoli, in a work dedicated to Giacomini, *Trattato degl'elementi del parlar toscano* (Florence, 1584), stated, taking the eleven-syllable line as an example, "... non pare, che nasca da l'acutezza di sillabe... ma da la lunghezza per la evidente dimora fatta maggiore che altrove, su la quarta e su la decima sempre lunghe, o su la sesta e su la decima pur necessariamente lunghe..." (pp. 48-9). Although my limited knowledge in this area does not permit me to say how widespread this opinion was, I note with interest that Bardi warned contemporary singers "di non guastare mai il verso cantando, facendo la lunga breve, e la breve lunga..." (*Discorso sopra la musica antica*, p. 245; the passage is omitted in Strunk), and Caccini inveighed against "la moltitudine di passaggi, tanto nelle sillabe brevi quanto lunghe" (*Le nuove musiche*, Preface; in Solerti, *Le origini*, p. 57). The rigorous historian Doni, however, maintained that "il Ritmo de' nostri versi si regge solo dagli accenti, come da essi si formano anco i versi, e che le sillabe accentuate si reputano come lunghe, e ad esse corrispondono.... E perciò vana si dee reputare la fatica di quelli, che nelle tre lingue corrotte... hanno cercato di rimettere in uso i versi misurati all'antica" (*Discorso della ritmopeia de' versi latini e della melodia de' cori tragichi*, in *Lyra Barberina*, vol. 2, p. 205). In view of both Mei's and Bartoli's theories, Walker's statement that "no 16th-century writer on the meter of modern verse mentions any rhythmic principle other than that of a fixed number of syllables and that of the caesura" ("Musical Humanism . . . ," p. 303, note 192) requires modification.

71. "Qualunche sillaba ha il suo accento; il quale, se l'innalza, si chiama acuto, se l'abbassa, grave, e se l'innalza e abbassa, circumflesso" (Benedetto Varchi, *L'Ercolano*, Florence, 1570). Varchi's definition is quoted in the *Vocabolario della Crusca* (vol. 1, p. 94) where the next meaning given is "E per Tono di voce esprimente i diversi affetti dell'animo."

72. This is still the primary meaning given by the *Grande dizionario della lingua italiana* (ed. Salvatore Battaglia, Editrice Torinese, 1961), the most recent etymological dictionary of Italian, apparently still in progress: "Elevazione della voce, che conferisce un tono più intenso a una determinata sillaba nel corpo della parola (accènto tonico)" (vol. 1, p. 72). In the early Baroque period, *accenti* also referred to a particular group of ornaments which developed out of the sixteenth-century tradition of free ornamentation. See Doni, *Trattato*, Chapter 24, pp. 69 ff., where the meaning is equated with "strascino: un passeggetto breve vocale, o instrumentale, che non ripercuote le voci."

73. *Del verso...*, fol. 52r.

74. The early sixteenth century had witnessed a revival of Platonic and Pythagorean formulations of the Beautiful and the Good in terms of exact relationships of numbers and parts. At the same time that Leonardo and Michelangelo were

deriving their empirical canon of proportions of the human body, works such as *De divina proportione* (1509) by Luca Paciolo were composed. (Cf. Benedetto Croce, *Aesthetic* [8th ed., trans. Douglas Ainslie, 1963], pp. 179-80.) Thus, Mei was not innovating in his endeavor to provide an aesthetic basis for Tuscan poetry at least partially rooted in neo-Pythagorean mathematics, and obviously took as his model Augustine's *De musica*, a work which he probably encountered in one or more manuscript versions during his early researches in Rome.

75. "... è fatto il verso principalmente per esser' sentito e approvato dall'udito. Per la qualcosa essendo il sensorio, che è ministro del sentimento, à chi quello appartiene, cosa formata e' materiale, fà di bisognio à tutti gli obbietti suoi insieme con la tal' forma di più anche della materia conveniente; la quale oltrà l'esser' tale e' talmente formata, hà necessità d'esser tanta, quanta ella possa esser proporzionata per il fine, à che la sua tutta essenza debba servire, all'orecchie altrui" (*Del verso...*, fol. 53v). Cf. some of Descartes' observations in his *Compendium* on music, a handbook which begins in a rather unorthodox way with a section on rhythmics: "Remarquez premièrement que tous les sens sont capables de quelque plaisir. Secondement, que ce plaisir des sens consiste en une certaine proportion et correspondance de l'objet avec les sens;... En quatrième lieu, cet objet est plus aisément aperçu par les sens dont les parties moins différentes entre elles. En cinquième lieu, ces parties-là ont moins de différence entre elles lesquelles il y a plus de proportion..." (*Oeuvres*, ed V. Cousin [Paris, 1824], vol. 5, pp. 446-47).

76. "... quella forma di verso si debbe allhor' estimar' più perfetta, che meglio ne sia sentita, per qualsivoglia sua proprietà, sia ella ò di grandezza ò d'altro, far lo più accomodamente e' più quasi vivamente apparire" (*Del verso...*, fol 55r).

77. "... il verso che nasce dà quelle [proporzioni], non essendo di tanta quantità, che l'orecchie se ne soddisfacciano à pieno, apparisce al senso, che n'è proprio giudice, non sò come quasi mozzo, e per la velocità sua di troppa leggerezza" (ibid.).

78. "... in queste... si tratti, ò di cose leggiere, ò almen' leggiermente, come... nelle frottole; ò di cose leggiadre e' delicate, come nelle canzoni; e non di gravi, stabili, e (come si dice) di nervo" (ibid.).

79. Ibid., fol. 55v.

80. Ibid., fol. 56v. See Chapter Four, below.

81. "... L'acutezza e' gravità d'accento son' nella voce due effetti, i quali nascono il primo dalla velocità, e' l'altro dalla lentezza del moto, che la produce, e' son' trà sè opposti come contrari... Acutezza e' gravità manifestamente son' due termini trasportati alle due prime differenze del tuono, l'uno preso dalla forma dell'angolo più atto a penetrare, e' l'altro dalla proprietà a' natura men commoda à esser' dal moto non natural soprafatta e' sforzata.... Parimente nella voce l'effetto generato dalla prestezza, per la sua (chiamandola hor' così) unitezza, atta alla violenza, facendosi quasi far luogo per forza, penetra più gagliardamente; dove quello, che nasce dalla tardità... venendo agevolmente impedito da ogni contrarietà, che nel

suo proceder' innanzi gli s'opponga,.... e' così più tosto infragnie, che egli punga" (fols. 1r-2r). Cf. *On the Soul* ii.8 (420a. 29-420b. 4).

82. *Del verso...*, fol. 2v. Mei's use of the word *spirito* in this context must be taken to mean simply "breath." Cf. his own definition later in this same passage: "... lo spirito... altro non è che l'aria dentro raccolta dalla nostra respirazione..."

83. *On the Soul* ii.8 (420b. 14-15).

84. *Sopra la prosa toscana*, fols. 2r-2v. Cf. *On the Soul* 420a. 3-5: "What has the power of producing sound is what has the power of setting in movement a single mass of air which is continuous from the impinging body up to the organ of hearing. The organ of hearing is physically united with air, and because it is in air, the air inside is moved concurrently with the air outside;" and Aristotle's *Problems* xix.27 (919b. 25-35): "Why is it that of all things which are perceived by the senses that which is heard alone possesses moral character? For music, even if it is unaccompanied by words, yet has character. Is it because that which is heard alone has movement . . . ? This movement resembles moral character both in the rhythms and in the melodic disposition of the high and low notes, but not in their commingling . . . Now these movements are connected with action, and actions are indicative of moral character." Also see Walker, "Ficino's *Spiritus* . . . ," p. 134 and p. 28 of the present chapter.

85. "Una tal qualità di compositura... la quale proporzionata a quel' concetto che si voleva exprimere, nell'essere da l'orecchio sentita, restandone in certo modo sodisfatto, quasi perfettamente contentava l'intelletto" (*Sopra la prosa...*, fol. 1r).

86. In the section on the composition of words in *Sopra la prosa...* (fol. 22v), Mei stated further that the effectiveness of words lies in their ability to imitate ("per virtù della sua imitazione") by means of an appropriate mixture of consonants and vowels, the peculiar quality of that which is intended to be understood; this is accomplished because the imitation makes the quality of its object sensible to the ear, and thereby has a marvellous ability to make its impression on the soul ("ha la forza maravigliosa nel far' apparir' quanto si ha in animo").

87. See p. 36.

88. See his first letter to Galilei, dated 8 May 1572 (ed. Palisca, p. 98); cf. Galilei's objections to the transposition of music to "unsingable pitches" (*Dialogo*, p. 87; Strunk, p. 317) as well as his condemnation of the enlarged range of modern music beyond the Pythagorean system, which he considered to be "veramente contro ogni natura di affetto, conciosiache come può sentire ogn'uno comunemente che si lamenta, non si parte mai dalle corde acute; e per contrario chi è mesto non si allontana mai dalle gravi se non una tale leggiera distanza" (*Dialogo*, pp. 83-84; omitted from the selections in Strunk).

89. "... il sentimento de la continuata delicatezza de' loro accordi, e consonanze, et cento altre soperchie maniere di artifizio che eglino sono iti quasi col fucellino, come si dice, cercando per allettare l'orecchio, è di sommo impedimento à

commovere l'animo ad affezzione alcuna,..." (Letter, 8 May 1572, p. 97). Cf. Galilei: ". . . the continual sweetness of the various harmonies, combined with the slight harshness and bitterness of the various dissonances (besides the thousand other sorts of artifice that the contrapuntists of our day have so industriously sought out to allure our ears, . . .) these are, as I have said, the greatest impediment to moving the mind to any passion" (*Dialogo*, p. 87; translation quoted from Strunk, p. 314).

90.   "... la inestimabile stracuratezza de nostri musici intorno al numero e ritmo... il quale infinite volte per non dir sempre mai in tutte queste è contrario à la natura de la cosa che vuole esprimere il concetto che significa da le parole,..." (Letter, 8 May 1572, p. 98).

91.   Cf. Bardi, *Discorso sopra la musica antica...*, in Strunk, pp. 293-94; and Galilei, *Dialogo*, p. 82 (Strunk, p. 308).

92.   To be sure, the principle of the imitation of nature was one which many sixteenth-century musical humanists, not all of whom were reformers, held in common. But, in the words of Armen Carapetyan, "Insofar as the search for right expressiveness in music—combined with neo-classic ideas of music and drama—was the chief reason for change in aesthetics and style, and insofar as naturalism was an impelling force in the development of the urge for expressiveness, at the end of the sixteenth century the concept of imitation of nature becomes a force in the development of style." (See "The Concept of *Imitazione della natura* in the Sixteenth Century," *Journal of Renaissance and Baroque Music* 1 [1946]: 58.) I would add that the differences between, for example, Zarlino and Galilei, involve the extent to which each of them was a "searcher for right expressiveness;" for Zarlino, it was necessary to adapt the principle of imitation to the ideal "natura" of a Pythagorean universe, and to the tenets of modern counterpoint (as he did in his *Istitutioni* part 4, ch. 32: "In qual maniera le harmonie si accommodino al soggetto delle parole" [translation in Strunk, pp. 255-59]; because, although he agreed that ancient music was in fact monodic, Zarlino believed that counterpoint represented an artistic advance on ancient monody. Cf. Walker, "Musical Humanism . . . ," p. 308, and note 40 to the present chapter.

93.   Not a quality of speech, rhyme was unessential in Mei's view ("La Rima non è cosa necessaria all'essenza del verso toscano..." [fol. 85v]), and therefore had to be subordinated to the manner of imitation required by the subject. The parallel between rhyme, an "ornament of locution," and the fugues and diminutions of counterpoint, or the "hundred other excessive means of artifice" in music, is clear; in each case, Mei condemned the use of such ornamentation for its own sake.

94.   See *Dialogo*, pp. 88-90; translation in Strunk, pp. 315-19.

95.   Preface to *Euridice*; see Appendix B below, p. 297. Also see p. 26 and note 34 above.

96.   "... poi che non potevano [tali musici] muovere l'intelletto senza l'intelligenza delle parole, mi venne pensiero introdurre una sorta di musica, per cui altri non potesse

quasi che in armonia favellare..." (*Le nuove musiche*, Preface, in Solerti, *Le origini*, p. 57). Cf. Hitchcock, p. 44.

97. "... in questo stile serve molto più l'intelligenza del concetto e delle parole, il gusto e l'imitazione di esso così nelle corde affettuose come nello esprimerlo con affetto cantando, che non serve il contrappunto..." (ibid., in Solerti, p. 60); cf. Hitchcock, p. 47.

98. Palisca, *Girolamo Mei: Letters*, Introduction, p. 81. One of the instruments of the "new orientation" was Galilei's counterpoint treatise (1588-91) in which he anticipated principles expounded in the following decade by Giulio Cesare Monteverdi in his *Dichiarazione* of the second practice — viz., that the most essential consideration of the new style was the affective expression of the text, to which the rules of counterpoint were to be subordinated, and that the dissonance had a positive function as a valuable means of expression to be not merely tolerated, but even exploited. Cf. Palisca, "Vincenzo Galilei's Counterpoint Treatise: A Code for the *Seconda prattica*," *JAMS* 9 (1956): 82. Also see Palisca's chapter, "The Artusi-Monteverdi Controversy," in *The Monteverdi Companion*, ed. Arnold and Fortune (London, 1968), pp. 133 ff.

99. "La qualità di [suoni e voci] e lor differenzie nel esser' profferite" (*Sopra la prosa*, fol. 5r).

100. "... queste passioni vengon' giudicate in lor' dal senso nostro quasi incomprensibili" (*Del verso...*, fol 6r). It is difficult to judge whether Mei held the concept of a medical *spiritus*, for although he spoke frequently and specifically in these early works of the motions of the soul, he did not make clear what in his opinion moved, or was moved.

101. "... la gravità e l'acutezza son proprie passioni e frà lor contrarie, l'una generata dalla velocità, e l'altra dalla tardità del moto, onde ella nasce." ("Come potesse...," p. 15; see p. 39 and note 121.)

102. "... quasi tasti naturali, ubbediscon' all'anima nel volontariamente o necessariamente esprimer' quanto da' lei vien' comandato in quello stante" (ibid., p. 14).

103. "...si come naturalmente nella distanza, e spatio della voce chiamata da musici diastematica, e per dir cosi, intervallativa, i luoghi più acuti son' segno d'animo commosso, et i mediocri di animo quieto, nel medesimo modo nella voce, chiamata da medesimi... continova, l'acutezza naturale semplicemente paragonata nelle parole con la gravità, ritien' proporzionatemente le qualità medesime. Onde quelle parole, che hanno sole sillabe acute, quanto sian' molte insieme, fanno per questo apparir' viè più che l'altre, affetto così fatto, e perciò son' non so chome [sic] per dir cosi più simiglianti ad habito giovanile, che à costume grave, e di vecchio..." (fols. 20r-20v). Concerning the terms "diastematic" and "continuous," see below, p. 111 and note 122. Mei provided examples of both types of words on fols. 18v-19r. According to his reasoning, *ora, mele, humido, dubiti* all have a

"natural acuteness" principally by virtue of their "short" (or, as we would say, "closed") vowels, which render their pronunciation rapid, vivacious, and delicate, and thereby impart to them a kind of youthful vigor ("quasi vigor di gioventù"). On the other hand, words composed of syllables containing a greater number of "long" or open vowels – *desio, pazzia, viole* – are suitable for portraying *grandezza e gravità* since their pronunciation is more leisurely; also in this category are words which resound with many consonants ("per virtù delle molte consonanti sonore"), such as *ombra, scherzo,* and *perla.*

104. *Sopra la prosa...*, fols. 20v-21v.

105. "...i quali... fanno comparir seco ciaschun dispersè, e' tutti insieme, per sua proprietà costume qualificato, e modesto, dove il vestir corto, il parlar presto, l'andar ratto, e la voce squillante non hanno punto seco grado di maiestà; e i grandi huomini diligenti esaminatori de costumi nobili, e delle lor convenienze, hanno confermato al magnanimo il moto lento, la voce grave, e il parlar' quieto" (fol. 22r). Cf. *Rhetoric* iii. 7, especially 1408a. 26 ff: "Each class of men, each type of disposition will have its own appropriate way of letting the truth appear." Cf. also *On the Generation of Animals* vol. 7 (786b. 35-787a. 5), wherein pitch is treated not as a mathematical entity but rather as a biological phenomenon and, among other qualities of the voice, as a reflection of age, sex, health or sickness, and even of character.

106. "Diverse dispozioni [sic] hanno seco naturalmente congiunti anco movimenti diversi. Perche il troppo caldo induce prestezza, e' celerità, e' il troppo freddo tardità e lentezza, si come il temperato ha seco sempre mediocrità e' quiete. Onde è nella qualità della voce per la cagion medesima si sente, che dalli animi commossi, quando son' riscaldati, per la celerità de movimenti s'innacutiscono, per dir così, i tuoni di lei, e quando per il timore ò altro effetto tale sono impediti, s'ingraviscono, dove ne quiete non apparisce niuna di queste alterazioni" (*Sopra la prosa...*, fol. 54v). Note the similarity of Mei's account of the affections to Giacomini's (see above, p. 25 and note 29).

107. Ibid., fols. 54v-55r.

108. "... conciosiache ciascuna simiglianza, quasi destando naturalmente passioni simili à se, muova nel obietto nato al ricevergli proporzionatamente alla sua virtù sempre affetti simiglianti" (ibid., fol. 62r).

109. See *Girolamo Mei: Letters*, pp. 92-93.

110. Ibid., p. 105.

111. Mei reiterates this in several places; see ibid., pp. 90, 93, et passim. On pp. 93-94, for example: "che... tutti i cantanti insieme cantassero non solamente le medesime parole, ma il medesimo tuono, et la medesima aria, con la medesima quantità di tempo et con la medesima qualità di numero e ritmo, le quali tutte

cose insieme fussero per propria natura atte à produr l'effetto che l'artefice suo ingegnava et si proponeva in animo di condurre."

112. See ibid., p. 116; translated by Palisca in the Introduction, p. 71.

113. "... la musica de nostri tempi... portando in certo modo secon nel animo del'uditore à un medesimo tempo diverse e contrarie note di affetti mentre che ella mescola indistintamente insieme arie e tuoni dissimigliantissimi et di natura contrarii gli uni à gli altri, quantunque ciascuna di queste cose habbja da per se naturalmente propria qualità e forza atta à destare e muovere con la sua simiglianza proprie affezzioni, non ne puo communemente per se medesima commovere alcuna" (ibid., pp. 96-97).

114. Ibid., p. 116.

115. See ibid., pp. 105-6.

116. Venice, Ciotti, 1602. For the rather complicated history of this work, see pp. 9-10 of Palisca's Introduction to *Mei: Letters*, p. 90 note 4, and the *Addendum* to pp. 9-11.

117. "... ben sapevano quei gran Filosofi intendenti della natura, che nella voce grave è il tardo, ed il sonnolento, nella mezzana la quiete, la maestà, e la magnificenza, e nell'acuta il ferir tosto l'orecchia e' il lamentevole. Ora chi non sà, che gli ebrj, e sonnolenti per lo più parlano in tuono grave, e tardo, e che gli uomini di grande affare con voce mezzana, magnifica, e quieta ragionano; ... al qual proposito dice Aristotile nel fine della Politica, che ne' Ritmi sono l'effige dell'ira e della mansuetudine, della fortezza, della temperanza, e d'ogni altra virtù morale, e di tutte le cose, che a questo contrarie sono, allegando poco di sotto le ragioni, dicendo così, nelle melodie sono le mutazioni di costumi; perchè non si stà in un medesimo modo al udire ciaschuna di esse..." (in G.B. Doni, *Lyra Barberina*, vol. 2, p. 240). The passage is omitted from the translation in Strunk.

118. *Dialogo*, p. 62.

119. "Ne è punto da maravigliarsi, che la diversità del suono circa l'acutezza & gravità, insieme con la differenza del moto, & dell'intervallo, partorisca varietà d'harmonia, & d'affetto; avvenga che la Natura non produce per l'ordinario i simili con cose contrarie, ne queste con mezzi della medesima qualità; ma si bene per l'opposito. Alla consideratione delle quali cose, quando fussi aggiunto la convenienza del Ritmo, & la conformità de' concetti,... tale melodia... sarebbe atta come già era di piegar gli animi degli uditori in quella parte, che al perito Musico piacesse" (ibid., pp. 75-76).

120. *Dialogo*, p. 89 (Strunk, p. 318).

121. Paris, Bibliothèque Nationale, Ms. lat. 7209[2]: "Trattato di musica fatto dal signor Hieronimo Mei Gentilhuomo Fiorentino," a sixteenth-century copy in 113 pages.

It is interesting to note the similarity between the use of the word *potesse* in Mei's opening sentence and its reappearance in Rinuccini's dedication to *Euridice* (cf. above, p. 21), as well as in Peri's preface to the readers of his score.

122. See "Come potesse...," p. 20; Mei borrowed these terms from Aristoxenus (*Harmonic Elements* i. 8-9).

123. Aristeides was a Greek rhetorician of the 2nd century A.D., and author of *De musica libri iii.* According to D.P. Walker (whose acquaintance with Mei's writings at the time of his "Musical Humanism . . . " was limited to the *Discorso* mentioned on p. 38 above) only Doni, Mersenne, and Salinas quoted Aristeides (see p. 4); but for the evidence and circumstances concerning Mei's knowledge of this source, see Palisca's Introduction to *Mei: Letters*, pp. 60-61.

124. "... mezzano trà i due, ... del quale essi spezzialmente si servivano nel pronunziar' i lor' versi nel leggerli" ("Come potesse...," p. 20).

125. "... stimai che gli antichi Greci e Romani... usassero un'armonia, che avanzando quella del parlare ordinario, scendesse tanto dalla melodia del cantare che pigliasse forma di cosa mezzana" (in Appendix B below, p. 297). Cf. Galilei's thoughts on singing in the Greek manner expressed in a late treatise (in Palisca, "Galilei and Links Between 'Pseudo-Monody' and Monody," *MQ* 46 [1960]: 358.)

126. "Come potesse...," pp. 65-66.

127. Ibid., pp. 94 ff.

128. Ibid., pp. 104 ff.

129. Ibid., p. 98. Cf. *De modis musicis*, Book iv (pp. 157 ff., but separately paginated in the Ms.), p. 18, quoted in note 96 to Chapter One, above; also Peri's and Rinuccini's prefaces to *Euridice* in which they recorded their belief that the ancients, "secondo l'openione di molti, cantavano su le scene le tragedie intere."

130. "... cantandosi però sempre da qual si voglia moltitudine di cantanti insieme una aria sola di canto, senza haversi altra mescolanza di contrappunto ò varietà di voci consonanti fuor' che della sola diapason... la qual' aria veniva secondata dallo strumento uno ò più, ò fusse di fiato, ò fusse di corde, ò d'ammendue insieme" ("Come potesse...," pp. 100-1). Galilei paraphrases very closely some of the ideas found in this section of Mei's treatise in his *Dialogo*, p. 145: "... avvertite che le Tragedie, e le Comedie fussero veramente... cantate da Greci... In oltre, nel cantare lo Strione unisone (e non in consonanza come si è detto e provato) con lo strumento... veniva à essere da ciascuno de circunstanti maggiormente inteso, ed à meno stancarsi la voce di lui; e quello che più importava era, che il Tibicine, ò Citharista, come perito nell'arte musica, veniva col mezzo dello strumento ben temperato, à mantenere lo Strione in quella voce e Tuono circa l'acute e grave; ed à fargli profferire le sillabe..., hora con molto ed hora con poco suono e voce, secondo che conveniva alla qualità del concetto che con le parole cercava significare."

131. "... per quasi ristorar' gli animi, ò mantenerli in que' tali affettij... e molte volte nel privato ozzio di ciascuno dà sè, per isfogamento e quasi purgazzioni e alleggerimento delle passioni e affetti propri" ("Come potesse...," p. 102).

132. Ibid., p. 103. Robert L. Weaver discusses the sixteenth-century traditions which differentiated among the social and functional roles of the different types of instruments in "Sixteenth-Century Instrumentation," *MQ* 47 (1961): 363-78.

Chapter 3

1. The term *libretto*, which may be found in a few isolated documents of the fifteenth and sixteenth centuries, was not commonly used until the practice of printing the text of a performance in a "little book" became firmly established with the opening of the public theaters after 1637. See Ulderico Rolandi, *Il libretto per musica attraverso i tempi* (Rome, 1951), pp. 14-15. D'Ancona (*Origini*, vol: 2, p. 351) cites one appearance of the word in the late fifteenth century.

2. See *Le origini del melodramma; Gli albori del melodramma;* and *Musica, ballo e drammatica alla corte Medicea dal 1600 al 1637* (Florence, 1905; repr. 69). The bibliography at the end of this study gives some idea of the enormous extent of Solerti's writings related to this subject.

3. *The Italian Madrigal* (hereafter *Madrigal;* Princeton, 1949, 3 vols.), and other studies cited in the bibliography herein.

4. *I canti carnascialeschi nelle fonti musicali del XV e XVI secolo* (Florence, Rome, 1937); *Alle fonti della monodia* (Milian, 1940) and others listed in the bibliography.

5. The term was coined by Emilio de' Cavalieri on the title page of his score *"Rappresentazione / di Anima, et di Corpo /* Nuovamente posta in Musica dal Sig. Emilio del Cavalliere, / per recitar Cantando. / Data in luce da Alessandro Guidotti Bolognese. / ... Con Licenza de' Superiori. / In Roma / Appresso Nicolò Mutij l'Anno del Iubileo. MDC."

6. A. A. Abert, *Claudio Monteverdi und das musikalische Drama.* Abert's study, however, leaves much to be said, for her emphasis is placed upon Monteverdi's transformation of the musical drama in the seventeenth century rather than the evolution of the genre from sixteenth-century sources.

7. See my bibliography at the end of this study.

8. See the introduction to his *Drammi per musica, dal Rinuccini allo Zeno.*

9. Schild, *Die Musikdramen Ottavio Rinuccinis.*

10. Momigliano, "I melodrammi del Rinuccini", in *Studi di poesia,* 3d ed. rev. (Florence, 1960), pp. 89-93.

11. Einstein, *Madrigal*, vol. 1, p. 167. "As yet," he continues, "this study has hardly begun."

12. See Chapter Two above, and Nino Pirrotta, "Early Opera and Aria," a most important essay on this subject in *New Looks at Italian Opera, Essays in Honor of Donald J. Grout*, pp. 39-107. If this is indeed what Pirrotta means by the statement, "The rhythmic formulation of the dramatic text and its various degrees of emphasis become the criteria of naturalness and necessity, that is, the aria, of the dramatic melody" (p. 71), then we may consider his words to be, among other things, a good argument for the validity of seeing the poetry as an important partner in the formation of the new genre.

13. See Marco da Gagliano's Preface to *Dafne* (1608), quoted in note 112 to Chapter One. The poet and cleric Angelo Grillo similarly testified to Rinuccini's humanistic concerns in a letter of 1614 to Giudio Caccini: "After hearing this pastoral drama [*Euridice?*], people who regard the chorus in dramatized poetry as a vain thing may understand (as Ottavio himself explained to me) how and why the ancients used it and how important it is in such poems" (quoted by Einstein, "Abbot Angelo Grillo's Letters as Source Materials for Music History," in *Essays on Music* [New York, 1956], pp. 168-69). In speaking about the erudite gatherings which took place at the Corsi household, Giovanni Battista Doni explains Rinuccini's role in terms of the suitability of his poetry to music, saying "perchè... e la Poesia, e la Musica sono sorelle, e consorti; ciò diede [a Corsi e Rinuccini] occasione di perfezionare scambievolmente l'una, e l'altra, e comunicarne il piacere a quelle virtuose Adunanze." See *Trattato della musica scenica*, included in a posthumous collection of Doni's unpublished works edited by Antonio Francesco Gori, *Lyra Barberina Amphichordos* (Florence, 1763, 2 vols.), vol. 2, p. 24.

14. See Filippo Vitali's Preface to *Aretusa* (1620), in which he speaks of the new manner of singing having been born "dal nobil pensiero del sig. Ottavio Rinuccini, il quale, essendo dalle muse unicamente amato e dotato di particolar talento nell'esprimere gli affetti, avrebbe voluto che il canto più tosto accrescesse forza alle sue poesie che gliela togliesse: e discorrendo col sig. Jacopo Corsi... come fosse da fare, che la musica non solamente non impedisse l'intender le parole, ma giovasse ad esprimere maggiormente e più vivamente il senso e il concetto loro, chiamato a sè il Sig. Jacopo Peri..." (Solerti, *Le origini* p. 96). Also see Pietro Bardi's letter (1634) to G. B. Doni, "Grand'obbligo ebbe il Caccini e il Peri al signor Ottavio;..." (ibid., p. 146), and Doni's own statements, based on Bardi and others, "che prima il Peri e il Caccini, sì per l'industria loro e sapere, come per l'assistenza continua e aiuto che ebbero dal sig. Jacopo e dal sig. Ottavio, arriva-rono a quel segno che si vede, che in questo stile appena si può fare meglio; e parimente grandissimo aiuto ricevè il Monteverde dal Renuccini nell'*Arianna*, ancorchè non sapesse di musica (supplendo a ciò col suo giudizio finissimo e con l'orecchia esatissima che possedeva; come anco si può conoscere dalla qualità e testura delle sue poesie), poichè con molta docilità e attenzione questi tre musici ascoltarono sempre gli utimissimi insegnamenti che quei due gentiluomini gli somministravano, instruendoli di continuo di pensieri eccellenti e dottrina esquisita, quale si richiedeva in cosa sì nuova e pregiata... E così si conosce che i veri architetti di questa musica scenica sono propriamente stati li signori Jacopo Corsi e Ottavio Rinuccini; e li primi formatori di questo stile li tre musici mentovati..." (*Trattato*, p. 25). Thus does Anna Abert, in her study on Monteverdi, express the

opinion that Rinuccini materially influenced the composer in setting the text of *Arianna* (p. 107).

15. Monteverdi's narrative and expressive recitative styles contain many elements which closely' resemble Peri's setting (see pp. 93 ff. and pp. 122 ff.). The quetion of Monteverdi's debt to his predecessors in the *stile rappresentativo* was raised by Alexander Ringer in a review in which he challenges Leo Schrade's concept that Monteverdi was the sole creator of a new style (*JAMS 4* [1951]: 153-59). See also A. M. Vacchelli Monterosso, "Elementi stilistici nell' *Euridice* di Jacopo Peri in rapporto all'Orfeo di Monteverdi," in *Claudio Monteverdi e il suo tempo*, ed. R. Monterosso (Cremona, 1969), pp. 117-26. Peri's influence on Monteverdi is discussed as well by Palisca, *Baroque Music*, pp. 37 ff., and Pirrotta, "Monteverdi e i problemi dell'opera," in *Studi sul teatro Veneto fra Rinascimento ed età barocca*, ed. Muraro (Florence, 1971), pp. 321-43.

16. *Del verso toscano*, fols. 57 ff. The discussion of rhyme comprises the third of the so-called three books of the treatise, beginning "Che sia quello, che comunemente è chiamato *Rima* e se egli è cosa tanto necessaria ò utile al verso toscano, quanto molti la voglion' credere." Mei concludes that "la Rima non è cosa necessaria all'essenza del verso toscano, nè medesimamente suo ornamento; ma un ornamento di locuzione appartenente di sua natura indistintamente al parlar tanto in prosa quanto in versi, e in que' luoghi, dove la qualità delle cose, che allhor' s'esprimono con dovuto rispetto di tutte le circustanze ve lo comportano" (ibid., fol. 85 v).

17. The *Vocabolario della Crusca* gives the following definition under *Recitare*: "Raccontare, Narrare, o Dire a mente con disteso ragionamento; si dice anche del favellare i comici sulle scene ne' teatri." However, the only meaning given for *Recitativo* refers to the musical style and is taken from Doni: "Componimento musicale di stile andante, e differente da quello dell' ariette; che si usa nelle poesie narrative, ad imitazione del recitare nelle commedie."

18. "Perchè in que' principij tutti eran' pensier' giovenili, come laudi e' adulazion' di donne ò amori ò altre imprese tali... le quali tutte cose son' tutte da animo ozioso e oziosamente delicato [*Del verso*, fols. 77r-77v].... quelli che son' stati al tempo de' padri nostri e' nostro, per dir così, divinissimi, havendo con l'industria loro, aiutata dalla sperienza, scoperto nuove maniere, ed emendati molti errori de' lor' maestri, le hanno di mano in mano aggiunto tanto di perfezione... [ibid., fol. 78r]. La poesia pervenne a quelle maniere d'imitazione, nelle quali ella cominciò ad haver continova necessità dell'azione, e' dove, per esser' essa per la maggior' e' più importante parte recitativa, i luoghi oziosi eran' radi e' piccioli, che furon' quelle maniere di poemi, che noi ancora co' nomi antichi chiamiamo Tragedia e Commedia [ibid., fol. 81v]... Perchè i poeti mossi dall'esemplo della troppo semplice... e' mal' commoda locuzione à questa nuova maniera d'imitare, delle rappresentationi, state in tanto favore appresso la rozza età de' nostri maggiori, e' insieme del Orfeo del Politiano, e' delle tragedie d'altri poeti di minor' nome, state scritte in rima; essendo... che questo tale ornamento non era punto utile all'azione, cominciarono finalmente à pensar' di valersi del modo... [ibid., fol. 82r]."

19. "... e così il Trissino nella Sofonisba [1515], e il Rucellai nella Rosamunda [1515],

e il Martelli [d. 1531] nella Tullia prima di tutti si risolvenino in que' luoghi, dove egli appariva di danno al disegno dell'imitazion' loro, senza altro rispetto interamente d'abbandonarlo... [ibid., fol. 82r]." In another passage [fol. 78v], Mei also cites two prose comedies by Ariosto, *I Suppositi* and *La Cassaria.* With respect to the early date of this treatise (see Chapter Two above, pp. 31-32), it is interesting to note that all of the works cited were written before 1533. The accuracy of Mei's grasp of history is reaffirmed by Marvin Herrick: "When the full impact of the classical revival was felt, unrhymed Italian verse, similar to the later English blank verse, was developed for both comedy and tragedy. This unrhymed verse did not become prominent, however, until the second decade of the sixteenth century, and at the close of the fifteenth century rhyme still ruled in all forms of the veracular drama." See *Italian Tragedy in the Renaissance* (Urbana, Illinois, 1965), p. 24.

20.   Angelo Ingegneri was concerned with these problems in *Della poesia rappresentativa e del modo di rappresentare le favole sceniche* (Ferrara, 1598). He outlines certain rules for the use of *intermedi* in tragedy, comedy, and pastoral, requiring that choruses be introduced in a natural manner, especially in the last genre, for country people are not ordinarily seen in crowds. Among the kinds of occasions which serve well as excuses for introducing a chorus are "festività, nozze, balli, giuochi, freschi, e diporti..." (p. 23). Also, care must be taken that the *intermedi* be distinct from the action of the pastoral, yet not wholly incongruous. See pp. 23-25.

21.   One exception is Beccari's *Il sacrificio d'Abramo,* performed in Ferrara in 1554 with music by Alfonso della Viola; in this instance, the music appears in a manuscript appendix to a copy of the play extant in Florence. See Solerti, "I precedenti del melodramma," *RMI* 10 (1903): 216 ff.; and ibid., *Albori,* vol. 1, insert between pp. 12-13.

22.   These were *Il satiro* and *La disperazione di Fileno,* both by Laura Guidiccioni Lucchesini, performed at carnival time in 1591 (1590, Florentine style); a third pastoral, *Il giuoco della cieca,* was adapted by the same poetess from Guarini's *Pastor fido* and produced in October 1595. See Alessandro Guidotti's preface to *Rappresentazione di Anima, et di Corpo,* reprinted in Solerti, *Le origini,* pp. 7-8; also, Pirrotta, "Cavalieri," in *Encicl. spett.,* vol. 2, cols. 256-58.

23.   *Trattato della musica scenica,* Chapter 9, "Dell'origine che ebbe a tempi nostri il cantare in scena" (pp. 22 ff.).

24.   "Conviene però sapere, che quelle melodìe sono molto differenti dalle odierne, che si fanno in stile, comunemente detto *Recitativo;* non essendo quelle altro, che ariette con molti artifizj, di ripetizioni, echi, e simili..." (ibid., p. 22).

25.   Concerning the poetic style, Guidotti expresses Cavalieri's opinion that the poem be "facile et pieno di versetti, non solamente di sette sillabe, ma di cinque e di otto, et alle volte in sdruccioli; e con le rime vicine, per la vaghezza della musica, fa grazioso effetto" (Solerti, *Le origini,* p. 8).

26. Such examples as *Il sacrificio d'Abramo* (Ferrara, 1554) and Andrea Gabrieli's choruses for *Edipo tiranno* (Vicenza, 1585), are isolated, and geographically scattered, and therefore do not represent a consistent stylistic tradition. As for the sixteenth-century *intermedio*, although it was entirely in music and did have some relation to the development of opera, it belonged more to the declining tradition of the madrigal than to the new ideal of dramatic music.

27. See the documents quoted by Solerti in *Musica, ballo e drammatica*; also see Pirrotta, "Tragédie et comédie dans la *camerata fiorentina*," p. 294. The title page of the earliest printed libretto, Rinuccini's *Dafne,* declares itself a *favola pastore.* See Appendix A, below, p. 245.

28. But see my argument against this point of view in Chapter One above.

29. "... io direi, che siccome questa specie suole avere più del poetico, e astratto, che le Commedie, e la Rappresentazioni, e si usa comporle quasi sempre di soggetti amorosi, e con stile fiorito, e soave,... così anco se gli potesse concedere di avere la melodia in tutte le sue parti, massime perchè vi si rappresentano Deità, Ninfe, e Pastori di quell'antichissimo secolo, nel quale la Musica era naturale, e la favella quasi poetica" (*Trattato*, Chapter 6, p. 15).

30. In 1486 a Florentine musician known as Giampietro della Viola furnished the music for a performance in Mantua of the so-called *Festa del lauro.* According to Alessandro d'Ancona (*Origini del teatro italiano*, vol. 2, p. 350, note 3), this work was probably identical to a *Rappresentatione di Phebo et di Phetonte (Pitone),* or alternatively, *di Phebo et di Daphné.* The latter appears in an undated codex together with a version of Poliziano's *Orfeo*, of which it is obviously an imitation, combining as it does mythological and pastoral figures and events. For the history of *Dafne* as an *intermedio* subject, see Schild, p. 28, and Yves F.-A. Giraud, *La fable de Daphné: Essai sur un type de métamorphose végétale dans la littérature et dans les arts jusqu'à la fin du XVIIe siècle* (Geneva, 1969), pp. 387ff.

31. See B. R. Hanning, "Glorious Apollo: Poetic and Political Themes in the First Opera," *The Renaissance Quarterly* 32 (1979): 485-513.

32. The question of the genre of Poliziano's *Orfeo* is confusing since the play is variously referred to as a tragedy (cf. Mei's remark above, p. 45) a secularized *rappresentazione sacra* or a dramatic ecolgue (Einstein, *Madrigal,* vol. 1, p. 35), and as the link between the allegorical style of the *rappresentazione sacre* and the mythological, secular style of the later pastoral play (M. Herrick, *Tragicomedy,* p. 126). Mario Apollonio discusses the problematic provenance of *Orfeo* in his essay, "Paesaggio dell'*Orfeo*," in *Il Poliziano e il suo tempo* (Atti del IV convegno internazionale di studi sul Rinascimento, Firenze, 1957), pp. 69-80. The date of the work and the occasion of its performance have been contested; see Momigliano's edition (*Le stanze, l'Orfeo, e le rime,* ["Collezione di classici italiani," vol. 55], Turin, 1921), p. 107, note to 11. 148-51.

33. See *Del verso toscano*, quoted above, p. 45 and note 18.

34. According to Walter W. Greg, "the *favola* as originally put forth continued to be reprinted without alteration, till 1776, when Ireneo Affò published the *Orphei*

Tragoedia from a collation of two manuscripts." This version, divided into five acts, with the addition of a chorus, was at that time thought to be an attempt by Poliziano himself to give the play a more sophisticated form. It is now known to be a reworking of the original by Antonio Tebaldeo for a performance at Ferrara. See *Pastoral Poetry and Pastoral Drama* (London, 1906), p. 157. A bibliography of the fifteenth- and sixteenth-century printings of *Orfeo* is given by Giosuè Carducci in his introduction to *Le stanze, l'Orfeo e le rime* (Florence, 1863), entitled "Delle poesie toscane di Messer Angelo Poliziano," pp. lxxxii-xcvii. also see Nino Pirrotta's discussion, "L'Orfeo degli strambotti," in *Li due Orfei,* pp. 5-44.

35. See below, pp. 52 ff.

36. Poliziano was for a time a member of Lorenzo's household as companion and tutor to his children. The two men remained lifelong friends and *fratres in Platone* in the so-called Platonic academy, an informal fraternity with Marsilio Ficino as its main figure, dedicated to the discussion of Platonic ideas.

37. The standard edition of Poliziano's Italian works is by Giosuè Carducci, *Le stanze, l'Orfeo e le rime... rivedute su i codici e su le antiche stampe.* A synopsis of the play is given by Greg, pp. 158 ff. *L'Orfeo* is translated by J. A. Symonds in *Sketches and Studies in Italy and Greece* (London, 1898), vol. 2, p. 345, and by Louis E. Lord, *Orpheus and Aminta* (London, 1931).

38. See note 1 to Chapter One above and Appendix B-2 below.

39. *Gli albori del melodramma,* vol. 3, pp. 242 ff. For reasons which can only be hypothetical, Monteverdi's score for Striggio's drama, first published in Venice two years after the first performance – i.e., in 1609 – resolves the fate of Orfeo in a less offensive manner by resorting to a *deus ex machina* (see below, pp. 128 ff.). Apollo descends out of pity for the bereeaved poet and leads him to heaven with the prospect of gazing upon Euridice fixed among the stars. The discrepancies between the 1607 libretto and the subsequent score are recorded by Solerti, who places the latter version in footnotes and italics. Della Corte's edition of the libretto (*Drammi per musica,* vol. 1, pp. 160-93) contains a garbled version of the fifth act in which he mistakenly combines Solerti's edition of the original libretto with the altered version given in his footnotes. For the reader's convenience, I include Striggio's libretto in Appendix E below, pp. 305 ff., with the alterations from the last act of Monteverdi's published score presented on pp. 326 ff.

40. Silvia announces Euridice's death (ll. 214-18) before giving the details of the woodland setting and serpent's bite to the striken Orfeo, who remains dumb. See Appendix E below, p. 312.

41. Cf. *Amores* ii. 12, ll. 1,2,5, and 16.

42. *Canzoniere,* no. 245 (ed. Emilio Bigi [Milan, 1963], p. 178). In addition to overt quotations, there are in these works many passages which contain, more subtly, paraphrase from the later pastoral literature. Anna Abert points out several places in the early opera libretti in which Orfeo and Euridice merely echo the sentiments

and expressions of those woodland figures who populated the idyllic poems of Guarini and Tasso. See her *Monteverdi*, pp. 100 ff., and 331 ff.

43. For a study of the political implications of Orpheus for the early sixteenth-century Florentine court, see Karla Langedijk, "Baccio Bandinelli's Orpheus: A Political Message," *Mitteilungen des Kunsthistorischen Institutes in Florenz* 20 (1976): 33-52.

44. See Kenneth R. R. Gros Louis, "Robert Henryson's *Orpheus and Euridice* and the Orpheus Traditions of the Middle Ages," *Speculum* 41 (1966): 643-55. Among other traditions, the author describes the popular or artistic tradition of Orpheus in the Middle Ages, "one which most certainly arises from the oral tradition, and which is related to the prominent position in medieval society of the singer of tales – the *scop [jongleur]*, the minstrel, or the *minnesinger*" (p. 643).

45. See D. P. Walker, "Le chant orphique de Marsile Ficin," in *Musique et poésie au XVIe siècle* (Paris, 1954), p. 18. Also see the quotation from Ficino in Chapter Two, above, p. 27: "Remember that song is the most powerful imitator of all things . . ."

46. The sculpture is part of a series depicting the seven liberal arts; Orpheus was surrounded by similar representations of Grammar, Logic, and Dialectic, Geometry, Arithmetic, and Music (the last personified by Tubal). A reproduction of the work may be seen in the frontispiece of this volume.

47. See D. P. Walker, "Orpheus the Theologian and the Renaissance Platonists," *Journal of the Warburg and Courtauld Institutes* 16 (1953): 100-120. For a survey of representations of Orpheus in antiquity, see Kathi Meyer-Baer, *Music of the Spheres and the Dance of Death* (Princeton, 1970), pp. 257-68.

48. See Gros Louis, "Henryson's *Orpheus . . .*," p. 644.

49. See ll. 17-25 and 93-100.

50. W. W. Greg calls attention to a small circular painting in *chiaroscuro* by Luca Signorelli (c. 1445-1523) "among the arabesques of the *cappella nova* in the cathedral at Orvieto. It represents the youthful Orpheus crowned with the laureate wreath playing before Pluto and Proserpine upon a fiddle or crowd of antique pattern. At his feet lies Eurydice, while around are spirits of the other world." See *Pastoral Poetry*, p. 161, note 1.

51. "Orfeo genuflesso a Plutone dice così." It is likely that Orfeo continued to sing here, in the same style as that which he used for his two preceding octaves (ll. 214-29), where the rubric reads "Orfeo cantando giugne all'inferno." This assumption is supported by the final couplet of Proserpina's speech immediately following, "Dunque tua dura legge a lui si pieghi,/ Pel canto per l'amor pe' giusti prieghi" (ll. 292-93). On the style of the music, see pp. 59 ff.

52. J. Kerman, *Opera as Drama* (New York, 1956), p. 28.

53. Kerman reconstructs a hypothetical "ideal scheme" for an act, in which Striggio would begin with a "static situation, follow it by a single important action, show Orpheus' reaction to it, and then sum up in a choral conclusion" (*Opera as Drama*, p. 34).

54. In all three versions, Orfeo's skill enables him to pass into the realm of the immortals – a feat equivalent to the Elizabethan sonneteer's artistic immortalization of his mortal love in defiance of the ravages of devouring time.

55. As Denis Arnold points out (*Monteverdi*, [London and New York, 1963], pp. 112-13, note 1), Caronte or Charon is a figure drawn from the sixteenth-century *intermedi*, in which hell-scenes were frequently portrayed, for they provided a splendid opportunity for the machinist to display his talents. Schild suggests that Rinuccini's appeal to the authority of Sophocles in his dedication to *Euridice* referred to the violation of the "unity of place" in his libretto, where the change in scenery appropriate to the *intermedi* was theoretically inadmissable in tragedy and comedy. See *Die Musikdramen...*, p. 25.

56. Hans Redlich (*Claudio Monteverdi: Leben und Werk* [Olten, 1949], p. 107) quotes the following passage from one of the composer's letters to Striggio, to illustrate that Monteverdi in fact considered Orfeo's plea, along with Arianna's lament, as "psychological axes" of their respective dramas: "... come caro Sig.^re potrò io imitare il parlar de venti, se non parlano! et come potrò io con il mezzo loro movere li affetti! Mosse l'Arianna per esser donna, et mosse parimenti Orfeo per essere homo et non vento;... L'Arianna mi porta ad un giusto lamento; et l'Orfeo ad una giusta preghiera" (9 Dec. 1616). I quote Malipiero's edition of the letter reproduced in his *Claudio Monteverdi* (Milan, 1929), p. 166; or see *Monteverdi: Lettere, dediche e prefazioni*, ed. Domenico de' Paoli (Rome, 1973), p. 87.

57. Cf. A. Abert, *Monteverdi*, p. 27.

58. See Einstein, *Madrigal*, vol. 1, pp. 97 ff.

59. See Chapter Four, p. 165 for a discussion of Monteverdi's setting of the *terzine*.

60. *Del verso toscano*, fol. 82r. See above, pp. 44-45 and note 18 of the present chapter.

61. "Perchè, volendo muover' in altrui ò l'ira ò il timore ò l'amore ò qualsivoglia altra perturbazione, fà di mestier', che quel' mezo, di che tu vuoi servirti per questo effetto, apparisca fermamente per le parole tue cosa vera, e' non fatta à studio e' pensatamente;... conciosiache altramente tutto si mostra cosa finta, e' apparisce che altri non dica di cuore. E chi s'accorge che non gli è parlato dà cuore, ma con arte e' maliziosamente, temendo d'inganno, và cauto e' non crede à quel' tale; e' non gli credendo, non se ne lascia portar' dalle sue parole, e' non si commuove. Hor' l'andar si occupando in cosifatte... soverchie delicature, le quali tutti son cose da animo ozioso e' discosto da ogni affetto, leva tosto altrui senza altro ogni fede" (ibid., fols. 71v-72r).

62. "... (la forma dell'imitare) non havendo necessità di rappresentar'altrui le cose come in fatto per esser' di sua proprietà *narrativa*, e' non, dicendo al presente così, *recitativa*, può nasconder' molte imperfezioni,..." (ibid., fol. 74v; italics mine).

63.   See above, pp. 44-45 and note 16 of the present chapter.

64.   These include *Rappresentazione di San Giovanni e Paulo* by Poliziano's patron, Lorenzo il Magnifico, *Rappresentazione di San Panunzio* by Feo Belcari, and several others by unknown authors such as *Rappresentazione di San Giovanni Gualberto, di Sant'Ignazio, di Sant'Antonio,* etc.   See Alessandro d'Ancona, ed., *Sacre rappresentazioni dei secoli XIV, XV e XVI* (Florence, 1872, 3 vols.), vols. 2 and 3.

65.   The *Rappresentazioni di Santa Barbara* and *di Constantino imperatore* both date from the early sixteenth century.   In both plays the octaves give way to terza rima at the point where one of the early church fathers delivers a sermon (see d'Ancona, *Sacre rappresentazioni,* vol. 2, pp. 81, 187.)   Moreover, *Constantino* includes an octosyllabic *lauda* (p. 219) and a "canzona con suoni gentili" (p. 200), also in octosyllabic verse with a four-line refrain, the rhythm of which lends itself extremely well to the type of setting later characteristic of the *canzon' a ballo* or the *canzonette:*

Quant è grande   la dolcezza
Di gustar   cibo suave
Tanto è duro;   crudo e grave
Star digiun con   grande asprezza.

66.   The ultimate verse, "Ma ecco Tirsi che del monte sdrucciola" contains a pun on its own structure, a *verso sdrucciolo.*

67.   The fragmentation of the octave among two or more characters engaged in dialogue occurs in the *rappresentazione sacra* as well.   See, for example, the *Rappresentazione di San Giovanni Gualberto* in d'Ancona's anthology, vol. 3, pp. 160 ff.

68.   See p. 53 above.

69.   See Mario Fubini, *Metrica e poesia: Lezioni sulle forme metriche italiane* (Milan, 1962, reprinted 1966), pp. 222-26, and especially p. 224: "... nel Quattrocento la terzina venne a trovarsi accanto a una nuova forma, l'ottava: di fronte all'ottava che si andava nobilitando per gli esempi classici, a poco a poco la terzina assunse la funzione più modesta di un discorse quotidiano."

70.   "L'ottava   rima cantava; la terzina discorreva, berteggiava, satirizava, esprimeva la parte prosaica e reale della vita." Quoted by Fubini, p. 225, note 2.

71.   The *rappresentazioni,* of course, had neither chorus nor regularly spaced lyrical highpoints to separate the various episodes of the action, except when they were performed with *intermedi.*   *La rappresentazione di Santa Uliva,* of which the earliest known edition is 1568 (Florence), has survived with its *intermedi.*   Here, aside from some choral singing of psalms, there are octaves intended to be sung by soloists as well as strophic passages for one or more solo voices which depart

from the ottave rime of the *rappresentazione* proper. See d'Ancona, *Sacre rappresentazioni*, vol. 3, pp. 235 ff. *Orphei tragoedia*, the reworking by Antonio Tebaldeo, was both divided into acts and provided with a chorus after the model of classical tragedy. See above, note 34 of the present chapter.

72. According to some historians, there is insufficient evidence to prove that *Orfeo* was ever performed. See Momigliano's edition, notes to pp. 101-2 and 107-8. More recently Nino Pirrotta has reviewed the problems of dating the work and considers 1480 to be the most probable year of its performance in Mantua. See "L'Orfeo degli strambotti," pp. 5 ff.

73. *Madrigal*, vol. 1, pp. 34-5.

74. See Einstein's section on the *strambotto*, ibid., pp. 87 ff. Further on Ugolini, see Pirrotta, "L'Orfeo degli strambotti," pp. 23-24.

75. The rubric at this point in the text begins: "Orfeo, cantando sopra il monte in su la lira e' seguenti versi latini..."

76. In fact, Einstein was able to trace several texts among the Petrucci *frottola* prints to precisely this type of dramatic origin; see *Madrigal*, vol. 1, p. 99.

77. Although Pirrotta's list of probable sung sections differs from mine by including more of Orfeo's stanzas (ll. 198-229) and excluding some lyrical verses assigned to other characters (Aristeo: ll. 125-37; Euridice: ll. 306-11), he nevertheless moves towards a reconstruction of the music by a similar procedure, suggesting musically plausible analogies from the contemporary *frottola* literature. See "L'Orfeo degli strambotti," pp. 20 ff.

78. Einstein, ibid., pp. 92 ff.

79. See Einstein, ibid., pp. 97 ff.

80. See Einstein, ibid., pp. 98-99. The piece is fourth in the *frottola* collection, printed in 1505.

81. This example was taken from the Smith College Music Archives' collection of *Madrigals of the Sixteenth and Seventeenth Century* copied by Albert Einstein, vol. 81. In his discussion of the piece in the section on the *capitolo (Madrigal*, vol. 1, p. 99), Einstein says, "The upper voice is a mixture of declamation with the most extravagant melismatic writing that harks back, as it were, to the ballata of the Trecento, while at the same time foreshadowing the exuberant coloratura of the monodists, of Caccini and the Monteverdi of the *Orfeo*. Such lyrical compositions of terze rime were certainly culminating points of the dramatic eclogue and of the pastoral drama which was to grow out of it."

82. See pp. 72 ff. of this chapter.

83. A few composers, particularly Monteverdi and Cavalli, remained faithful to the early operatic ideal of a continuity in nuance and variety of expression. Thus, they frequently interrupted a formal series of strophes with recitative, or punctuated their recitatives with short *arioso* passages. See, for example, *L'incoronazione di Poppea,* II. 13 and *Giasone,* I. 3. After the middle of the century, however, the structural implications of a given libretto were evidently accepted as fixed limitations.

84. For a discussion of the musical settings by Peri and Caccini, see pp. 87 ff. and examples 6 and 7. See Appendix B below, pp. 270 ff. for the complete text of the libretto.

85. I have adopted the practice used by Mario Fubini, in *Metrica e poesia,* indicating the eleven-syllable verses with upper case letters, those of seven syllables with lower case ones; the letters themselves, of course, signify the occurrence of rhyme.

86. Other solutions were being sought for the musical stage, all of them employing rhyme to some extent. For example, a *favola pastorale* by Ascanio Ordei (Milanese), *I fidi amanti,* was entirely set to music "a quattro voci" by Gasparo Torelli (da S. Sepolcro) in 1599. According to Solerti ("Precedenti del melodramma," p. 468), the play was derived from Tasso's eclogue *Il convito di pastori.* The verse style of the libretto, which is printed in an appendix to Solerti's article (see pp. 471 ff.) occupies a place midway between the stylized, isometric couplets of Cavalieri's *Rappresentazione,* and Rinuccini's irregular combination of long and short verses with occasional unrhymed lines. Ordei's verses are of mixed length but the rhymes tend to proceed in couplets. The *favola* has three acts, the first two of which are followed by *intermedi.* The third concludes with the only stable chorus in the work. Printed by Luigi Torchi in *L'arte musicale in Italia* ([Milan, 1897 ff.], vol. 4, pp. 73-147), the music is in four-part madrigal style throughout.

87. The occurrence of unrhymed lines in Rinuccini's poetry seems frequently to be associated with a new thought. Elsewhere, unrhymed lines are used with some degree of regularity only in the elusive position of second verse of a tercet in the rapid-moving *parti recitative.* (See, e.g., p. 69.) The passage may be found in Appendix B below, p. 273.

88. Although there is no extant evidence, the verse style of the *Rappresentazione* may have been very similar to Cavalieri's earlier pastorals, written by Laura Guidiccioni in conformity with the composer's intentions, for these plays (*Il satiro* and *La disperazione de Fileno*) are cited by Guidotti as examples of the poetic style best suited for representation on stage. See his preface to the *Rappresentazione* in Solerti, *Le origini,* p. 8 and note 90 below. Concerning Cavalieri's collaboration with the poet from Lucca see Solerti, "Laura Guidiccioni Lucchesini ed Emilio de' Cavalieri," *RMI* 9 (1902): 797-829.

89. See numbers 4-14 of the facsimile edition (ed. Francesco Mantica, Rome, 1912), pp. iiii-v, and "Scena Quarta" of the libretto included at the end of the score. The libretto is also given in Solerti, *Le origini,* pp. 13-139. See Appendix F, pp. 331-32 below, for the text of the passage discussed here.

90. Hendecasyllabic couplets were occasionally used to mark the close of a dialogue, as in the example above. It was Cavalieri's belief that "Il poema non dovrebbe passare settecento versi, e conviene che sia facile et pieno di versetti, non solamente di sette sillabe, ma di cinque e di otto, et alle volte in sdruccioli; e con le rime vicine, per la vaghezza della musica, fa grazioso effetto. E ne' Dialoghi le proposte et risposte non siano molto lunghe; e le narrative d'un solo siano più brevi che possano." See Guidotti's preface, in Solerti, *Le origini*, p. 8.

91. See the quotation from Guidotti in the preceding note, especially, "e con le rime vicine, per la vaghezza della musica, fa grazioso effetto."

92. See ll. 531-34, discussed below, p. 71 and again ll. 710-13 (cf. Appendix B, p. 293).

93. It will be remembered that the prologue, which, like Dafne's recitation, is essentially narrative in content, is also organized into quatrains. Dafne's verses, however, begin interposed into a dialogue, are made to simulate the freer style of prose with their mixed seven- and eleven-syllable lines, rather than the more measured style of the hendecasyllabic verses of the prologue.

94. Scene 1, ll. 73-81; see above, p. 66, and Appendix B below, pp. 272 ff.

95. See pp. 68 ff, and Appendix B below, pp. 274 ff. and 283 ff.

96. See G. B. Doni, *Trattato della musica scenica*, chapter 13, pp. 33 ff. Also see Doni's *Annotazioni sopra il Compendio de' generi, e de' modi della musica* (Rome, 1640), pp. 60-62.

97. "... potrà usare maggiore libertà servendosi anco di quello stile semplice, che possiamo chiamare narrativo; perchè si adopra nelle narrazioni di alcuni messi, descrizioni, e simili ragionamenti quieti; o proprio recitativo, perchè conviene alle recitazioni col canto di qualche Poema eroico, o Romanzo, quale in effetto si sente nelle arie di queste ottave rime, che si cantano familiarmente;..." (*Trattato*, p. 33). The "properly recitational" style will be discussed in connection with the strophic poetry in Chapter Four below.

98. It will be recalled that, in speaking of the "grandissimo aiuto" Monteverdi received from Rinuccini during their collaboration on *Arianna*, Doni praises the poet for his "giudizio finissimo" and "orecchia esatissima." See *Trattato...*, p. 25 quoted in note 14 to the present chapter.

99. "Chi vorrà dunque puntualmente esprimere quegli accenti stessi, e piegamenti di voci, che naturalmente si fanno favellando... gli farà di bisogno di grande attenzione, e lungo esercizio, e di un instrumento a posposito [*sic*]; ma soprattutto di un orecchia molto delicata. Doverà perciò osservare diligentemente quali sillabe s'intuonano con accento uniforme, ed equabile, e in quali si alza, o abbassa la voce, e insino a che segno, o intervallo, ponendo mente a quei transiti veloci, che si fanno intorno le sillabe accentate, e tutte le varietà che si fanno principalmente da' più leggiadri, ed esperti Dicitori secondo il costume, affetto, e sentimento di quello, che si dice, come nelle interrogazioni, minacce, ed ogni sorte di

interiezione, e parlare figurato" (*Trattato*, p. 34). Compare this statement with Galilei's advice to "moderni prattici" who wish to learn "l'imitazione delle parole: Quando vanno... alle Tragedie & Comedie, che recitano i Zanni,... osservino di gratia in qual maniera parla, con qual voce circa l'acutezza & gravità, con che quantità di suono, con qual sorte d'accenti & di gesti, come profferite quanto alla velocità & tardità del moto, l'uno con l'altro quieto gentilhuomo. Attendino un poco la differenza che occorre tra tutte quelle cose, quando uno di essi parla con un suo servo... quando al supplicante nel raccomandarsi; come ciò faccia l'infuriato ò concitato;... come quelli che si lamenta; come quelli che grida; come il rimoroso; e come quelli che esulta d'allegrezza." (see *Dialogo*, p. 89 and Chapter Two above, p. 39.) Also note the similarity of both Doni's and Galilei's concept of "accenti" to Mei's formulation involving acuteness and gravity; see Chapter Two above, pp. 32 ff.

100.   On the verse characteristics of the *luoghi oziosi*, see Chapter Four below, pp. 137 ff.

101.   Doni, *Trattato*, p. 32. In the same passage, he condemns the use of this recitative style altogether in tragedies and comedies; for these genres should not be performed entirely in music, but only those sections which are themselves full of affection should be sung.

102.   "... servendosi con molto giudizio di note veloci, e trattenendosi assai nella istessa corda; perchè l'istesso si fa anco quando col parlar semplice alcuna cosa si racconta" (*Trattato*, p. 34).

103.   Doni distinguished between *stile recitativo* and *stile rappresentativo* (see ibid., chapter 11 ff., beginning on p. 28). The first is modeled upon ordinary speech, and includes not only theatrical monody but also that solo style used in church, chamber, and oratory as well. *Stile rappresentativo* applies only to that imitation of speech in song which is used in scenic representation. This style is almost the same as the *stile recitativo*, but incorporates the imitation of actions, gestures, and manners. *Stile rappresentativo* is by nature imitative, however, and only accidentally narrative, as in messenger scenes, etc. In the passages quoted above, Doni is concerned with *recitativo scenico*, or *stile rappresentativo*, which may be narrative, recitational, or affective (see above, p. 72). A similar categorization of the styles possible within the *stile recitativo scenico* was set forth by Doni in *Annotazioni sopra il Compendio de' generi, e de' modi della musica* (Rome: Andrea Fei, 1640), pp. 60-62.

104.   I disagree with Schrade that "Doni abstracted his ideas of *stile recitativo* from (Monteverdi's) *lettere* [Due lettere amorose]" for it is quite obvious that he had read Peri's preface carefully and accepted its premises, at the same time voicing a few reservations in his treatise. In fact, Schrade goes on to suggest that Monteverdi's *lettere*, unique among his madrigals, constitute themselves a deliberate imitation of the principles prescribed by the Florentine innovators. See *Monteverdi, Creator of Modern Music* (New York, 1950), pp. 290-91.

105.   Concerning the reference to the affections, see Chapter Two above, especially p. 26 where portions of this same passage are quoted.

106. "Conobbi, parimente,..." (see Appendix B below, p. 297). My translation differs in several respects from that given in Strunk, pp. 374-75. Peri's preface may also be found in Solerti's editions, *Albori*, vol. 2, pp. 108-10 and *Le origini*, pp. 45-49.

107. "... stimai che gli antichi Greci e Romani... usassero un armonia, che avanzando quella del parlare ordinario, scendesse tanto dalla melodia del cantare che pigliasse forma di cosa mezzana" (cf. Appendix B below, p. 297).

108. "E questa è la ragione, onde veggiamo in quelle poesie aver'avuto luogo il jambo, che non si innalza come l'esametro, ma pure è detto avanzarsi oltr' a' confini de ragionamenti familiari" (ibid.).

109. Cf. J. B. Greenough, et al. (eds.), *Allen and Greenough's New Latin Grammar* (Boston, 2d ed. rev., 1903; repr., 1931), pp. 411 ff.

110. Palisca, *Baroque Music*, p. 29.

111. "... mi venne pensiero introdurre una sorte di musica, per cui altri potesse quasi che in armonia favellare, usando in essa (come altre volte ho detto) una certa nobile sprezzatura di canto, trapassando talora per alcune false; tenendo però la corda del basso ferma, eccetto che quando io me ne volea servire all'uso comune, con le parti di mezzo tocche dall'instrumento per esprimere qualche affetto, non essendo buone per altro" (*Le nuove musiche*, Preface; in Solerti, *Le origini*, p. 57). Cf. Hitchcock's translation, pp. 44-5.

112. Palisca, *Baroque Music*, p. 29.

113. In another passage, Caccini speaks of expressing *il gusto* of the text in *corde affettuose*. See *Le nuove musiche*, Preface, in Solerti, *Le origini*, p. 60 and note 97 of Chapter Two above.

114. See Chapter Two above, pp. 23 ff.

115. See Mei's letter of 8 May 1572 in Palisca's edition, p. 116. A translation of this passage is given in the Introduction, p. 71.

116. Putnam Aldrich (*Rhythm in Seventeenth-Century Italian Monody* [New York, 1966], pp. 12-13) points out that both types of rhythm may be seen in the prints of the early monodists. He cites Caccini's "Amarilli, mia bella" as an example of free rhythm, and "Udite, udite amanti" as illustrating the use of "strict" rhythm. Both are from *Le nuove musiche*. It is my conviction that these traits had not yet become polarized in Peri's style.

117. See *Discorso sopra la musica antica e 'l cantar bene*, p. 240. The passage is quoted in Chapter Two above, pp. 38-39 and note 117.

118. See Chapter Four, p. 156.

119.   See Chapter Two above, pp. 32-33 and note 77.

120.   Of course the word is intended here in its general sense, as used by Castiglione in *The Courtier*, where it describes the ease and nonchalance which the perfect courtier brings to everything he does.   See Wayne A. Rebhorn, *Courtly Performances: Masking and Festivity in Castiglione's "Book of the Courtier"* (Detroit, 1978), pp. 33-44; and Pirrotta, "Early Opera and Aria," p. 54 and note 41.

121.   See Caccini's Preface to *Euridice*, dedicated to Bardi, and reprinted in Appendix B below, pp. 299-300 (as well as in Solerti, *Albori*, vol. 2, pp. 111-12, and *Le origini*, pp. 50-52): "Nella qual maniera di canto, ho io usata una certa sprezzatura, che io ho stimato, che habbia del nobile, parendomi con essa di essermi appressato quel più alla natural favella."

122.   "... la quale ha sempre fatte degne del cantar suo le musiche mie..." (italics mine). See Appendix B below, p. 298.

123.   In his preface to *Euridice* Caccini also mentions Vittoria Archilei in this connection. "Io era stato di parere con l'occasione presente di fare un discorso a i lettori del nobil modo di cantare,... e con la nuova maniera de passaggi, e raddoppiate inventati da me i quali hora adopera cantando l'opere mie già è molto tempo, Vittoria Archilei, cantatrice di quella eccellenza, che mostra il grido della sua fama." See Appendix B below, p. 300.

124.   The "architectonic end," which belongs solely to comedy, is to purge the minds of the evil feeling of melancholy.   See Chapter Two above, p. 30 and below, the following note.

125.   From *Il Verrato*, quoted and translated in Weinberg, *HLC*, vol. 2, p. 1080.

126.   See Herrick, *Tragicomedy*, p. 141, where this passage is quoted in translation from Guarini's *Compendio della poesia tragicomica* (1601).

127.   Both Tasso and Guarini use enjambment frequently, especially in passages consisting entirely of hendecasyllables, where the same effect is obtained as that which results from the interposition of short lines. Enjambment is almost entirely absent in Rinuccini's verse, where the frequent seven-syllable lines serve the same function – to approximate the cadence of ordinary speech.

128.   See Chapter Four, pp. 131 ff.

129.   In *Pastor fido*, at the ends of Acts II, III and V; in *Aminta*, also at the ends of Acts II, III and V; Act IV concludes with an apparently through-composed madrigal, which is however identified by Luigi Fassò as the first strophe of a *canzone* written by Tasso for the wedding of Virginia de' Medici. See p. 92 of the edition cited in Chapter One above, note 19.

130. On this matter, see Arnold Hartmann, "Battista Guarini and *Il pastor fido*," *MQ* 39 (1953): 419-22.

131. Ibid., pp. 422 ff. Hartmann offers the suggestion, "The very quantity of such settings confirms an impression that composers in Italy at this time had to satisfy an inexhaustible demand for madrigal music for private use, whereas stage music rarely outlived the original occasion of its performance, having been associated from its inception with stage machinery, ballet, and the general spectacle."

132. Hartmann mentions several other extant settings of the "Giuoco della cieca" – by Gabriele Fattorini (1598), Gastoldi (1602), Casentini (1609), Brognonico (1612), Usper (1623), and Biandra (1626). See ibid., pp. 420-21. Ghizzolo's version is distinguished by being the only one in the monodic style. Solerti compares the text of the madrigal version by Marsilio Casentini with Guarini's play in an appendix to his article. "Laura Guidiccioni...," pp. 824-29. Of course, the Guidiccioni-Calieri version of 1595, *Giuoco della cieca* ("una pastorella tutta in musica" performed at the Pitti "nella sala delle statue dove si ballava"), has not survived. See Solerti, ibid., pp. 814-15.

133. "*Madrigali et arie per sonare et cantare nel chitarone, liuto o clavicembalo, a 1 et 2 di Giovanni Ghizzolo da Brescia col giuoco della cieca, et una Mascherata de' Pescatori.* Libro Primo, In Venetia, Raverii, MDCIX." Ghizzolo was born at Brescia in the second half of the sixteenth century, and died at Novara in 1625. He was a pupil of Costanzo Porta, but he adopted the monodic and concertato styles early in his career, the above-mentioned publication having been preceded by only one book of polyphonic compositions, *Madrigali a 5 voci, Libro I°* (Venice: Raverii, 1608).

134. The choral sections will be discussed in Chapter Four; I am here concerned only with the recitative verse and music.

135. *Il pastor fido*, III.2, ll. 128-36.

136. In this and other examples in which I have changed the barring in the interest of clarity, I have indicated the position of the original barlines by short vertical lines in the upper staff.

137. This passage may be found on p. 11 of the facsimile edition of Peri's *Euridice* (Rome, 1934). All other musical citations of *Euridice* refer to this edition. New facsimiles of the Florence, 1601 edition have been published by Broude Bros. (New York, 1973), and Forni (Bologna, 1969). The opera also appears in L. Torchi, ed., *L'arte musicale in Italia* (Milan, 1897-191?), vol. 6.

138. See pp. 66 ff. and p. 70 above.

139. These remarks are not related to the theory described by Putnam Aldrich in *Rhythm in Seventeenth-Century Italian Monody*, which is rooted principally in an analysis of verse structure in terms of arsic and thetic motion. It may be possible, however, to draw an analogy between Peri's use of harmonic rhythm and the

principles governing the alternation of motion and repose in the verse structure, although I do not believe that the two are interrelated, nor that Peri's music is susceptible to such formalization. Further on Peri's and Caccini's settings of *Euridice*, see Palisca, *Baroque Music*, chapter 3, and Howard M. Brown, "How Opera Began: An Introduction to Jacopo Peri's *Euridice*," in *The Late Italian Renaissance 1525-1630*, Eric Cochrane, ed. (London, 1970), pp. 401-43.

140.   The examples from Caccini's score are taken from the original edition, *L'Euridice posta in musica in stile rappresentativo da Giulio Caccini detto Romano* (Florence, Marescotti, 1600), printed in facsimile editions by Ricordi (Milan, 1880) and Forni (Bologna, c. 1978). The work also appears (incomplete) in Eitner (ed.), *Publikationen älterer praktischer und theoretischer Musikwerke*, vol. 10: *Die Oper von ihren ersten Anfängen bis zur Mitte des 18. Jahrhunderts* (Leipzig, 1881).

141.   Cf. Doni's praise of Peri's "prolation" (*Trattato*, p. 76).

142.   Cf. Caccini, *Euridice*, pp. 13-15.

143.   The music is from the facsimile edition of the score, p. II.

144.   The *due lettere* were printed in Monteverdi's seventh book of madrigals (1619); following the heading of each piece is the rubric "si canta senza battuta." See *Tutte le opere di Claudio Monteverdi*, ed. G. Francesco Malipiero (Asolo, 1926-42), vol. 7, pp. 160-75.

145.   The text, which is to my knowledge unidentified, is here taken from the score itself.

146.   The date of composition of these works is a problem in view of the fact that, as Leo Schrade comments, "they are definitely obsolete by 1619 and have no forerunners in Monteverdi's own work." Schrade also ventured the cautious opinion that "deliberate imitation [of the Florentines] is not impossible in Monteverdi's work" (*Monteverdi*, p. 297).

147.   The Ms. is Codex 704 *olim* 8750. See Porter, "Peri and Corsi's *Dafne*: Some New Discoveries and Observations," *JAMS* 18 (1965): 173-74. The fragment is reprinted as Example 4 in Porter's article (p. 180). I find the musical style fairly consistent with, for example, "Per quel vago boschetto."

148.   "*La / Dafne di Marco / Da Gagliano / Nell'Accademia degl'Elevati / L'Affannato / Rappresentata in Mantova. / ... / In Firenze. / Appresso Cristoforo Marescotti. MDCVIII. / ...*" My quotations from the score are taken from the copy of the printed score in the Magliabecchiana collection of the Biblioteca Nazionale Centrale in Florence (Mus. ant. 36). There is now a facsimile edition published by Forni (Bologna, 1970) as well as a performing edition, with a translation of the composer's preface by James Erber (London, Cathedral Music, c. 1978). The work also appears (incomplete) in *Publikationen älterer praktischer und theoretischer Musikwerke*, vol. 10. The revised libretto is given in Solerti, *Albori*, vol. 2, pp. 65-104, and in della Corte, *Drammi*, vol. 1.

149. On Gagliano, see Emil Vogel, "Marco da Gagliano, zur Geschichte des florentiner Musiklebens von 1570-1650," *Vierteljahrsschrift für Musikwissenschaft* 5 (1889): 396-442, 509-68.

150. Pirrotta makes a similar distinction between, on one hand, the sometimes erratic chordal accompaniments of Peri and Caccini, and on the other, the more fluent and linear style of Cavalieri's bass, and suggests that such a distinction in part depended upon the composers' respective instrumental skills. See "Early Opera and Aria," pp. 55-56.

151. A later work by Peri, *Iole lusinghiera* — a lament from a poem by Andrea Salvadori — manifests a greater degree of tonal coherence than that which characterizes his early operas. According to Ademollo, *(La bell'Adriana* [Città di Castello, 1888], pp. 149-51), *Iole* dates from about 1628. The piece is reproduced in Solerti, *Albori*, vol. 1, facing p. 32. A facsimile and transcription has also been published in J. Peri, *Lamento di Jole*, ed. N. Anfuso and A. Gianuario (Florence: Centro Studi Rinascimento Musicale, 1976).

152. See above, pp. 86 ff. of the present chapter.

153. See p. 68 above for a schematic representation of the verse, part of which appears in example 17; also see Appendix F below, pp. 331-32.

154. See p. 72 above and note 99 to the present chapter.

155. Peri does occasionally lapse into the old madrigalistic technique of depicting the meaning of isolated words of the text rather than imitating the tenor of their expression. See, for instance, Dafne's narration "Per quel vago boschetto" in which "E volti gl'occhi al cielo" is set to a rising triad.

156. Hugo Riemann credited Gagliano with initiating this "späterhin stereotype Endformel für Fragen." See *Handbuch der Musikgeschichte*, vol. 2, part 2 (Leipzig, 1922), p. 212. However, examples may be found in Peri's score, although perhaps not as consistently as they appear in Gagliano's. See, for instance, the chorus on p. 24: "Ma tu, perchè tardavi a darle aiuta?" and Arcetro on p. 13: "Ohimè! che fia giammai?"

157. *"L'Arianna / Tragedia / Del Sig. Ottavio Rinuccini, / Gentilomo Della Camera / Del Re Cristianissimo / Rappresentata in Musica / Nelle Reali Nozze del Sereniss. / Principe di Mantova, / E della Serenissima Infanta / Di Savoia / ...* In Mantova. / Presso gli Heredi di Francesco Osanna Stampator Ducale. 1608 / ..." The libretto was also printed in Florence and Venice in the same year, as well as included in a chronicle of the Mantuan festivities of 1608 by Federico Follino, *Compendio delle sontuose feste...* (Mantua: Aurelio et Lodovico Osanna, 1608). Solerti includes Follino's description. See Chapter One above, note 35.

158. Another example may be seen at the end of Rinuccini's *Ballo delle Ingrate*, performed at the Mantuan festivities of 1608 and printed by Solerti with the

commentary from Follino's *Compendio*. See "Ahi, troppo, ahi troppo è duro" in *Albori*, vol. 2, p. 258. In addition to the word repetitions within the verses, a four-line refrain of text and music concludes the piece. See Monteverdi's *Opere*, vol. 8, part 2, pp. 344 ff.

159.   Such figures as analepsis (the immediate repetition of phrases), anaphora (the repetition of the same word or phrase in several successive clauses), and aposiopesis (the sudden halting of a speech, or its fragmentation into short phrases caused by numerous halts, usually symptomatic of violent emotions) are not difficult to discover in these verses.

160.   In Caccini's words, "... quella sorte di musica, che non lasciando bene intendersi le parole, guasta il concetto et il verso, ora allungando et ora scorciando le sillabe per accomodarsi al contrappunto, laceramento della poesia..." (*Le nuove musiche*, Preface, in Solerti, *Le origini*, p. 56). Cf. Hitchcock's translation, p. 44.

161.   The technique of refrain or repetition of an entire verse, or pair of verses, at intervals in the course of a monologue or scene, occurs in Tasso's *Aminta* as well. For example, cf. I.i, wherein variations of the couplet, "Cangia, prego, consiglio, / Pazzarella che sei," occur at various points in Dafne's long harangue. A similar technique lends formal organization on a large scale to another score by Monteverdi — Striggio's *Orfeo* — wherein the second act is buttressed by the poetic and musical repetition of a pair of verses: "Ahi caso acerbo! ahi fato empio e crudele! / Ahi stelle ingiuriose, ahi cielo avaro!"

162.   "Early Opera and Aria," p. 82.

163.   Ibid., p. 73.

164.   Performed in Mantua at the Accademia degli Invaghiti in 1607, the score was not published until 1609 (Venice: Ricciardo Amadino). A souvenir edition of the libretto, however, was issued in the year of its first performance (1607) and is reproduced in Solerti, *Albori*, vol. 3, pp. 241 ff. See p. 47 above, and note 39 to the present chapter. For the reader's convenience, the original libretto is given below in Appendix E, p. 305, followed by the revised ending from Monteverdi's score, p. 326.

165.   See Grout, "The Chorus in Early Opera," in *Festschrift Friedrich Blume zum 70. Geburtstag*, ed. Abert and Pfannkuch (Kassel, 1963), p. 159.

166.   See Appendix E below, p. 306.

167.   Except for the dissonance (a seventh) which occurs on "sconsolato core," there are no affective intervals in the speech. Cf. Monteverdi's *Orfeo* (ed. Malipiero, *Opere*, vol. 11, pp. 12-13), and p. 125 below. Other editions include those by G. Benvenuti (in *I Classici musicali italiani*, 9, 1942), A. Wenziger (Kassel, 1955), and Denis Stevens (London, 1967). All references to Monteverdi's score in this study, however, are to the Malipiero edition, except for the musical examples, which are from the 1609 score.

168. Both of these strophic pieces will be discussed further in Chapter Four. See pp. 157 ff. and 165.

169. Cf. Monteverdi's *Orfeo*, p. 12.

170. Cf. example 13 above (p. 108) and Monteverdi's score, pp. 56 ff.

171. See *Orfeo*, pp. 58-59. In a discussion concerning "l'uso della melopeia," Doni recommends the practice of assigning a suitable range or *tuono* to each character according to his age, station, etc. The critic cites Peri's treatment of the shepherds as a good illustration of the potential effect of this concept. (See *Trattato*, pp. 85-86, and scene 5 of *Euridice*, pp. 41 ff., entirely between Arcetro and Aminta.) The idea that a particular range or *tonos* be assigned to each character is in keeping with Mei's understanding of ancient modal theory.

172. Cf. example 18 above (p. 113) "Non piango e non sospiro."

173. This example, and the previous one, are taken from the first edition of the score (Venice, 1609.) In keeping with my practice throughout this study, I have reduced the note values by half, even though "Tu se' morta" is generally performed at a slow tempo. Concerning the barring, it seems to me that the lack of coincidence between the placement of barlines and text accents (compared to, e.g., example 21 – "Rosa del ciel") is, along with frequent syncopations, part of Monteverdi's technique in representing Orfeo's distraught state. Therefore, I have made no attempt to regularize the barring nor to minimize the rhythmic syncopations.

174. See the outlines given in the present chapter, pp. 47 ff. and note 39.

175. See Herrick, *Tragicomedy*, pp. 126-27; also M. Doran, *Endeavors of Art*, pp. 189-91, and W. W. Greg, *Pastoral Poetry and Pastoral Drama*, pp. 164-68.

176. *Pastoral Poetry*, pp. 168-69.

177. The possibility exists, however, that the threat of the Bacchantes was very much present in the revised version of 1609. In his *Baroque Music*, p. 37, Prof. Palisca states that "the endings of the libretto and score are not incompatible. A *Moresca*, which in the theater is usually a battle-dance, is the last item in the score. This may well have accompanied the hostile movements of the Bacchantes, from which Apollo provides Orpheus a convenient escape."

178. See Hanning, "Glorious Apollo. . . ."

179. The 1609 alterations of the final act begin at l. 612. See Appendix E below, p. 328.

Chapter 4

1. Cf. *Poetics* 1456a.25; also Ingegneri, *Della poesia rappresentativa*, pp. 18 ff.

2. See Donald J. Grout, "The Chorus in Early Opera," p. 158.

3.   See ibid., pp. 128-29, et passim.

4.   See Chapter One above, note 27, and Sternfeld, "The First Printed Opera Libretto." This earliest *Dafne* libretto is given in Appendix A below, pp. 245-60, and differs in some small ways from the 1600 version printed in Solerti, *Albori*, vol. 2, pp. 75-99.

5.   On the basis of this and other structural similarities between Rinuccini's libretti, I must take exception to Grout's remark that *Dafne* "is not, properly speaking, an opera, but rather a pair of intermedi . . ." ("The Chorus in Early Opera," p. 159).

6.   See Solerti's edition in *Albori*, vol. 2, pp. 25-6. another precedent may be seen in *Il pastor fido*, IV.6, wherein the antiphonal exchange of a chorus of hunters and one of shepherds comprises the entire scene.

7.   See note 37 to Chapter One above. The libretto appears in *Albori*, vol. 2, pp. 189 ff., where it is divided by Solerti into five acts.

8.   See also Act 5, ll. 1015 ff., and *Arianna*, scene 4, ll. 576 ff. In the latter example, Solerti indicates the possibility that *cori spezzati* were intended (*Albori*, vol. 2, pp. 143 ff.); the libretto also appears in Della Corte, *Drammi*, vol. 1, pp. 111-56.

9.   The play remained in Ms. until the early nineteenth century when it was printed in Rome by the curator of the Barberini library, Luigi Maria Rezzi. See Solerti's bibliographical introduction to *Albori*, vol. 2, pp. v and x. Also see Chapter One above, note 37.

10.   The problem of the musical treatment of the chorus had been encountered many times earlier. Cf. the account of an anonymous chronicler concerning a performance of the tragedy *Alidoro* in 1568:

I know that in our time choruses have been performed in a number of different ways; some have made a single member of the chorus speak in continuously grave and eloquent tones. . . . Others have allotted them to a solo singer, unsupported by any accompaniment. . . . Others still have preferred to let the whole crowd sing together. . . .

(The passage is quoted by Pirrotta in "Temperaments and Tendencies in the Florentine Camerata," p. 185.) Galilei believed that, whereas the Greek choruses sang in unison, the accompanying instrumentalists played consonances with the vocal line. (Cf. *Dialogo*, p. 83.) This belief might be seen to be reflected in the apparent practice of using monodic choruses in certain passages in the first operas; see above, p. 133 and note 35 in the present chapter.

11.   See the fascimile edition of the score, pp. 2-4, and Appendix B below, p. 273.

12.   Ibid., pp. 21 and 24; in scene 5, pp. 41-42.

13. Ibid., pp. 42 ff.

14. Cf. the facsimile edition of Caccini's score, pp. 20 ff. (scene 3), pp. 40 ff. (scenes 5 and 6).

15. Solerti reproduces the altered rubrics of Gagliano's score, as well as the singers' names inserted by an unknown hand, probably in connection with a later performance in Florence. See the notes to his edition of the libretto in *Albori*, vol. 2, pp. 77 ff. The singers were "Domenico Poggi, Cecchino, Piero, Adamo, Nicc.°, and Orazio Brandi (Brandino);" the name "Tonino" is added a few pages later. According to Stuart Reiner, Caterina Martinelli played only the role of Venus in the 1608 version of *Dafne*. Furthermore, the song with which she is associated in Gagliano's preface, "Chi da lacci d'amor" (ll. 151-58) was incorrectly assigned to Cupid by Solerti and others, but rightly belongs to Venus. See Reiner, "La vag' Angioletta (and others)," *Analecta Musicologica*, 14 (1974): 44 ff. Also see above, pp. 170 ff.

16. "The Chorus in Early Opera," p. 153. However, in Gagliano's preface to the 1608 score, the composer writes, "non vorrebbe essere formato il coro di manco che di sedici o diciotto persone" (in Solerti, *Albori*, vol. 2, p. 70).

17. On p. 2 of the original score, at the lines "E quando mai per queste piagge..."

18. The idea that "Tonino Cecchino" might be one and the same person is dispelled by the notation on p. 4 of the score (subsequently deleted), indicating one name on each of two vocal lines in one of the quatrains *a due* mentioned above.

19. See *Orfeo* (in vol. 11 of Monteverdi's *Opere*), pp. 11 and 64-65. and Appendix E below, pp. 306 ff.

20. Ibid., p. 118; on the *ottave* settings, see above, pp. 166 ff.

21. Ibid., p. 127.

22. The line (53) is from Petrarch's 205th sonnet, "Due rose fresche e colte in paradiso," which, according to Einstein, had been set often as wedding music (*Madrigal*, vol. 1, p. 191). Also see Chapter Three above, note 42.

23. See *Euridice*, p. 4.

24. For a discussion of the structure of these choruses, see pp. 137 ff.

25. Thus, for example, Orfeo's song, "Antri, ch'a miei lamenti," in the static first half of the second scene of *Euridice*, before the appearance of the messenger, is composed of rhymed, mixed verse, and built up into two assymetrical stanzas. By contrast, the parallel section of Striggio's work in Act 2 consists of a series of isometric and strophic quatrains – 12 before the messenger's entrance – which in effect, gather momentum toward Orfeo's dance song, "Vi ricorda, o boschi ombrosi."

26.   See Chapter Three, pp. 119-20.   One is an invocation, the other a *balletto* similar to Peri's "Al canto, al ballo," in madrigal style at the end of the first scene.   See Monteverdi's score, pp. 11 and 14-16.

27.   See Chapter Three, pp. 80 ff., where I discuss a recitative setting of the non-choral passages.

28.   See "The Chorus in Early Opera," p. 157.

29.   See Chapter One, note 68.

30.   See "The Chorus . . . ," p. 158.

31.   In the original *Dafne* libretto, these occur at the ends of the first and fourth scenes: "Almo Dio, che 'l carro ardente" and "Non si nasconde in selva," respectively.   In each, the refrain is only a single verse, and in the case of "Almo Dio," it occurs only at the end of the first two strophes.

32.   See Chapter Four, p. 136.

33.   See Peri's *Euridice*, pp. 7-8; and pp. 7-8 in Caccini's score.   It is unlikely that this device of framing solo recitative with polyphonic choral refrain was used in the original *Dafne* production, in which the only refrain verse, in the chorus "Non si nasconde in selva" (ll. 276 ff.), is not separable from the strophes which it concludes.

34.   See *Orfeo*, pp. 16-17 and Peri's *Euridice*, pp. 7-8.

35.   Cf. Peri, pp. 19-21 and Monteverdi, pp. 68-74.   The opening strophe of "Cruda Morte" in both the Peri and Caccini scores was apparently intended for a monodic chorus, although it is unlikely that the men's voices sang the basso continuo line, which, while it is more rapid than the sustained style characteristic of recitative, does not contain enough notes to accommodate the text.

36.   See *Orfeo*, pp. 130-35.

37.   In fact, Monteverdi eliminates the latter half of the text, organizing the rest into sections of two or three verses composed in a variety of textures (for 2, 3 and 5 parts) over a repeating bass and further unified by an independent instrumental ritornello.   See *Orfeo*, pp. 32-39.

38.   See Chapter Three above, pp. 129-30.

39.   See Peri's score, pp. 19-21.   In this and the subsequent diagrams, the Roman numerals represent different stanzas of music, arabic numbers designate the strophes of the text, and "R" stands for "refrain" or "ritornello."

40.   See Peri's score, pp. 39-40.

41. Schrade paraphrases at length the description of the performance written by Filippo Pigafetta. Cf. *La représentation d'Edipo tiranno* (Paris, 1960), p. 50.

42. See Schrade, ibid., pp. 37-39.

43. See Peri's *Euridice*, pp. 50-52.

44. See Caccini's *Euridice*, pp. 37-39.

45. See ibid., pp. 17 ff. and 50-51.

46. Among the tragedies, Mussato's *Ecerinis*, Trissino's *Sofonisba*, Aretino's *Orazia*, and Leonico's *Il Soldato* appear in an anthology edited by Federico Doglio, *Il teatro tragico italiano* (Parma, 1960).

47. "... a la quale osservanza risponde in parte quella de poeti nostri ne le lor canzoni, dove tutte le stanze di ciascuna debbon esser equali, così di numero come di qualità di versi..." Cf. Letter no. 6 to Galilei (in Palisca, *Mei: Letters*, p. 167), in which he also describes the characteristics of the parts of the ancient ode.

48. Cf. *Del verso toscano*, fols. 21r-v, and Chapter Two above, pp. 32-33; also see Galilei's remarks above, p. 156.

49. "... dovendo queste tali composizioni sentirsi più, essendo cantate, che semplicemente leggendosi, venendone agevolmente ricoperti dal canto con l'aria e modi suoi questi tali difetti, ne potevan' essi venir' anche considerati meno; e per ciò più liberamente trascurati da que' tali artefici, come interveniva anche appresso gli antichi poeti greci in que' tempi, che i medesimi solevan' esser' poeti, e musici; de' quali si legge, che tutti quelli, che accompagnavan' i lor versi col canto non eran' tanto stretti nell'osservanza d'ogni lor' perfezione, come eran' gli altri che gli facevano come se essi havesser' ad esser solamente letti, i quali e nelle misure e ordine loro erano squisitissimi" (*Del verso toscano*, fol. 21v). Concerning the use of the word *modi* again here, cf. Peri's words in Chapter Two above, p. 26 and note 34.

50. Cf. Carlo Angeleri, *Bibliografia delle stampe popolari* (Florence, 1953).

51. Cf. Federico Ghisi's study, *I canti carnascialeschi nelle fonti musicali del XV e XVI secolo* (Florence, 1937).

52. See Chapter One above, pp. 13-14. I use the word in its narrow, poetic sense to refer specifically to certain metrical forms found in the works of Chiabrera and Rinuccini, without meaning necessarily to imply the various musical connotations associated with the word by Einstein, for example, in *Madrigal*, vol. 2, pp. 576 ff.

53. "Peri and Corsi's *Dafne...*," pp. 189-91.

54. *Narciso* has two interlude choruses of exactly the same structure — one a chorus of nymphs in the middle of the first act (ll. 134-45), and another of hunters at the beginning of the second (ll. 249-72). *Dafne* and *Euridice* each have another

chorus similar to the *canzonetta* in design, the only difference being that they are composed entirely in *ottonari*: "Almo Dio, ch'il carr'ardente" (*Dafne*, ll. 67-84) and "Se de' boschi i verdi onori" (*Euridice*, ll. 372-89), both consisting of six-line strophes divided into symmetrical halves: abc-abc. However, except for the characteristic rhythmic alternation between triple and duple meter, I do not see any musical relationship between the Peri and Caccini settings of the *Euridice* chorus and that of "Almo Dio" reprinted by Porter from the Brussels Ms. (ibid., pp. 177-78).

55. The chorus in *Oritia*, "Non fu lieve la saetta" at the end of scene 2 (ll. 246-59), contains a variation of the pattern, manifesting Chiabrera's nascent baroque feeling for design; the strophe is rendered assymetrical by the addition of a seventh verse: abab-bcc (8888-488). In *Pianto d' Orfeo* ("Cinto il crin d'oscure bende," ll. 229 ff.) and *Galatea* ("Tempo rio, che tosto voli," ll. 377 ff.), the structure of the strophe remains unvaried. Chiabrera's libretti may be found in Solerti, *Albori*, vol. 2 (see pp. 70, 99, and 129, respectively). Concerning the early date of these three libretti, see Solerti, "Le 'favolette da recitarsi cantando' di G. Chiabrera," *Giornale storico e letterario della Liguria* 4 (1903): 227-37.

56. A five-part madrigal by Marco da Gagliano on a text very similar to Striggio's closing chorus appears in his Sixth Book (Venice, 1617):

> Evoè Padre Lieo
> Tioneo
> Bromio Bacco Dionigi
> Evoè Padre Leneo
> Bassareo
> Ecco io seguo i tuoi vestigi.

This strophe forms a five-voiced refrain, separating three other stanzas of music for two voices and basso continuo. The music of the refrain utilizes the hemiola rhythm characteristic of the other *canzonetta* settings discussed below. The piece is given in Torchi (ed.), *L'arte musicale in Italia* (Milan, 1897 ff.), vol. 4, pp. 23-24.

57. Follino gives the following interesting particulars of its performance (printed in Solerti, *Albori*, vol. 2, p. 185):

> Bacchus, preceded by the lovely Arianna and Cupid, were seen to appear on stage . . . in the presence of, and surrounded by, many pairs of Soldiers wearing beautiful arms with superb plumes on their heads; who, wherever they were on the set, took up their instruments which were on hand to play a nice dance tune (*aria da ballo*). One group of Soldiers did a very delightful dance, performing many figures; and while they were dancing, another group of Soldiers began to accompany the music and the dance with the following words:

> Spiega omai, giocondo Nume,
> L'auree piume;
> Vien pur lieto; Amor t'appella.
> etc.

In the same chronicler's description of the 1608 *intermedi* by Chiabrera, written for a performance of Guarini's *Idropica* in Mantua, the celestial chorus which closes the fifth and final *intermedio*—"Da quel dì che l'auree strade," again a *canzonetta* following the pattern described above—is also called *aria da ballo.* See Solerti, *Albori*, vol. 3, p. 233.

58. *Il rapimento* was the climax of the Florentine festivities of 1600, towering above *Euridice* in the lavish amount of preparation and attention it received. Cf. Palisca, "The First Performance of 'Euridice', pp. 3-4, and Nagler's description in *Theatre Festivals of the Medici*, pp. 96-100.

59. Concerning Chiabrera's libretti, see the article by Solerti cited in note 55 of this chapter; also Anna Abert, *Monteverdi*, pp. 108 ff., and Cesare Garboli, in *Encicl. spett.*, vol. 3, cols. 624-25.

60. Cf. Anna Abert, *Monteverdi*, p. 109, where the development of Chiabrera's libretti is discussed with particular reference to his experimentation with "immer neuer, raffiniertere Strophenformen."

61. "... Veramente alcuni riguardando, che il verseggiatore in scena rappresenta il favellare vicendevole, vogliono per rappresentare in ciò maggiormente la verità, che le rime se ne sbandiscano affatto. Alcuni altri stimano, che 'l verso toscano privo della rima, rimanga privo di sua propria soavità, e forza, e sulle Scene l'hanno rimato, ma senza ordine certo, e con una larga licenza; onde si viene a soddisfare alla grazia del verso, ed al debito delle Scene: quale sia l'opinione migliore io non so: credo, che nell'uno, e nell'altro modo si possa verseggiare senza colpa niuna. Ed hora ho preso consiglio di non abbandonare le rime.... Ed il Coro rappresentando un popolo, io reputo che non debba luogo avere in azione privata: laonde io mi sono ritenuto di frapporvelo." See *Delle opere di Gabriello Chiabrera* (Venice, 1805; 5 vols.) vol. 4, p. 116.

62. *Gelopea*, a *favola boschereccia* in five acts, probably dates from about 1600; see ibid., pp. 153 ff.

63. Only in *Il pianto d'Orfeo* is the chorus regularly absent from the scene-endings. See Solerti, *Albori*, vol. 3, pp. 91 ff.

64. According to Solerti, ("Le favolette...," p. 233), the libretto dates from 1608 or before, although it was not performed until 1614. *Galatea* is printed by Solerti in *Albori*, vol. 3, pp. 105 ff., with the expanded version of 1617 (*Gli amori di Aci e Galatea*) in footnotes. For the reader's convenience, I have taken the liberty of reproducing the 1614 libretto, taken from Solerti, in Appendix G below. Another *favoletta*, *Polifemo geloso*, has an overall form extremely similar to Striggio's *Orfeo*, although it is not clear whether the Chiabrera work antedates the other. *Polifemo* appears in *Albori*, vol. 3, pp. 75 ff.

65. It will be recalled that both Rinuccini and Striggio eliminate from their versions Orfeo's rival for Euridice's affections—the young shepherd Aristeo, who had appeared prominently in Poliziano's *favola*. See the comparative outlines in Chapter Three above, pp. 47-51.

66.   See Appendix G below, ll. 34-60.

67.   The scheme given above represents ll. 313-34; see Appendix G below.

68.   See her discussion of the libretto in *Monteverdi*, p. 102.

69.   See Solerti, *Albori*, vol. 2, p. 78 (footnotes) and Appendix A below, pp. 262-63.

70.   Cf. Appendix A below, pp. 263-64, and the first edition of Gagliano's score, "*La / Dafne di Marco / Da Gagliano / Nell'Accademia degl'Elevati / L'Affannato / Rappresentata in Mantova. /* ... In Firenze. / Appresso Cristoforo Marescotti. MDCVIII. / ...,*" pp. 8-11. An incomplete edition of the score appears in *Publikationen ältere...Musikwerke*, vol. 10 (hereafter *PaM*), pp. 86 ff. The chorus "Oimè! che veggio" may also be found in Schering, *Geschichte der Musik in Beispielen* (Leipzig, 1931), example 175. There is now a facsimile edition as well, published by Forni (Bologna, 1970).

71.   See the score, *Dafne*, pp. 12-14 (*PaM*, pp. 91-93). Also concerning "Almo Dio, ch'il carr'ardente," see note 54 of this chapter.

72.   See pp. 3-5 of the score (*PaM*, pp. 81-83) and example 26 above. In Solerti's edition of the libretto (*Albori*, vol. 2, p. 78), a verse was omitted from the last strophe, which should read:

> Pera, pera il rio veleno,
> Non attoschi il mondo più;
> Verde il prato, e 'l ciel sereno
> Torni omai, torni qual fù.

See Appendix A below, pp. 262-63.

73.   Cf. Solerti, *Albori*, vol. 2, p. 95 (footnotes) and Appendix A below, pp. 266-67; also see the score, *Dafne*, pp. 41-46 (*PaM.*, pp. 102 ff.).

74.   Similarly, *Narciso's* world is populated by a chorus of hunters, and one of nymphs; the latter enjoys the same prominence as the fishermen in *Arianna*, occupying the stage literally for the duration of the opera. Thus Rinuccini refers to them as the "Coro di Ninfe *stabile*" in the index of characters appearing in the Ms.; cf. Solerti, *Albori*, vol. 2, p. 190.

75.   See Chapter One above, note 36.

76.   See "The Chorus in Early Opera," pp. 160-61. In note 19, Grout suggests that *Arianna* anticipates Landi's opera in the placement of the main choral climax at the end of the last act. However, as I remark below, the largest choral scene in *Arianna* occurs near the beginning of the play as it generally did in the early libretti. For the ensuing discussion of *Arianna*, see Rinuccini's libretto in Solerti, *Albori*, vol. 2, pp. 146 ff.

77. Indeed, Rinuccini's last libretto (*Narciso*) ends not with a strophic *canzona* but rather with an unequivocal madrigal text, in which a moral is derived from the transfiguration of the expired Narciso.

78. I do not include the narrative recitations of the early court masques, which were usually presented in long series of ottave rime, since they seem to me to represent a separate tradition from the *intermedi* and perhaps one that is less relevant for the beginnings of opera. See below, p. 167.

79. Examples are Arion's song from the fifth *intermedio*, "Dunque fra torbid'onde," composed and performed by Jacopo Peri; "Dalle più alte sfere" from the first *intermedio*, by Antonio Archilei, and "Io che dal ciel farei la luna" by Caccini.

80. See Porter, "Peri and Corsi's *Dafne* . . . ," p. 173. Concerning Corsi (d. 1604), the noble amateur musician and patron of the arts whose home in Florence was the scene of a quasi-academy in the last decade of the sixteenth century, as well as the site of the first performance of *Dafne* in 1598, see Nino Pirrotta's article in *Encicl. spett.*, vol. 3, col. 1525.

81. Porter suggests that two tercets assigned to Venus in the fourth scene (ll. 247-52) may have been set "in a light canzonetta style." The text in question is organized into a symmetrical pattern resembling the *canzonette* described above: abB acC. See "Peri and Corsi's *Dafne* . . . ," p. 195.

82. The third is Orfeo's plea to the Underworld gods, "Funeste piagge" (ll. 418 ff.), which is organized into three unequal stanzas of mixed verse with occasional unrhymed lines, united by the refrain, "Lagrimate al mio pianto, Ombre d'Inferno."

83. Cf. Doni's remark concerning the appropriateness of music to tragicomedy, quoted in Chapter Three, note 29.

84.
> Se d'amor nel regno crudo
> Mercè speri ei dà dolori;
> Se richezze e gran tesori,
> Mira ben ch'il vedrai nudo.
>
> Pensi forse andarne seco
> Per securo e bel cammino?
> Non è sol leggier bambino,
> Ma pennuto, e vola cieco.
> etc.

Perhaps Rinuccini, hoping that Monteverdi would set his latest libretto too, even had the strains of Orfeo's tune in mind as he wrote the text.

85. Concerning Rinuccini's position among the composers of solo song at the end of the sixteenth century, see William Porter, *The Origins of the Baroque Solo Song: A Study of Italian Manuscripts and Prints from 1590-1610* (Yale University: diss., 1962; 2 vols.), Chapter 3.

86. See Chapter Two above, pp. 32-33.

87. *Dubbi intorno a quanto io ho detto dell'uso dell'enharmonio con la solutione di essi,* intended as a partial supplement to his *Prattica del contrapunto,* is preserved in Florence, Biblioteca Nazionale, Mss. Galileiani, Anteriori a Galileo, vol. 3, fols. 62r-68r. The treatise is discussed by Claude Palisca, "Vincenzo Galilei and Some Links Between 'Pseudo-Monody' and Monody," *MQ* 46 (1960): 344-60.

88. See Palisca, "Galilei and Some Links . . . ," p. 347.

89. Quoted in translation by Palisca; see ibid.

90. Quoted by Palisca, ibid., p. 360.

91. See ibid., pp. 357-58.

92. See Striggio's *Orfeo,* ll. 351 ff. (in Appendix E below, p. 316) and Monteverdi's score (*Opere,* vol. 11), pp. 81-83. All references to the music are to Malipiero's edition, with the exception of the musical examples, which are taken from the first edition.

93. Concerning the prologues, see above, pp. 171 ff. The poetic form of Caronte's strophes and of the examples by Rinuccini and Chiabrera discussed below are all exactly the same as that of the prologues, rhyming ABBA.

94. See the score, pp. 41 ff. Note that Monteverdi also perpetuates the convention, begun by Peri, of associating the shepherds' song with the sound of duetting flutes (cf. ritornello, p. 45).

95. See Striggio's libretto, ll. 500 ff., and pp. 121-23 of Monteverdi's score.

96. See Solerti, *Albori,* vol. 2, pp. 256-57. It is interesting to note that the *Ballo,* presented in Mantua in 1608, has no prologue.

97. The *Ballo delle Ingrate* is printed in Malipiero's complete edition of Monteverdi's works in vol. 8, part 2; see pp. 337-44.

98. Two numbers from *Cefalo,* however, are known to have survived in Caccini's *Le nuove musiche.* These are the final chorus, "Ineffabile ardore" and Titone's solo in terza rima from the opening of Act 2, "Chi mi conforta ahimè!" about which see above, p. 165.

99. Perhaps it is significant to note that Chiabrera called a large group of verses composed in this form "canzoni morali." See *Opere,* I, 259 ff.

100. See Chapter Three above, p. 72.

101. Solerti omits the third verse of the aria. According to Caccini's setting, the opening tercet should read: "Chi mi conforta ahimè! chi più consolami? / Or che 'l mio sol, che si bei raggi adornano, / Il desiato lume ahi lasso involami."

102. See Solerti, *Albori*, vol. 2, pp. 347 ff. Besides a short, strophic, but unrhymed *coro d'angeli*, the work consists entirely of a long monologue by the angel Gabriel.

103. Porter reproduces this setting in his article "Peri and Corsi's *Dafne* . . . ," pp. 181-82, upon which I rely.

104. Einstein reproduces the piece in *Madrigal*, vol. 3, no. 9. For the text, with his comments on the piece, see *Madrigal*, vol. 1, p. 97.

105. See *Madrigal*, vol. 1, p. 97.

106. See the score of *Orfeo*, pp. 84-100. It is interesting to remark that a particular "aria in terza rima" (no. 63) by Cosimo Bottegari from the Bottegari Lutebook, dating from the last quarter of the sixteenth century, has a last line which matches fairly closely the corresponding passge in Monteverdi's setting. See Carol MacClintock, ed., *The Bottegari Lutebook* ("The Wellesley Edition," no. 8 [Wellesley, Mass., 1965]), p. 75.

107. The collection, entitled *Fioretti di frottole, barzellette, capitoli, strambotti, e sonetti*, was copied by Einstein, and appears in vol. 83 of the Smith College Music Archives (Madrigals of the Sixteenth and Seventeenth Centuries). The text of this piece, the twentieth item in the collection ("Tema chi teme io de temer non curo") does not extend to the fourth line of music; presumably the last line of the tercet was to be repeated, or the music was taken up by instruments.

108. Printed as the last song in *Le nuove musiche*; cf. Hitchcock's edition, p. 137.

109. See the 1608 score, pp. 49-51 (*PaM*, pp. 111-13).

110. These may be found in Solerti, *Albori*, vol. 2, pp. 2 ff.

111. Cf. the descriptions of two of these performances printed by Solerti, ibid., pp. 44 and 58.

112. See ibid., pp. 45-49.

113. Florence, Biblioteca Nazionale Centrale, Cl.XIX, cod. 66 and the Brussels Ms., cited in Chapter Three, note 147. The piece is published by Ghisi, *Alle fonti della monodia*, p. 47.

114. See his section on the *strambotto* in *Madrigal*, vol. 1, pp. 87 ff. In his articles on the *Ruggiero* ("Die Aria di Ruggiero," *Sammelbände der Internationalen Musikgesellschaft* 13 [1911-12]: 444-54; and "Ancora sull'aria di Ruggiero," *RMI* 41 [1937]: 163-69), Einstein gives the erroneous impression that this tune and the *Romanesca* were bass formulas used to support any number of melodies; but cf. Palisca, "Vincenzo Galilei and Some Links," especially p. 354, and notes 34-35. Also see Warren Kirkendale, *L'Aria di Fiorenza, id est il Ballo del Gran Duca* (Florence, 1972), passim.

115. See *Madrigal*, vol. 1, p. 285.

116. See *Madrigal*, vol. 3, no. 31. Also see ibid., vol. 1, p. 285, where another melodic
      formula is given.

117. Examples are nos. 8, 31, 38, 53, 54; see ed. cit., Chapter Four, note 106 above.

118. Cf. Nagler, *Theatre Festivals of the Medici*, pp. 116-18.

119. "Furon le soprascritte ottave composte musicalmente dall'istesse donne che le
      cantarono: la prima fu cantata con la solita sua grazia e voce angelica dalla
      signora Vittoria Archilei, romana; la seconda con ogni suprema esquisitezza dalla
      signora Settimia, e la terza con l'usata prontezza ed ammirazione universale dalla
      signora Francesca, ambidue figliuole del celebratissimo Giulio Romano; e la quarta
      ottava composta dalla medesima signora Francesca con stile graziosissimo e vago,
      fu dalle predette unitamente cantata con sî belle fughe e passaggi..." (in Solerti,
      Albori, vol. 2, p. 288).

120. For example, "Quest'aria cantò solo con altri passaggi secondo il suo stile Jacopo
      Peri," and "Quest'aria cantò solo parte con i propri passaggi, e parte a suo gusto
      il famoso Francesco Rasi" (*Le nuove musiche*, pp. 21-22). Chiabrera's strophes are
      not octaves, but are composed of five lines of hendecasyllables. Nevertheless, it is
      interesting to note that the bass line is very similar to Monteverdi's setting of the
      terzine of "Possente spirto."

121. However, it must be said that after 1608 ottave rime appear only sporadically in
      the masque texts, which inevitably absorbed the recitative style in their dialogue
      passages. In fact Peri took part in several of these productions, for example, the
      Mascherata di Ninfe di Senna of 1611, for which he reportedly composed the
      recitative portions. Cf. Solerti, *Albori*, vol. 2, p. 285.

122. See Porter, "Peri and Corsi's *Dafne* . . . ," p. 179.

123. See pp. 19-20 (*PaM*, pp. 98-100).

124. In Monteverdi's *Opere*, vol. 8, part 2, pp. 317-19, and vol. 11, p. 118, respectively.

125. See Chapter Three, above, p. 72.

126. "Peri and Corsi's *Dafne* . . . ," pp. 186-88; the piece is preserved in two Mss. in
      the Biblioteca Estense in Modena, for which Porter gives the sigla.

127. See example 33 and p. 167. Also see Riccardo Allorto, "Il prologo dell' *Orfeo*;
      note sulla formazione del recitativo Monteverdiano," in *Claudio Monteverdi e il
      suo tempo*, ed. R. Monterosso (Cremona, 1969), pp. 157-68.

128. See, for example, Antonio Belloni, *Il seicento*, 2d ed. (Milan, 1929), p. 124.

129. To quote Einstein (*Madrigal*, vol. 1, p. 285), ". . . in the streets and squares and on the canals."

130. See above, p. 137. The corollary is that the increased use of the chorus in the early years of the century and the expansion of its role as a formal prop preceding its eventual decline corresponds to a lessening of interest in terza and ottava rima solos.

131. See Solerti, *Albori*, vol. 2, pp. 313-18. Chiabrera's last full-fledged libretto, *Angelica in Ebuda* (1615), has the same verse characteristics; cf. *Albori*, vol. 3, pp. 137 ff.

132. Cf. ibid., vol. 2, pp. 335 ff.

Appendix A

Rinuccini, *La Dafne*

The version of Rinuccini's *Dafne* reproduced here is taken from the earliest printed edition of the libretto, which probably dates from 1598, and which is therefore also the earliest example of any printed opera libretto:

Rappresentazione / di Dafne / favola pastorale / composta dal Signor / Ottavio Rinuccini / et fatta recitare in musica dal Signor / Jacopo Corsi.

The text is a transcription of the only known exemplar of this 1598 libretto, which survives in the Special Collections of the Music Division of the New York Public Library at Lincoln Center. I have made no editorial changes or corrections except that 1) I have occasionally added some punctuation to the verse endings and 2) to avoid confusion, I have followed modern orthographic usage rather than the original text only in distinguishing between u and v (for example, *fugitivo cervo* instead of *fugitiuo ceruo*).

The alternate prologue assigned to La Musica for one of the post-1600 performances (pp. 260-61), and the alterations to scenes 1 and 5, which partially represent the revisions Rinuccini introduced for Marco da Gagliano's 1608 setting of *La Dafne* (pp. 261-67), are excerpted from Solerti, *Gli Albori del melodramma*, vol. 2, pp. 77 ff.

Original Libretto, 1598

[La Dafne]

OVIDIO.

Da fortunati campi où i mortali
Godonsi all'ombra de' frondosi mirti
I graditi del ciel felici spirti
Mostromi in questa notte à vòi mortali.

Quel mi son io che su la dotta lira   5
Cantai le fiamme de celesti amanti
E trasformati lor varii sembianti
Soave sì ch'il mondo ancor m'ammira.

Indi l'arte insegnai come si deste
In un gelato sen fiamma d'amore,   10
E come in libertà ritorna un core
Cui son d'amor le fiamme aspre è moleste.

Ma qual par che tra l'ombre il ciel rischiari
Nuova luce, e splendor di rai celesti,
Qual maestà vegg'io son forse questi   15
Gl' eccelsi Augusti miei felici e chiari.

Ah riconosco io ben l'alta Regina
Gloria e splendor de Lottaringi Regi
Il cui nome immortal gl'alteri fregi
Celebra 'l mondo, e'l nobil arno inchina.   20

Seguendo di giovar l'antico stile
Con chiaro esempio à dimostrarvi piglia
Quanto sia donne, e cavalier periglio
La potenza d'Amor recarsi à vile.

Vedrete lagrimar quel Dio ch'in cielo   25
Porta in bel carro d'or la luce e 'l giorno,
E dell'amata ninfa il lume adorno
Adorar dentro al trasformato stelo.

[Scene One]

PRIMO CHORO.

Tra quest'ombre segrete
S'inselva e si nasconde   30
L'horrida belva cauti il piè movete.
Ninfe e Pastori, ah non scotete fronde.

Choro.
Dunque senza timor senza spavento
Per nostri dolci campi
Non guiderem mai più gregge od armento.   35

Choro.

    Giove immortal che tra baleni e lampi
    Scoti la terra e'l cielo,
    Mandane ò fiamma ò telo,
    Che da mostro si rio n'affidi, e scampi.

Choro.

    Deh quando mai per queste piaggie o quelle   40
    Fronda corremo ò fiore,
    Misere pastorelle,
    Che di terror non ci s'agghiacci il core.

Choro.

    Ebra di sangue in quest'oscuro bosco
    Giacea pur dianzi la terribil fera.   Era   45
    Dunque piu non attosca
    Nostre belle contrade altrove è gita.   Ita
    Farà ritorno più per questi poggi?   Oggi
    Ohimè chi n'assicura
    S'hoggi tornar pur deve il mostro rio?   Io   50

    Chi se' tu, che n'affidi e ne console?   Sole
    Il Sol tu sei, tu sei di Delo il Dio?   Io
    Hai l'arco teco per ferirlo Apollo?   Ollo
    S'hai l'arco tuo, saetta infin che mora
    Questo mostro crudel che ne divora?   Ora   55

          Qui Apollo saetta il Pitone.

    Pur giacque estinto al fine
    In sul terren sanguigno
    Dall' invitt'arco mio l'Angue maligno.
    Securi itene al bosco
    Ninfe e Pastori ite securi al prato   60
    Non più di fiamma è tosco
    Infetta il puro Ciel l'horribil fiato
    Tornin le belle rose
    Ne le guancie amorose
    Torni tranquillo il cor sereno il volto   65
    Io l'alma el fiato al crudo serpe ho tolto.

CHORO SECONDO.

Almo Dio ch'il carro ardente
Per lo Ciel volgend'intorno
Vesti il di d'un aureo manto
Se tra l'ombra horrid' algente   70
Splend'il Ciel di lumi adorno
E pur tua la gloria e'l vanto.

Se germoglian frondi e fiori
Selve e prati e' rinnovella
L'ampia terra il suo bel manto   75
Se de suoi dolci tesori
Ogni pianta si fa bella
E pur tua la gloria e'l vanto.

Per te vive e per te gode
Quanto scerne occhio mortale,   80
O rettor del carro eterno
Ma si tacci ogn'altra lode
Sol dell'arco è dello strale
Voli il grido al ciel superno.

Nobil vanto il fier dragone   85
Di velen di fiamme armato
Su'l terren versat'hà l'alma
Per trecciar fregi, e corone
Al bel crin di raggi ornato
Qual fia degno edera o palma.   90

[Scene Two]

AMORE. VENERE. APOLLO.

Amore.
    Che tu vadia cercando ò giglio ò rosa
    Per infiorarti il crine,
    Non ti vo creder nò Madre vezzosa.

Venere.
    Che cerco dunque ò figlio.

Amore.
    Rosa non già ne giglio   95
    Cerchi d'Adone, ò d'altro vie più bello
    Leggiadro pastorello.

Venere.
    Ah tristo tristo ecco'l Signor di Delo
    Pe boschi oggi sen van gli Dei del Cielo.

Apollo.
    Dimmi possente Arciero   100
    Qual fera attendi ò qual serpente al varco
    Ch'ai la faretra, e l'arco.

Amore.
    Se da quest'arco mio
    Non fu Pitone ucciso
    arcier non son però degno di riso,   105
    E son del ciel Apollo un nume anch'io.

Apollo.
    Sollo, ma quando scocchi
    L'arco, sbendi tu gl'occhi,
    O ferisci all'oscuro arciero esperto.

Venere.
    S'hai di saper desio   110
    D'un cieco arcier le prove,
    Chiedilo al Re dell'onde,
    Chiedilo in Cielo à Giove,
    E tra l'ombre profonde
    Del regno horrid' oscuro,   115
    Chiedi chiedi à Pluton se fu sicuro.

Apollo.
    S'in Cielo, in mare, in terra,
    Amor trionfi in guerra,
    Dove dove m'ascondo
    Chi nuovo ciel m'insegna, ò nuovo mondo.   120

Amore.
    So ben che non paventi
    La forza d'un fanciullo

Saettator di mostri è di serpenti
Ma prendi pur di me giuoco è trastullo.

Apollo.
    Ah tu t'ardiri à torto   125
    O mi perdoni amore,
    O se mi vuoi ferir rispiarma il core.

Venere.
  .   Vedrai che grave rischio è scherzar seco
    Bench'ei sia pargoletto ignudo è cieco.

Amore.
    S'in quel superbo core   130
    Non fo piaga mortale
    Più tuo figlio non son non sono amore.

Venere.
    Amato pargoletto
    Come giust'ira è sdegno
    Hoggi t'infiamma'l petto   135
    Si spero al nostro regno
    Veder l'altero Dio servo è suggetto.

Amore.
    Non havrò posa mai, non havrò pace
    Fin ch'io nol veggia lagrimar ferito
    Da quest'arco schernito, ·   140
    Madre ben mi dispiace
    Di lasciarti soletta,
    Ma toglie assai d'honor tarda vendetta.

Venere.
    Vanne pur lieto ò figlio
    Lieta rimango anch'io,   145
    Che troppo è gran periglio
    Haverti irato à canto
    Per queste selve intanto
    Farò dolce soggiorno
    Poscia faremo insieme al ciel ritorno.   150

Venere.
Chi da lacci d'amor vive disciolto
Della sua libertà goda pur lieto
Superbo nò d'oscura nube involto
Stassi per noi del ciel l'alto decreto
S'hor non senti d'amor poco nè molto   155
Havrai dimane il cor turbato e'nqueto
E Signor proverrai crud'è severo
Amor che dianzi disprezzasti altero.

CHORO TERZO.

Had'arcier che l'arco tendi,
Che velat'ambo le ciglia   160
Amirabil meraviglia
Mortalmente i cori offendi
Se così t'infiammi encendi
Vers'un Dio quai saran poi
Sovra noi gli sdegni tuoi.   165

D'un leggiadro giovinetto
Già de boschi honore è gloria
Suona ancor fresca memoria
Che m'agghiaccia il cor nel petto
Qual per entro un ruscelletto   170
Se mirando arse d'amore,
E tornò piangendo in fiore.

Ogni Ninfa in doglie e'n pianti
Posto havea per sua bellezza
Ma del cor l'aspra durezza   175
Non piegar l'afflitte amanti
Quelle voci è quei sembianti
Ch'havrian mosso un cor di fera
Schernia pur quell'alma altera.

Una al pianto in abbandono   180
Lagrimando uscì di vita
Che fu poi per gl'antri udita
Rimbombar nud'ombra è suono
Hor quì più non ha perdono
Più non soffre amore irato   185
L'impietà del cor ingrato.

Punt'il sen di piaga acerba
Da quell'armi ond'altri ancise
Non pria fine al pianto ei mise
Ch'un bel fior si fe su l'erba,   190
O beltà crud'è superba
Non fia più ch'in van m'insegni
Con irato amor si sdegni.

[Scene Three]

DAFNE. APOLLO. AMORE.

Dafne.
Del fugitivo cervo
Quest'è pur orma impressa   195
Fosse almen quì vicin la fera stessa.

Apollo.
Qual d'un bel ciglio adorno
Spira lume gentil ch'al cor mi giugne.

Dafne.
Certo non molto lunge
Se'l desir non m'inganna e qui d'intorno   200
Hor vedrò sel mio stral va dritto, e punge.

Apollo.
Ah ben sent'io se son pungenti i dardi
De' tuoi soavi sguardi,
Dimmi qual tu ti sei,
O Ninfa, ò Dea, che tale   205
Ressembra agl'occhi miei,
Che cerchi armata di faretra e strale?

Dafne.
Seguendo io me ne giva
Per quest'ombrosa selva,
I passi, e l'orma di fugace belva,   210
E son donna mortal non del ciel diva.

Apollo.
Se cotal luce splende
In bellezza mortale
Del ciel più non mi cale.

Dafne.

>Dove mi volgo, dove 215
>Moverò 'l passo, che la fera trove.

Apollo.

>Senza che dardo avventi o l'arco scocchi
>Valli cercando ò monti,
>Far nobil preda puoi co' tuoi begli occhi.

Dafne.

>Altra preda non bramo, altro diletto, 220
>Che fere e selve è son contenta è lieta
>Se damma errante, ò fer cignal saetto.

Apollo.

>Ah che non sol di fere
>Saettatrice sei,
>Ma contro à gl'alti Dei 225
>Saette avventi dalle luci altere.

Dafne.

>Del ciel gl'eterni Numi
>Humile honoro è colo,
>E per le selve solo
>Pongo su l'arco i dardi, 230
>Ma tu per gioco il mio cammin ritardi.

Apollo.

>Deh non sdegnar che teco
>Compagno venga, anch'io so tender l'arco,
>E quando non ti spiaccia
>Farem d'accordo dilettosa caccia. 235

Dafne.

>Altri che l'arco mio
>Non vo compagno addio.

Apollo.

>Ohimè non tanta fretta
>Aspetta Ninfa aspetta.

Amore.

>Ve che ti giunsi al varco, 240
>O impara a disprezzar l'etate, e l'arco.

Hor sù dall'alto cielo
Mirin gl'eterni Dei
Le glorie, e' vanti miei,
E voi quaggiù mortali   245
Celebrate il valor degl' aurei strali.

[Scene Four]

VENERE. AMORE.

Venere.
    Figlio, dolce diletto
    Del cor de gl'occhi miei
    Come si lieto, e baldanzoso sei,
    Dillo bel pargoletto,   250
    Dimmelo amor ch'anch'io
    Senta le gioie tue dentra 'l cor mio.

Amore.
    Madre di gemme e d'oro
    Un bel carro m'appresta.
    Pommi su l'aurea testa   255
    Nobil fregio d'honor cerchio frondoso,
    Vegghimmi hoggi gli Dei dell'alto cielo
    Trionfator pomposo
    Quel Dio ch'intorno gira
    Il carro luminoso   260
    Vinto dall'arco mio piange e sospira.

Venere.
    Qual de gli Dei del Cielo
    Della faretra invitta
    Non senti dentro il cor pungente telo
    Io che madre ti sono, ahi quanto ahi quanto   265
    Il molle sen trafitto,
    E in Cielo, e in terra ho lagrimato, e pianto.

Amore.
    S'hai lagrimato e pianto hai riso anchora.
    Dimmi piangevi all'hor
    Che del fabbro geloso   270
    Non potesti schivar l'inganno ascoso.

Venere.
    Taci taci bel figlio
    Pur troppo è tu lo sai,
    Il mio bel viso all'hor si fe' vermiglio,
    Ma di tornare al Cielo è tempo omai.   275

QUARTO CHORO.

    Non si nasconde in selva
    Sì dispietata belva,
    Ne sù per l'alto polo
    Spiega le penne à volo augel solingo;
    Ne per le piaggie ondose   280
    Tra le fere squammose alberga core,
    Che non senta d'amore.

    Arder mirian le piante
    L'una dell'altro amante
    E gl'elementi anchora   285
    Bel foco arde innamora, e'nsieme accorda
    Sol contr'à gl'aurei strali
    I semplici mortali armano il core,
    Che non senta d'amore.

    Questi l'albe è le sere   290
    Perde cacciando fere
    E quei s'al ciel rimbomba
    Di Marte altera tromba all'armi corre,
    Altri la mente vaga
    Di mortal fasto appaga e'ndura il core   295
    Che non senta d'amore.

    Ma se d'un ciglio adorno
    Mira le fiamme un giorno
    O pregio del bel volto
    Scherzai con l'aure sciolto un capel d'oro   300
    Già vinto ogn'altro affetto
    Trova ch'in human petto non è core,
    Che non senta d'amore.

[Scene Five]

NUNTIO. CHORO.

Nuntio.
>   Qual nova meraviglia
>   Vedut'han gl'occhi miei?   305
>   O sempiterni Dei,
>   Che per lo ciel volgete
>   Nostre sorti mortali, ò triste, ò liete,
>   Fu gastigo ò pietate/cangiar l'alma beltate?   /310

Choro.
>   Pastor deh narra à noi
>   Le nuove meraviglie
>   Che visto han gl'occhi tuoi.

Nuntio.
>   Non senza trar dal core
>   Lagrime di dolore   315
>   Udirete pastori
>   Il destin della bella cacciatrice
>   Pur troppo miserabile e'nfelice.

Choro.
>   Di pur saggio Pastore,
>   Che non senza dolore   320
>   Lagrima per pietate un gentil core.

Nunzio.
>   Quando la bella Ninfa
>   Sprezzando i preghi del celeste amante
>   Vidi, che per fuggir volse le piante,
>   Da voi mi tolsi anch'io   325
>   L'orme seguendo dell'acceso Dio,
>   Ella quasi cervetta
>   Ch'innanzi à crudo veltro il passo affretta
>   Fuggia veloce, è spesso
>   Si volgeva à mirar se lungi, ò presso   330
>   Havea l'odiato amante;
>   Ma fatt'accorta homai
>   Ch'era ogni fuga in vano
>   I lagrimosi rai
>   Al Ciel rivolse, è l'una è l'altra mano   335
>   E'n lamentevol suono
>   Ch'io non udii, che troppo era lontano

Sciolse la lingua, et ecco in un momento,
Che l'uno è l'altro leggiadretto piede
Che pur dianzi al fuggir parve aura ò vento   340
Fatto immobil si vede
Di salvatica scorza insieme avvinto,
E le braccia, e le palme al ciel distese;
Veste selvaggia fronde
Le crespe chiome, e bionde   345
Più non riveggio el viso e'l bianco petto
Ma del gentile aspetto
Ogni sembianza si dilegua, e perde
Sol miro un arboscel fiorito, è verde.

Choro.
    O miserabil fato, ò destin rio,   350
    Che fe' disse all'hora
    L'innamorato Dio.

Nunzio.
    All'alta novitate
    Fermò repente il passo,
    E confuso d'horrore è di pietate   355
    Restò per lungo spazio immobil sasso,
    Poscia alle frondi amate
    Levando gl'occhi sospirosi, e molli
    Stese le braccia e'l nobil tronco avvinse,
    E mille volte ribaciollo, e strinse;   360
    Piangean d'intorno le campagne, e i colli
    Sospiravan pietosi, è l'aure, e i venti,
    Et ei nel gran dolore
    Sciolgea si mesti accenti,
    Ch'io sentii di pietà mancarmi il core: 365
    Ma vedete lui stesso
    Che verso noi sen viene
    Tutto carco di pene,
    Deh come fuor del luminoso volto
    Traspare il duol ch'ha dentro il core accolto.   370

[Scene Six]

Apollo.
    Dunque ruvida scorza
    Chiuderà sempre la beltà celeste,

Lumi voi che vedeste
L'alta beltà ch'hà lagrimar vi sforza
Affisatevi pur in questa fronde,   375
Qui posa, è quì s'asconde
Il mio bene, il mio core, il mio tesoro
Per cui ben ch'immortal languisco, e moro.
Ninfa sdegnosa è schiva,
Che fuggendo l'amore d'un Dio del Cielo   380
Cangiasti in verde lauro il tuo bel velo,
Non fia però, ch'io non t'onori et ami
Ma sempre al mio crin d'oro
Faran ghirlanda le tue frondi, e rami;
Ma deh s'in questa fronde odi il mio pianto,   385
Senti la nobil cetra
Quai doni à te dal ciel cantando impetra;

Non curi la mia pianta, ò fiamma, ò gelo,
Sien del vivo smeraldo eterni i pregi,
Ne l'offenda giamai l'ira del Cielo.   390

I bei Cigni di Dirce, ei sommi Regi,
De verdeggianti rami al crin famoso
Portin segno d'honor ghirlanda, è fregi.

Gregge mai nè Pastor fia che noioso
Del verde manto suo la spoglie, e prive;   395
Alla grat'ombra il dì lieto, e gioioso
Tragghin dolce cantando, e Ninfe, e dive.

ULTIMO CHORO.

Bella Ninfa fuggitiva
Sciolt' e priva
Del mortal tuo nobil velo,   400
Godi pur pianta novella,
Casta è bella
Cara al mondo è cara al Cielo.

Tu non curi è nembi è tuoni
Tu coroni   405
Cigni Regi, e Dei celesti,
Geli il cielo o'nfiammi è scaldi

Di smeraldi
Liet'ogn'hor t'adorni è vesti.

Godi pur de doni egregi   410
I tuoi pregi
Non t'invidio, e non desio,
Io se mai d'amor m'assale
Aureo strale
Non vo guerra con un Dio.   415

S'à fuggir movo le piante
Vero amante
Contr'amor crud'è superba,
Venir possa il mio crin d'auro
Non pur lauro,   420
Ma qual'è più miser'herba.

Sia vil canna il mio crin biondo
Che l'immondo
Gregge ogn'hor schiant'è dirame,
Sia vil fien ch'a crudi denti   425
De gl'armenti
Tragga ogn'hor l'avida fame.

Ma s'a preghi sospirosi
Amorosi
Di pietà sfavillo et ardo,   430
S'io prometto all'altrui pene
Dolce speme
Con un riso, ò con un sguardo.

Non soffrir cortese amore
Ch'il mio ardore   435
Prend'à scherno alma gelata,
Non soffrir ch'in piaggia o'n lido
Cor infido
M'abbandoni innamorata.

Fa ch'al foco de miei lumi   440
Si consumi
Ogni gelo, ogni durezza
Ardi poi quest'alma all'hora

Ch'altri adora
Qual si sia la mia bellezza.   445

Il Fine

Alternate Prologue: La Musica

Prologo fatto alla Dafne recitatasi in casa del
Signor Don Giovanni Medici

LA MUSICA.

Germe immortal del luminoso regno
Diva son io, ch'il suono acuto e 'l grave
Con bell'arte temprar dolce e soave,
Scesa nel mondo, a voi mortali insegno.

Io le voci di Pindo e gl'aurei detti
Spargo soave sì d'almo concento,
Che lagrimosi o lieti a mio talento
Rendo cantando ne' teatri i petti.

Sotto tetto real leggiadre e snelle
Non pur sciolgono il piè donne e guerrieri,
Ma nel puro zaffir, sotto gl'imperi
Della cetera mia, danzan le stelle.

Già pregio fui delle famose scene
Che cotanto illustrar le Muse Argive,
Del Tebro poi su le superbe rive
Cantai, scorso l'onor d'Argo e Micene.

Indi dell'Arno alle fiorite sponde
Scòrgemi a riverir gentil pensiero
I Toschi regi, e di più gloria altero
Cingermi il crin pensai di nuove fronde.

Colme d'alto stupor le scene aurate
Della bell'Alba allor le voci udiro;
Allor gli abissi al gran cantor s'apriro,
E pianse Apollo su le frondi amate.

Ma quando mi credei per più bel canto
Di più famoso allor fregiar le chiome,
Turba, di cui ridir non degno il nome,
Tolsemi ogni mio pregio, ogni mio vanto.

E poteo sì che dal reale albergo,
Ove d'òr mi credea rinnovar gli anni,
Per sottrarmi d'invidia a' fieri inganni,
Volsi, sdegnando, disprezzata il tergo.

Ma forse ad onta di mia sorte rea
Spero di ritrovar non vil mercede
Là 've di gigli e d'òr superba siede,
Di virtù, di valor novella Astrea.

Fra tanto, o sol de' cavalier più degni,
Che me raccogli sì cortese e pio,
Il suon di questa cetra e 'l cantar mio
Il magnanimo cor d'udir non sdegni.

La Dafne — Excerpts from the Revisions of 1608

[Scene One]

CORO.
Tra queste ombre segrete
S'inselva e si nasconde   30'
L'orrida belva: cauti il piè muovete,
Ninfe e Pastori; ah, non scotete fronde.

Altro Pastore.
Dunque senza timor, senza spavento,
Pe' nostri dolci campi
Non guiderem mai più gregge od armento?   35'

Ninfa del Coro.
E quando mai per queste piagge e quelle
Fronda corremo o fiore,
Misere verginelle,
Che di terror non ci si agghiacci 'l core?

Tirsi.
> Giove immortal, che tra baleni e lampi   40′
> Scoti la terra e 'l cielo,
> Màndane o fiamma o telo
> Che da mostro sì rio n'affidi e scampi.

Pastore del Coro.
> Mira dal ciel, deh mira
> Nudi di fronde omai questi arboscelli,   45′
> Pallide l'erbe e torbidi i ruscelli.

> Mira dal ciel, deh mira
> Tra lagrime e lamenti
> Tender le palme al cielo
> Sconsolati pastor, ninfe innocenti.   50′

Pastor del Coro.
> Se lassù tra gli aurei chiostri
> Puote un cor trovar mercè,
> Odi il pianto e i preghi nostri,
> O del Ciel monarca e re.

Coro.
> Odi il pianto e i preghi nostri,   55′
> O del Ciel monarca e re.

Coro.
> Se a ferir la turba altera
> Che sovr'Ossa Olimpo alzò,
> D'atro foco ira severa
> Tra le nubi il Cielo armò,   60′

> Odi il pianto e i preghi nostri,
> O del Ciel monarca e re.

Coro.
> De la destra onnipotente
> Non vil pregio ancor sarà
> Sterminar crudo serpente   65′
> Che struggendo il mondo va.

> Odi il pianto e i preghi nostri,
> O del Ciel monarca e re.

Pastore del Coro.
 Pera, pera il rio veleno,
 Non attoschi il mondo più;   70'
 [Verde il prato e'l ciel sereno]
 Torni omai, torni qual fu.

 Odi il pianto e i preghi nostri,
 O del Ciel monarca e re.

Altro Pastore.
 Ma dove oggi trarrem tranquilla un'ora   75'
 Senza temer l'abominevol tosco?

Pastore del Coro.
 Ebra di sangue in questo oscuro bosco
 Giacea pur dianzi la terribil fera.   Era

Altro Pastore.
 Dunque più non attosca
 Nostre belle campagne, altrove è gita?   Ita 80'

Pastore del Coro.
 Farà ritorno più per questi poggi?   Oggi

Altro Pastore.
 Oimè! chi n'assecura
 S'oggi tornar pur deve il mostro rio?   Io
 Chi sei tu, che n'affidi e ne console?   Sole

Pastore del Coro.
 Il Sol tu sei? tu sei di Delo il Dio?   Dio 85'
 Hai l'arco teco per ferirlo, Apollo?   Hollo
 S'hai l'arco tuo, saetta infin che mora
 Questo mostro crudel che ne divora.

  Qui Apollo mette mano a l'arco e saetta il Fitone.

Coro.
 Oimè che veggio! o Divo, o Nume eterno,
 Ecco l'orribile angue: 90'
 Spenga forza del Ciel mostro d'inferno.

O benedetto stral! mirate il sangue!
O glorioso arciero!
Ah, mostro fero, ancor non cadi esangue?

Arma di nuovo stral l'arco possente.   95'
Vola, vola pungente;
Spezza l'orrido tergo,
Giungilo al cor dove ha la vita albergo.

Apollo.
Pur giacque estinto al fine
In su 'l terren sanguigno   100'
Da l'invitt'arco mio l'angue maligno.
Securi itene al bosco,
Ninfe e Pastori, ite securi al prato:
Non più di fiamma e tosco
Infetta 'l puro ciel l'orribil fiato.   105'
Tornin le belle rose
Ne le guancie amorose;
Torni tranquillo il cor; sereno 'l volto:
Io l'alma e 'l fiato al crudo serpe ho tolto.

CORO.

Almo Dio, che 'l carro ardente   110'
Per lo ciel volgendo intorno
Vesti 'l dì d'un aureo manto,
Se tra l'ombra orrida algente
Splende il ciel di lume adorno,
È pur tua la gloria e 'l vanto.   115'

[Three more strophes follow, as above.]

[Scene Five]

NUNZIO. CORO.

Nunzio.
Qual nova meraviglia
Veduto han gli occhi miei?   305'
O sempiterni Dei,
Che per lo ciel volgete

Nostre sorti mortali o triste o liete,
Fu castigo o pietate
Cangiar l'alma beltate? 310′

Coro.
Pastor, deh narra a noi
Le nove meraviglie,
Che visto han gli occhi tuoi.

Nunzio.
Non senza trar dal core
Lagrime di dolore 315′
Udirete, Pastori,
Il destin de la bella cacciatrice
Pur troppo miserabile e 'nfelice.

Coro.
Di' pur, saggio Pastore,
Che non senza dolore 320′
Lagrima per pietate un gentil core.

Nunzio.
Quando la bella Ninfa,
Sprezzando i prieghi del celeste amante,
Vidi che per fuggir movea le piante,
Da voi mi tolsi anch'io 325′
L'orme seguendo de l'acceso Dio.
Ella, quasi cervetta
Che innanzi a crudo veltro il passo affretta,
Fuggìa veloce, e spesso
Si volgeva a mirar se lungi o presso 330′
Avea l'odiato amante;
Ma, fatt'accorta omai
Ch'era ogni fuga in vano,
I lagrimosi rai
Al ciel rivolse e l'una e l'altra mano, 335′
E 'n lamentevol suono,
Ch'io non udii, chè troppo era lontano,
Sciolse la lingua: et ecco in un momento
Che l'uno e l'altro leggiadretto piede,
Che pur dianzi al fuggir parve aura o vento, 340′
Fatto immobil si vede

Di salvatica scorza insieme avvinto,
E le braccia e le palme al ciel distese
Veste selvaggia fronde:
Le crespe chiome e bionde   345′
Più non riveggo e 'l volto e 'l bianco petto;
Ma dal gentile aspetto
Ogni sembianza si dilegua e perde;
Sol miro un arboscel fiorito e verde.

Pastore del Coro.
O miserabil caso, o destin rio!   350′
Che fe', che disse allora
L'innamorato Dio?

Nunzio.
A l'alta novitate
Fermò repente il passo,
E, confuso d'orrore e di pietate,   355′
Restò per lungo spazio immobil sasso.
Poscia a le frondi amate,
Alzando gli occhi sospirosi e molli,
Stese le braccia e 'l nobil tronco avvinse
E mille volte ribaciollo e strinse.   360′
Piangean d'intorno le campagne e i colli,
Sospiravan pietosi e l'aure e i venti;
Et ei nel gran dolore
Sciogliea sì mesti accenti,
Ch'io sentii per pietà mancarmi il core.   365′

Pastore del Coro.
Ahi dura, ahi ria novella!
Mira, deh, Tirsi mio, che il ciel ne piange,
Senti gli augei lagnar tra' secchi rami
E le fere ulular per le campagne;
Odi come piangendo ognun la chiami.   370′

Ninfa del Coro.
Piangete, O Ninfe, e con voi pianga Amore;
Raccogliete le penne, aure celesti,
E voi pietosi e mesti
Fermate i pie' d'argento, o fonti, o fiumi;
Lagrimate ne l'alto eterni Numi.   375′

Coro.

    Sparse più non vedrem di quel fin oro
    Le bionde chiome a 'l vento;
    Ahi! nè più s'udirà tra 'l bel tesoro
    Di perle e di rubin l'alto concento.
    Ahi! ch'ecclissato e spento   380'
    È del ciglio seren l'almo splendore.
    Piangete, Ninfe, e con voi pianga Amore.

    Piangete, Ninfe, e con voi pianga Amore.

    Dov'è la bella man, dove il bel seno,
    Dove, dove il bel viso?
    E dov'è il dolce riso
    Dov'è del guardo il lampeggiar sereno?

Pastore del Coro.

    Ahi lagrime, ahi dolor'!
    Piangete, Ninfe, e con voi pianga Amore.

Coro.

    Piangete, Ninfe, e con voi pianga Amore.   390'

Appendix B

Rinuccini, *L'Euridice*

The texts reproduced here are taken from the first printed editions of the libretto and scores of *L'Euridice.* Rinuccini's dedication and libretto are from:

> L'Euridice / D'Ottavio / Rinuccini, / Rappresentata / nello sponsalitio / Della Christianiss. / Regina / di Francia, e di / Navarra./[emblem]/ In Fiorenza, 1600./ Nella Stamperia di Cosimo Giunti./ Con licenza de' Superiori.

Peri's dedication and preface (pp. 296-99) are from:

> Le Musiche / di Iacopo Peri / Nobil Fiorentino / sopra L'Euridice / del Sig. Ottavio Rinuccini / Rappresentate Nello Sponsalizio / della Cristianissima / Maria Medici / Regina di Francia / e di Navarra./[emblem]/ In Fiorenza / appresso Giorgio Marescotti./ MDC.

Caccini's preface (pp. 299-300) is from:

> L'Euridice / Composta in / Musica / in stile rappresentativo / da Giulio Caccini / detto Romano./[emblem]/ In Firenze / appresso Giorgio Marescotti./ MDC.

The texts are given in their original form, unedited except for the addition of some punctuation to the prose sections, and occasionally to the verse endings as well.

Dedication to the Libretto, 1600

Alla Christianissima Maria Medici Regina di Francia, e di Navarra.

È stata openione di molti Christianiss. Regina, che gl'antichi Greci, e Romani cantassero su le Scene le Tragedie intere; ma sì nobil maniera di recitare non che rinnovata, ma ne pur che io sappia fin quì era stata

tentata da alcuno, e ciò mi credev'io per difetto della Musica moderna di
gran lunga all'antica inferiore; ma pensiero sì fatto mi tolse interamente
dell'animo M. Iacopo Peri, quando udito l'intentione del Sig. Iacopo
Corsi, e mia mise con tanta gratia sotto le note la favola di Dafne
composta da me solo per far una semplice prova di quello, che potesse il
canto dell'età nostra, che incredibilmente piacque a que pochi, che
l'udirono; onde preso animo, e dato miglior forma alla stessa favola, e di
nuovo rappresentandola in casa il Sig. Iacopo, fu ella non solo dalla
nobiltà di tutta questa Patria favorita, ma dalla Serenissima Gran
Duchessa, e gl'illustrissimi Cardinali Dal Monte, e Montalto udita, e
commendata; ma molto maggior favore, e fortuna ha sortito l'Euridice
messa in Musica dal medesimo Peri, con arte mirabile, e da altri non più
usata havendo meritato dalla benignità, e magnificenza del Sereniss.
Gran Duca d'essere rappresentata in nobilissima Scena alla presenza di
V. M. del Cardinale Legato, e di tanti Principi, e Signori d'Italia, e di
Francia; la onde cominciando io a conoscere, quanto simili
rappresentationi in Musica siano gradite, ho voluto recar in luce queste
due, perche altri di me più intendenti si ingegnino di accrescere, e
migliorare si fatte Poesie, di maniera, che non habbiano invidia a quelle
antiche tanto celebrate da i nobili scrittori. Potrà parere ad alcuno, che
troppo ardire sia stato il mio in alterare il fine della favola d'Orfeo, ma
cosi mi è parso convenevole in tempo di tanta allegrezza, havendo per
mia giustificatione esempio di Poeti Greci, in altre favole; e il nostro
Dante ardì dì affermare essersi sommerso Ulisse nella sua navigatione,
tutto che Omero, e gl'altri Poeti havessero cantato il contrario. Cosi
parimente ho seguito l'autorità di Sofocle nel l'Aiace in far rivolger la
Scena non potendosi rappresentar altrimenti le preghiere, e i lamenti
d'Orfeo. Riconosca V. M. in queste mie ben che piccole fatiche l'humil
devotione dell'animo verso di lei, e viva lungamente felice per ricever da
Iddio ogni giorno maggior grazie, e maggior favori.
Di Firenze il dì [4] d'Ottobre 1600.

> Di V. M. Humiliss. Servitore
> Ottavio Rinuccini.

Libretto

[L'EURIDICE]

INTERLOCUTORI.

La Tragedia.
Euridice.

Orfeo.

Arcetro. ⎫

Tirsi. ⎬ Pastori

Aminta. ⎭

Dafne Nuntia.

Venere.

Choro di Ninfe, e Pastori

Plutone.

Proserpina.

Radamanto.

Caronte.

Choro di ombre, e Deità d'Inferno.

LA TRAGEDIA.

Io che d'alti sospir vaga e di pianti
Spars'or di doglia, or di minaccie il volto
Fei negl'ampi Teatri al popol folto
Scolorir di pietà volti, e sembianti,

Non sangue sparso d'innocenti vene   5
Non ciglia spente di Tiranno insano,
Spettaccolo infelice al guardo humano
Canto su meste, e lagrimose scene.

Lungi via lungi pur da regi tetti
Simolacri funesti, ombre d'affanni,   10
Ecco i mesti coturni, e i foschi panni
Cangio, e desto ne i cor più dolci affetti.

Hor s'avverrà, che le cangiate forme
Non senza alto stupor la terra ammiri,
Tal' ch'ogni alma gentil' ch'Apollo inspiri   15
Del mio novo cammin calpesti l'orme.

Vostro Regina fia cotanto alloro
Qual forse anco non colse Atene, o Roma,
Fregio non vil su l'onorata chioma
Fronda Febea fra due corone d'oro.   20

Tal per voi torno, e con sereno aspetto
Ne Reali Imenei, m'adorno anch'io,

E su corde più liete il canto mio
Tempro al nobile cor dolce diletto.

Mentre Senna Real prepara intanto   25
Altro diadema, onde il bel crin si fregi,
E i manti, e seggi de gl'antichi Regi
Del Tracio Orfeo date l'orecchia al canto.

[Scene One]

CHORO.

Ninfe ch'i bei crin d'oro
Sciogliete liete allo scherzzar de' venti,   30
E voi ch'almo tesoro
Dentro chiudete a bei rubini ardenti,
E voi ch'all' Alba in Ciel togliete i vanti
Tutte venite, o Pastorelle amanti,
E per queste fiorite alme contrade   35
Risuonin liete voci, e lieti canti:
Oggi à somma beltade
Giunge sommo valor santo Imeneo,
Avventuroso Orfeo,
Fortunata Euridice,   40
Pur vi congiunse il Cielo, o dì felice.

Ninf. del Cho.
Raddoppia, e fiamm', e lumi
Al memorabil giorno
Febo ch'il carro d'or rivolgi intorno.

Past.
E voi Celesti Numi   45
Per l'alto Ciel con certo moto erranti,
Rivolgete sereni
Di pace, e d'amor pieni
Alle bell'alme i lucidi sembianti.

Ninf.
Vaghe Ninfe amorose   50
Inghirlandat' il crin d'alme viole
Dite liete, e festose
Non vede un simil par d'amanti 'l Sole.

Eur.

    Donne, ch'a' miei diletti
    Rasserenate sì lo sguardo, e'l volto,   55
    Che dentr'a vostri petti
    Tutto rassembra il mio gioir raccolto,
    Deh come lieta ascolto
    I dolci canti, e gli amorosi detti
    D'amor, di cortesia graditi affetti.   60

Past.

    Qual in sì rozo core
    Alberga alma sì fera, alma si dura
    Che di sì bell'amor' l'alta ventura
    Non colmi di diletto e di dolcezza?
    Credi Ninfa gentile   65
    Pregio d'ogni bellezza
    Che non è fera in bosco, augello in fronda,
    O muto pesce in onda,
    Ch'oggi non formi, e spiri
    Dolcissimi d'amor sensi, e sospiri,   70
    Non pur son liete l'alme, e lieti i cori
    De vostri dolci amori.

Eur.

    In mille guise, e mille
    Crescon le gioie mie dentro al mio petto
    Mentre ogn'una di voi par che scintille   75
    Dal bel' guardo seren riso, e diletto;
    Ma deh compagne amate
    Là tra quell'ombre grate
    Moviam di quel'fiorito almo boschetto
    E quivi al suon de limpidi cristalli   80
    Trarrem liete carole, e lieti balli.

Cho.

    Itene liete pur, noi qui fra tanto
    Che sopragiunga Orfeo
    L'ore trapasserem' con lieto canto.

    CHORO.

    Al canto, al ballo, all'ombre, al prato adorno   85
    Alle bell'onde, e liete

Tutti, o Pastor correte
Dolce cantando in si beato giorno.

Al canto, al etc.

Selvaggia Diva, e boschereccie Ninfe
Satiri, e voi Silvani   90
Reti lasciat', e cani
Venite al suon delle correnti linfe.

Al canto, al etc.

Bella Madre d'Amor dall'alto Coro
Scendi a nostri diletti
E, co bei pargoletti   95
Fendi le nubi, e'l Ciel con l'ali d'oro.

Al canto, al etc.

Corran di puro latte, e rivi, e fiumi
Di mel distilli, e manna
Ogni selvaggia canna,
Versat' ambrosia e voi Celesti Numi.   100

Al canto, al etc.

[Scene Two]

Or.

Antri ch'a' miei lamenti
Rimbombaste dolenti amiche piaggie,
E voi piante selvaggie;
Ch'alle dogliose rime
Piegaste per pietà l'altere cime,   105
Non sia più nò, che la mia nobil cetra
Con flebil canto a lagrimar v'alletti,
Ineffabil mercede, almi diletti
Amor cortese oggi al mio pianto impetra;
Ma deh perche sì lente   110
Del bel carro immortal le rotte accese
Per l'eterno cammin tardono il corso?
Sferza Padre cortese

A volanti destrier, le groppe, e'l dorso.
Spegni nell'onde omai,   115
Spegni, o nascondi i fiammeggianti rai.
Bella Madre d'Amor dall'onde fora
Sorgi, e la nott'ombrosa
Di vaga luce scintillando indora;
Venga deh venga omai la bella Sposa   120
Tra'l notturno silentio, e i lieti orrori
A temprar tante fiamme, e tanti ardori.

Arcet.
Sia pur lodato amore
Che d'allegrezza colmo
Pur nella front'un dì ti vidi il core.   125

Orf.
O mio fedel' ne pur picciola stilla
A gl'occhi tuoi traspare
Dell'infinito mare
Che di dolcezza amor nel cor distilla.

Arc.
Hor non ti riede in mente   130
Quando fra tante pene
Io ti dicea sovente,
Armati il cor di generosa spene,
Che de fedeli amanti
Non ponno al fin delle Donzelle i cori   135
Sentir senza pietà le voci, e pianti?
Ecco ch'a tuoi dolori
Pur s'ammolliro al fine
Del disdegno cor gl'aspri rigori.

Orf.
Ben conosc'hor, che tra pungenti spine   140
Tue dolcissime rose
Amor serbi nascose, hor veggio, e sento
Che per farne gioir ne dai tormento.

Tirsi
Nel puro ardor della più bella Stella
Aurea facella   di bel foco accendi   145

    E quì discendi   sù l'aurate piume
    Giocondo Nume,   e di celeste fiamma
    L'anime infiamma.

    Lieto Imeneo d'alta dolcezza un nembo
    Trabocca in grembo   a' fortunati amanti,   150
    E tra bei canti   di soavi amori
    Sveglia ne' cori   una dolce aura, un riso
    Di Paradiso.

Arc.

    Deh come ogni Bifolco, ogni Pastore
    A tuoi lieti Imenei   155
    Scopre il piacer ch'entro racchiude il core.

Tirsi

    Del tuo beato amor gl'alti contenti
    Creschano ognor come per pioggia suole
    L'onda gonfiar de' rapidi torrenti.

Orf.

    E per te Tirsi mio liete, e ridenti   160
    Sempre le notti, e i dì rimeni il Sole.

Daf. Nunzia.

    Lassa, che di spavento, e di pietate
    Gelami il cor nel seno.
    Miserabil beltate
    Come in un punto ohime venisti meno.   165
    Ahi che lampo, o baleno
    In notturno seren ben ratto fugge,
    Ma più rapida l'ale
    Affretta humana vita al dì fatale.

Arc.

    Ohime che fia già mai?   170
    Pur hor tutta gioiosa
    Al fonte degl'allor costei lasciai.

Orf.

    Qual così ria novella
    Turba il tuo bel sembiante
    In questo allegro dì gentil Donzella?   175

Daf.

O del gran Febo, e delle sacre Dive
Pregio sovran di queste selve onore
Non chieder la cagion del mio dolore.

Orf.

Ninfa deh sia contenta
Ridir perche t'affanni 180
Che taciuto martir troppo tormenta.

Nun. [Dafne]

Com'esser può già mai
Ch'io narri, e ch'io reveli
Sì miserabil caso? ò fato, ò Cieli,
Deh lasciami tacer, troppo il saprai. 185

Cho.

Dì pur sovente, del timor l'affanno
E dell'istesso mal men grave assai.

Daf.

Troppo più del timor fia grave il danno.

Orf.

Ah non sospender più l'alma dubbiosa.

Daf.

Per quel vago boschetto 190
Ove rigando i fiori
Lento trascorre il fonte de gl'Allori,
Prendea dolce diletto
Con le compagne sue la bella Sposa,
Chi Violetta, o Rosa 195
Per far ghirlande al crine
Togliea dal prato, e dall'acute spine,
E qual posando il fianco
Sù la fiorita sponda
Dolce cantava al mormorar dell'onda. 200
Ma la bella Euridice
Movea danzando il piè sù'l verde prato,
Quando ria sorte acerba
Angue crudo, e spietato,

Che celato giacea tra fiori, e l'erba   205
Punsele il piè con sì maligno dente,
Ch'impallidì repente
Come raggio di Sol che nube adombri,
E dal profondo core
Con un sospir mortale   210
Che spaventoso ohime, sospinse fore
Che quasi havesse l'ale
Giunse ogni Ninfa al doloroso suono,
Et ella in abbandono
Tutta lasciossi all'or nell'altrui braccia.   215
Spargea il bel volto, e le dorate chiome
Un sudor via più freddo assai che ghiaccio.
Indi s'udio il tuo nome
Tra le labbra sonar fredde e tremanti
E volti gl'occhi al Cielo   220
Scolorito il bel viso, e i bei sembianti
Restò tanta bellezza immobil gelo.

Arc.

Che narri, ohime, che sento?
Misera Ninfa, e più misero Amante
Spettaccol di miseria, e di tormento.   225

Orf.

Non piango, e non sospiro
O mia cara Euridice
Che sospirar, che lagrimar non posso.
Cadavero infelice,
O mio core, o mia speme, o pace, o vita.   230
Ohime chi mi t'ha tolto
Chi mi t'ha tolto, ohime dove se gita?
Tosto vedrai, ch'in vano
Non chiamasti morendo il tuo consorte;
Non son, non son lontano   235
Io vengo, o cara vita, o cara morte.

Arc.

Ahi morte invida, e ria
Così recidi il fior de l'altrui speme?
Così turbi d'amor gl'almi contenti?
Lasso ma indarno a' venti   240

Ove l'empia n'assal volan le strida;
Fia più senno il seguirlo, acciò non vinto
Da sovverchio dolor se stesso uccida.

Daf.

Va' pur ch'ogni dolor si fa men grave   245
Ove d'amico fido
Reca conforto il ragionar soave.

Ninf.

Dunque è pur ver, che scompagnate, e sole
Tornat' o Donne mie,
Senza la scorta di quel vivo Sole?

Amin.

Sconsolati desir gioie fugaci   250
O speranze fallaci
E chi creduto havrebbe
In sì breve momento
Veder il Sol d'ogni bellezza spento?

Ninf.

Bel dì ch'in su'l mattin si lieto apristi   255
Deh come avanti sera
Nube di duol t'adombra oscura, e nera;
O gioie, o risi, o canti
Fatti querele, e pianti.

Past.

O voi cotanto alteri   260
Per fior di giovanezza
E voi che di bellezza
Sì chiari pregi havete
Mirate donne mie quel che voi sete.

Cho.

Cruda morte ahi pur potesti   265
Oscurar sì dolci lampi
Sospirate aure celesti
Lagrimate o Selve, o Campi.

Quel bel volto almo fiorito
Dove Amor suo seggio pose   270

Pur lasciasti scolorito
Senza Gigli, e senza Rose.
      Sospirate aure, etc.
Fiammeggiar di negre ciglia
Ch'ogni Stella oscuri in prova
Chioma d'or guancia vermiglia   275
Contr'à morte ohime che giova?
      Sospirate aure, etc.
S'Appenin nevoso il tergo
Spira giel che l'onde affrena
Lieto foco in chiuso albergo
Dolce April per noi rimena.   280
      Sospirate aure, etc.
Quand'a rai del Sol cocenti
Par che il Ciel s'infiammi, e'l Mondo
Fresco rio d'onde lucenti
Torna il dì lieto e giocondo.
      Sospirate aure, etc.
Spoglia sì di fiamm' e tosco   285
Forte carme empio serpente
Ben si placa in selve, o'n bosco
Fier Leon nell'ora ardente.
      Sospirate aure, etc.
Ben Nocchier costante, e forte
Sa schernir marino sdegno   290
Ahi fuggir colpo di morte
Già non val mortal ingegno.
      Sospirate aure, etc.

[Scene Three]

Arc.

Se fato invido, e rio
Di quest' amate piaggie ha spento il Sole
Donne, ne riconsole   295
Che per celeste aita
Il nobile Pastor rimaso è in vita.

Cho.

Benigno don de gl'immortali Dei
S'ei vive pur da tanta angoscia oppresso

Ma tu perche non sei 300
In sì grand'uopo al caro amico appresso?

Arc.

Con frettoloso passo
Come tu sai dietro li tenni, or quando
Da lungi il vidi, che dolente, e lasso
Sen già com' huom d'ogni allegrezza in bando 305
Il corso alquanto allento,
Pur tuttavia da lunge
Tenendo al suo cammin lo sguardo intento;
Et ecco al loco ei giunge
Dove fe' morte il memorabil danno. 310
Vinto da l'alto affanno
Cadde su l'herba, e quivi
Si dolenti sospir dal cor gl'usciro
Che le fere, e le piante, e l'herbe, e i fiori
Sospirar seco, e lamentar s'udiro; 315
Et egli: o fere, o piante, o fronde, o fiori
Qual di voi per pietà m'addita il loco
Dove ghiaccio divenne il mio bel foco?
E come porse il caso, o volle il fato
Girando intorno le dolenti ciglia 320
Scorse sul verde prato
Del bel sangue di lei l'herba vermiglia.

Cho.

Ahi lagrimosa vista, ahi fato acerbo.

Arc.

Sovra'l sanguigno smalto
Immobilmente affisse 325
Le lagrimose luci, e'l volto esangue,
Indi tremando disse
O sangue, o caro sangue
Del mio ricco tesor misero avanzo
Deh co' miei baci insieme 330
Prendi del alma ancor quest' aure estreme.
E quasi ei fosse d'insensibil pietra
Cadde su l'herba, e quivi
Non dirò fonti, o rivi

Ma di lagrime amare   335
Da quegl'occhi scorgar pareva un mare.

Cho.

Ma tu perche tardavi a dargli aita?

Arc.

Io che pensato havea di starmi ascoso
Fin che l'aspro dolor sfogasse alquanto
Quando su'l prato erboso   340
Cader lo vidi, e crescer pianto, a pianto
Mossi per sollevarlo, O meraviglia.
Et ecco un lampo ardente
Da l'alto Ciel mi saettò le ciglia;
Allor gl'occhi repente   345
Rivolsi al folgorar del novo lume,
E sovr' human costume
Entro bel carro di zaffir lucente
Donna vidi celeste, al cui sembiante
Si coloriva il Ciel di luce, e d'oro.   350
Avvinte al carro avante
Spargean le penne candidette, e snelle
Due Colombe gemelle,
E qual le nubi fende
Cigno che d'alto alle bell'onde scende   355
Tal con obliqui giri
Lente calando là fermaro il volo,
Ove tra rei martiri
Lo sconsolato amante
Premea con guancia lagrimosa il suolo;   360
Ivi dal Carro scese
L'altera Donna, e con sembiante humano
Candida man per sollevarlo stese.
Al celeste soccorso
La destra ei porse, e fe' sereno il viso.   365
Io di sì lieto avviso
Per rallegrarvi il cor mi diedi al corso.

Cho.

A te qual tu ti sia de gl'alti Numi
Ch'al nobile Pastor recasti aita

Mentre havran queste membra, e spirto, e vita   370
Canterem lodi ogn'or tra incensi, e fumi.

CHORO.

Se de boschi i verdi onori
Raggirar su nudi campi
Fa stridor d'orrido Verno
Sorgono anco, e frond'e fiori   375
Appressando i dolci lampi
Della luce il carro eterno.

S'al soffiar d'Austro nemboso
Crolla in Mar gli scogli alteri
L'onda torbida spumante,   380
Dolce increspa il tergo ondoso
Sciolti i nembi oscuri, e feri
Aura tremula, e vagante.

Al rotar del ciel superno
Non pur l'aer, e'l foco intorno,   385
Ma si volve il tutto in giro.
Non è il ben nel pianto eterno;
Come or sorge, or cade il giorno,
Regna quì gioia, o martiro.

Past.
  Poi che dal bel sereno   390
In queste piagge umil tra noi mortali
Scendon li Dei pietosi a nostri mali,
Pria che Febo nasconda a Teti in seno
I rai lucenti, e chiari
Al Tempio a i sacri Altari   395
Andiam devoti, e con celeste zelo
Alziam le voci, e'l cor cantando al Cielo.

Quì il Choro parte, e la Scena si tramuta.

[Scene Four]

Ven.
Scorto da immortal guida
Arma di speme, e di fortezza l'alma
Ch' havrai di morte ancor trionfo, e palma.   400

Orf.

    O Dea Madre d'Amor figlia al gran Giove,
    Che fra cotante pene
    Ravvivi il cor con sì soave spene
    Per qual fosco sentier mi scorgi? e dove
    Rivedrò quelle luci alme, e serene?   405

Ven.

    L'oscuro varco, onde siam giunti a queste
    Rive pallide, e meste,
    Occhio non vide ancor d'alcun mortale,
    Rimira intorno, e vedi
    Gl'oscuri campi, e la Città fatale   410
    Del Re che sovra l'ombre ha scettro, e regno;
    Scogli il tuo nobil canto
    Al suon dell'aureo legno,
    Quanto morte t'ha tolto ivi dimora;
    Prega, sospira, e plora   415
    Forse avverrà, che quel soave pianto
    Che mosso ha il Ciel pieghi l'Inferno ancora.

Orf.

    Funeste piaggie ombrosi orridi campi,
    Che di Stelle, o di Sole
    Non vedeste giamai scintill'e lampi,   420
    Rimbombate dolenti
    Al suon dell'angosciose mie parole,
    Mentre con mesti accenti
    Il perduto mio ben con voi sospiro;
    E voi deh per pietà del mio martiro,   425
    Che nel misero cor dimora eterno,
    Lagrimate al mio pianto ombre d'Inferno.

    Ohime che sù l'aurora
    Giunse all'occaso il Sol de gl'occhi miei
    Misero è sù quell'ora   430
    Che scaldarmi a bei raggi mi credei
    Morte spense il bel lume, e freddo, e solo
    Restai fra pianto, e duolo
    Com'angue suole in fredda pioggia il verno;
    Lagrimate al mio pianto ombre d'Inferno.   435

E tu mentre al Ciel piacque
Luce di questi lumi
Fatti al tuo dipartir fontan' e fiumi
Che fai per entro i tenebrosi orrori?
Forse t'affliggi, e piangi   440
L'acerbo fato, e gl'infelici amori;
Deh se scintilla ancora
Ti scalda il sen di quei sì cari ardori,
Senti mia vita, senti,
Quai pianti, e quai lamenti   445
Versa il tuo caro Orfeo dal cor interno.
Lagrimate al mio pianto ombre d'Inferno.

Plutone.
Ond'è cotanto ardire
Ch'avanti al dì fatale
Scend'a' miei bassi regni un'huom mortale?   450

Orf.
O de gl'orridi, e neri
Campi d'Inferno, o dell'altera Dite
Eccelso Rè, ch'alle nud'ombre imperi,
Per impetrar mercede
Vedovo amante a quest' abisso oscuro   455
Volsi piangendo, e lagrimando il piede.

Plu.
Si dolci note, e si soavi accenti
Non spargeresti in van, se nel mio regno
Impetrasser mercè pianti, o lamenti.

Orf.
Deh se la bella Diva   460
Che per l'acceso monte
Mosse a fuggirti in van ritrosa, e schiva
Sempre ti scopra, e giri
Sereni i rai della celeste fronte,
Vagliami il dolce canto   465
Di questa nobil cetra
Ch'io ricovri da te la Donna mia;
L'alma deh rendi a questo sen dolente,
Rendi a quest' occhi il desiato Sole,

A queste orecchie il suono   470
Rendi delle dolcissime parole;
O me raccogli ancora
Tra l'ombre spente, ov'il mio ben dimora.

Plu.

Dentro l'infernal porte
Non lice ad huom mortal fermar le piante;   475
Ben di tua dura sorte
Non sò qual novo affetto
M'intenerisce il petto,
Ma troppo dura legge,
Legge scolpita in rigido diamante   480
Contrasta a preghi tuoi misero amante.

Orf.

Ahi che pur d'ogni legge
Sciolto è colui, che gl'altri affrena, e regge;
Ma tu del mio dolore
Scintilla di pietà non senti al core.   485
Ahi lasso, e non rammenti
Come trafigga Amor, come tormenti.
E pur su'l monte dell'eterno ardore
Lagrimasti ancor tù servo d'amore.
Ma deh se'l pianto mio   490
Non può nel duro sen destar pietate,
Rivolgi il guardo a quell'alma beltate,
Che t'accese nel cor si bel desio;
Mira Signor, deh mira
Come al mio lagrimar dolce sospira   495
Tua bella sposa, e come dolce i lumi
Rugiadosi di pianto a me pur gira.
Mira signor deh mira,
Quest'ombre intorno, e quest'oscuri Numi;
Vedi come al mio duol come al mio pianto   500
Par che ciascun si strugga, e si consumi.

Pros.

O Re nel cui sembiante
Mi appago si ch'il Ciel sereno, e chiaro
Con quest'ombre cangiar m'è dolce e caro,
Deh se gradito amante   505

Già mai trovasti in questo sen raccolto
Onda soave a l'amorosa sete,
S'al cor libero, e sciolto
Dolci fur queste chiome, e laccio, e rete
Di sì gentil amante aqueta il pianto.   510

Orf.

A sì soavi preghi
A sì fervido amante
Mercede anco pur nieghi?
Che fia però se fra tant'alme, e tante
Riede Euridice a rimirare il Sole?   515
Rimarran queste piaggie ignude, e sole?
Ahi che me seco, e mille, e mille insieme
Diman teco vedrai nel tuo gran regno;
Sai pur che mortal vita all'ore estreme
Vola più ratta che saetta al segno.   520

Orf. [Plutone]

Dunque dal regno oscuro
Torneran l'alme al Ciel, et io primiero
Le leggi spezzerò del nostro impero.

Rad.

Sovra l'eccelse Stelle
Giove a talento suo comanda, e regge.   525
Nettuno il Mar corregge
E move a suo voler turbi, e procelle
Tu sol dentr'a i confin d'angusta legge
Havrai l'alto governo
Non libero Signor del vasto Inferno?   530

Plu.

Romper le proprie leggi è vil possanza.
Anzi reca sovente, e biasmo, e danno.

Orf.

Ma degl'afflitti consolar l'affanno
E pur di regio cor gentil usanza.

Caron.

Quanto rimira il sol volgendo intorno   535
La luminosa face

Al rapido sparir d'un breve giorno
Cade morendo, e fa qua giù ritorno
Fà pur legge o gran Rè quanto a te piace.

Plu.

Trionfi oggi pietà ne campi Inferni,   540
E sia la gloria, e'l vanto
Delle lagrime tue del tuo bel canto;
O della Regia mia ministri eterni
Scorgete voi per entro all'aere scuro
L'amator fido alla sua donna avante;   545
Scendi gentil amante
Scendi lieto, e sicuro
Entro le nostre soglie,
E la diletta Moglie
Teco rimena al Ciel sereno, e puro.   550

Orf.

O fortunati miei dolci sospiri,
O ben versati pianti,
O me felice sopra gl'altri amanti.

Choro d'Ombre, e Deità d'Inferno.

Poi che gl'eterni imperi
Tolto dal Ciel Saturno   555
Partiro i figli alteri
Da quest'orror notturno
Alma non tornò mai
Del Ciel a' dolci rai.

Unqua ne mortal piede   560
Calpestò nostre arene,
Che d'impetrar mercede
Non nacque al mondo spene
In quest'abisso dove
Pietà non punge, e muove.   565

Or di soave pletro
Armato, e d'aurea cetra
Con lagrimoso metro
Canoro amante impetra,

Ch'il Ciel riveggha, e viva 570
La sospirata Diva.

Si trionfaro in guerra,
D'Orfeo la cetra e i canti,
O figli della terra
L'ardir frenat'e i vanti; 575
Tutti non sete prole
Di lui che regge il Sole.

Scender al centro oscuro
Forse fia facil opra
Ma quanto ahi quanto è duro 580
Indi poggiar poi sopra;
Sol lice alle grand'alme
Tentar sì dubbie palme.

Si rivolge la Scena, e torna come prima.

[Scene Five]

Arc.
Già del bel carro ardente
Rotan tepidi i rai nel Ciel sereno 585
E già per l'Oriente
Sorge l'ombrosa notte, e'l di vien meno,
Ne fà ritorno Orfeo,
Ne pur di lui novella ancor si sente.

Cho.
Già temer non si dee di sua salute, 590
Se da campi celesti
Scender Nume divin per lui vedesti.

Arc.
Vidilo, e sò ch'il ver quest'occhi han visto,
Ne regna alcun timor nel petto mio;
Ma di vederlo men dolente, e tristo 595
Struggemi l'alma, e'l cor caldo desio.

Amin.
Voi che sì ratte il volo
Spiegate aure volanti,
Voi de' fedeli amanti

Per queste piaggie, e quelle   600
Spargete le dolcissime novelle.

Cho.

Ecco il gentil Aminta
Tutto ridente in viso;
Forse reca d'Orfeo giocondo avviso.

Amin.

Non più, non più lamenti   605
Dolcissime compagne
Non fia chi più si lagne
Di dolorosa sorte
Di fortuna, o di morte, il nostro Orfeo,
Il nostro Semideo,   610
Tutto lieto, e giocondo,
Di dolcezza, e di gioia
Nuota in un mar, che non ha riva, o fondo.

Cho.

Come tanto dolore
Quetossi in un momento?   615
E chi cotanto ardore
In sì fervido cor sì presto ha spento?

Amin.

Spento è il dolor ma vive
Del suo bel foco ancor chiare, e lucenti,
Splendon le fiamme ardenti;   620
La bella Euridice
Ch'habbiam cotanto sospirato, e pianto
Più che mai bella è viva
Lieta si gode al caro sposo a canto.

Cho.

Vaneggi Aminta o pure   625
Ne speri rallegrar con tai menzogne?
Assai lieti ne fai, se n'assecuri
Ch'il misero Pastore
Prenda conforto nel mortal dolore.

Amin.

    O del regno celeste   630
    Voi chiamo testimon superni Numi,
    S'il ver parlo, e ragiono;
    Vive la bella Ninfa, e questi lumi
    Pur or miraro il suo bel viso, e queste
    Orecchie udir delle sue voci il suono.   635

Cho.

    Quai dolci, e care nove
    Ascolto, o Dei del Cielo, o sommo Giove
    Ond'è cotanta gratia, e tanto dono?

Amin.

    Quando al Tempio n'andaste io mi pensai
    Ch'opra forse saria non men pietosa   640
    Dell'infelice sposa
    Gl'afflitti consolar vecchi parenti
    E la ratto n'andai
    Ove tra schiera di pastori amici
    La sventurata sorte   645
    Lagrimavan que vecchi orbi e'nfelici;
    Or mentre all'ombra di quell'elci antiche
    Ch' giro al prato fanno
    Con dolci voci amiche
    Eramo intenti a disaprir l'affanno   650
    Come in un punto appar baleno, o lampo
    Tal a nostri occhi avanti
    Sovraggiunti vegghiam gli sposi amanti.

Cho.

    Pensa di qual stupor, di qual diletto
    Ingombrò l'alme, e i cori   655
    Della felice coppia il dolce aspetto.

Amin.

    Chi può del Cielo annoverar le Stelle,
    O i ben di Paradiso
    Narri la gioia lor, la festa, e'l riso,
    Ridite piaggie voi campagne, e monti,   660
    Ditelo fiumi, e fonti,
    E voi per l'alto Ciel Zeffiri erranti,

Qual fù gioia mirar sì cari amanti,
Qual pallidetto giglio
Dolcemente or languia la bella sposa   665
Or qual purpurea rosa
Il bel volto di lei venia vermiglio;
Ma sempre, o che il bel ciglio
Chinasse a terra, o rivolgessi in giro
L'alme beava, e i cor d'alto martiro;   670
Ardea la terra, ardean gl'eterei giri,
A'gioiosi sospiri
Dell'uno, e l'altro innamorato core,
E per l'aer sereno
S'udian musici chori   675
Dolci canti temprar d'alati amori.
Io fra l'alta armonia
Per far liete ancor voi mi misi in via.

Cho.

O di che bel seren s'ammanta il Cielo
Al suon di tue parole   680
Fulgido più, ch'in sul mattin non suole
E più ride la terra, e più s'infiora
Al tramontar del dì ch'in sù l'Aurora.

[Scene Six]

Orf.

Gioite al canto mio selve frondose
Gioite amati colli, e d'ogni intorno   685
Ecco rimbombi dalle valli ascose.

Risorto è il mio bel Sol di raggi adorno,
E co begl'occhi onde fa scorno a Delo,
Raddoppia foco all'alme, e luce al giorno

E fa servi d'amor la terra, e'l Cielo.   690

Cho.

Tù sei tù sei pur quella
Ch'in queste braccia accolta
Lasciasti il tuo bel velo alma disciolta.

Eur.

    Quella, quella son io, per cui piangeste,
    Sgombrate ogni timor Donzelle amate,   695
    A che più dubbie, a che pensose state?

Cho.

    O sempiterni Dei
    Pur veggio i tuoi be lumi, e'l tuo bel viso
    E par ch'anco non creda a gl'occhi miei.

Eur.

    Per quest'aer giocondo   700
    E spiro, e vivo anch'io,
    Mirate il mio crin biondo
    E del bel volto mio
    Mirate Donne le sembianze antiche
    Riconoscete omai gl'usati accenti,   705
    Udite il suon di queste voci amiche.

Cho.

    Ma come spiri, e vivi?
    Forse il gran regno Inferno
    Spoglian de pregi suoi gl'Eterei Divi?

Eur.

    Tolsemi Orfeo dal tenebroso regno.   710

Arc.

    Dunque mortal valor cotanto impetra?

Orf.

    Dell'alto don fu degno
    Mio dolce canto, e'l suon di questa cetra.

Amin.

    Come fin giù ne tenebrosi abissi
    Tua nobil voce udissi?   715

Orf.

    La bella Dea d'Amore
    Non sò per qual sentiero
    Scorsemi di Pluton nel vasto impero.

Daf.

    E tu scendesti entro l'eterno orrore?

Orf.

    Più lieto assai, ch'in bel giardin Donzella.   720

Amin.

    O magnanimo core,
    Ma che non puote Amore?

Cho.

    Come quel crudo Rege
    Nudo d'ogni pietà placar potesti?

Orf.

    Modi or soavi hor mesti,   725
    Fervidi preghi, e flebili sospiri
    Temprai si dolce, ch'io
    Nell'implacabil cor destai pietate;
    Così l'alma beltate
    Fù mercè, fù trofeo del canto mio.   730

Cho.

    Felice Semideo, ben degna prole
    Di lui che sù nell'alto
    Per celeste sentier rivolge il Sole,
    Rompersi d'ogni pietrà il duro smalto
    Vidi a tuoi dolci accenti,   735
    E'l corso rallentar fiumi, e tormenti,
    E per udir vicini
    Scender da gl'alti monti abeti, e pini;
    Ma vie più degno vanto oggi s'ammira
    Della famosa lira,   740
    Vanto di preggio eterno
    Mover gli Dei del Ciel, piegar l'Inferno.

CHORO.

    Biondo arcier che d'alto monte
    Aureo fonte
    Sorger fai di sì bell'onda,   745
    Ben può dirsi alma felice

Cui pur lice
Appressar l'altera sponda.

Ma qual poi del sacro umore
Sparge il core   750
Tra i mortal può dirsi un Dio;
Ei de gl'anni il volo eterno
Prende a scherno
E la morte e'l fosco oblio.

Se fregiat' il crin d'alloro   755
Bel tesoro,
Reca al sen gemmata lira,
Farsi intorno alma corona
D'Elicona
L'alte Vergini rimira.   760

Del bel coro al suon concorde
L'auree corde,
Sì soave indi percote,
Che tra boschi Filomena,
Ne Sirena   765
Tempra in mar sì care note.

S'un bel viso, ond'arde il petto
Per diletto
Brama ornar d'eterno vanto,
Sovra'l Sol l'amata Diva   770
Bella, e viva
Sa ripor con nobil canto.

Ma se schiva a bei desiri
Par che spiri
Tutto sdegno un cor di pietra,   775
Del bel sen l'aspra durezza,
Vince, e spezza
Dolce stral di sua faretra.

Non indarno a incontrar morte
Pronto, e forte   780
Move il piè Guerriero, o Duce,
Là 've Clio da nube oscura,

Fa secura
L'alta gloria ond'ei riluce.

Ma che più? s'al negro lito   785
Scende ardito
Sol di cetra armato Orfeo,
E del Regno tenebroso
Lieto sposo
Porta al Ciel palma, e trofeo.   790

IL FINE

Dedication to *Le Musiche sopra L'Euridice*, 1601 (Peri)

Alla Cristianissima Maria Medici, Regina di Francia, e di Navarra.

Poichè Le nuove Musiche fatte da me, nello sponsalizio della
Maestà Vostra (Cristianissima Regina) riceverono tanto favore dalla sua
presenza, che puo non pure adempiere ogni loro difetto, ma sopravanzare
infinitamente, quanto di bello, e di buono potevano ricevere altronde;
Vengo sicuro a dedicarle al suo gloriosissimo nome.   E s'ella non ci
riconoscerà cosa, ò degna di lei, ò almeno proporzionata alle perfezioni
di questo nuovo Poema; Ove il Signor Ottavio Rinuccini, e nell'ordinar,
e nello spiegar sì nobil favola, adornandola tra mille grazie, e mille
vaghezze, con maravigliosa unione di quelle due, che si difficilmente
s'accompagnano Gravità, e Dolcezza; ha dimostrato d'esser al par, de' piu
famosi Antichi, Poeta in ogni parte mirabile, ci scorgerà almeno quella
nobile qualità, che trassero dalla presenza sua, quando si compiacque
ascoltarle, et udire il mio canto, sotto la persona d'Orfeo.   Gradiscale
dunque la Maestà Vostra, come nobili, e degne, non da altro, che dalla
grandezza di lei medesima, che l'ha honorate.   Et accetti in esse
un'affetto umilissimo dell'antica servitù mia, con il quale insieme con
queste Musiche, le dedico di nuovo me stesso, e le prego da Dio il colmo
delle sue grazie, e de suoi favori.
Di Firenze il di vi. di Febbraio 1600.

Di V. M. Cristianissima

Umilissimo Servitore
Iacopo Peri.

Preface to *Le Musiche sopra L'Euridice*, 1601 (Peri)

A LETTORI.

Prima ch'io vi porga (benigni Lettori) queste Musiche mie, ho stimato convenirmisi farvi noto quello, che m'ha indotto a ritrovare questa nuova maniera di canto, poichè di tutte le operazioni humane la ragione debbe essere principio, e fonte; E chi non puo renderla agevolmente da a credere, d'haver'operato a caso. Benchè dal Sig. Emilio del Cavaliere, prima che da ogni altro, ch'io sappia, con maravigliosa invenzione ci fusse fatta udire la nostra Musica su le Scene; Piacque nondimeno a' Signori Iacopo Corsi, ed Ottavio Rinuccini (fin l'anno 1594) che io adoperandola in altra guisa, mettesi sotto le note la favola di Dafne, dal Signor Ottavio composta, per fare una semplice pruova di quello, che potesse il canto dell'età nostra. Onde veduto, che si trattava di poesia Dramatica, e che però si doveva imitar col canto chi parla (e senza dubbio non si parlò mai cantando), stimai, che gli antichi Greci, e Romani (i quali secondo l'openione di molti cantavano su le Scene le Tragedie intere) usassero un' armonia, che avanzando quella del parlare ordinario, scendesse tanto dalla melodia del cantare, che pigliasse forma di cosa mezzana; E questa è la ragione, onde veggiamo in quelle Poesie, haver' havuto luogo il Iambo, che non s'innalza, come l'Esametro, ma pure e detto avanzarsi oltr'a confini de' ragionamenti familiari. E per cio tralasciata qualunque altra maniera di canto udita fin quì, mi diedi tutto a ricercare l'imitazione, che si debbe a questi Poemi; e considerai, che quella sorte di voce, che dagli Antichi al cantare fu assegnata, la quale essi chiamavano Diastematica (quasi trattenuta, e sospesa) potesse in parte affrettarsi, e prender temperato corso tra i movimenti del canto sospesi, e lenti, e quegli della favella spediti, e veloci, et accomodarsi al proposito mio (come l'accomodavano anch'essi, leggendo le Poesie, et i versi Eroici) avvicinandosi all'altra del'ragionare, la quale continuata appellavano; Il che i nostri moderni (benchè forse ad altro fine) hanno ancor fatto nelle musiche loro. Conobbi parimente nel nostro parlare alcune voci, intonarsi in guisa, che vi si puo fondare armonia, e nel corso della favella passarsi per altre molte, che non s'intuonano, finchè si ritorni ad altra capace di movimento di nuova consonanza; et havuto riguardo a que' modi, et a quegli accenti, che nel dolerci, nel rallegrarci, et in somiglianti cose ci servono, feci muovere il Basso al tempo di quegli, hor più, or meno, secondo gli affetti, e lo tenni fermo tra le false, e tra le buone proporzioni, finchè scorrendo per varie note la voce di chi ragiona, arrivasse a quello, che nel parlare ordinario intonandosi, apre la via a nuovo concento; e questo non solo, perchè il corso del ragionare non ferisse l'orecchio (quasi intoppando negli incontri delle ripercosse corde, dalle consonanze più spesse,) ò non paresse in un certo modo ballare al moto del Basso, e principalmente nelle cose, ò meste, ò gravi, richiedendo per natura l'altre più liete, più spessi movimenti: Ma ancora perchè l'uso delle false, ò scemasse, ò ricoprasse quel vantaggio, che ci s'aggiugne dalla necessità dell'intonare ogni nota, di che per cio fare potevan forse haver manco bisogno l'antiche Musiche. E però, (sì come io non ardirei affermare questo essere il canto nelle Greche, e nelle Romane favole usato), così ho creduto esser quello, che solo possa donarcisi dalla nostra Musica, per accomodarsi alla nostra favella.   Onde fatta udire a quei Signori la mia openione, dimostrai loro questo nuovo modo di cantare, e piacque sommamente, non pure al Signor Iacopo, il quale haveva di gia composte arie bellissime per quella favola, ma al Signor Piero Strozzi, al Signor Francesco Cini, et ad altri molti intendentissimi gentilhuomini (che nella nobiltà fiorisce hoggi la Musica) come anco a quella famosa, che si puo chiamare Euterpe dell'età nostra, la Signora Vettoria Archilei, la quale ha sempre fatte degne del cantar suo le Musiche mie, adornandole, non pure di quei gruppi, e di quei lunghi giri di voce, semplici, e doppi, che dalla vivezza dell'ingegno suo son ritrovati ad ogni hora, più per ubbidire all'uso de' nostri tempi, che, per ch'ella stimi consistere in essi la bellezza, e la forza del nostro cantare, ma anco di quelle, e vaghezze, e leggiadrie, che non si possono scrivere, e scrivendole non s'imparano da gli scritti.   L'udì, e la commendò Messer Giovanbattista Iacomelli, che in tutte le parti della musica eccellentissimo, ha quasi cambiato il suo cognome col Violino, in cui egli è mirabile: E per tre Anni continui, che nel Carnovale si rappresentò, fu udita con sommo diletto, e con applauso universale ricevuta, da chiunque vi si ritrovovo.   Ma hebbe miglior ventura la presente Euridice, non perchè la sentirono quei Signori, et altri valorosi huomini, ch'io nominai, e di più il Signor Conte Alfonso Fontanella, et il Signor Orazio Vecchi, testimoni nobilissimi del mio pensiero, ma perchè fu rappresentata ad una Regina si grande, et a tanti famosi Principi d'Italia, e di Francia, e fu cantata da più eccellenti Musici de nostri tempi; Tra i quali il Signor Francesco Rasi, nobile Aretino rappresentò Aminta, il Signor Antonio Brandi Arcetro, et il Signor Melchior Palantrotti, Plutone; e dentro alla Scena fu sonata da Signori per nobiltà di sangue, e per eccellenza di musica illustri, il Signor Iacopo Corsi, che tanto spesso ho nominato, sonò un Gravicembalo; et il Signor Don Grazìa Montalvo, un Chitarrone; Messer Giovanbattista dal Violino, una Lira grande; e Messer Giovanni Lapi, un Liuto grosso: E benchè fin allhora l'havessi fatta nel modo appunto, che hora viene in luce: Non dimeno Giulio Caccini (detto Romano) il cui sommo valore è noto al

Mondo, fece l'arie d'Euridice, et alcune del Pastore, e Ninfa del Coro, e de' Cori, *Al canto, al ballo, Sospirate,* e *Poi che gli eterni imperi.* E questo, perchè dovevano esser cantate da persone dipendenti da lui, le quali Arie si leggono nella sua composta, e stampata pur dopo, che questa mia fu rappresentata a sua Maestà Cristianissima.

Ricevetela però benignamente cortesi Lettori, e benchè io non sia arrivato con questo modo fin dove mi pareva di poter giugnere (essendo stato freno al mio corso il rispetto della novità), graditela in ogni modo; e forse avverrà, ch'in altra occasione io vi dimostri cosa piu perfetta di questa: Intanto mi parrà d'haver fatto assai, havendo aperta la strada al valor' altrui, di camminare per le mie orme alla gloria, dove a me non è dato di poter pervenire. E spero, che l'uso delle false, sonate, e cantate senza paura, discretamente, et appunto (essendo piaciute a tanti, e sì valorosi huomini) non vi saranno di noia, massime nell'arie più meste, e più gravi, d'Orfeo, d'Arcetro, e di Dafne, rappresentata con molta grazia da Iacopo Giusti, fanciulletto Lucchese. E vivete lieti.

[Iacopo Peri]

Preface to *L'Euridice*, 1600 score (Caccini)

All'Illustr.^{mo} Sign.^{re} il Sig. Giovanni Bardi de Conti di Vernio, Luogotenente Generale dell'una e dell'altra Guardia di N.° S.^{re} Suo Osser.^{mo}

Havendo io composto in musica in stile rappresentativo la favola d'Euridice, e fattola stampare, mi è parso parte di mio debito dedicarla à V. S. Illustriss. alla quale, io son sempre stato particolar servitore, et à cui mi truovo infinitamente obligato. In essa ella riconoscerà quello stile usato da me altre volte, molti anni sono come sa V. S. Illustriss. Nell' Egloga del Sanazzaro, *Iten'all'ombra de gli ameni faggi,* et in altri miei madrigali di quei tempi: *Perfidissimo volto, Vedro'l mio Sol, Dovrò dunque morire,* e simili; E questa e quella maniera altresì la quale ne gli anni, che fioriva la Camerata sua in Firenze, discorrendo ella diceva insieme con molti altri nobili virtuosi, essere stata usata da gli antichi Greci nel rappresentare le loro Tragedie, et altre favole adoperando il canto. Reggesi adunque l'armonia delle parti, che recitano nella presente Euridice sopra un basso continovato, nel quale ho io segnato le quarte, seste, e settime; terze maggiori, e minori più necessarie rimettendo nel rimanente lo adattare le parti di mezzo à lor luoghi nel giudizio, e nell'arte di chi suona, havendo legato alcune volte le corde del basso, affine che nel trapassare delle molte dissonanze, ch'entro vi sono, non si

ripercuota la corda, e l'udito ne venga offeso; Nella qual maniera di canto, ho io usata una certa sprezzatura, che io ho stimato, che habbia del nobile, parendomi con essa di essermi appressato quel più alla natural favella. Ne ho ancora fuggito il riscontro delle due ottave, e due quinte, quando due soprani cantando con l'altre parti di mezzo fanno passaggi, pensando perciò, con la vaghezza, e novità loro, maggiormente di dilettare, e massimamente poi che senza essi passaggi, tutte le parti sono senza tali errori. Io era stato di parere con l'occasione presente di fare un discorso à i lettori del nobil modo di cantare, al mio giudizio il migliore, co'l quale altri potessi esercitarsi, con alcune curiosità appartenenti ad esso, e con la nuova maniera de passaggi, e raddoppiate inventati da me i quali hora adopera cantando l'opere mie già è molto tempo, Vittoria Archillei, cantatrice di quella eccellenza, che mostra il grido della sua fama; ma perche non è parso al presente ad alcuni miei amici (à i quali non posso, ne devo mancare far questo) mi sono perciò riserbato ad altra occasione, riportando io per hora questa sola sodisfazione di essere stato il primo à dare alla stampa simile sorte di canti, e lo stile, e la maniera di essi, la quale si vede per tutte l'altre mie musiche, che son fuori in penna, composti da me più di quindici anni sono in diversi tempi, non havendo mai nelle mie musiche usato altr' arte, che l'immitazione de' sentimenti delle parole, toccando quelle corde più, e meno affettuose, le quali ho giudicato più convenirsi per quella grazia, che più si ricerca per ben cantare; la qual grazia, e modo di canto, molte volte mi ha testificato essere stata costà in Roma accettata per buona universalmente V. S. Illustriss.; la quale prego in tanto à ricevere in grado l'affetto della mia buona volontà, et à conservarmi la sua protezione, sotto il quale scudo spererò sempre potermi ricoverare, et esser difeso dai pericoli, che sogliono soprastare alle cose non più usate, sapendo che ella potrà sempre far fede non essere state discare le cose mie à Principe grande, il quale havendo occasione di esperimentare tutte le buone arti, giudicare ottimamente ne può; con il che baciando la mano à V. S. Illustriss. prego Nostro Signore la faccia felice.
Di Firenze li 20 di Dicembre 1600.

    Di V. S. Illustrissima

                      Servitore Affettionatissimo, et Obbligatissimo,
                                Giulio Caccini.

Appendix C

Prologue to *L'Arianna* (Text by Rinuccini)

(From the first edition of the libretto, which appeared in Federico Follino, *Compendio dalle sontuose feste fatte l'anno MDCVIII nella città di Mantova. . .* , as given in Solerti, *Gli Albori del melodramma*, vol. 2, pp. 147-48.)

APOLLO.

Io, che ne l'alto a mio voler governo
La luminosa fa e e 'l carro d'oro,
Re di Permesso e del soave Coro,
De la lira del ciel custode eterno,

Non perché serpe rio di tosco immondo
Avveleni le piagge e 'l cielo infetti,
Non perché mortal guardo il cor saetti,
Stampo d'orme celesti il basso mondo.

Di cetra armato, e non di strali o d'arco,
Donna, c'hai su 'l bel Mincio e scettro e regno,
Per dilettarti il cor, bramoso vegno,
Di magnanime cure ingombro e carco.

Ma gli alti pregi tuoi, le glorie e l'armi
Non udrai risuonar corde guerriere:
Pieghino al dolce suon l'orecchie altere
Su cetera d'amor teneri carmi.

Si chiaro omai su gloriose piume
Sorvoli di splendor guerrieri e regi,
Che di Pindo non pon' ghirland'e fregi
Crescer nova chiarezza al tuo gran lume.

Odi, Sposa real, come sospiri
Tradita amante in solitaria riva:
Forse avverrà che de la scena argiva
L'antico onor ne' novi canti ammiri.

Appendix D

Prologue to *Il Narciso* (Text by Rinuccini)

(From Solerti, *Gli Albori del melodramma*, vol. 2, pp. 191-92.)

GIULIO ROMANO.

Io che quasi pastor tra questi boschi
A voi davanti, alta Regina, or vegno,
Son quei ch'al vario suon d'un cavo legno
Fo si dolci sentir gli accenti toschi.

Là dove ricco al mar d'antichi pregi
Rivolge il Tebro altier le torbid'onde
Nacqui, ma d'Arno a le fiorite sponde
Aura mi scorse de' Medicei regi.

Ivi de l'auree Muse in sen nutrito
Appresi di cantar si dolci modi,
Ch'ove in pregio è virtù, con chiare lodi
Fu il nobil suon de la mia voce udito.

Non senz'alto ammirar l'estense Duce
Piegò su 'l Po l'orecchie al mio bel canto,
E quei non men ch'in venerabil canto
Per tre corone in Vatican riluce.

Ma di più chiaro onor più calda spene
Alzò gl'ingegno a più sublimi studi
Poscia ch'a rimirar le pompe e i ludi
Rivolsi il cor de la famosa Atene,

E di musico mel gli alti concetti
Per tal arte temprai d'almi poeti
Ch'io valsi a mio desir dogliosi e lieti
Render cantando ne' teatri i petti.

Colme d'alto stupor le scene aurate
De la bell'Alba allor le voci udiro,
Allor gli abissi al gran cantor s'apriro
E pianse Apollo su le fronde amate.

Per gioia tua, benchè da gli anni stanco,
O sostegno e splendor d'Arno e Loreno,
Note più care ancor trarrò dal seno
Cigno canoro più, quanto più bianco.

Mentre a le regie tue superbe Nuore
Via più sacra armonia Pindo riserba,
Odi, Donna immortal, come tra l'erba
Un misero fanciul cangiossi in fiore.

Appendix E

Striggio, *La favola d'Orfeo*

The text of Striggio's *Orfeo* reproduced here is transcribed, unedited, from the first printed edition of the libretto:

> La / Favola d'Orfeo / Rappresentata in Musica / Il Carnevale
> dell'Anno M.D.CVII. / Nell'Accademia de gli Invaghiti di Mantova /
> Sotto i felici auspizij del Serenissimo Sig. Duca / benignissimo lor
> protettore. / [emblem] / In Mantova, per Francesco Osanna stam-
> pator Ducale. / Con licenza de' Superiori 1607.

The alterations of the fifth act (pp. 326-29), which appeared for the first time in Monteverdi's score (Venice, 1609), are taken from Solerti, *Gli Albori del melodramma*, vol. 3, pp. 270-72.

Libretto, 1607

[LA FAVOLA D'ORFEO]

PROLOGO.

LA MUSICA.

Dal mio Permesso amato à vio ne vegno
Incliti Eroi, sangue gentil di Regi,
Di cui narra la Fama eccelsi pregi,
Nè giugne al ver perch'è tropp'alto il segno.

Io la Musica son ch'à i dolci accenti   5
Sò far tranquillo ogni turbato core,
Et hor di nobil ira, et hor d'amore
Posso infiammar le più gelate menti.

Io sù cetera d'or cantando soglio
Mortal orecchia lusingar sonora   10
E in guisa tal de l'armonia sonora
De le rote del Ciel più l'alme invoglio.

Quinci à dirvi d'Orfeo desio mi sprona
D'Orfeo che trasse al suo cantar le fere,
E servo fè l'Inferno à sue preghiere   15
Gloria immortal de Pindo e d'Elicona.

Hor mentre i canti alterno hor lieti, hor mesti
Non si mova augellin fra queste piante,
Nè s'oda in queste rive onda sonante,
Et ogni Auretta in suo camin s'arresti.   20

ATTO PRIMO.

PASTORE.
In questo lieto e fortunato giorno
C'hà posto fine à gli amorosi affanni
Del nostro Semideo cantiam Pastori
Con sì soavi accenti
Che sien degni d'Orfeo nostri concenti.   25

Oggi fatt'è pietosa
L'alma già sì sdegnosa
De la bella Euridice.
Oggi fatt'è felice
Orfeo nel sen di lei, per cui già tanto   30
Per queste selve ha sospirato, e pianto.

Dunque in sì lieto e fortunato giorno
C'hà posto fine à gli amorosi affanni
Del nostro Semideo cantiam Pastori
Con sì soavi accenti   35
Che sien degni d'Orfeo nostri concenti.

CHORO.
Vieni Imeneo, deh vieni,
E la tua face ardente
Sia quasi un Sol nascente
Ch'apporti à questi i dì sereni,   40
E lunge homai disgombre
De gli affanni e del duol le nebbie e l'ombre.

NINFA.
Muse honor di Parnaso, amor del Cielo
Gentil conforto à sconsolato core

Vostre cetre sonore   45
Squarcino d'ogni nube il fosco velo:
E mentre oggi propizio al vostro Orfeo
Invochiamo Imeneo
Sù ben temprate corde
Co'l vostro suon, nostr'armonia s'accorde.   50

CHORO.
Lasciate i monti
Lasciate i fonti
Ninfe vezzose e liete,
E in questi prati
A i balli usati   55
Leggiadro il piè rendete.

Quì miri il Sole
Vostre carole
Più vaghe assai di quelle,
Ond' à la Luna   60
A l'aria bruna
Danzano in Ciel le stelle.

Poi di bei fiori
Per voi s'honori
Di questi amanti il crine,   65
C'hor de i martiri
De i lor desiri
Godon beati il fine.

PASTORE.
Ma tu gentil cantor s'à' tuoi lamenti
Già festi lagrimar queste campagne,   70
Perc'hor al suon de la famosa cetra
Non fai teco gioir le valli e i poggi?
Sia testimon del core
Qualche lieta canzon che detti Amore.

ORFEO.
Rosa del Ciel, gemma del giorno, e degna   75
Prole di lui che l'Universo affrena
Sol ch'il tutto circondi e'l tutto miri,
Da gli stellanti giri

Dimmi vedestù mai
Alcun di me piu fortunato amante?   80
Fù ben felice il giorno
Mio ben che pria ti vidi,
E più felice l'hora
Che per te sospirai,
Poich'al mio sospirar tù sospirasti: 85
Felicissimo il punto
Che la candida mano
Pegno di pura fede à me porgesti,
Se tanti Cori havessi
Quant'occhi ha il Ciel sereno, e quante chiome   90
Sogliono i Colli haver l'Aprile e'l Maggio,
Colmi si farien tutti e traboccanti
Di quel piacer ch'oggi mi fà contento.

EURIDICE.

Io non dirò qual sia
Nel tuo gioire Orfeo la gioia mia,   95
Che non hò meco il core,
Ma teco stassi in compagnia d'Amore;
Chiedilo dunque à lui s'intender brami
Quanto lieta i' gioisca e quanto t'ami.

CHORO.

Lasciate i monti   100
Lasciate i fonti
Ninfe vezzose e liete,
E in questi prati
A i balli usati
Leggiadro il piè rendete.   105

Quì miri il Sole
Vostre carole
Più vaghe assai di quelle,
Ond'à la Luna
A l'aria bruna   110
Danzano in Ciel le stelle.

CHORO.

Vieni Imeneo, deh vieni,
E la tua face ardente
Sia quasi un Sol nascente

Ch'apporti à questi amanti i dì sereni,   115
E lunge homai disgombre
De gli affanni e del duol le nebbie e l'ombre.

PASTORE.

Ma s'il nostro gioir dal Ciel deriva
Com'è dal Ciel ciò che quà giù n'incontra,
Giusto è ben che divoti   120
Gli offriamo incensi e voti.
Dunque al Tempio ciascun rivolga i passi
A pregar lui ne la cui destra è il Mondo,
Che lungamente il nostro ben conservi.

CHORO.

Alcun non sia che disperato in preda   125
Si doni al duol benche talhor n'assaglia
Possente sì che nostra vita inforsa.
Che poiche nembo rio gravido il seno
D'atra tempesta inorridito hà il Mondo
Dispiega il Sol più chiaro i rai lucenti,   130
E dopò l'aspro gel del verno ignudo
Veste di fior la Primavera i campi.
Orfeo di cui pur dianzi
Furon cibo i sospir bevanda il pianto,
Oggi felice è tanto   135
Che nulla è più che da bramar gli avanzi.
Ma perche tal gioire
Dopo tanto martire? Eterni Numi
Vostr'opre eccelse occhio mortal non vede
Che splendente caligine le adombra;   140
Pur se lece spiegar pensiero interno
Sol per cangiarlo ove l'error si scopra,
Direm, ch'in questa guisa
Mentre i voti d'Orfeo seconda il Cielo,
Prova vuol far di sua virtù più certa.   145
Ch'il soffrir le miserie è picciol pregio,
Ma'l cortese girar di sorte amica
Suol dal dritto camin traviar l'alme.
Oro così per foco è più pregiato.
Combattuto valore   150
Godrà così di più sublime honore.

Il fine del primo Atto.

ATTO SECONDO

ORFEO.
    Ecco pur ch'à voi ritorno
    Care selve e piagge amate,
    Da quel Sol fatte beate
    Per cui sol mie notti han giorno.   155

PASTORE.
    Mira ch'à se n'alletta
    L'ombra Orfeo di que' faggi,
    Hor ch'infocati raggi
    Febo da Ciel saetta.

    Sù quelle erbose sponde   160
    Posiamci, e'n varij modi
    Ciascun sua voce snodi
    Al mormorio de l'onde.

DUE PASTORI.
    In questo prato adorno
    Ogni selvaggio Nume   165
    Sovente hà per costume
    Di far lieto soggiorno.

    Quì Pan Dio de' Pastori
    S'udi talor dolente
    Rimembrar dolcemente   170
    Suoi sventurati amori.

DUE PASTORI.
    Qui le Napee vezzose
    (Schiera sempre fiorita)
    Con le candide dita
    Fur viste à coglier rose.   175

CHORO.
    Dunque fà degni Orfeo
    Del suon de l'aurea lira
    Questi campi ove spira
    Aura d'odor Sabeo.

ORFEO.

    Vi ricorda ò boschi ombrosi   180
    De' miei lunghi aspri tormenti
    Quando i sassi a' miei lamenti
    Rispondean fatti pietosi?

    Dite, allor non vi sembrai
    Più d'ogni altro sconsolato?   185
    Hor fortuna hà stil cangiato
    Ed hà volti in festa i guai.

    Vissi già mesto e dolente,
    Hor gioisco, e quegli affanni
    Che sofferti hò per tant'anni   190
    Fan più caro il ben presente.

    Sol per tè bella Euridice
    Benedico il mio tormento,
    Dopò'l duol viè più contento,
    Dopò'l mal viè più felice.   195

PASTORE.

    Mira, deh mira Orfeo, che d'ogni intorno
    Ride il bosco e ride il prato,
    Segui pur co'l plettro aurato
    D'addolcir l'aria in sì beato giorno.

MESSAGGIERA.

    Ahi caso acerbo, ahi fato empio e crudele,   200
    Ahi Stelle ingiuriose, ahi Cielo avaro.

PASTORE.

    Qual suon dolente il lieto dì perturba?

MESSAGGIERA.

    Lassa, dunque debb'io
    Mentre Orfeo con sue note il Ciel consola
    Con le parole mie passargli il core?   205

PASTORE.

    Questa è Silvia gentile
    Dolcissima compagna

De la bella Euridice: ò quanto è in vista
Dolorosa: hor che fia? deh sommi Dei
Non torcete da noi benigno il guardo.   210

MESSAGGIERA.
Pastor lasciate il canto,
Ch'ogni nostra allegrezza in doglia è volta.

ORFEO.
Donde vieni? ove vai? Ninfa che porti?

MESSAGGIERA.
A te ne vengo Orfeo
Messaggiera infelice   215
Di caso più infelice e più funeste.
La tua bella Euridice.   ORF. Ohime che odo?
La tua diletta sposa è morta.   ORF. Ohime.

MESSAGGIERA.
In un fiorito prato
Con l'altre sue compagne   220
Giva cogliendo fiori
Per farne una ghirlanda à le tue chiome,
Quando angue insidioso
Ch'era fra l'erbe ascoso
Le punse un piè con velenoso dente,   225
Ed ecco immantinente
Scolorissi il bel viso e ne' suoi lumi
Sparir que' lampi, ond'ella al Sol fea scorno.
Allhor noi tutte sbigottite e meste
Le fummo intorno richiamar tentando   230
Gli spirti in lei smarriti
Con l'onda fresca e co' possenti carmi;
Ma nulla valse, ahi lassa,
Ch'ella i languidi lumi alquanto aprendo,
E tè chiamando Orfeo,   235
Dopò un grave sospiro
Spirò frà queste braccia, ed io rimasi
Piena il cor di pietate e di spavento.

PASTORE.
Ahi, caso acerbo, ahi fato empio e crudele.
Ahi stelle ingiuriose, ahi Cielo avaro.   240

PASTORE.
    A l'amara novella
    Rassembra l'infelice un muto sasso,
    Che per troppo dolor non può dolersi.

PASTORE.
    Ahi ben havrebbe un cor di Tigre o d'Orsa
    Chi non sentisse del tuo mal pietate,   245
    Privo d'ogni tuo ben misero amante.

ORFEO.
    Tu se' morta mia vita, ed io respiro?
    Tu se', tu se' pur ita
    Per mai più non tornare, ed io rimango?
    Nò, che se i versi alcuna cosa ponno   250
    N'andrò sicuro a' più profondi abissi,
    E intenerito il cor del Rè de l'Ombre
    Meco trarròtti a riveder le Stelle:
    O se ciò negheràmmi empio destino
    Rimarrò teco in compagnia di morte,   255
    A dio terra, à dio Cielo, e Sole à dio.

CHORO.
    Ahi caso acerbo, ahi fato empio e crudele,
    Ahi stelle ingiuriose, ahi Cielo avaro.
    Non si fidi huom mortale
    Di ben caduco e frale   260
    Che tosto fugge, e spesso
    A gran salita il precipizio è presso.

MESSAGGIERA.
    Ma io ch'in questa lingua
    Hò portato il coltello
    C'hà svenata d'Orfeo l'anima amante,   265
    Odiosa à i Pastori et à le Ninfe,
    Odiosa à me stessa, ove m'ascondo?
    Nottola infausta il Sole
    Fuggirò sempre e in solitario speco
    Menerò vita al mio dolor conforme.   270

CHORO.
    Chi ne consola ahi lassi?
    O pur chi ne concede

Ne gli occhi un vivo fonte
Da poter lagrimar come conviensi
In questo mesto giorno   275
Quanto più lieto già tant'hor più mesto?
Oggi turbo crudele
I due lumi maggiori
Di queste nostre selve
Euridice, et Orfeo,   280
L'una punta da l'angue,
L'altra dal duol trafitto, ahi lassi ha spenti;

Ahi caso acerbo, ahi fato empio e crudele,
Ahi stelle ingiuriose, ahi Cielo avaro.

Ma dove, ah dove hor sono   285
De la misera Ninfa
La belle e fredde membra,
Che per suo degno albergo
Quella bell'alma elesse
Ch'oggi è partita in su'l fiorir de' giorni?   290
Andiam Pastori andiamo
Pietosi à ritrovarle,
E di lagrime amare
Il dovuto tributo
Per noi si paghi almeno al corpo esangue.   295

Ahi caso acerbo, ahi fato empio e crudele,
Ahi stelle ingiuriose, ahi Cielo avaro.

Ma qual funebre pompa
Degna fia d'Euridice?
Portino il gran feretro   300
Le Grazie in veste nera,
E con lor chiome sparse
Le Muse sconsolate
L'accompagnin cantando
Con flebil voce i suoi passati pregi.   305
Di Nubi il Ciel si cinga
E con oscura pioggia
Pianga sopra il sepolcro:
E poich'egli havrà pianto
Languida luce spieghi,   310

E lampanda funesta
Sia di nobil tomba il Sol dolente.

Ahi caso acerbo, ahi fato empio e crudele,
Ahi Stelle ingiuriose, ahi Cielo avaro.

Quì si muta la Scena.

Il fine del Secondo Atto.

ATTO TERZO

ORFEO.

  Scorto da te mio Nume   315
  Speranza unico bene
  De gli afflitti mortali, homai son giunto
  A questi regni tenebrosi e mesti
  Dove raggio di Sol giamai non giunse.
  Tù mia compagna e duce   320
  Per così strane e sconosciute vie
  Reggesti il passo debile e tremante,
  Ond'oggi ancora spero
  Di riveder quelle beate luci
  Che sole à gli occhi miei portano il giorno.   325

SPERANZA.

  Ecco l'atra palude, ecco il nocchiero
  Che trae gli spirti ignudi à l'altra sponda,
  Dov'hà Pluton de l'ombre il vasto impero.
  Oltra quel nero stagno, oltra quel fiume,
  In quei campi di pianto e di dolore,   330
  Destin crudele ogni tuo ben t'asconde.
  Hor d'uopo è d'un gran core e d'un bel canto.
  Io fin quì t'hò condotto, hor più non lice
  Teco venir, ch'amara legge il vieta.
  Legge scritta co'l ferro in duro sasso   335
  De l'ima reggia in sù l'orribil soglia
  Che in queste note il fiero senso esprime,
  Lasciate ogni speranza ò voi ch'entrate.
  Dunque se stabilito hai pur nel core
  Di porre il piè ne la Città dolente,   340
  Da te me'n fuggo e torno
  A l'usato soggiorno.

ORFEO.
    Dove, ah dove te'n vai
    Unico del mio cor dolce conforto?
    Poiche non lunge homai   345
    Del mio lungo camin si scopre il porto,
    Perche ti parti e m'abbandoni, ahi lasso,
    Su'l periglioso passo?
    Qual bene hor più m'avanza
    Se fuggi tù dolcissima Speranza?   350

CARONTE.
    O tu ch'innanzi morte à queste rive
    Temerario te'n vieni, arresta i passi;
    Solcar quest'onde ad huom mortal non dassi,
    Nè può co' morti albergo haver chi vive.

    Che? vuoi forse nemico al mio Signore   355
    Cerbero trar da le Tartaree porte?
    O rapir brami sua cara consorte
    D'impudico desire acceso il core?

    Pon freno al folle ardir, ch'entr' al mio legno
    Non accorrò più mai corporea salma,   360
    Sì de gli antichi oltraggi ancor ne l'alma
    Serbo acerba memoria e giusto sdegno.

ORFEO.
    Possente Spirto e formidabil Nume,
    Senza cui far passaggio à l'altra riva
    Alma da corpo sciolta in van presume.   365

    Non viv'io nò, che poi di vita è priva
    Mia cara sposa il cor non è più meco,
    E senza cor com'esser può ch'io viva?

    A lei volt'hò'l camin per l'aër cieco,
    A l'Inferno non già, ch'ovunque stassi   370
    Tanta bellezza il paradiso hà seco.

    Orfeo son io che d'Euridice i passi
    Seguo per queste tenebrose arene,
    Dove giamai per huom mortal non vassi.

O de le luci mie luci serene,   375
S'un vostro sguardo può tornarmi in vita,
Ahi chi nega il conforto à le mie pene?

Sol tu nobile Dio puoi darmi aita,
Nè temer dei, che sopra un'aurea Cetra
Sol di corde soavi armo le dita   380

Contra cui rigid'alma in van s'impetra.

CARONTE.
    Ben solletica alquanto
    Dilettandomi il core
    Sconsolato Cantore
    Il tuo pianto e'l tuo canto.   385
    Ma lunge, ah sia da questo petto.
    Pietà di mio valor non degno affetto.

ORFEO.
    Ahi sventurato amante,
    Sperar dunque non lice
    Ch'odan miei preghi i Cittadin d'Averno?   390
    Onde qual ombra errante
    D'insepolto cadavero infelice
    Privo sarò del Cielo e de l'Inferno?
    Così vuol empia sorte
    Ch'in questi orror di morte   395
    De te mio cor lontano
    Chiami tuo nome in vano,
    E pregando, e piagnendo mi consumi?
    Rendetemi 'l mio ben Tartarei Numi.

    Ei dorme, e la mia cetra   400
    Se pietà non impetra
    Ne l'indurato core, almeno il sonno
    Fuggir al mio cantar gli occhi non ponno.
    Sù dunque, à che più tardo?
    Tempo è ben d'approdar sù l'altra sponda,   405
    S'alcun non è ch'il neghi
    Vaglia l'ardir se foran vani i preghi.
    E' vago fior del Tempo
    L'occasion, ch'esser dee colta à tempo.

Quì entra nella barca, e passa cantando

Mentre versan questi occhi amari fiumi   410
Rendetemi 'l mio ben, Tartarei Numi.

CHORO DI SPIRITI INFERNALI.
　　Nulla impresa per huom si tenta in vano
　　Nè contra lui più sà natura armarse,
　　Et de l'instabil piano
　　Arò gli ondosì campi, e'l seme sparse   415
　　Di sue fatiche, ond'aurea messe accolse.
　　Quinci perche memoria
　　Vivesse di sua gloria,
　　La Fama à dir di lui sua lingua sciolse,
　　Che pose freno al Mar con fragil Legno,   420
　　Che sprezzò d'Austro e d'Aquilon lo sdegno.

　　Per l'aëree contrade à suo viaggio
　　L'ali lievi spiegò Dedalo industre.
　　Nè di Sol caldo raggio
　　Ne distemprò sue penne humor palustre,   425
　　Ma novo augel sembrando in suo sentiero
　　A l'alata famiglia
　　Fece per maraviglia
　　Perch'arridea fortuna al gran pensiero
　　Fermar il volo, e starsi e l'aure e i venti 430
　　A rimirar cotanto ardire intenti.

　　Altri dal carro ardente e da la face
　　Ch'accende il giorno in terra al Ciel salito
　　Furò fiamma vivace.
　　Ma qual cor fù giamai cotanto ardito   435
　　Che s'aguagli à costui ch'oggi si vede
　　Per questi oscuri chiostri
　　Fra larve e serpi e Mostri
　　Mover cantando baldanzoso il piede?
　　L'orecchie in van Caronte à i preghi ha sorde, 440
　　E in vano homai Cerbero latra e morde.

Il fine del Terzo Atto.

ATTO QUARTO.

PROSERPINA.

    Signor quell'infelice
    Che per queste di morte ampie campagne
    Và chiamando Euridice,
    Ch'udito hai tù pur dianzi   445
    Così soavemente lamentarsi,
    Moss'hà tanto pietà dentro al mio core
    Ch'io torno un'altra volta à porger preghi
    Perch'il tuo Nume al suo pregar si pieghi.
    Deh se da queste luci   450
    Amorosa dolcezza unqua traesti,
    Se ti piacque il seren di questa fronte
    Che tù chiami tuo Cielo, onde mi giuri
    Di non invidiar sua sorte à Giove;
    Pregoti per quel foco   455
    Con cui già la grand'alma Amor t'accese,
    D'Orfeo dolente il lagrimar consoli,
    E fà che la sua Donna in vita torni
    Al bel seren de i sospirati giorni.

PLUTONE.

    Benche severo et immutabil fato   460
    Contrasti amata sposa à tuoi desiri,
    Pur nulla homai si neghi
    A tal beltà congiunta à tanti preghi.
    La sua cara Euridice
    Contra l'ordin fatale Orfeo ricovri.   465
    Ma pria ch'i tragga il piè da questi abissi
    Non mai volga ver lei gli avidi lumi,
    Che di perdita eterna
    Gli fia certa cagione un solo sguardo.

    Io così stabilisco. hor nel mio Regno   470
    Fate ò Ministri il mio voler palese
    Sì che l'intenda Orfeo
    E l'intenda Euridice,
    E di cangiarlo hor più tentar non lice.

CHORO DI SPIRITI INFERNALI.

    O de gli habitator de l'ombre eterne   475
    Possente Rè legge ne fia tuo cenno,

Che ricercar altre cagioni interne
Di tuo voler nostri pensier non denno,
Trarrà da queste orribili caverne
Sua sposa Orfeo, s'adoprerà suo senno   480
Si che no'l vinca giovanil desio,
Ne i gravi imperi tuoi sparga d'oblio.

PROSERPINA.
Quali grazie ti rendo
Hor che si nobil dono
Concedi à' preghi miei signor cortese?   485
Sia bendetto il dì che pria ti piacqui,
Benedetta la preda e'l dolce inganno,
Poiche per mia ventura
Feci acquisto di tè perdendo il Sole.

PLUTONE.
Tue soavi parole   490
D'Amor l'antica piaga
Rinfrescan nel mio core,
Cosi l'anima tua non sia più vaga
Di celeste diletto,
Si ch'abbandoni il marital tuo letto.   495

CHORO DI SPIRITI
Pietate oggi et Amore
Trionfan ne l'Inferno.
Ecco il gentil cantore
Che sua sposa conduce al Ciel superno.

ORFEO.
Qual honor di te fia degno   500
Mia cetra onnipotente,
S'hai nel Tartareo Regno
Piegar potuto ogn'indurate mente?

Luogo havrai fra le più belle
Imagini celesti,   505
Ond'al tuo suon le stelle
Danzeranno co' giri hor tardi hor presti.

Io per te felice à pieno
Vedrò l'amato volto,

E nel candido seno   510
De la mia Donna oggi sarò raccolto.

Ma mentre io canto (ohime) chi m'assicura
Ch'ella mi segua? ohime chi mi nasconde
De l'amate pupille il doce lume?

Forse d'invidia punte   515
La Deità d'Averno
Perch'io non sia qua giù felice à pieno
Mi tolgono il mirarvi
Luci beate e liete
Che sol co'l guardo altrui bear potete?   520

Ma che temi mio core?
Ciò che vieta Pluton comanda Amore.
A Nume più possente
Che vince huomini e Dei
Ben ubbidir devrei.   525

> Quì si fa strepito dietro alla Scena.

Ma che odo ohime lasso?
S'arman forse à' miei danni
Con tal furor le furie innamorate
Per rapirmi il mio bene, ed io'l consento?

> Quì si volta.

O dolcissimi lumi io pur vi veggio,   530
Io pur: ma qual Eclissi ohime v'oscura?

UNO SPIRITO.
Rott'hai la legge, e se' di grazia indegno.

EURIDICE.
Ahi vista troppo dolce e troppo amara:
Così per troppo amor dunque mi perdi?
Et io misera perdo   535
Il poter più godere
E di luce e di vita, e perdo insieme
Tè d'ogni ben più caro, ò mio Consorte.

CHORO DI SPIRITI.
    Torna à l'ombre di morte
    Infelice Euridice,   540
    Nè più sperar di riveder il Sole
    C'homai fia sordo à' preghi altrui l'Inferno.

ORFEO.
    Dove te'n vai mia vita? ecco i' ti seguo.
    Ma chi me'l vieta ohime: sogno, o vaneggio?
    Qual poter, qual furor da questi orrori,   545
    Da questi amati orrori
    Mal mio grado mi tragge, e mi conduce
    A l'odiosa luce?

CHORO DI SPIRITI.
    E la virtute un raggio
    Di celeste bellezza   550
    Fregio de l'alma ond'ella sol s'apprezza:
    Questa di Tempo oltraggio
    Non teme, anzi maggiore
    Divien se più s'attempa il suo splendore.
    Nebbia l'adombra sol d'affetto humano,   555
    A cui talhor invano
    Tenta opporsi ragion, ch'ei la sua luce
    Spegne, e l'huom cieco à cieco fin conduce.

    Orfeo vinse l'Inferno e vinto poi
    Fù da gli affetti suoi.   560
    Degno d'eterna gloria
    Fia sol colui c'havrà di sè vittoria.

              Quì di nuovo si volge la Scena.

              Il fine del Quarto Atto.

ATTO QUINTO.

ORFEO.
    Questi i campi di Tracia, e questo è il loco
    Dove passommi il core
    Per l'amara novella il mio dolore.   565

Poiche non hò più spene
Di ricovrar pregando
Piagnendo e sospirando
Il perduto mio bene,
Che poss'io più? se non volgermi à voi   570
Selve soave un tempo
Conforto a' miei martir, mentre à Dio piacque,
Per farvi per pietà meco languire
Al mio languire.

Voi vi doleste ò Monti, e lagrimaste   575
Voi sassi al dispartir del nostro sole,
Et io con voi lagrimerò mai sempre,
E mai sempre dorròmmi, ahi doglia, ahi pianto.
                Eco. Hai pianto.

Cortese Eco amorosa
Che sconsolata sei   580
E consolar mi vuoi ne' dolor miei,
Benche queste mie luci
Sien già per lagrimar fatte due fonti,
In così grave mia fiera sventura
Non ho pianto però tanto che basti.   585
                Ec. Basti.

Se gli occhi d'Argo havessi
E spandessero tutti un Mar di pianto,
Non fora il duol conforme à tanti guai.
                Ec. Ahi.

S'hai del mio mal pietade, io ti ringrazio
Di tua benignitate.   590
Ma mentre io mi querelo
Deh perche mi rispondi
Sol con gli ultimi accenti?
Rendimi tutti integri i miei lamenti.

Ma tu anima mia se mai ritorna   595
La tua fredd'ombra à queste amiche piagge,
Prendi hor da me queste tue lodi estreme
C'hor à te sacro la mia cetra e'l canto
Come à te già sopra l'altar del core
Lo spirto acceso in sacrifizio offersi.   600

Tu bella fusti e saggia, e in te ripose
Tutte le grazie sue cortese il Cielo
Mentre ad ogni altra de suoi don fù scarso
D'ogni lingua ogni lode à te conviensi
Ch'albergasti in bel corpo alma più bella,   605
Fastosa men quanto d'honor più degna.
Hor l'altre Donne son superbe e perfide
Ver chi le adora dispietate instabili,
Prive di senno e d'ogni pensier nobile
Ond'à ragione opra di lor non lodansi,   610
Quinci non fia giamai che per vil femina
Amor con aureo strale il cor trafiggami.
Ma ecco stuol nemico
Di Donne amiche à l'ubbriaco Nume,
Sottrar mi voglio a l'odiosa vista   615
Che fuggon gli occhi ciò che l'alma aborre.

CHORO DI BACCANTI.
Evohe padre Lieo
Bassareo
Te chiamiam con chiari accenti,
Evohe liete e ridenti   620
Te lodiam padre Leneo,
Hor c'habbiam colmo il core
Del tuo divin furore.

BACCANTE.
Fuggito è pur da questa destra ultrice
L'empio nostro avversario il Trace Orfeo   625
Disprezzator de' nostri pregi alteri.

UN'ALTRO BACCANTE.
Non fuggirà, che grave
Suol esser più quanto più tarda scende
Sovra nocente capo ira celeste.

DUE BACCANTI.
Cantiam di Bacco intanto, e in varij modi   630
Sua Deità si benedica e lodi.

CHORO DI BACCANTI.
Evohe padre Lieo
Bassareo

Te chiamiam con chiari accenti,
Evohe liete e ridenti   635
Te lodiam padre Leneo
Hor c'habbiam colmo il core
Del tuo divin furore.

BACCANTE.
Tu pria trovasti la felice pianta
Onde nasce il licore   640
Che sgombra ogni dolore,
Et a gli egri mortali
Del sonno è padre e dolce oblio de i mali.

CHORO.
Evohe padre Lieo
Bassareo   645
Te chiamiam con chiari accenti,
Evohe liete e ridenti
Te lodiam padre Leneo,
Hor c'habbiam colmo il core
Del tuo divin furore.   650

BACCANTE.
Te domator del lucido Oriente
Vide di spoglie alteramente adorno
Sopr'aureo carro il portator del giorno.

BACCANTE.
Tu qual Leon possente
Con forte destra e con invitto core   655
Spargesti et abbattesti
Le Gigantee falangi, et al furore
De le lor braccia ferreo fren ponesti.
Allhor che l'empia guerra
Mosse co' suoi gran figli al Ciel la Terra.   660

CHORO.
Evohe padre Lieo
Bassareo
Te chiamiam con chiari accenti,
Evohe liete e ridenti
Te lodiam padre Leneo,   665

Hor c'habbiam colmo il core
Del tuo divin furore.

BACCANTE.
Senza te l'alma Dea che Cipro honora
Fredda e insipida fora,
O d'ogni human piacer gran condimento   670
E d'ogni afflitto cor dolce contento.

CHORO.
Evohe padre Lieo
Bassareo
Te chiamiam con chiari accenti,
Evohe liete e ridenti   675
Te lodiam padre Leneo
Hor c'habbiam colmo il core
Del tuo divin furore.

Il fine del Quinto Atto.

Text of Act V of Monteverdi's Score, 1609

[Altered Ending]

ATTO QUINTO.

ORFEO.
Questi i campi di Tracia e questo è il loco
Dove passommi il core
Per l'amara novella il mio dolore.   565'

Poichè non ho più spene
Di ricovrar pregando
Piangendo e sospirando
Il perduto mio bene,
Che poss'io più se non volgermi a voi,   570'
Selve soavi, un tempo
Conforto ai miei martir mentre a Dio piacque,
Per farvi per pietà meco languire
Al mio languire?

Voi vi doleste, o monti, e lagrimaste   575'
Voi, sassi, al dipartir del nostro sole,

Et io con voi lagrimerò mai sempre,
E mai sempre dorrommi, ahi doglia, ahi pianto!
              Eco. Ahi pianto.

Cortese Eco amorosa,
Che sconsolata sei   580′
E consolar mi vuoi ne' dolor miei,
Benchè queste mie luci
Sien già per lagrimar fatte due fonti,
In così grave mia fiera sventura
Non ho pianto però tanto che basti.   585′
              Eco. Basti.

Se gli occhi d'Argo avessi
E spandessero tutti un mar di pianto,
Non fora il duol conforme a tanti guai.
              Eco. Ahi.

S'hai del mio mal pietade, io ti ringrazio
Di tua benignitate.   590′
Ma, mentre io mi querelo,
Deh, perchè mi rispondi
Sol con gli ultimi accenti?
Rendimi tutti integri i miei lamenti.

Ma tu, anima mia, se mai ritorna   595
La tua fredd'ombra a queste amiche piagge,
Prendi or da me queste tue lodi estreme
Ch'or a te sacro la mia cetra e 'l canto
Come a te già sopra l'altar del core
Lo spirto acceso in sacrifizio offersi.   600′
Tu bella fusti e saggia, e in te ripose
Tutte le grazie sue cortese il cielo
Mentre ad ogni altra de' suoi don fu scarso;
D'ogni lingua ogni lode a te conviensi
Ch'albergasti in bel corpo alma più bella,   605′
Fastosa men quanto d'onor più degna.
Or l'altre donne son superbe e perfide,
Ver' chi le adora dispietate instabili,
Prive di senno e d'ogni pensier nobile,
Ond'a ragione opra di lor non lodasi;   610′

Quinci no fia giamai che per vil femina
Amor con aureo strale il cor trafiggami.

APOLLO, discende in una nuvola cantando.

Perch'a lo sdegno et al dolor in preda
Così ti doni, o figlio?
Non è, non è consiglio   615′
Di generoso petto
Servir al proprio affetto.
Quinci biasmo e periglio
Già sovrastar ti veggio
Onde movo dal ciel per darti aita;   620′
Or tu m'ascolta e n'avrai lode e vita.

ORFEO.
Padre cortese, al maggior uopo arrivi,
Ch'a disperato fine
Con estremo dolore
M'avean condotto già sdegno et amore.   625′
Eccomi dunque attento a tue ragioni,
Celeste padre; or ciò che vuoi, m'imponi.

APOLLO.
Troppo. troppo gioisti
Di tua lieta ventura,
Or troppo piagni   630′
Tua sorte acerba e dura. Ancor non sai
Come nulla qua giù diletta e dura?
Dunque se goder brami immortal vita
Vientene meco al ciel ch'a sè t'invita.

ORFEO.
Si non vedrò più mai   635′
De l'amata Euridice i dolci rai?

APOLLO.
Nel sole e ne le stelle
Vagheggerai le sue sembianze belle.

ORFEO.
Ben di cotanto padre
Sarei non degno figlio,   640′
Se non seguissi il tuo fedel consiglio.

APOLLO et ORFEO ascende cantando al cielo.
    Saliam cantando al cielo
    Dove ha virtù verace
    Degno premio di sè, diletto e pace.

CORO.
    Vanne, Orfeo, felice a pieno   645′
    A goder celeste onore,
    Là 've ben non vien mai meno,
    Là 've mai non fu dolore,
    Mentr'altari, incensi e voti
    Noi t'offriam lieti e devoti.   650′

    Così va chi non s'arretra
    Al chiamar di nume eterno,
    Così grazia in ciel impetra
    Chi qua giù provò l'inferno,
    E chi semina fra doglie   655′
    D'ogni grazia il frutto coglie.

[MORESCA]

Appendix F

Excerpt from Emilio de' Cavaliere, RAPPRESENTATIONE DI ANIMA ET DI CORPO (Rome, 1600).

(The text, by Padre Agostino Manni, is taken from Solerti, *Le origini del melodramma*, pp. 20-21.)

SCENA QUARTA

CORPO ET ANIMA.

CORP.   Anima mia che pensi?
                    Perche dogliosa stai
                    Sempre traendo guai?

ANI.   Vorrei riposo, e pace:
                    Vorrei diletto e gioia,
                    E trovo affanno e noia.

C.   Ecco i miei sensi prendi
                    Qui ti riposa, e godi
                    In mille varij modi.

A.   Non vò più ber quest'acque.
                    Che la mia sete ardente
                    S'infiamma maggiormente.

C.   Prendi l'honor del Mondo,
                    Què gioir quanto vuoi
                    Què satiar ti puoi.

A.   Nò nò, ch'io so per prova,
                    Con quanto assenzio, e fele
                    Copre il suo falso mele.

C.   Alma d'ogn'altra cosa
                    Tu sei più bella, e vaga:
                    In te dunque t'appaga.

A. Già non mi feci io stessa:
    E come in me potrei
    Quetar gli affetti miei?

C. Lasso che di noi fia!
    Se ritrosa sei tanto
    Starenci sempre in pianto?

A. Questo nò, se m'ascolti,
    E se meco rimiri
    A più alti desiri.
    Terra perchè mi tiri
    Pur alla terra? hor segui il voler mio
    Et amendue riposerenci in Dio.

Appendix G

LA GALATEA by Gabriello Chiabrera

The text reproduced here is taken from the first printed edition of the libretto:

La Galatea / Favola maritima / [heraldic device of Cardinal Ferdinand Gonzaga] / In Mantova, presso Aurelio et Lodovico / Osanni fratelli stampatori ducali / 1614. Con licenza de' Superiori.

as given in Solerti, *Gli Albori del melodramma*, vol. 3, pp. 105-36.

GALATEA

PROLOGO.

IRIDE.
    Scesa dal ciel del folgorante Giove
    Eterna messaggiera a voi ne vegno,
    Di Teti poi nel fluttuoso seno
    Ratta m'ascondo e'l piè rivolgo altrove.

    Tra queste, ch'or mirate, onde spumanti   5
    Vedrete Galatea pianger d'amore,
    E de l'egro suo cor l'aspro dolore
    Vòlto (pietà del cielo) in dolci canti.

    Dunque, mentre io vi lascio, irati venti
    Non conturbino 'l sen del mare infido,   10
    Onda non franga e non percota 'l lido,
    Ferminsi i pesci a le sue note intenti.

[SCENA I.]

ACI.
    Questi, nati nel mar, perle e coralli
    Onde s'ornano il crin l'eterne dive,

Oggi del mio bel sole   15
Faran ghirlanda a l'aurea chioma e bionda
Di rose in vece e pallide viole.

PRIMO PESCATORE
    Aci, tutto giocondo
    A' tuoi dolci diletti
    Par che s'allegri il ciel, gioisca il mondo.   20

IDRILLO.
    Così de' nostri petti
    Mira la gioia sfavillar nel volto,
    E qual diletto abbiam nel seno accolto
    Leggilo in fronte a quest'amica schiera;
    Per te lieto il mattin, lieta la sera.   25

ACI.
    Come a l'altrui martire
    Si raddoppia il tormento in gentil core,
    Tale al vostro gioire
    Maggior contento in me dispensa Amore,
    Ma del mio caro ardore   30
    Non scorgo in questo loco
    I dolci amati lampi
    Ond'io son tutto foco.

PRIMA PESCATRICE.
    Forse ne' fondi algosi
    In grembo al sonno ella n'avvien che pose: 35
    Chè là giù non traspare
    Sì tosto com' a noi l'alba di rose.
    Scogliam la voce al canto,
    Invitiamla co' prieghi,
    Oggi è propizio a le tue voglie il Fato,   40
    Nulla al tuo desiar fia che si nieghi.

CORO.
    Vieni, deh vieni, o Galatea vezzosa,
    Rida al seren de' tuoi soavi lumi
    Sovra l'arena d'òr l'onda amorosa.

SECONDA PESCATRICE.
Vieni, deh vieni, or che più chiaro splende 45
Febo ne l'alto ciel di luce adorno,
Tra le sals'onde a noi, deh, fa ritorno
Con quel vago splendor ch'ogn'alma accende:
Vieni al nostro pregar, vieni festosa.

Replica il CORO.
Vieni, deh vieni, o Galatea vezzosa, 50
Rida al seren de' tuoi soavi lumi
Sovra l'arena d'òr l'onda amorosa.

LE DUE PESCATRICI.
Vieni, deh vieni, ove tra dolci canti
Sovra il tranquillo suol d'instabil mare
Attende tua beltà, che può beare 55
Schiera fedel d'avventurosi amanti;
Vieni, e'n grembo al tuo ben dolce riposa.

Replica il CORO.
Vieni, deh vieni, o Galatea vezzosa,
Rida al seren de' tuoi soavi lumi
Sovra l'arena d'òr l'onda amorosa. 60

ACI.
Gitene, e sian di preda
Carche l'occhiute reti:
Io, fin che l'alma dèa di grembo a Teti
Non mi discopra il bel del suo sembiante,
Non moverò le piante. 65

SECONDO PESCATORE.
Andiam, chè chiaro il sole
Cangia le rose de la vaga Aurora
In bell'oro lucente,
A portar guerra a la spumosa prole.

IDRILLO.
Aci, lodato il ciel che di contento 70
Colmo ti veggio il seno,
E, quel che men sperai,
Adorator di due sereni rai.

ACI.

 Non è sì duro petto e non è core
 Ogn'or libero e sciolto,   75
 Che non sospiri il bel seren d'un volto.
 Amor, tardi o per tempo, ogn'alma assale;
 Nè variar di cielo
 Nè grave soma di passati giorni
 Sono a le piaghe suo schermo o riparo;   80
 E, qual colpo di morte,
 Così comune è l'amorosa sorte.
 Pensa qual de' mortali
 Trarrà disciolto il piè da sue catene,
 Se fra tormenti e pene   85
 Langue ogni nume al balenar d'un ciglio
 Colmo di fiamme e di pungenti strali.

IDRILLO.

 Felice pescatore,
 Miracol di contento in fra gli amanti,
 Ogn'or fra risi e canti   90
 In quest'umida riva
 Riposi in grembo a l'adorata Diva,
 Colmo di foco il sen, di gioia il core.

ACI.

 Così dispensa Amor le sue dolcezze,
 Così rende beati i servi suoi.   95

IDRILLO.

 Per bellezza immortale
 Aver piagato il petto,
 Dove non puoi temer che venga meno
 Il contento o 'l diletto,
 Perchè sian preda del vorace Tempo   100
 Le rose del bel volto,
 I bianchi gigli del lattato seno,
 Somma felicità, somma dolcezza.
 Ma, sin che de' suoi rai
 Ti faccia Galatea lieto e contento,   105
 Sciogli le voci al vento,
 E fa ch'in mille modi

Quest'onde e questi scogli
Odin il suo bel nome, odin sue lodi.

ACI.

Son tuoi begl'occhi, o Galatea gentile,   110
Cari dispensator de' miei contenti,
E de la vita mia stelle lucenti.

De 'l tuo volto seren vincon le rose
Quelle più vaghe, onde superba infiora
La strada al sol la rugiadosa Aurora.   115

Caro languir per così bella fiamma,
Caro a sì dolce ardor venirsi meno,
Caro è piaga d'Amor raccorre in seno.

Viva pur nel tuo cor l'istesso foco,
Nè spenga novo amor vecchio desio,   120
O soave cagion del viver mio.

Ma non è Polifemo
Quel che move le piante
Fra quei sassosi scogli,
Del mio sol, del mio cor misero amante?   125
Volghiam la prora altrove,
Ratti l'ira fuggiam d'un tanto mostro.

[SCENA II]

POLIFEMO.

Qui, dove in riva a l'onde
Sovente il mio bel sol move le piante,
Sfogherò il mio dolor, misero amante,   130
Mentre da gl'antri oscuri
A l'aspre mie querele Eco risponde.

O Galatea, che 'l pregio sei
Del vasto regno, del crudo amor,
Ond'io traggo dolenti e rei   135
I mesti giorni piangendo ogn'or,

Quando a' raggi di tua beltade
Me stesso diedi e la mia fe',

Io non curai mia libertade,
Io non curai nulla di me.   140

Soave speme, aura d'amore
Un tempo verde nel sen fiorì,
Un tempo lieto nel petto il core
A' tuoi bei lumi sè stesso aprì.

Ma s'io spargo le voci ai venti   145
Tu, fêra, altrove rivolgi il piè,
Sorda qual aspe a i miei lamenti:
A tanta fede, crudel, mercè!

Ma non mir'io di Ninfe un vago stuolo
Mover 'l piè ver' quest'aurata arena?   150
Forse nel bel seren del volto amato
Avrò conforto a la mia dura pena;
M'asconderò vicino,
Poichè quanto mi strugge
Altrettanto mi fugge.   155

[SCENE III]

CORO.
      L'aure, ch'in ciel rimenano
      La rugiadosa Aurora
      E 'l zaffiro serenano
      Ch'il sol di luce indora,
      Mentre soavi spirano   160
      I nostri cor respirano.

      A' suoi fiati dolcissimi
      In grembo all'erbe e fiori
      Sciogliam canti lietissimi
      Da' fortunati cori;   165
      Il crin di rose infiorisi,
      E 'l vago giorno onorisi.

SECONDA PESCATRICE.
      Qui dimorar sovente,
      Qui sovente danzar fra l'erbe e i fiori
      Mentre fervono in ciel gl'estivi ardori   170

Suol Galatea, ch'ogni anima innamora
Quando la chioma bionda
Tragge, qual novo sol, da l'onde fuori.

PRIMA PESCATRICE.
  Già da lungi mirar parmi il bel ciglio
  E la divina luce   175
  Che più ch'in uman volto in lei riluce;
  Avventurate arene,
  E scogli fortunati,
  Per cotanta beltà lieti e beati.

GALATEA.
  Soavissimo gioire!   180
  Ecco 'l fin de' lunghi affanni,
  Ecco 'l fin di quel martire
  Che soffert'ho cotant'anni;
  O tormenti, o pene, o danni,
  Lungi omai da questo petto;   185
  Qui s'annida almo diletto
  Qui soggiorna almo desire;
  Soavissimo gioire!

SECONDA PESCATRICE.
  Ecco il pregio de l'onde
  Ecco la vaga e bella Galatea,   190
  Che di soavi accenti
  Fa risonar queste marine sponde,
  E co 'l lucido lampo ogn'alma bea.

IDRILLO.
  Scendi, possente diva,
  In queste arene, scendi   195
  In quest'algosa riva:
  Infioreranti il crine
  Vaghe rose e vïole
  Còlte allor che nel ciel sorgeva 'l sole.

GALATEA.
  Cari pregi adorati,   200
  Gemme de' vaghi prati,
  Ecco di voi m'adorno,
  Di voi formo ghirlanda al crin d'intorno.

CORO.

    Il crin, che vago infiora
    Costei di gigli e rose,   205
    Sembra il crin de l'Aurora
    Quando precorre il sole
    E le piagge del ciel fa luminose;
    Anzi l'istessa luce.
    Onde il sereno giorno Apollo adduce.   210

IDRILLO.

    Ecco su l'alta rupe
    Il mostro orrendo, ecco l'etneo gigante:
    Volgiam altrove omai, Ninfe, le piante.

PRIMA PESCATRICE.

    Ma che temiam se nostra schiera affida
    Immortal diva, al cui poter non vale   215
    Furor d'ira mortale?

[SCENE IV]

POLIFEMO.

    O Dea, ch'io non so mai se Cipro o Gnido
    Più vaga adori o còla,
    Perchè sorda al mio dir, cruda a' miei pianti,
    Fuggi d'udir di queste voci il grido?   220
    Già sai quanti ogn'or vibri in questo seno
    Strali per tua beltate
    Il pargoletto Arciero:
    Arcier che, bench'infante,
    Atterra ogni gigante.   225

GALATEA.

    Queta i sospiri e i pianti,
    Ed a sen che più molle
    A' tuoi desir si pieghi
    Porgi d'amore affettuosi i prieghi;
    Che se d'alta beltade   230
    Amor serva mi fece,
    Vano è sperar al tuo dolor pietade.

POLIFEMO.
    Crudel! cotanta fede
    Merta tanto martir per sua mercede?
    Ma, deh, svelane al meno   235
    Qual sì beato seno
    Ricetto è di tuo core,
    E qual ciglio ti fe' serva d'Amore?

GALATEA.
    Aci, di queste sponde
    Il più bello, il più vago;   240
    Aci, di cui quest'onde
    Mormoran sempre in mille guise e mille;
    Aci, con le sue vaghe alme faville
    Questo cor dolcemente accende e sface;
    Aci mio ben, Aci mio cor, mia pace.   245

POLIFEMO.
    Dunque mentr'io mi moro
    Fra mille affanni e doglie,
    Un pescator mi toglie
    La mia vita, il mio ben, il mio tesoro?
    Or or movo le piante: 250
    Fin di mia dura sorte
    Sarà di quel garzon l'acerba morte.

GALATEA.
    O cielo, o Dei, quanto furor l'assale!

IDRILLO.
    Egli, d'ira già colmo a noi s'invola,
    E 'l siegue Galatea tutta dolente,   255
    Crudo timor d'innamorata mente.

CORO.
    D'Amor le fiamme ed i pungenti strali
    Or ancidono un petto,
    Or son dolci e vitali,
    Or cagion di tormento, or di diletto;   260
    E con diversa sorte
    Dànno a' miseri amanti
    Or dolci risi, or pianti, or vita, or morte.

CORO.
    Qual balen fra le nubi,
    Amorosa dolcezza si dilegua;
    Fugge, qual strale al vento,
    Ogni gioia d'Amor in un momento.

[SCENE V]

EURILLO, nunzio.
    Sconsolata beltà, funesto giorno!
    Non così tosto affretta
    Al destinato segno   270
    Pennuto dardo o rapida saetta,
    Come nel basso regno
    Battè veloci l'ale
    Nel fior de gl'anni suoi beltà mortale.

SECONDA PESCATRICE.
    Qual lacrimevol suon l'aria perturba?   275

IDRILLO.
    Queste d'Eurillo son note dolenti:
    Temo d'infausta sorte,
    D'Aci pavento il caso,
    E del Ciclope la sdegnosa faccia
    Ancor nel petto mio morte minaccia.   280

EURILLO, nunzio
    Pescator, che gioiste
    Al gioir de la Dea che l'onde onora,
    Piangete il duol ch'il molle petto accora.
    Aci estinto si giace; Aci, conforto
    Del suo bel seno, è morto!   285

PRIMA PESCATRICE.
    E come? Ohimè, già tutto giaccio ho il core
    Di pietà, di dolore!

EURILLO, nunzio.
    Sotto rupe che 'l mar bagna e circonda,
    Stava attendendo la sua bella sposa
    Aci, ed al canto suo tutta festosa   290

Sovra l'arena d'or muoveasi l'onda,
Quand'ecco Polifemo irato giunse
(L'aspro cor colmo d'ira
Ben dimostrava accolto
Nel torbid'occhio e nel sanguigno volto);   295
Poscia svelse crudele
Sasso, cima di monte,
E l'avventò: nè cadde il colpo in vano
Ond'estinto il garzon giacque su 'l piano.

SECONDA PESCATRICE.
Ahi dolente novella! Ahi duro fato!   300

EURILLO, nunzio.
Guinse la vaga diva
Ch'egli spirava l'ultimo sospiro,
E fra la braccia sue mesta l'accolse;
Qual possente martiro
Gl'ingombrasse la mente   305
Dicanlo i scogli pur, chi'l suon dolente
Udir di sue querele,
Dica l'arena d'oro
Quelle misere voci: — Ahi, ch'io non moro! —
Così tra i pianti e l'ire   310
Doleasi sol di non poter morire.

PRIMA PESCATRICE.
Miserabil successo! Empio destino!

PRIMO PESCATORE.
O fior di giovinezza,
O pregio di bellezza,
Come languendo in un breve baleno   315
Così te 'n vieni meno!
A così dure pene
Piangete, o scogli, e lacrimate, arene.

CORO.
Piangete, o scogli, e lacrimate, arene.

SECONDA PESCATRICE.
Sol, che ne l'oriente   320
Di sì tenera età sorgendo fuora

Avesti de' tuoi dì bellezza, aurora,
Deh, come a l'occidente
Ne lo spuntar rapido affretti il corso!
A così dure pene   325
Piangete, o scogli, e lacrimate, arene.

CORO.
Piangete, o scogli, e lacrimate, arene.

CORO.
Dove, dove è 'l crin d'oro,
Dove le rose de le guance amate,
E dove il bel tesoro   330
Di quelle vaghe luci alme e beate?
Ahi, che spente, eclissate,
Chiusero seco ogni più dolce bene!
Piangete, o scogli, e lacrimate, arene.

CORO.
Spegni ne l'alto, o Febo, i rai lucenti,   335
Acciò che non ritorni
Il fosco a noi di sì funesti giorni;
E questo infausto dì non abbia loco
Tra bei giorni de l'anno,
O giorno a noi di sempiterno affanno!   340
Turbo o procella ria d'atra tempesta
Avvolga l'empia notte,
E seren non si miri
Lampeggiar fra' zaffiri,
O precorrere il dì lucenti albori,   345
Nè aurora sia che il ciel di rose infiori.

[SCENA VI]

POLIFEMO.
Or che per questa destra
Giace il vil pescator privo di vita,
E 'n van chiamando aita
Ne le braccia di lei se 'n venne meno;   350
Io, già libero il seno,
Canterò 'l gioir mio,
Onde, al vostro soave mormorio.
                                        Eco. rio. rio.

PRIMA PESCATRICE.
  Con duplicata voce il ciel lo chiama
  Di tal misfatto rio.   355

POLIFEMO.
  Voce, che mi rispondi e rio mi chiami,
  Me già non incolpar, ma l'empia e dura
  Che m'accese nel cor fiamma d'amore.
                            Eco. more. more.

POLIFEMO.
  Non può morir, che diva
  Non fa soggetta il Fato a mortal scempio.   360
                            Eco. empio. empio.

PRIMA PESCATRICE.
  Empio ben sei, che l'immortal suo seno
  D'immortal morte e di dolor colmasti.

POLIFEMO.
  Empio ad altrui, a me medesmo pio:
  Con la sua morte a me diedi la vita
  E spensi co 'l suo sangue il foco mio,   365
  Che, per timor di sue beltà caduta,
  In questo cor più non s'avviva e sorge.
                            Eco. sorge. sorge.

POLIFEMO.
  Sorga pur, s'egli può: pianga colei;
  Ne le sventure sue
  Forse ramembrerà gl'affanni miei.   370

SECONDO PESCATORE.
  Vanne pur, vanne altiero
  Di gloriose prove.
  Nel ciel l'eterno Giove
  Con fulmine o saetta
  Del duol di Galatea prenda vendetta!   375

CORO.
  Tempo rio, che tosto voli
  E n'involi

Ogni gioia, ogni diletto,
Sol eterni e doglie e pianti
De gl'amanti   380
Nel ferito acceso petto;

Qual più vaga innostra e infiora
Bell'Aurora
Gioventù di mortal seno,
Si dilegua in un momento   385
Il contento:
Ogni dolce ha il suo veneno.

Ch'attendiamo in un sospiro
Di martiro
O di dolce e lieta sorte,   390
S'al fuggir di rapid'ore
Atro orrore
Poi ne fa preda di morte?

[SCENA VII]

PRIMO PESCATORE.
Ma, dal profondo sen de l'ampio mare
Sorger mirate Galatea dolente;   395
Sue doglie acerbe, amare,
Nel pallor del bel volto
Dimostra il core accolto.

GALATEA.
Onde spumose, e voi
Algosi lidi e numerose arene,   400
Ch'al mio gioir gioiste,
Or lacrimate a le mie dure pene;
Turbate al mio dolore,
Spumosi flutti, al mar l'immenso seno,
Procellose fremente;   405
Mostrate in questa guisa
Come al mio sospirar meco piangete!

SECONDO PESCATORE.
Se ne' divini petti
Tanto martir soggiorna e tanti mali,
Meno infelici son gli egri mortali: 410

GALATEA.
    Poichè a gli sguardi, a' risi
    Di mortal giovinetto,
    Misera, offersi il petto,
    Mia libertade in me medesma uccisi;
    Egli nel fior de' suoi più lieti giorni   415
    Cadde, fatto di gelo;
    Io, per infausto don d'irato cielo
    Fatta diva immortale,
    Perchè languendo e non sperando aita
    Sempre morissi senza uscir di vita,   420
    Lacrimo il mio contento, il mio conforto.
    Aci mio, tu sei morto?
    Aci, mio cor, mio pace
    Chiudesti in sonno eterno
    Le dolci tue pupille,   425
    Fonti de l'ardor mio, di mie faville!
    Aci, di questo sen gioia e tesoro,
    Se l'afflitta mia voce e i mesti accenti,
    Alma disciolta, senti,
    Deh, mira il mio martoro,   430
    Mira mia vita, mira
    Com'io d'immortal morte ognor mi moro.
    E sopra questo porporino e vago
    Corallo, ch'a me desti,
    Vedi quai versi intanto   435
    Da' languid'occhi miei fiumi di pianto.

IDRILLO.
    Udite il flebil suon de' mesti accenti!
    Come s'affanna e come
    Chiama piangendo ogn'or l'amato nome!

PROTEO.
    Bella Diva del mar, che mentre versi   440
    D'amarissimo pianto acerbi fiumi
    Crescer fai le sals'onde,
    Omai rasciuga i lagrimosi lumi.

GALATEA.
    E qual conforto in così rio martire
    Fia che consoli il mesto cor dolente,   445

Se fra l'estinta gente
Si giace ogni mio ben, ogni desire?

PROTEO.
    Vedrai l'amato volto
    Più lucido, vedrai
    Più lieti sfavillar gl'accesi rai.   450
    Tal ne gl'immensi abissi
    Fra l'eterno secreto
    Avvolge immobil Fato alto decreto.

GALATEA.
    Così soave speme il cor lusinga
    Al suon di tue parole   455
    Che, come nebbia al sole,
    Par ch'ogni mio dolor si venga meno,
    E sol d'alto desir si colmi il seno!
    Ma come, o quando o dove
    Fia che 'l mio ben ritrove?   460

PROTEO.
    Mossi a' tuoi mesti accenti,
    Il gran Rettor del mar e 'l sommo Giove
    A l'estinto garzon reser la vita,
    E d'immortalità vestir sue membra.
    Più quell'Aci non sembra   465
    Che dianzi un pescator tendea le reti:
    Splendon più vaghi e lieti
    Gli occhi, d'immortal luce ogn'or ridenti,
    Ma no 'l vedi o conosci? ecco fra l'onde
    Ei sorge, a te se'n viene: 470
    Lungi dunque i martir', lungi le pene.

ACI.
    Amor, s'il tuo veneno
    Di sì caro gioir mesci e confondi,
    Se tanto ben nascondi
    Sotto pochi respiri e poche stille,   475
    Sempre fia questo seno
    Esca a le tue faville;
    E, se dopo il morire
    Concede eterno fato

Così dolce gioire,   480
Soavissimo duol, morir beato!

SECONDO PESCATORE.
    Avventurati amanti,
    Godano i vostri cori
    Frutti soavi di felici amori;
    Nè tra querele e pianti   485
    D'intorno rimbombar s'oda quest'onda,
    Ma sol voce di gioia il ciel confonda.

PROTEO.
    Non fia che vi disgiunga
    Ira d'aspro rivale,
    Nè più turbar potrà colpo mortale   490
    I soavi diletti
    De' vostri eterni petti.

GALATEA.
    Care lagrime mie,
    Ben versati sospiri,
    E ben sofferte ancor pene aspre e rie: 495
    Se tanto a' miei desiri
    Premio concede 'l fato,
    Care lagrime mie, pianto beato!

PRIMO PESCATORE.
    Non più qual si solea
    Aci fra noi s'inviti,   500
    Divo immortal, di sì vezzosa Dea
    Per decreto del ciel consorte e sposo;
    A cui pregi sì chiari
    Or devoti ergerem tempii ed altari.

EURILLO, nunzio.
    Ma, deh, perchè non sciogli,   505
    Diva, dal lieto sen voci canore?
    Or ch'è propizio a le tue voglie Amore,
    Fa rimbombar quest'onde e questi scogli.

GALATEA.
    Chi 'l bell'arco possente e la faretra,
    Ch'in sè nasconde mille aurati strali,   510

Chi canterà sovra soave cetra
De l'immortal arcier lodi immortali?
A soccorrer un cor non mai s'arretra,
Ed al grand'uopo altrui veloci ha l'ali:
Dio, per cui gira il ciel, mantiensi 'l mondo   515
Ne le fere amarezze ancor giocondo.

EURILLO, nunzio.
Ecco l'alma Anfitrite,
Come sorgendo fuora
Del vasto impero di Nettun spumante,
Diva del mar, tua deitade onora.   520

ANFITRITE.
Anime fortunate,
Felici amanti, avventurosi numi,
Sempre volin per voi l'ore beate,
Nè sia fero dolor che vi consumi.
Colmi di gioia il ciel gl'alti diletti   525
De' vostri eterni innamorati petti.
Sempre con voi felicità soggiorni,
Sian eterni, contenti
Qual son di vostra vita eterni i giorni.

CORO.
Lieto splendi e fortunato   530
Giorno a noi d'alti contenti
Rida ogn'erba in grembo al prato,
Scopra Febo i rai lucenti.

Oggi Amor benigno accoppia,
Donator d'alto diletto,   535
Fortunata e lieta coppia,
Due desiri in un sol petto.

Questo dì lieto e beato
Onoriam con dolci accenti;
Rida ogn'erba in grembo al prato,   540
Scopra Febo i rai lucenti.

Lieto splendi e fortunato
Giorno a noi d'alti contenti,

Rida ogn'erba in grembo al prato
Scopra Febo i rai lucenti.   545

IL FINE.

Bibliography

I. Primary Sources

A. Theoretical Works and Chronicles

Accademia degli Alterati. Extracts from the *Diario* (Ms. Ashburnham 558 of the Biblioteca Medicea Laurenziana of Florence). Published by Bernard Weinberg, "Argomenti di discussione letteraria nell'Accademia degli Alterati (1570-1600)," *Giornale storico della letteratura italiana*, 131 (1954): 175-94.

Aristotle. *Works*. Edited by W. D. Ross and J. A. Smith. Oxford: Clarendon Press, 1908-1952. 12 vols. *De anima*, trans. J. A. Smith (vol. 3, 1931); *De generatione animalium*, trans. Arthur Platt (vol. 5, 1912); *Problemata*, trans, E. S. Forster (vol. 7, 1927); *Politica*, trans. B. Jowett (vol. 10, 1921); *Rhetorica*, trans. W. Rhys Roberts; *De poetica*, trans. I. Bywater (vol. 11, 1952).

Bardi, Giovanni de'. "Discorso mandato... a Giulio Caccini sopra la musica antica e 'l cantar bene," in *Lyra Barberina Amphichordos*. Edited by Antonio Francesco Gori. 2 vols., pp. 233-48. Florence: Caesareis, 1763.

Bartoli, Giorgio. *Trattato degl'elementi del parlar toscano*. Florence: Giunti, 1584.

Castelvetro, Lodovico. *Poetica d'Aristotele vulgarizzata et sposta*. Vienna: G. Stainhofer, 1570.

Descartes, René. *Compendium*, in *Oeuvres*. Edited by V. Cousin, vol. 5, pp. 446 ff. Paris: F. G. Levrault, 1824-26.

Doni, Giovanni Battista. *Lyna Barberina Amphichordos*. Edited by Antonio Francesco Gori. 2 vols. Florence: Caesareis, 1763.

_____. *Annotazioni sopra il Compendio de' generi, e de' modi della musica*. Rome: Andrea Fei, 1640.

Follino, Federico. *Compendio delle sontuose feste fatte l'anno MDCVIII nella città di Mantova..*. Mantua: Aurelio et Lodovico Osanna, 1608. Reprinted in part by A. Solerti in vol. 2 of *Gli albori del melodramma*, pp. 145 ff. Milan: Sandron, [1904].

Galen. *On the Natural Faculties*. Translated by A. J. Brock. London: J. M. Dent, 1916.

Galilei, Vincenzo. *Dialogo della musica antica, e della moderna*. Florence: Giorgio Marescotti, 1581. Edited in facsimile by Fabio Fano. Rome: Reale accademia d'Italia, 1934.

Giacomini de' Tebalducci Malespini, Lorenzo. "Lezione... sopra la purgatione della tragedia," in *Prose fiorentine raccolte dallo Smarrito [Carlo Dati] accademico della Crusca*, pt. 2, vol. 4 (1729), pp. 212-50. Florence: Santi Franchi, 1716-1745.

Giraldi Cintio, Giovanni Battista. *Scritti estetici di..*. Edited by G. Antimaco. ("Biblioteca rara," vols. 52-53.) Milan, 1864.

Guarini, Giovanni Battista. *Compendio della poesia tragicomica, tratto dai duo Verati*. Venice: G. B. Ciotti, 1601.

Ingegneri, Angelo. *Della poesia rappresentativa e del modo di rappresentare le favole sceniche*. Ferrara: Vittorio Baldini, 1598.

Mei, Girolamo. "Come potesse tanto la musica appresso gli antichi..." ("Trattato di musica..."). Paris: Bibliothèque Nationale, Ms. lat. 7209^2. 113 pp. Sixteenth-century copy.

_____. "Del verso toscano Trattato del Signor Hieronimo Mei Gentiluomo fiorentino

distinto in tre libri." Florence: Biblioteca Riccardiana, Ms. Ricc. 2597. 91 fols.
Seventeenth-century copy.

_____. *Letters on Ancient and Modern Music to Vincenzo Galilei and Giovanni Bardi.*
Edited with an introduction and notes by Claude V. Palisca. Rome: American
Institute of Musicology, "Musicological Studies and Documents," no. 3 (1960).

_____. "Trattato di... sopra la prosa toscana, e della composizione delle parole in due
libri." Florence: Biblioteca Nazionale Centrale, Magliabecchiana, Cl. 6, cod. 34. 72
fols. Autograph.

_____. "De modis Musicis antiquorum ad Petrum Victorium Libri III. Autoris
Autographum." Vaticanus latinus Ms. 5323. 155, 44 pp. [1567-73].

Michele, Agostino, *Discorso... come si possono scrivere con molta lode le comedie, e le
tragedie in prosa.* Venice: G. B. Ciotti, 1592.

Patrici, Francesco. *Della poetica.* Ferrara: Baldini, 1586.

Rossi, Bastiano de'. *Descrizione dell'apparato e degl'intermedi fatti per la commedia
rappresentata in Firenze nelle nozze de' Serenissimi Don Ferdinando Medici a Madama
Cristina di Lorena, Gran Duchi di Toscana.* Florence: Anton Padovani, 1589.
Reprinted in part by A. Solerti in vol. 2 of *Gli albori del melodramma,* pp. 16 ff.
Milan: Sandron, [1904]

Solerti, Angelo, ed. *Le origini del melodramma; testimonianze dei contemporanei.* Turin:
Fratelli Bocca, 1903. Reprint Bologna, Forni, 1969.

Sommi, Leone de'. *Quatro dialoghi in materia di rappresentazioni sceniche.* Edited by
F. Marotti. Milan: Il Polifilo, 1968.

Strunk, Oliver, ed. *Source Readings in Music History.* New York: Norton, 1950.

Varchi, Benedetto. *Lezzioni... lette da lui publicamente nell'Accademia fiorentina, sopra
diverse materie, poetiche, e filosofiche...* Florence: Giunti, 1590.

Zarlino, Gioseffo. *Le institutioni harmoniche.* Venice: [Pietro da Fino?], 1558.

B. Poetry and Music

Ancona, Alessandro d', ed. *Sacre rappresentazioni dei secoli XIV, XV, e XVI., 3 vols.*
Florence: Successori Le Monnier, 1872.

Beccari, Agostino. *Il Sacrificio.* Reprinted in vol. 17 of *Parnaso italiano, ovvero Raccolta
de' poeti classici italiani.* Edited by A. Rubbi. 56 vols. Venice, 1784-91.

Bottegari, Cosimo. *The Bottegari Lutebook.* Edited by Carol Mac Clintock. ("The
Wellesley Edition," no. 8.) Wellesley, Mass.: The Wellesley Press, 1965.

Caccini, Giulio. *L'Euridice composta in musica in stile rappresentativo da Giulio Caccini
detto Romano.* Florence: Giorgio Marescotti, 1600.

_____. *L'Euridice.* Reprinted in facsimile by Ricordi. Milan, 1880.

_____. *L'Euridice.* Reprinted in facsimile by Forni. Bologna, n. d.

_____. *Euridice.* Edited by Robert Eitner, in *Publikationen älterer praktischer und
theoretischer Musikwerke,* vol. 10: *Die Oper von ihrem ersten Anfängen bis zur Mitte
des 18 Jahrhunderts.* Leipzig: Breitkopf & Härtel, 1881.

_____. *Le nuove musiche.* Florence: Marescotti, 1601 [1602]. Edited in facsimile
with a preface by F. Vatielli. Rome: Reale accademia d'Italia, 1934.

_____. *Le nuove musiche.* Edited with translation by H. Wiley Hitchcock. (Recent
Researches in the Music of the Baroque Era, vol. 9) Madison, Wisc.: A-R Editions, 1970.

Cavalieri, Emilio de'. *La rappresentazione di anima, et di corpo novamente posta in
musica dal sig. Emilio del Cavaliere per recitar cantando.* Rome: Mutii, 1600. Edited
in facsimile by Francesco Mantica with an introduction by Domenico Alaleona.
Roma: Casa editrice Claudio Monteverdi, 1912.

Chiabrera, Gabriello. *Delle opere di G. C.* 5 vols. bound in 3. Venice, 1805.

_____. *Dialoghi dell'arte poetica con altre prose e lettere.* Venice, 1830.

_____. *Il rapimento di Cefalo* and other libretti. Edited by Angelo Solerti, in vol. 3 of *Gli albori del melodramma,* pp. 3 ff. Milan: Sandron [1905].

_____. *Rime.* Edited by Giuseppe Paolucci. 3 vols. Rome: Salvioni, 1718.

Corte, Andrea della, ed. *Drammi per musica dal Rinuccini allo Zeno.* 2 vols. ("Classici italiani," vol. 57.) Turin: Unione tipografico-editrice torinese [1958].

_____. *Ottavio Rinuccini, Drammi per musica: Dafne, Euridice, Arianna.* Turin: Unione tipografico-editrice torinese, 1926

Doglio, Federico, ed. *Il teatro tragico italiano.* Parma: Guanda, 1960.

Fioretti di frottole, barzellette, capitoli, strambotti, e sonetti libro secondo (1519). Copied by Einstein and preserved in the Smith College Music Archives; Madrigals of the Sixteenth and Seventeenth Centuries. Vol. 83. Northampton, Mass.

Gagliano, Marco da. *La Dafne... nell'accademica degl'Elevati l'Affannato rappresentata in Mantova.* Florence: Cristoforo Marescotti, 1608. Annotated copy belonging to the Biblioteca Nazionale Centrale in Florence, Magliabecchiana collection, Mus. ant. 36.

_____. *La Dafne.* Reprinted in facsimile by Forni. Bologna, 1970.

_____. *La Dafne.* Edited by James Erber. London, Cathedral Music, c. 1978.

_____. *La Dafne* (incomplete). Edited by Robert Eitner, in *Publikationen älterer praktischer und theoretischer Musikwerke,* vol. 10. Leipzig: Breitkopf & Härtel, 1881.

Ghizzolo, Giovanni. *Madrigali et arie per sonare et cantare... col giuoco della cieca, et una Mascherata de' Pescatori.* Venice: Raverii, 1609.

Giraldi Cinthio, Giovanni Battista. *Eglè.* Reprinted in vol. 24 of *Parnaso italiano, ovvero Raccolta de' poeti classici italiani.* Edited by A. Rubbi. 56 vols. Venice, 1784-91.

_____. *Le tragedie di...* Venice: G. C. Cagnacini, 1583.

Guarini, Giovanni Battista. *Il pastor fido.* In *Teatro del Seicento.* Edited by Luigi Fassò. "La letteratura italiana; storia e testi," vol. 39, Milan: pp. 97-323. Riccardo Ricciardi, [1967].

Jacquot, J. and D. P. Walker, ed. *Musique des intermèdes de 'La Pellegrina'.* Vol. 1 of *Les fêtes de Florence (1589).* ("Le choeur des Muses.") Paris: Centre National de la Recherche Scientifique, 1963.

Monteverdi, Claudio. "Due lettere amorose," in *Concerto, Settimo libro de madrigali a 1, 2, 3, 4 & sei voci.* Vol. 7 of *Tutte le opere di C. M.* Edited by G. Francesco Malipiero. 16 vols. in 17. Asolo, 1926-42.

_____. "Il ballo delle Ingrate." In *Madrigali guerrieri, et amorosi, libro ottavo.* Vol. 8 of *Tutte le opere di C. M.*

_____. "Il lamento di Arianna." In vol. 11 of *Tutte le opere di C. M.*

_____. *Lettere, dediche, e prefazioni.* Edited by Domenico de Paoli. Rome: De Santis, 1973.

_____. *L'Orfeo Favola in musica da Claudio Monteverdi rappresentata in Mantova l'anno 1607, et novamente data in luce.* Venice: Ricciardo Amadino, 1609.

_____. *L'Orfeo.* Edited by G. Francesco Malipiero in vol. 11 of *Tutte le opere di C. M.*

Peri, Jacopo. *Le musiche di Iacopo Peri Nobil Fiorentino sopra l'Euridice del sig. Ottavio Rinuccini rappresentate nello sposalizio della Cristianissima Maria Medici Regina di Francia e di Navarra.* Florence: Giorgio Marescotti, 1600 [1601].

_____. *Le musiche di Iacopo Peri... sopra l'Euridice del sig. Ottavio Rinuccini.* Facsimile edition by Enrico Magni Dufflocq. Rome: Reale accademia d'Italia, 1934.

_____. *Le musiche... sopra l'Euridice.* Facsimile of the Florence, 1601 print. Bologna, Forni, 1969.

_____. *Le musiche... sopra l'Euridice.* Facsimile of the Florence, 1601 print. New York: Broude Bros., 1973.

_____. *L'Euridice.* Edited by L. Torchi in vol. 6 of *L'arte musicale in Italia.* Milan: Ricordi, 1897-191?

Petrucci, Ottaviano de'. *Frottole libro sexto.* Venice, 1505. Copied by Einstein and preserved in the Smith College Music Archives; "Madrigals of the Sixteenth and Seventeenth Centuries." Vol. 81. Northampton, Mass.

Poliziano (Angelo Ambrogini). *Le stanze, L'Orfeo, e le rime.* Edited with an introduction by Giosuè Carducci. Florence, 1863.

_____. *Le stanze, l'Orfeo, e le rime.* Edited with an introduction by A. Momigliano. ("Collezione di classici italiani," 55.) Turin: Unione tipografico-editrice torinese [1921].

_____. *L'Orfeo.* Translated by J. A. Symonds in *Sketches and Studies in Italy and Greece.* Vol. 2, pp. 345 ff. London, 1898.

_____. *Orpheus and Aminta.* Translated by Lewis E. Lord. London, 1931.

Rinuccini, Ottavio. *Rappresentazione di Dafne favola pastorale...* [Florence: Marescotti, 1598?]

_____. *L'Euridice d'Ottavio Rinuccini rappresentata nello sposalitio della Christianiss. Regina di Francia, e di Navarra.* Florence: Giunti, 1600.

_____. *Dafne, Euridice, Arianna.* Edited by Andrea della Corte. Turin: Unione tipografico-editrice torinese, 1926.

_____. *Dafne, Euridice, Arianna.* Edited by Andrea Rubbi, in vol. 17 of *Parnaso italiano, ovvero, Raccolta de' poeti classici italiani.* 56 vols. Venice, 1784-91.

_____. *Intermedi, Mascherate, Dafne, Euridice, Arianna, Narciso, Balletto delle Ingrate,* and other poems intended for music. Edited by A. Solerti, in vol. 2 of *Gli albori del melodramma.*

Solerti, Angelo. *Gli albori del melodramma.* Milan: Sandron [1904-5]; reprint Hildesheim, G. Olms, 1969. 3 vols. Vol. 2: Works by Ottavio Rinuccini; vol. 3: Works by Gabriello Chiabrera and Alessandro Striggio.

Striggio, Alessandro. *La favola d'Orfeo rappresentata in musica il carnevale dell'anno MDCVII.* Mantua: Francesco Osanna, 1607.

Tasso, Torquato. *L'Aminta.* Edited with an introduction and notes by Luigi Fassò. 3d ed. Florence: Sansoni, n. d.

II. Reference Works

Accademia della Crusca. *Vocabolario.* Fifth printing. Florence: Tipografia Galileiana di N. Cellini, 1863 ff.

Ambros, August Wilhelm. *Geschichte der Musik.* Vol. 4. 3d ed., revised and enlarged by Hugo Leichtentritt. Leipzig: Leuchart, 1909.

Angeleri, Carlo. *Bibliografia delle stampe popolari.* Florence: Sansoni Antiquariato, 1953.

Belloni, Antonio. *Il seicento.* 2d ed. Milan: Casa editrice dottor Francesco Vallardi, 1929.

Enciclopedia dello spettacolo. Edited by D'Amico. 10 vols. Rome: Le Maschere, 1954-66.

Greenough, J. B. et al. (ed.). *Allen and Greenough's New Latin Grammar.* 2d ed. revised. Boston: Ginn & Co., 1903. Reprinted, 1931.

Grout, Donald J. *A Short History of Opera.* 2d ed. revised. New York: Columbia University Press, 1965.

Musik in Geschichte und Gegenwart. Edited by Friedrich Blume. Kassel: Bärenreiter, 1949.

Riemann, Hugo. *Handbuch der Musikgeschichte.* Vol. 2, part 2: *Das Generalbasszeitalter, die Monodie des 17. Jahrhunderts und die Weltherrschaft der Italiener.* Edited by Alfred Einstein. 2d ed. revised. Leipzig: Breitkopf und Härtel, 1922.

Rilli, Jacopo. *Notizie letterarie, ed istoriche intorno agli uomoni illustri dell'Accademia fiorentina,* part 1. Florence: Per P. Matini, Stampatore Arcivescovale, 1700.

Solerti, Angelo. *Musica, ballo e drammatica alla corte Medicea dal 1600 al 1637.* Florence: R. Bemporad, 1905. Reprint Bologna: Forni, 1969.

Weinberg, Bernard. *A History of Literary Criticism in the Italian Renaissance.* 2 vols. Chicago: University of Chicago Press, 1961.

III. Secondary Sources

Abert, Anna Amalie. *Claudio Monteverdi und das musikalische Drama.* Lippstadt: Kistner & Siegel, 1954.

Ademollo, A. *La Bella Adriana ed altre virtuose del suo tempo alla corte di Mantova.* Città di Castello: Lapi, 1888.

Aldrich, Putman. *Rhythm in Seventeenth-Century Italian Monody.* New York: Norton, 1966.

Allorto, Riccardo. "Il prologo dell' *Orfeo*; note sulla formazione del recitativo Monteverdiano" In *Claudio Monteverdi e il suo tempo.* Edited by R. Monterosso, pp. 157-68. Cremona, 1969.

Ancona, Alessandro d'. *Origini del teatro Italiano.* 2d ed. 2 vols. Turin: E. Loescher, 1891.

Apollonio, Mario. "Paesaggio dell'*Orfeo*," in *Il Poliziano e il suo tempo.* (Atti del IV convegno internazionale di studi sul Rinascimento.) Florence: G. C. Sansoni, 1957, pp. 69-80.

Arnold, Denis. *Monteverdi.* In "The Master Musicians Series." Edited by Jack Westrup. London: J. M. Dent, 1963.

Brand, C. P. *Torquato Tasso: A Study of the Poet and of His Contribution to English Literature.* Cambridge: Cambridge University Press, 1965.

Brown, Howard Mayer. "How Opera Began: An Introduction to Jacopo Peri's *Euridice* (1600)," in *The Late Italian Renaissance, 1525-1630.* Edited by Eric Cochrane, pp. 401-43. London: Macmillan, 1970.

_____. *Sixteenth-Century Instrumentation: The Music for the Florentine Intermedii.* (Musicological Studies and Documents, 30) American Institute of Musicology, 1973.

Calcaterra, Carolo. *Poesia e canto, studi sulla poesia melica italiana e sulla favola per musica.* Bologna: Nicola Zanichelli, 1951.

Carapetyan, Armen. "The Concept of *Imitazione della Natura* in the Sixteenth Century," *Journal of Renaissance and Baroque Music* 1 (1946): 47-67.

Carducci, Giosuè. *Su l'Aminta di T. Tasso.* Florence: G. C. Sansoni, 1896.

Comte, C. and P. Laumonier. "Ronsard et les musiciens du XVIe siècle," *Revue d'histoire littéraire de la France* 7 (1900): 341-81.

Croce, Benedetto. *Aesthetic.* 8th ed. revised. Translated by Douglas Ainslie. New York: Noonday Press, 1960.

Doran, Madeleine. *Endeavors of Art, A Study of Form in Elizabethan Drama.* Madison, Wis.: University of Wisconsin Press, 1954.

Einstein, Alfred. "Abbot Angelo Grillo's Letters as Source Materials for Music History," in *Essays on Music.* New York: Norton, 1956, pp. 153-73.

_____. "Ancora sull'aria di Ruggiero," *Rivista musicale italiana* 41 (1937): 163-69.

_____. "Die Aria di Ruggiero," *Sammelbände der Internationalen Musikgesellschaft* 13 (1911-12): 444-54.

_____. *The Italian Madrigal.* Translated by Alexander H. Krappe, Roger H. Sessions, and Oliver Strunk. 3 vols. Princeton, N.J.: Princeton University Press, 1949.

_____. *Madrigals of the Sixteenth and Seventeenth Centuries,* copied by Einstein and preserved in the Smith College Music Archives, vol. 81 and 83. Northampton, Mass.

Fano, Fabio, ed. *La Camerata fiorentina; Vincenzo Galilei.* Vol. 4 of *Istituzioni e monumenti dell'arte musicale italiana.* Milan: Ricordi, 1934.

Fubini, Mario. *Metrica e poesia: Lezioni sulle forme metriche italiane.* Milan: Feltrinelli, 1962. Reprinted 1966.

Gallico, Claudio. *Monteverdi: Poesia musicale, teatro, e musica sacra.* Turin: Einaudi, 1979.

Garboli, Cesare. "Chiabrera," in *Enciclopedia dello spettacolo,* vol. 3, cols. 624-5.

Ghisi, Federico. *Alle fonti della monodia: Due nuovi brani della 'Dafne'; il 'Fuggilotio musicale' di G. Caccini.* Milan: Bocca, 1940.

_____. *I canti carnascialeschi nelle fonti musicali del XV e XVI secolo.* Florence, Rome: L. S. Olschki, 1937.

_____. "Carnival Songs and the Origins of the *Intermezzo giocoso,*" *The Musical Quarterly* 25 (1939): 325-33.

_____. "La tradition musicale des fêtes florentines et les origines de l'opéra," in *Musique des intermèdes de 'La Pellegrina.'* ("Le Choeur des Muses," ed. J. Jacquot.) Paris: Centre National de la Recherche Scientifique, 1963.

Giamatti, A. Bartlett. "Italian." In *Versification: Major Language Types: Sixteen Essays.* Edited by W. K. Wimsatt, pp. 148-64. New York: Modern Language Association, 1972.

Girardi, Enzo Noè. *Esperienza e poesia di Gabriello Chiabrera.* (Pubbl., Univ. catt. del Sacro cuore. Nuova ser., vol. 33.) Milano: Vita e pensiero, 1950.

Giraud, Yves F.-A. *La fable de Daphné: Essai sur un type de métamorphose végétale dans la littérature et dans les arts jusqu'à la fin du XVIIe siècle.* Geneva: Droz, 1969.

Greg, Walter W. *Pastoral Poetry and Pastoral Drama.* London: A. H. Bullen, 1906. Reprinted, New York: Russell & Russell, 1959.

Gros Louis, Kenneth R. R. "Robert Henryson's *Orpheus and Euridice* and the Orpheus Traditions of the Middle Ages," *Speculum* 41 (1966): 643-55.

Grout, Donald J. "The Chorus in Early Opera," in *Festschrift Friedrich Blume zum 70. Geburtstag.* Edited by Anna Amalie Abert and Wilhelm Pfannkuch. Kassel, etc., Bärenreiter, 1963, pp. 151-61.

Hanning, Barbara Russano. "Apologia pro Ottavio Rinuccini," *Journal of the American Musicological Society* 26 (1973): 240-62.

_____. "Glorious Apollo: Poetic and Political Themes in the First Opera," *The Renaissance Quarterly* 32 (1979): 485-513.

Hartmann, Arnold. "Battista Guarini and Il Pastor Fido," *The Musical Quarterly* 39 (1953): 415-25.

Hathaway, Baxter. *The Age of Cristicism: The Late Renaissance In Italy.* Ithaca, New York: Cornell University Press, 1962.

Herrick, Marvin T. *Italian Tragedy in the Renaissance.* Urbana, Illinois: University of Illinois Press, 1965.

_____. *Tragicomedy.* Urbana, Illinois: University of Illinois Press, 1955. Reprint 1962.

Katz, Ruth Torgovnik. "The Origins of Opera: The Relevance of Social and Cultural Factors to the Establishment of a Musical Institution." Ph.D. Dissertation, Columbia University, 1963.

Kerman, Joseph. *Opera as Drama.* New York: Knopf, 1956.

Kirkendale, Warren. *L'aria di Fiorenza, id est il Ballo del Gran Duca.* Florence: Olschki, 1972.

Langedijk, Karla. "Baccio Bandinelli's Orpheus: A Political Message." *Mitteilungen des Kunsthistorischen Institutes in Florenz* 20 (1976): 33-52.

Lippman, Edward A. *Musical Thought in Ancient Greece.* New York and London: Columbia University Press, 1964.

Lowinsky, Edward. Review of *Der musikalische Humanismus im 16. und im fruehen 17. Jahrhunderts* by D. P. Walker. *The Musical Quarterly* 37 (1951): 285-89.

Malipiero, Francesco. *Claudio Monteverdi.* Milan: Fratelli Treves, 1929.

Martin, Henriette. "'La Camerata' du comte Bardi et la musique florentine du XVIe siècle," *Revue de musicologie* 16 (1932): 63-74, 152-61, 227-34; 17 (1933): 92-100, 141-51.

Maugain, G. *Ronsard en Italie.* (Fasc. 2.°, Deuxième série des Publications de la Faculté des Lettres de Strasbourg) Paris: Belles-Lettres, 1926.

Meyer-Baer, Kathi. *Music of the Spheres and the Dance of Death: Studies in Musical Iconology.* Princeton, N.J.: Princeton University Press, 1970.

Momigliano, Attilio. "I melodrammi del Rinuccini." In *Studi di poesia.* 3d ed. revised, pp. 89-93. Messina: G. D'Anna, 1960.

Monti, G. M. *Le villanelle alla napolitana e l'antica lirica dialettale.* Naples: Città di Castello, 1925.

Nagler, Alois M. *Theatre Festivals of the Medici.* New Haven: Yale University Press, 1964.

Neri, Ferdinando. *Il Chiabrera e la Pléiade francese,* Turin: Bocca, 1920.

Osthoff, Wolfgang. *Theatergesang und darstellende Musik in der italienischen Renaissance (15. und 16. Jahrhundert).* 2 vols. Tutzing: Schneider, 1969.

Palisca, Calude V. "The Alterati of Florence: Pioneers in the Theory of Dramatic Music." In *New Looks at Italian Opera, Essays in Honor of Donald J. Grout.* Edited with an Introduction by William W. Austin, pp. 9-38. Ithaca: Cornell University Press, 1968.

_____. "The Artusi-Monteverdi Controversy" In *Monteverdi Companion.* Edited by Arnold and Fortune. London: Faber and Faber, 1968.

_____. *Baroque Music.* Englewood Cliffs, N. J.: Prentice Hall, 1968.

_____. "The *Camerata fiorentina:* A Reappraisal," *Studi musicali* 1 (1972): 203-34.

_____. "The First Performance of 'Euridice'." In the *Twenty-fifth Anniversary Festschrift of Queens College.* New York: City University of New York, 1964.

_____. *Girolamo Mei: Letters on Ancient and Modern Music to Vincenzo Galilei and Giovanni Bardi.* A Study with Annotated Texts. American Institute of Musicology, "Musicological Studies and Documents," no. 3 (1960).

_____. "Musical Asides in the Diplomatic Correspondence of Emilio de' Cavalieri," *The Musical Quarterly* 49 (1963): 339-55.

_____. "Vincenzo Galilei and Some Links Between 'Pseudo-Monody' and Monody." The Musical Quarterly 46 (1960): 344-60.

_____. "Vincenzo Galilei's Counterpoint Treatise: A Code for the *Seconda prattica,*" *Journal of the American Musicological Society* 9 (1956): 81-96.

Perella, Nicholas J. "The Autonomy of Poetry in Battista Guarini's Polemical Tracts," *Forum Italicum* 7 (1973): 338-52.

Pirrotta, Nino. "Bardi." In *Enciclopedia dello spettacolo.* Vol. 1, cols. 1498-9.

_____. "Camerata fiorentina." In *Enciclopedia dello spettacolo.* Vol. 2, cols. 1563-68.

_____. "Cavalieri." In *Enciclopedia dello spettacolo.* Vol. 3, cols. 256-58.

_____. "Corsi." In *Enciclopedia dello spettacolo.* Vol. 3, col. 1525.

_____. *Li due Orfei, da Poliziano a Monteverdi.* Turin: Einaudi, 1969. Reprinted 1975.

_____. "Early Opera and Aria." In *New Looks at Italian Opera, Essays in Honor of Donald J. Grout.* Edited with an Introduction by William W. Austin, pp. 39-107. Ithaca: Cornell University Press, 1968.

_____. "Monteverdi e i problemi dell'opera," in *Studi sul teatro Veneto fra Rinascimento ed età barocca.* Edited by M.-T. Muraro, pp. 321-43. Florence: Olschki, 1971.

_____. "Rinuccini." In *Enciclopedia dello spettacolo.* Vol. 8, cols. 1003-4.

_____. "Temperaments and Tendencies in the Florentine Camerata," *The Musical Quarterly* 40 (1954): 169-89.

_____. "Tragédie et comédie dans la Camerata fiorentina." In *Musique et poésie au*

XVIe siècle, pp. 287-97. (Colloques internationaux du Centre National de la Recherche Scientifique, vol. 5.) Paris: Editions du Centre National, 1954.

Planiscig, Leo. *Luca della Robbia*. Vienna: Verlag Anton Schroll, [1940].

Porter, William V. *The Origins of the Baroque Solo Song: A Study of Italian Manuscript and Prints from 1590-1610*. 2 vols. Ph.D. dissertation. Yale University, 1962.

————. "Peri and Corsi's *Dafne*: Some New Discoveries and Observations," *Journal of the American Musicological Society* 18 (1965): 170-96.

Raccamdoro-Ramelli, F. *Ottavio Rinuccini*. Fabriano: Tipografia gentile, 1900.

Rebhorn, Wayne. *Courtly Performances: Masking and Festivity in Castiglione's "Book of the Courtier."* Detroit: Wayne State University Press, 1978.

Redlich, Hans. *Claudio Monteverdi: Leben und Werk*. Olten, O. Walter, 1949.

Reiner, Stuart. "La vag' Angioletta (and Others)," *Analecta Musicologica* 14 (1974): Studien zur Italienisch-Deutschen Musikgeschichte, 9: 26-88.

Ringer, Alexander. Review of *Monteverdi, Creator of Modern Music*, by Leo Schrade, *Journal of the American Musicological Society* 4 (1951): 153-59.

Rolandi, Ulderico. *Il libretto per musica attraverso i tempi*. Rome: Ateneo, 1951.

Rossi, Vittorio. *Battista Guarini ed il Pastor fido*. Turin: E. Loescher, 1886.

Schild, Marion. *Die Musikdramen Ottavio Rinuccinis*. Ph. D. dissertation, University of Munich, 1933.

Schrade, Leo. *Monteverdi, Creator of Modern Music*. New York: Norton, 1950.

————. *La représentation d'Edipo tiranno*. Paris: Centre National de la Recherche Scientifique, 1960.

————. *Tragedy in the Art of Music*. Cambridge, Mass.: Harvard University Press, 1964.

Solerti, Angelo. "Le 'favolette da recitarsi cantando' di Gabriello Chiabrera," *Giornale storico e letterario della Liguria* 4 (1903): 227-37.

————. "Laura Guidiccioni Lucchesini ed Emilio de' Cavalieri," *Rivista musicale italiana*, 9 (1902): 797-829.

————. "I precedenti del melodramma," *Rivista musicale italiana* 10 (1903): 207-33, 466-70.

Sonneck, O. G. "*Dafne*, the First Opera," *Sammelbände der internationalen Musikgesellschaft* 15 (1913-14): 102-10.

Sternfeld, F. W. "The First Printed Opera Libretto," *Music and Letters* 59 (1978): 121-38.

Stevens, Denis. *Monteverdi: Sacred, Secular, and Occasional Music*. Rutherford, New Jersey: Fairleigh Dickinson University Press, 1978.

Strainchamps, Edmond. "New Light on the Accademia degli Elevati of Florence," *The Musical Quarterly* 62 (1976): 507-35.

Tiersot, Julien. "Ronsard et la musique de son temps," *Sammelbände der Internationalen Musikgesellschaft* 4 (1902-03): 70-142.

Tomlinson, Gary. "Ancora su Ottavio Rinuccini," *Journal of the American Musicological Society* 28 (1975): 351-56.

————. "Ottavio Rinuccini and the *favola affettuosa*," *Comitatus* 6 (1975): 1-27.

————. "Rinuccini, Peri, Monteverdi, and the Humanist Heritage of Opera." Ph.D. dissertation, University of California at Berkeley, 1979.

Vacchelli Monterosso, A. M. "Elementi stilistici nell' *Euridice* di Jacopo Peri in rapporto all'*Orfeo* di Monteverdi." In *Claudio Monteverdi e il suo tempo*. Edited by R. Monterosso, pp. 117-26. Cremona, 1969.

Vogel, Emil. "Marco da Gagliano, zur Geschichte des florentiner Musiklebens von 1570-1650," *Vierteljahrsschrift für Musikwissenchaft* 5 (1889): 396-442, 509-68.

Walker, D. P. "Ficino's Spiritus and Music," *Annales musicologiques* 1 (1953): 131-50.

————. "Le chant orphique de Marsile Ficin." In *Musique et poésie au XVIe siècle*, pp. 17-33. (Colloque internationaux du Centre National de la Recherche Scientifique, Vol. 5.) Paris: Editions du Centre National, 1954.

————. "La musique des intermèdes florentins de 1589." In *Les fêtes de la renaissance*, pp. 133-44. Paris: Centre National de la Recherche Scientifique, 1956.

————. "Musical Humanism in the 16th and Early 17th Centuries," *Music Review* 2 (1941): 1-13, 111-21, 220-27, 288-308; 3 (1942), 55-71.

————. "Orpheus the Theologian and the Renaissance Platonists," *Journal of the Warburg and Courtauld Institutes* 16 (1953): 100-20.

Warburg, Aby. "I Costumi teatrali per gli intermezzi del 1589...," in *Commemorazione della riforma melodrammatica.* ("Atti dell'accademia del R. Istituto musicale di Firenze," Anno XXXIII.) Florence: Tipografia Galletti e Cocci, 1895.

Weaver, Robert L. "Sixteenth-Century Instrumentation," *The Musical Quarterly* 47 (1961): 363-78.

Weaver, R. and N. A *Chronology of Music in the Florentine Theater, 1590-1750*. Detroit, 1978.

Index

Cover illustrations: watermark examples selected from the *French Harpsichord Music of the 17th Century* by Bruce Gustafson, published by UMI Research Press.